DEMOCRACY'S BEGINNING

DEMOCRACY'S BEGINNING
THE ATHENIAN STORY

THOMAS N. MITCHELL

YALE UNIVERSITY PRESS
NEW HAVEN AND LONDON

For information about this and other Yale University Press publications, please contact:
U.S. Office: sales.press@yale.edu   www.yalebooks.com
Europe Office: sales@yaleup.co.uk   www.yalebooks.co.uk

Typeset in Minion Pro by IDSUK (DataConnection) Ltd
Printed in Great Britain by TJ International Ltd, Padstow, Cornwall

Library of Congress Cataloging-in-Publication Data

Mitchell, Thomas N., 1939–
   Democracy's beginning: the Athenian story/Thomas N. Mitchell.
     pages   cm
   ISBN 978-0-300-21503-8 (hardback)
1. Democracy—Greece—Athens—History—To 1500.   2. Greece—Politics and government—To 146 B.C.   3. Athens (Greece)—Politics and government.   I. Title.
   JC75.D36M58 2015
   320.938—dc23
                                                                              2015023656

A catalogue record for this book is available from the British Library.

10 9 8 7 6 5 4 3 2 1

Contents

Illustrations and Maps

15 Terracotta hydria attributed to the Class of Hamburg depicting women
    collecting water at a fountain house, c. 510–500 B.C. The Metropolitan
    Museum of Art, Rogers Fund, 1906 (06.1021.77). Image © The
    Metropolitan Museum of Art.

Maps

Acknowledgements

This book has been long in gestation and I am indebted to the many people who helped along the way. I began work on the book during a semester as a Visiting Fellow at the Hoover Institution at Stanford University in 2002. I received warm hospitality at the Institution, and learned a great deal from the impressive gathering of experts there in modern democracy, who were very eager to discuss democracy's beginning and the Athenian experience. I got great stimulus and many insights from my time among them.

The work continued at Trinity College Dublin, where I received valuable help from my classical colleagues, in particular Brian McGing, who read the entire text of an early draft, and whose broad knowledge of the subject saved me from many errors and identified many ways in which the book could be more sharply focused and improved. I am also grateful to my colleague Christine Morris, who helped with selection of the illustrations used in the book.

The reviewing process by Yale University Press was the most thorough and helpful that I have experienced. The readers, whose expertise was clearly evident, provided detailed, constructive critiques which indicated where more work was needed and where improvements could be made. I am very grateful to them for the time and effort they devoted to making this a better book. I also want to thank my publisher at the Press, Heather McCallum, for her efficiency, graciousness and supportive attitude at all stages of the process.

Special thanks are also due to my daughter-in-law, Leone Mitchell, who prepared the manuscript and proved a most able research assistant. But my greatest debt is owed to my wife, Lynn, and I want to thank her for her patience and encouragement during the writing of this book, and for her unfailing support throughout my professional career. I dedicate this book to her and to our four children, Noel, Sean, Kevin and Tara, who have brought us great happiness.

Abbreviations

Ancient Authors and Texts

Aesch.	Aeschines
Aeschyl.	Aeschylus
Supp.	*Suppliants*
Eum.	*Eumenides*
Andoc.	Andocides
Arist.	Aristotle
Ath. Pol.	*Athenaion Politeia*
Eth. Nic.	*Nicomachean Ethics*
Pol.	*Politics*
Rhet.	*Rhetoric*
Aristoph.	Aristophanes
Ach.	*Acharnians*
Eccl.	*Ecclesiazusae*
Plut.	*Plutus*
Cic.	Cicero
Acad.	*Academia*
Brut.	*Brutus*
Cluent.	*Pro Cluentio*
Leg.	*De Legibus*
Off.	*De Officiis*
Or.	*De Oratore*
Rep.	*De Republica*
Sest.	*Pro Sestio*
Tusc.	*Tusculan Disputations*
Dem.	Demosthenes
Din.	Dinarchus

Diod.	Diodorus Siculus
Diog. Laert.	Diogenes Laertius
Dion. Hal.	Dionysius of Halicarnassus
Eur.	Euripides
Supp.	*Suppliants*
FGrH	F. Jacoby, *Die Fragmente der griechischen Historiker*, 3 vols, 1923–58
frg(s)	fragment(s)
Hdt.	Herodotus
Hell. Oxy.	*Hellenica Oxyrhynchia*, a papyrus containing fragments of a history of the Greek world in the early fourth century
Hes.	Hesiod
Theog.	*Theogony*
WD	*Works and Days*
Homer	
Il.	*Iliad*
Od.	*Odyssey*
Hyper.	Hyperides
Euxen.	*On Behalf of Euxenippus*
IG I³, IG II²	*Inscriptiones Graecae*, 3rd edition of first volume, and 2nd edition of second volume
Isocr.	Isocrates
Antid.	*Antidosis*
Areop.	*Areopagiticus*
Panegyr.	*Panegyricus*
Panath.	*Panathenaicus*
Lyc.	Lycurgus
Leoc.	*Against Leocrates*
Lys.	Lysias
Nepos	Cornelius Nepos
Milt.	*Miltiades*
Paus.	Pausanias
Philoch.	Philochorus (fl. c. 300 B.C.), author of an *Atthis*, a form of literature centred on the history of Athens. Only fragments survive
Philostr.	Philostratus (late second century A.D.), author of *Vitae Sophistarum* (*VS*)

Plato
- *Alc.* — *Alcibiades*
- *Apol.* — *Apology*
- *Char.* — *Charmides*
- *Clit.* — *Clitopho*
- *Gorg.* — *Gorgias*
- *Hipp. Min.* — *Hippias Minor*
- *Menex* — *Menexenus*
- *Prot.* — *Protagoras*
- *Rep.* — *Republic*
- *Symp.* — *Symposium*
- *Theaet.* — *Theaetetus*

Plut. — Plutarch
- *Ages.* — *Agesilaus*
- *Alc.* — *Alcibiades*
- *Alex.* — *Alexander*
- *Arist.* — *Aristides*
- *Cim.* — *Cimon*
- *Cleom.* — *Cleomenes*
- *Dem.* — *Demosthenes*
- *Lyc.* — *Lycurgus*
- *Lys.* — *Lysander*
- *Nic.* — *Nicias*
- *Pelop.* — *Pelopidas*
- *Per.* — *Pericles*
- *Phoc.* — *Phocion*
- *Them.* — *Themistocles*

Polyb. — Polybius

Ps. Andoc. — Pseudo-Andocides

Ps. Xen. — Pseudo-Xenophon, commonly referred to as the Old Oligarch, anonymous author of the *Constitution of Athens*

Schol. — Scholia, explanatory marginal notes on ancient text

Soph. — Sophocles

Thuc. — Thucydides

Xen. — Xenophon
- *Anab.* — *Anabasis*
- *Apol.* — *Apology*

Hell.	*Hellenica*
Lak. Pol.	*Lakedaimoniōn Politeia*
Mem.	*Memorabilia*
Oec.	*Oeconomica*
Symp.	*Symposium*

Modern Works

AJAH	*American Journal of Ancient History*
Ath. Trib. Lists	*The Athenian Tribute Lists*, by B.D. Meritt, H.T Grey and M.F. McGregor, 4 vols, Cambridge, Mass., 1939–53
CA	*Classical Antiquity*
CJ	*Classical Journal*
C&M	*Classica et Mediaevalia*
CQ	*Classical Quarterly*
Dem. Emp. Arts	*Democracy, Empire and the Arts*, ed. Deborah Boedeker and Kurt Raaflaub, Cambridge, Mass., 1998
Democracy. 2500?	*Democracy 2500? Questions and Challenges*, ed. Ian Morris and Kurt Raaflaub, Dubuque, Ia, 1998
DK	H. Diels and W. Kranz, eds, *Die Fragmente der Vorsokratiker*, 6th edn., 3 vols, Berlin, 1951–52
GRBS	*Greek, Roman and Byzantine Studies*
Hansen, *Ath. Dem.*	Mogens Hansen, *Athenian Democracy in the Age of Demosthenes*, Bristol, 1999
HCT	A Historical Commentry on Thucydides by A.W. Gomme, A. Andrews and K.J. Dover, 5 vols, Oxford 1948–81
HSCP	*Harvard Studies in Classical Philology*
JHS	*Journal of Hellenic Studies*
Jones, *Ath. Dem.*	A.H.M. Jones, *Athenian Democracy*, Baltimore, Md, 1977
ML	Russell Meiggs and D.M. Lewis, *A Section of Historical Inscriptions to the End of the Fifth Century B.C.*, 2nd edn., Oxford, 1988
PP	*La Parola del passato*
Rhodes, *Com. Ath. Pol.*	P.J. Rhodes, *A Commentary on the Aristotelian Athēnaiōn Politeia*, Oxford, 1981
Tod, GHI II	M.N. Tod, *A Selection of Greek Historical Inscriptions, Vol. II, 402–323 B.C.*, Oxford, 1958
Yale Class. St.	*Yale Classical Studies*

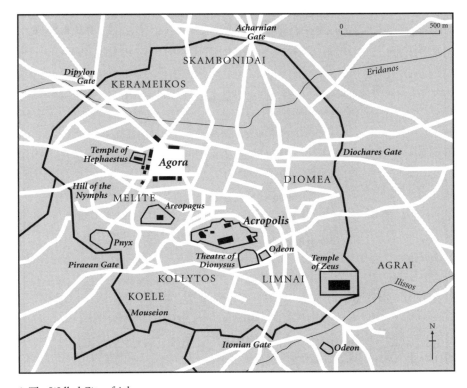

1. The Walled City of Athens.

PAEONIA

THRACE

ILLYRIA

PELLA

AMPHIPOLIS

ABDERA

STAGEIRA

Thasos

AEGAE
(VERGINA)•

CHALCIDICE

ELIMEA

OLYNTHUS

DION•

POTIDAEA

PERRHAEBIA

Mt Olympus▲

MOLOSSIA

AEGEAN
SEA

THESSALY

PHERAE

CORCYRA

PHARSALUS•

ARTEMISIUM

Scyros

*Ionian
Islands*

THERMOPYLAE

PHOCIS

EUBOEA

LOCRIS

ITHACA

DELPHI

PHOCIS

CHALCIS

LOCRIS

CHAERONEA

BOEOTIA

ERETRIA

DELIUM

THEBES

TANAGRA

PLATAEA

MARATHON

ATTICA

ELEUSIS

CEPHISIA

CARYSTUS

MEGARA

ATHENS

ELIS

CORINTH

PIRAEUS

ELIS

ARCADIA

PHLIUS

CLEONAE

LAURIUM

OLYMPIA

MYCENAE

Aegina

MANTINEA

ARGOS

EPIDAURUS

SUNIUM

Ceos

*IONIAN
SEA*

TRIPHYLIA

TEGEA

MEGALOPOLIS

MESSENIA

MESSENE

PYLOS•

SPARTA

LACONIA

Melos

TAENARUM

N

MEDITERRANEAN   SEA

0   100 miles

0   150 km

2. Mainland Greece.

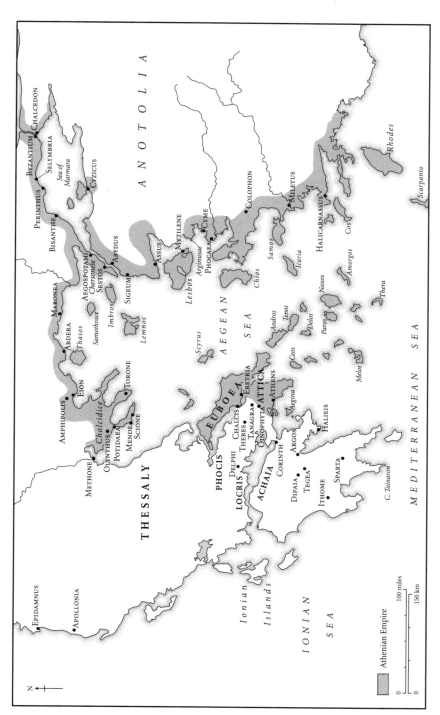

3. Greece and the Athenian Empire (shaded).

OROPOS

PLATAEA

RHAMNUS

PARNES MOUNTAINS

PHYLE

DECELEA

MARATHON

Cephisus

Pentelikon Mts

ACHARNAE

CEPHISIA

ELEUSIS

Aigaleos Mts

COLONUS

ATHENS

Ilisos

BOUDORON

PHALERUM

PIRAEUS

ERCHIA

PAEANIA

BRAURON

Salamis

Hymettos Mts

SPHETTUS

Saronic Gulf

Aegina

AEGILIA

THORICUS

ANAPHLYSTUS

Laureion Mines

SUNIUM

N

MEDITERRANEAN   SEA

0   10 miles

0   15 km

4. Attica.

Introduction

Democracy is at a particularly critical and fascinating point in its history. The collapse of communism in 1989 brought a wave of euphoria among proponents of democracy, and extravagant references to the end of history and of mankind's journey towards a universally acceptable political order. To many, democracy had emerged as a clear victor over competing political and economic ideologies, the natural form of polity for civilised societies, the agent of progress, the means to prosperity, political stability and international peace, and to secure protection of human rights and human dignity.

The reality over the past twenty-five years has not quite matched the euphoria. There was certainly a significant and sustained increase in the number of democratic states after 1989. In the late 1980s about sixty states, or 36 per cent of the total number, could be classified as free democracies. Ten years later, as a new millennium began, the number had grown to eighty-six, or 45 per cent of the world's countries, and the number of so-called electoral democracies, i.e. those conducting free and fair elections, stood at 120.

But over the last decade and a half the expansion of democracy and its values has virtually ceased. The 2013 Freedom House Survey of the world's 195 states shows a steady decline in global freedom in recent years and an expansion and strengthening of authoritarianism. There has been virtually no increase in the number of states that can be ranked as free in more than a decade, and there has been a significant drop in the number of electoral democracies, which had reached 123 in 2005, and now stands at 117. Only 43 per cent of the world's population live in societies that can be classed as free. Democracy has had particular difficulties taking hold in North Africa, the Middle East and Central Asia, where authoritarian traditions and cultural and religious barriers to many basic democratic tenets remain strong.

The overall experience of the decade and a half, including the tragic situations in Iraq and Afghanistan, illustrates the difficulty of rooting democracy on a firm, stable basis. The entire history of democracy confirms that difficulty. Donald Kagan in his book on Pericles has aptly described democracy as 'one of rarest, most delicate and fragile flowers in the jungle of human experience'.[1] It has been a fleeting phenomenon in the history of government and has lain outside the experience of the vast majority of the peoples of the world down the ages. It originated and flourished in Athens for almost two centuries 2,500 years ago, about the same time that a closely related form, republicanism, began to evolve in Rome. But by the birth of Christ both democracy and republicanism had disappeared root and branch from human experience, and for the following 1,700 years or more survived only in the history books and in the reflections of the intelligentsia.

The rebirth of democratic ideals and systems, which began in the middle of the seventeenth century, was slow and halting, and fully developed liberal democracy, as we know it, has had a very short history indeed. The impediments are many. Even within the cultural tradition that created democracy, there have always been divisions about its character, purposes and merits. Many of the best minds in the history of western thought, beginning with Socrates, Plato and Aristotle, have rejected democracy's basic tenets outright, especially its view of political equality. Many modern intellectuals, from Madison to more recent influential figures such as Michels, Weber and Schumpeter, have had reservations about the stability and effectiveness of a system that gives power to the people. The idea of giving control to the masses rather than the meritorious few can seem a perversion of justice and common sense, creating equality where none exists, and risking faction-ridden, elite-driven or rudderless government, or even a tyranny of an improvident majority.

A further difficulty is a lack of agreement about what constitutes a genuine democracy. This leaves scope for regimes with scant respect for the rule of law or the rights of citizens to lay claim to the title in an attempt to legitimise their rule, creating a danger that the term may become so elastic as to be meaningless. Even among political scientists there is limited agreement about the essence of democracy. Since the late 1950s there has been a general shift in political science towards a more empirical, scientific method that concentrates on description and explanation of things as they are, and that eschews so-called normative judgements and theorising about the right and the ideal. In line with that trend there has been a tendency to move the discussion of democracy away from the theoretical level and issues related to the idea of democracy and its ideals and principles to the empirical level and the way in which democracy functions in actual states. Joseph Schumpeter is generally considered to have originated this trend in his wide-ranging book *Capitalism, Socialism and Democracy*, first published in 1942. He dismissed traditional approaches, which he considered flawed by speculative theorising, and put forward what was regarded as a more true-to-life empirical view designed to explain how actual democracies worked. He saw democracy in narrow terms as an 'institutional arrangement for arriving at political decisions in which individuals acquire power to decide by means of a competitive struggle for the people's vote'. In other words, democracy was merely a method or process by which the governed could select and confer power on their rulers through a competitive electoral process. Elections had to be periodic to be meaningful and, to be truly competitive, had to be open, free and fair, which required the existence of certain rights such as freedom of expression, and freedom of assembly and organisation.

Schumpeter's views had a major impact and brought a concentration on the narrow concept of democracy centred on a particular method of choosing leaders. What else democracy aimed to offer, what other role or rights it claimed for citizens, what rulers should do once in office, all such issues were seen as separate questions. The electoral method was seen as the essential defining characteristic of democracy and the means by which political systems could be analysed with precision and democratic institutions better understood. Samuel Huntington, in his influential book *The Third Wave* (1992), expresses succinctly the view of Schumpeter's disciples when he states that 'elections, open, free and fair, are the essence of democracy, the inescapable sine qua non', and insists that the definition in terms of procedures for constituting government provides 'the analytical precision and empirical referents that make the concept a useful one. … Fuzzy norms do not yield useful analysis.'[2]

No one can deny the value of empirical studies of how actual democracies work. It is equally obvious that an electoral process that secures for the people the right to say who will govern them lies at the heart of representative democracy, and that a study of its operation is a useful tool for the measurement of the vitality and stability of particular democratic regimes. But the idea that open, free and fair elections – concepts which are themselves fuzzy norms – encompass all that is significant and tangible in the democratic ideal is untenable, or even absurd.

Democracy is concerned with more than procedures for electing leaders. It is an ideology, a set of political ideals derived from a particular view of the nature, dignity and social needs of human beings. The procedures and institutions of democracy are dictated by these ideals, designed to make them a reality. It is these ideals that form the defining characteristics of democracy. Their realisation is the end, the procedures and institutions are the means.

These ideals first emerged in their full form in Athens at the end of a long search for a durable, broadly acceptable political order. The Athenians rejected the time-honoured belief that political power belonged to the privileged few, and replaced it with a new vision of the state as a community or partnership (*koinonia*) of political equals, equal in freedom, equal in political rights, equal in justice under a communally sanctioned rule of law, with a form of government that was of the people, by the people, for the people, and with a form of citizenship that entailed civic participation and promotion of the common good. Procedures and institutions were evolved to implement and protect these ideals.

These are the ideals that have inspired democratic movements since their re-emergence since the revolutions of the later eighteenth century. The procedures and institutions to implement them followed on from the guiding principles. They can and have varied widely, and there are vast differences between the form and functioning of the constitution of Athens and the constitutional structures of modern democracies. The interpretation of the ideals has, of course, also evolved and now contains elements not envisaged by the Athenians. But there is a core of first principles that has prevailed, and that will always constitute the heart of the democratic ideal. If these principles are ignored, or seriously diluted, or perverted, democracy will become what Ronald Syme once called the Roman republican constitution, 'a screen and a sham', and will never achieve the high expectations that it can create a more enlightened social and political order for all humanity. These principles and their full implications must remain at the centre of democratic debate, alongside empirical investigation of the political structures that can best achieve their realisation.[3]

The place of Athens as the progenitor of the ideological foundations of democracy, and the first paradigm of a remarkably stable democracy based on them, will always make the Athenian experience a crucial aid to a better understanding of the merits, challenges and weaknesses of democratic systems. Recent classical scholarship has shown an awareness of this. The wealth of varied, detailed and innovative studies of Athenian democracy that has appeared in recent times is testimony to the enduring relevance of the Athenian revolution and what followed to the political dialogue of the modern world. I have hesitated about adding another book to that high volume of existing literature, but the enduring importance of the Athenian story and the need to keep harvesting the legacy provide a strong justification. There is still scope for a better understanding of the roots and character of democracy, and the debate should continue.

The idea for this book arose from my experience as a Visiting Fellow at the Hoover Institution at Stanford University in 2002. The diversity and richness of the work being done there on modern democracies, and the degree of interest in democracy's beginning and its first manifestation in Athens, caused me to look anew at the world's first democracy, at what inspired it, what political beliefs underpinned it, why it took hold so firmly, what made it work, what accounted for its success in building an empire, for its cultural and creative genius, and for its survival for almost two hundred years, and what flaws brought it revolution and, eventually, domination by Macedonia.

The book attempts to answer these questions by doing two particular things that, it is hoped, will better illustrate the character and significance of the Athenian achievement. It tells the full story of democracy's beginning, its roots in the traditions of the *polis* and in the revolutionary movements that swept through the Aegean in the seventh and sixth centuries B.C., its maturing at Athens, the principles and institutions that underpinned it, gave it stability and sustained it for almost two centuries. It also deals with the flaws that contributed to its eventual demise, when it failed to find a way of coping with the might of Macedonia. Secondly, it gives prominence to both theory and practice, and the interaction between them. It is not only the story of the evolution of the democratic constitution and the ideals and principles that inspired it, but is also an empirical study of how it worked and coped in the historical context in which it operated. It shows the democracy in action, implementing a new vision of how society should be organised and governed, finding its way, evolving with the tide of history, revealing both its strengths and weaknesses as it confronted the challenges of a troubled world of war and power struggles. There is a full narrative of historical events, providing a necessary context for a clearer understanding of the functioning and character of the system.

The interaction of theory and practice was especially important in the case of Athens. The democracy was theory-based. Solon had laid down the basic principles of a just society. They were carried further by the constitution of Cleisthenes which represented the climax of a sustained progression in the Greek world towards a form of society characterised by *isonomia*, equality before the law and equality of political rights, principles seen as the guarantors of freedom. But the development and fortunes of the later democracy were also heavily affected by ideological forces and the theoretical political speculations that became increasingly part of the experience of the class that continued to provide the bulk of the political leadership. Leading figures such as Pericles, Thucydides, Alcibiades and his circle, Antiphon, Theramenes and Critias, and the foremost orators of the fourth century were all products of the vibrant intellectual milieu created by the Sophists, in which political debate and theorising were very much to the fore. The rise of flourishing schools such as those of Plato, Isocrates and Aristotle in the fourth century, with their sharp focus on political principles and systems, particularly democracy and the perceived vagaries of the Athenian form of it, shows an ongoing preoccupation among the intelligentsia with political theory and theory-based forms of government and distribution of power. The impact of this culture of ideology on Athenian leadership and on the course of Athenian democracy will be carefully examined at relevant points in the book. The study also confronts some of the more controversial constitutional and historical questions, but in general it is aimed at a far wider audience than the *cognoscenti*, and it is hoped that it will be of particular interest and value to students of the classics, history and the social sciences as a whole, and to all who have an interest in the history of government.

CHAPTER 1

The Greek *Polis*: Cradle of Democracy

The story of the emergence of Greek democracy has its roots in the dominant form of political organisation that developed in the Greek world between 800 and 500 B.C., and that is known as the *polis* or city-state. By the end of the fifth century there were over eight hundred such city-states throughout the Greek world and, while many showed marked differences in their political structures and ideals, they all had many common characteristics and similarities of political culture, out of which emerged seminal political principles and ideals that became embedded in western political thought and provided the bedrock of the democratic ideal.[1]

The Beginnings

The form and character of the early stages in the evolution of the *polis* are difficult to determine, the evidence coming only from archaeological remains and sparse literary sources, but in its developed form at the end of the so-called Archaic Age (c. 500 B.C.), it can be described as a self-governing territory with a major urban centre which was generally walled and had an acropolis or high place that served as a stronghold. The word *polis* is also used in our sources to describe the urban centre, but when it denoted a political entity, it included the urban centre and its hinterland with no distinction between town and country. The *polis* was essentially its people, and those who lived in the remoter areas of its territory were as much a part of it as those who lived in the city.

The urban centre did, however, play a central role in the lives of all citizens. It was the seat of government and contained all the state's civic buildings. It was the site of the main temples, theatres and gymnasia. It had the public gathering place, the Agora, which became the main marketplace and trading place. Much of the population lived in the city, and it was the final refuge for the whole population in times of serious danger from war. The urban centre was therefore a unifying focal point for all, residents and non-residents: meeting place, marketplace, centre of religious, cultural and intellectual life, of education and entertainment, and the place where the citizen body functioned as a political community.

A further defining characteristic of the *polis* was smallness. Almost 80 per cent of Greek *poleis* had territories of no more that 80 square miles (207 square kilometres), and only 10 per cent measured more that 200 square miles (518 square kilometres). Just thirteen are recorded with territories over 400 square miles (1,036 square kilometres). Sparta was by far the largest city-state in the Greek world, controlling an area of about 3,200 square miles (8,288 square kilometres), but the bulk of that comprised the subjugated neighbouring territory of Messenia. Athens was also among the five largest, with an area of about 1,000 square miles (2,590 square kilometres).

Populations are more difficult to determine. Recorded figures generally refer to adult male citizens or able-bodied citizens of military age. The numbers in the rest of the population, which comprised the wives and children of citizens, resident aliens or metics, and slaves, can only be conjectured, a task made more difficult by the fact that there must have been wide variations in the proportion of metics and slaves in different states, depending on such factors as location and levels of prosperity.

A large state, such as Corinth, with an area of about 35 square miles (90 square kilometres) and a capacity to field an army as large as 5,000 hoplites, is estimated to have had a total population of about 70,000 in the fifth century. Athens, by far the most populous of all the Greek states, had an adult male population of 40,000–50,000 in the mid-fifth century, could muster citizen armies as large as 26,000, and must have had a total population well in excess of 250,000. According to Aristotle, Sparta at its peak had a citizen population of 10,000. But these states were exceptions, and all the evidence suggests that the average *polis* had no more than 500–2,000 adult male citizens.[2]

The political and social ideals and values that evolved with the development of this very particular form of political organisation are reasonably well documented in the various strands of the writings of the Greeks from Homer onwards. The word *polis* is mentioned 250 times in the Homeric epics, now generally dated to the eight century B.C., and central features of the classical *polis* are already evident in those references – a territory with a main settlement, which is generally surrounded by a wall and contains temples, a gathering place and residences of the leading nobles (*basileis*).

The more developed Homeric *polis* was a self-governing community, controlled by a group of nobles who held the title of *basileus*, which later came to mean 'king'. This largely hereditary aristocracy would have comprised the households (*oikoi*) that had the greatest wealth and power, derived from the size of their estates, the extent of their kinsmen, retainers and connections, and the esteem that their lineage and personal achievements gave them. There was one dominant *basileus*, who was, however, more a *primus inter pares* than an absolute monarch, his position dependent on maintaining the power-base on which his dominance rested.

Neither the literary sources nor archaeology provide much information about the rest of the population, which would have comprised a significant body of independent farmers and a lower class of tenant farmers, sharecroppers, farm labourers, artisans and retainers in the noble households. There was also a number of slaves. Whether all of the lower classes enjoyed full freedom, or lived in serflike conditions, remains unclear. But all of the lower classes would have been to some degree dependent on the local 'big man' for their economic welfare, the maintenance of law and order, and the settlement of disputes in accordance with customary law and procedure. There is some evidence, however, that the class division between the aristocracy and the independent farmer was narrow, and that social mobility was not precluded.[3]

At the level of the *polis*, the nobles controlled affairs of government under the leadership of the chief *basileus*, with whom they met in council to deliberate and decide on issues of public importance. Interestingly, at this level a role was given to the broader mass of people, the *demos*, the bulk of whom were presumably the independent farmers who would have formed the main mass of the army. The *demos* were formally assembled to receive information and hear debates on occasions when matters of major public interest were at issue. They did not vote and had no real opportunity to influence decisions, but there was a recognition that they had a legitimate interest in political affairs and needed to be informed and, if possible, persuaded of the rightness of proposed courses of action. This was a far cry from any concept of political equality, but it was an important acknowledgement of the interest of all in what concerns all, and marked a sharp difference between the Greeks, even in the early stages of their political development, and the people around them, who were ruled by despotic regimes that left no room for any consideration of the worth and welfare of the individual.

Nonetheless, Homer's world was a sharply divided, feudal society. The aristocracy saw themselves as the *aristoi*, the best, and they were accepted as such. In return, however, they were expected to behave with justice (*dike*) towards all, and to work for the common good and to bear the brunt of the burden of protecting the state. The Homeric aristocracy lived by a strict code, their lives dominated by the pursuit of honour (*time*) and a drive to prove their merit (*arete*), which meant being foremost in strength, skill and martial prowess and in service to their homeland. The *Iliad* and *Odyssey* present, of course, an idealised portrayal of heroic figures, but they obviously reflect the qualities and moral values sought and admired in leaders in the world of Homer's audience.

Overall, the picture of the *polis* in the developed and more ideal form that emerges from the Homeric poems represents a superior, civilised form of living with all the benefits of social communion – order, justice and security under the benign governance of a worthy nobility motivated by concern for the public good as well as personal glory. The ordinary citizen had a place and a role in the workings of the body politic, and a right to expect that his political masters would treat him fairly and protect his interests.[4]

A more consciously political writer than Homer appeared around the end of the seventh century in Hesiod of Boeotia. Hesiod provides a very different perspective on life and on the *polis* from Homer. In the *Works and Days*, his didactic poem on farming, he is the voice of the lower class, describing the work of the peasant farmer and its values. It is a world that contrasts sharply with the lofty aristocratic code of the heroes of epic. The farmer finds his way to *arete* by a humbler route: honest toil on the land. Hesiod exalts the value of work. It is an honourable road to respectability and prosperity, and the farmer's priority must remain his work and the need to fill his barns and provide for his household. He does not have time for politics or the distractions of the Agora.[5]

But in both the *Works and Days* and his other main surviving poem, the *Theogony*, whose subject is the origin and genealogies of the gods, Hesiod combines his didactic purpose with strong political messages about the principles that must direct the interrelationships and governance of a political community. His concern is not with power or privilege or how they are distributed. He accepts the class divisions of his day and acknowledges that the nobles have the right and capacity to rule. His preoccupation is with the right use of power and the broader moral underpinnings of the *polis* and their preservation.

Hesiod is the first to set down a clear ethical basis for the *polis*. All facets of life in the *polis* must be directed by justice (*dike*), the great ethical foundation of human relations, signifying what is fair and what is due. For Hesiod, political association is possible only because all human beings have been given the capacity for justice by Zeus, so that human behaviour, unlike that of all other animals, would be governed by its tenets. To illustrate the driving force in the animal kingdom, he tells the tale of the hawk and the nightingale, the hawk mocking the nightingale caught in its claws for its pleas for mercy and asserting that the stronger will do as he pleases. This is the law of 'might is right', but Hesiod warns that it is not a law that can prevail in human society. Mankind must opt for justice as the better way and place it above the forces opposed to it, violence (*bia*) and arrogant pride (*hybris*). And this applies to ruler and ruled alike. Hesiod is insistent that his brother Perses, with whom he was in dispute, must live by justice as faithfully as the *basileis*.[6]

In both the *Works and Days* and the *Theogony, dike* is personified as a divine power and is given a dignity and status commensurate with Hesiod's view of her importance in the life of the *polis*. She is presented as the daughter of Zeus and Themis (whose name became another word for the right and the just), revered by all the gods, who watches the deeds of men and is the eyes and ears of Zeus in monitoring wrongdoing. In the *Theogony* she is built into a cosmic force, part of the universal order, since justice in Hesiod underlies the workings of the entire cosmos, the kingdom of Zeus being its great model and exemplar. *Dike* is also presented as the sister of two other powerful forces essential for a stable, just and peaceful society, *Eunomia* and *Eirene*. *Eunomia* personified the power that produced the well-ordered, well-governed state and the law-abiding citizen. *Eirene* was the spirit of peace.

Hesiod declares in the *Works and Days* that these three 'look after the works of mortals'. He also associates with justice another benign force that influences human relations and behaviours, *aidos*, the antithesis of *hybris*, denoting a sense of shame that makes wrongdoing uncomfortable and imposes restraint through regard for the feelings and opinions of others. These are the four main forces of social order in Hesiod. They provide the bonds of society and represent the qualities, embedded in the human psyche, that create in human beings a unique moral sensibility and a high social aptitude. Hesiod's repeated message is that on the preservation of these qualities depend the stability, prosperity and survival of political associations, and the chance for citizens to reap the benefits of life in the *polis*. He is equally emphatic that their absence will ultimately bring divine retribution on wrongdoers and ruin on the entire community.[7]

But Hesiod was keenly aware that humanity is susceptible to forces of evil as well as forces of good, and he believed this was especially true in his own day. He saw evil all around, malicious strife as opposed to healthy rivalry, along with greed, dishonesty, shamelessness, perjury, violence and bribe-devouring nobles who pervert justice by their crooked judgements, are driven by *hybris*, and do not fear the gods. He blames it all on a progressive moral degeneration in human history. He uses myth, in the familiar tradition of epic, as a cautionary example and means of presenting the message more graphically, telling the tale of the five ages of the world, during which mankind went through a steady moral decline from the golden age, when men lived like gods, to the age of iron, when Hesiod lived, when the race is headed for destruction, caught in a spiral of depravity, which will end with justice and shame abandoning the earth. His deep pessimism about the state of his world gave added urgency to his exhortations to the way of justice, order and peace, and to his dire warnings of the consequences of the departure from them.[8]

Hesiod's importance in the history of western political thought seldom gets the prominence it deserves. He was the first of the Greeks to articulate in a structured way a concept of the state as a community of citizens whose relations and institutions must be based on justice. He has a well-developed concept of what justice means, presenting it as an intrinsic human quality that predisposes human beings to have regard for each other, to give each his due, to live together in accordance with accepted norms of behaviour in a manner that ensures order, harmony and concern for the common good. These were ideas that remained at the heart of subsequent Greek political thought and that became an important part of the Greek legacy to the western political tradition.

The Age of Revolution

The evolution of the *polis* beyond the stage depicted in Homer and Hesiod is poorly documented, but such evidence as exists indicates that by the middle of the seventh century the *polis* had developed into a more tightly organised and more integrated political community with more formalised political institutions. The aristocracy had formed into a more tightly knit, exclusive ruling elite, the dominance of a single *basileus* had disappeared, and control of government was firmly in the hands of an oligarchy, a council of the leading families which chose a rotating executive from its members.

But rapidly changing circumstances in the late seventh and early sixth centuries put severe strains on the ascendancy of this hereditary nobility and ushered in an era of revolutionary strife (*stasis*) both within the upper class and between the upper and lower classes. This was to lead to major social and political change, and to a significantly different concept of the *polis* and of how it should be governed.

The main catalyst for these developments was an expansion of economic opportunity. This led to a growth in the size and affluence of the middle class, which eroded the monopoly on wealth of the traditional aristocracy and weakened the political power derived from it. The wider prosperity came mainly from increased commerce, which was stimulated by two waves of colonisation that began in Greece as early as 750 B.C., the first wave directed mainly westwards towards Sicily and southern Italy, the second wave moving eastwards during the latter half of the seventh century into the Hellespont and along the shores of the Black Sea. The main motive was to relieve overcrowding in the mother cities, but an important effect was to create greatly increased trading opportunities, as the new settlements sent back grain and other food products and themselves became markets for the output of the skilled artisans of the homeland. There emerged alongside the relatively prosperous free farmers further groups of the well-to-do, comprising those, such as manufacturers, merchants and shipowners, who were able to capitalise on the expanded international trade.

Linked to this growth and wider dispersal of wealth was another development of far-reaching significance: a radically different battle array for Greek armies, the so-called hoplite phalanx, which massed infantry, equipped with thrusting spears and circular shields and extensive body armour, in close formation, presenting a seemingly impenetrable body of fighters to the enemy. The phalanx proved so effective that it had become the regular formation in the Greek world by the end of the seventh century.

The emergence of the phalanx had political as well as military effects. It was a mass infantry army. It required larger numbers to be effective and was made possible only because growing prosperity was extending the numbers of citizens able to equip themselves for military service. But the involvement of a broader section of the citizenry in the defence of the state lessened the dependence of the public for protection on the traditional aristocracy and had a levelling effect, diluting the power the aristocracy had derived from its monopoly of the military role.

The power-base of the ruling elite was being eroded on many sides. The dependent feudal existence of the masses in Homeric society was giving way to a new order. Prosperity gained from free enterprise and individual entrepreneurial initiative naturally fostered a spirit of independence and individualism, and the expanded military responsibilities of the better-off also gave the newly prosperous a greater stake in their society and claims to a greater say in its management.[9]

There are many other signs that the winds of change were blowing through the Greek world in the late seventh and early sixth centuries, Ionia providing the main inspiration for many of the new trends. A growing sense of self and of personal autonomy can be seen in the highly creative and innovative literary life of the period. The great era of heroic narrative poetry, centred on aristocratic exploits and preoccupations, gave way to new literary forms focused on the free expression of the poet's own thoughts and feelings about all types of subjects, grave and gay. New meters were created for new genres, which have been variously classified as melic, lyric, elegiac and iambic. The new poetry was endlessly varied in theme, tone and purpose, ranging from the polemical, satirical and hortatory, to lyrical meditations on the fragility and intensity of human emotions, especially love, and more light-hearted musings on the more trivial, hedonistic diversions of the human spirit.

But all of it was neoteric, and all of it was personal, sometimes deeply subjective and self-revealing. All human life was its concern, the ordinary as well as the extraordinary. The universality of its themes and sentiments transcended class. It had a frank and free quality, the individual expressing individual experience as he or she saw fit. Some of it had an iconoclastic quality, representing something of a spiritual liberation or revolution. It signalled a society of growing individualism and intellectual freedom, creative and innovative, with a penchant for what the Romans later called *res novae* (revolutionary change).[10]

There were other cultural developments in a similar vein. The art of the period shows the impact of colonisation and broader contacts with foreign peoples and cultures. Greek vase-painting and metalwork went through an Orientalising phase, with figure-drawing, animal motifs and floral designs replacing the earlier Geometric patterns, and with distinctive variations evolving in different *poleis*. Bronze work showed even greater changes and produced such striking innovations as the well-known griffin heads and siren handles. There was a willingness to embrace new forms, and to borrow ideas and techniques that appealed.[11]

But the most far-reaching and fundamental form of change in the period began to emerge at the end of the seventh century, an intellectual revolution that originated in the Ionian city of Miletus. The creative energy and intellectual vibrancy that mark this entire era began to turn in a new direction and to ask new questions about old mysteries – the origin of the universe, what it is made of, whether there is an order and cosmic law controlling it, why it is the way it is. The answers were sought not in myth or traditional concepts of divine forces, but in human powers of observation and the capacity of the informed mind for reasoned analysis, hypothesis and logical argument.

This was the birth of a new mode of enquiry – rational, systematic thinking – which later, in the time of Socrates and Plato, assumed the name philosophy, and it had profound effects on Greece and on the whole development of western civilisation. Its scrutiny of the world of nature and its search for order and system within it proceeded to the more practical study of humanity itself, the nature and needs of human beings, and the form of society and the principles of conduct that could best advance human well-being and happiness. It also embraced the critical evaluation of its own methodology in the study of logic and epistemology. Greek philosophy maintained and extended its appeal and influence until Justinian, to protect Christian teaching, shut down the Greek philosophical schools in A.D. 529, after more than a thousand years of continuous activity. Neoplatonism, however, continued to have a strong influence for a great deal longer, especially in the Alexandrian School, in Byzantine mediaeval thought and in the works of great mediaeval philosophers such as John Scotus Eriugena. The legacy of Greek philosophy, of course, still endures.

The rise of philosophy at the end of the seventh century says important things about the mentality of the Greeks of that early period. Philosophy exalted the power of the mind, the life of the mind and the cultivation of the mind. It responded to the impulses that drive curiosity and enquiry. It stood for the free, independent search for truth and the challenging of untested, traditional assumptions. These were not attributes that offered obvious material benefits or that were likely to be easily appreciated by the general public, and the signs are that initially there was indeed a degree of scepticism about both the philosophers and their activities. But in spite of that, philosophy gained a firm foothold and went on to flourish, and that could only have happened in a society that valued freedom of thought and expression, had a disposition to respect intellectual prowess and endeavour, and had the openness and confidence to countenance new ways of looking at fundamental issues.[12]

Against this background of economic, cultural and psychological change, it is not surprising that the old social order and its political apparatus came under challenge. The pressures for political reform were given further impetus by deterioration in the rule of the aristocracy. Greed, *hybris*, crooked judgements and a general disregard for justice are recurring charges against the ruling elite in the fragments of the poets from Hesiod to Solon. Corruption in those who controlled the administration of justice in a system of unwritten law brought the threat of oppression. It was an assault on personal freedom, and was especially unlikely to be tolerated by the hoplite class, who had a new place and power in their society.

Corruption also had the effect of weakening the cohesion of the nobility and gave rise to more intense flare-ups of the *stasis* to which all narrow oligarchies are prone. The competitive strife was worsened by the new economic conditions. Some noble families had taken advantage of the new opportunities and flourished. Others had not. The parity among peers, so vital to the stability of oligarchies, was eroded. Many of the newly enriched merchant class invested in land, intermarried with the old nobility and sought entry to the ruling elite, further upsetting the established order. The staunchly conservative poet Theognis blames much of the ills of his day on these nouveaux riches.[13]

A further destabilising factor was a widening chasm between rich and poor. The new prosperity had passed by the mass of the poorer classes, the sharecroppers and small independent farmers and the many who lacked the means or the spirit of enterprise to avail themselves of the new opportunities. The position of the poor appears, in fact, to have worsened with the general increase in wealth as they faced new pressures from wealthy competitors. Harsh debt laws, such as existed in Athens, under which loans were made on the security of the person and default resulted in debt bondage, further increased the vulnerability of the poor and added to the discontent and to the general resentment that comes with gross inequality.

Out of this background there emerged across the Greek world in the late seventh and sixth centuries an upsurge of social unrest centred around issues of corruption, oppression and political exclusion. In some states the response was the appointment of a respected leader as a lawgiver, with the task of mediating grievances and addressing the rights of the citizen by drawing up a constitution (*politeia*) and a written code of law, in other words creating a system of constitutional government and the rule of law.

In other cases, opportunistic leaders exploited the dissent, rallied the dissenters, and were able to seize power and establish themselves as absolute rulers backed by force. They became known as tyrants (*tyrannoi*), a word, possibly of Lydian origin, that was used to describe a monarch whose power was usurped rather than inherited or legally bestowed. It was sometimes used interchangeably with *basileus*, and initially had no derogatory connotations, though it quickly developed them.[14]

The best-documented case studies of patterns of revolution are provided by Sparta and Athens. Both were large and far from typical city-states, but their experience is broadly illustrative of the problems besetting the Greek world in the revolutionary era. Their solutions also represent some of the most important advances in the evolution of the *polis* and in Greek thinking about the state and the citizen and the best form of government.

Sparta

The Spartans, part of a Dorian migration from the north into the Peloponnesus c. 1000 B.C., had consolidated their control of the fertile Eurotas valley in the heart of Laconia in the southern Peloponnesus by the middle of the eighth century. The earlier population were, unusually, neither driven out nor enslaved, but were kept in permanent subjugation in a condition of serfdom, tied to the land and forced to deliver fixed portions of the produce to their new masters. They became known as helots. Outlying communities in Laconia (*perioecoi*) were also reduced to dependent status, with local autonomy, but forced to accept Spartan foreign policy and to contribute troops to fight in Spartan wars under Spartan command. Spartan expansionism continued with an attack on their neighbours to the west, the Messenians, in the second half of the eighth century. The Messenians were conquered, their land was confiscated and distributed to Spartans, and the population was reduced to the status of helots, working their lands as serfs of their conquerors.

Conquest gave Sparta the means of dealing with population pressures at home that other Greek states resolved by colonisation, but the strategy came with the risk of insurrection by unhappy subjects. That risk materialised around the middle of the seventh century when the Messenians revolted on a grand scale. There followed a gruelling war, lasting seventeen years, which stretched Spartan resources and resolve, and caused disorder in the ranks and upheaval in the state as a whole. The unrest centred around problems that became familiar in other Greek states – an unacceptable inequality in the distribution of wealth, giving rise to calls for redistribution of land, hoplite discontent intensified by a punishing war and a general resentment of unfettered oligarchic rule.

Out of this crisis came a series of major social and political reforms. It is difficult to separate the new from the old in these changes, because our knowledge of earlier Spartan history is so meagre and the ancient tradition ascribed the whole developed Spartan constitutional order to one of the most shadowy figures of antiquity, the lawgiver Lycurgus, as if it all happened at once, the inspired creation of a legendary sage. The legend surrounding Lycurgus was further embellished by a tradition that the main elements of his constitutional arrangements were given to him, or sanctioned, by the Delphic Oracle. The text of the Delphi-linked code, which became known as the Great Rhetra, is recorded in Plutarch and paraphrased by Tyrtaeus, but its date cannot be determined.[15]

But whatever the stages and process by which the new order came into being, there was enacted in Sparta in the latter part of the seventh century a political system that gave the state long-term stability and that has fascinated all who have studied it down the ages, evoking reactions of both admiration and revulsion.

The new constitution retained an old and unusual tradition of two hereditary kings, who came from two leading noble families, who may originally have headed two distinct tribes who coalesced. They commanded the armies in the field, but, apart from certain priestly functions, had few powers in civilian government, merely serving as ordinary members of a Council of Elders (*gerousia*). This Council comprised thirty members, who had to be over sixty years of age at the time of election. They were elected for life from among those of highest merit, which meant in practice that they came from the nobility, as Aristotle makes clear. They were elected by acclamation by the body of citizens, the *damos*. The Council constituted Sparta's highest court, with a crucial role in criminal jurisdiction, and it also had probouleutic powers, which meant that it prepared all proposals going before the people. The *damos*, in addition to its electoral powers, also had the right to a say in shaping public policy, though it is clear it had no final decision-making power.

The main executive power rested with five magistrates known as Ephors (Overseers). They are not mentioned in the Rhetra, and it is not certain when they were established, but they had a dominant place in the seventh-century constitution. They held office for one year, were chosen by the people, and all citizens were eligible alike for the office. They had judicial powers, responsibility for maintaining law and order and for overseeing the conduct of all public officials, and exercised a general control that Aristotle refers to as sovereign and resembling a dictatorship.[16]

But the most far-reaching changes in the constitutional arrangements that evolved in Sparta in the latter part of the seventh century related to the concept and role of the citizen, and they had major social as well as political implications. The changes were clearly inspired by the Messenian War. The Spartan penchant for militarism, visible in its earlier history, was intensified by a conflict that strained morale and discipline, fomented unrest and revealed the scale of the threat from a majority population held in subjugation. As a result the concept of the citizen-soldier was born and Sparta became a military state, its citizens a military master-class.

Under its developed constitution all young males of citizen birth were subjected to a system of state education (the *agoge*) designed to produce fearless soldiers and fervent patriots. At the age of seven they had to leave home and become part of the communal educational system, which concentrated on developing physical stamina, military skills, iron discipline, unwavering courage and selfless devotion to country. When they entered their teens they each received a young adult mentor, who supervised and assisted the progress of his charge, with whom he was expected to develop a close relationship, generally sexual. Pederasty was accepted, especially in Dorian Greece, as an educational aid, developing qualities of loyalty and selfless devotion, and increasing the influence of the mentor in moulding strong moral character.

The *agoge* ended around age twenty, but the military life and training regimen continued. The men essentially lived in barracks and had to become members of a mess hall and dine there each evening, contributing a fixed amount of food. They were expected to marry and generally did in their twenties but, until their training ended at thirty and they received full rights of citizenship, they could not sleep at home and had little opportunity for family life. Even then, they were soldiers first and foremost and, to allow total concentration on their military mission, they were precluded from any other form of professional activity and were denied the use of coined money. The essential requirements of life were met through grants of land, which were worked by helots, who supplied the family's needs and the contributions to the mess hall.[17]

The iron discipline and steely courage of Spartan warriors became fabled in Greece and in later western history. The ethos that inspired it is memorably portrayed in a series of stirring elegies by Tyrtaeus, a celebrated Spartan poet of the seventh century and a commander in the Messenian War. He exalts martial valour as the highest virtue, the true *arete*. For him, the summit of manliness was standing firm in the face of bloody slaughter and summoning the courage to die, if necessary, in defence of family and fatherland (*patris*). This was the noblest form of human endeavour because it brought glory and benefit to the city and the whole people. It served the common good. He gives detailed descriptions of the rewards that were given to the brave. The Spartans were extravagant in celebrating their war heroes. Those who survived returned as revered members of their community with an honoured place for as long as they lived. Those who fell won immortal fame for themselves, their father, their children and their line.[18]

This was an ideal of *arete* with wider significance than the valour characteristic of the Homeric hero, whose heroism was driven by a preoccupation with his own honour and reputation. The new *arete* had an eye on glory too, but it was grounded in patriotism, in duty to one's native land (*gē*), in serving the common good, in being a good citizen. It was the spirit of Thermopylae, where three hundred Spartans with their king, Leonidas, stood against the Persian hordes, models of heroic valour in the face of impossible odds and of willing self-sacrifice for home and country.

The most significant political dimension of Spartan militarism was that the role of soldier was seen as inseparable from the role of citizen. The soldier was an integral part of a *polis*, of a fatherland (*patris*), of a community (*koinonia*). As such, the soldier's foremost responsibility was at one with his responsibility as a citizen, protecting and advancing the good of his community. In Spartan eyes that duty transcended all personal interests. The end of citizenship was serving the common good. The well-being of the state was therefore paramount, and the good citizen lived not for himself but for the fatherland.

Plutarch, an admirer of many facets of the Spartan constitution, emphasised the communitarianism underlying the so-called Lycurgan reforms: 'No-one was allowed to live as he wished but, as if in a camp, everyone had his regimen and way of life determined and was entirely focused not on himself but on his country.' In another summarising passage he described the organic nature of the Spartan community in which citizens were moulded to have neither the desire nor the capacity to live a private life but rather, like bees, to be integrated with society, clustering around their leader and transported by their fervour and ambition to belong totally to their country.[19]

But while the concept of the citizen-soldier meant unconditional, lifelong commitment to the security and service of the state, it also fully integrated the citizen and gave him benefits and status and a genuine role in the management of the state. Besides basic economic security and the honour attached to military service, citizens at Sparta enjoyed a level of social and political equality well beyond that which existed anywhere else in Greece in the seventh century. Citizens were known as *homoioi* (peers), those of like status, a term whose meaning is much debated but that was clearly designed to lift the citizen-soldier beyond class and create a degree of equality across the legal, political and social spheres that was genuine and substantial.

The legal equality is well attested. Spartan citizens lived under a rule of law that gave no legal or political privilege to anyone on the basis of purely external factors such as wealth or birth. In this sense the constitution conformed to Aristotle's concept of the most favourable state as a community of equals. Citizens were also politically equal in that all were theoretically eligible for public office. The Ephorate was unconditionally open to all citizens. Merit was the qualification for the *gerousia*, but that in theory gave every citizen the opportunity to reach it. All citizens again participated on an equal basis in the electoral and deliberative functions of the Popular Assembly, the *damos*. The system retained a powerful executive that left the major executive powers in the hands of a few, but it was designed, to an extent at least, to be a changing few, and every citizen could aspire to be part of it. The oligarchic nature of the executive was also mitigated by the fact that office was annual and, with the exception of the Ephorate, subject to a certain level of accountability.[20]

But the system went further and also sought to establish a significant degree of social equality. The whole structure of the educational regime and the way of life of the citizen-soldiers tended in this direction. Aristotle was impressed by the levelling effects of the system and what were regarded as its democratic features. He points out that the children of rich and poor were educated in the same way. The same equality continued into adolescence and adulthood. No difference was made between rich and poor: they shared the same food in the common mess and the dress of the rich was such as to be affordable by the poor. Aristotle rightly sees this as a determined effort to build an equalitarian ethos.

The Spartan concern with equality did, however, have its limits, as Aristotle also points out. It never extended to the distribution of wealth and, despite the prominence given to frugality and austerity in the Spartan tradition, rich and poor continued to exist without any evidence of dissent. Nor was there any real attempt to achieve equality in practice in the distribution of political power. Birth, wealth and the appeal to merit (the great catchword of aristocracies, frequently linked to birth and wealth) remained powerful forces in Sparta and ensured the continuing political domination of a largely hereditary nobility.

Nonetheless, the Spartan constitution brought the principle of equality among citizens to the fore and gave substantial validity to its description of its citizens as *homoioi*.[21]

The seventh-century reforms defused the unrest surrounding the Messenian War and brought a level of stability and loyalty to the constitution that left little scope for the factional strife and the intrigues of would-be tyrants that continued to plague much of the rest of the Greek world. Aristotle is enthusiastic in his praise of these aspects of the Spartan constitution, which he saw as a balanced blend of aristocratic and democratic elements. He frequently emphasises that, if a constitution is to survive, all elements, or at least the great majority of the citizenry, must be convinced of its merits, be satisfied with what it gives them, and accordingly have loyalty to it and want its continuance. Aristotle strongly believed in the principle of consent, and he found it operating in the Spartan system. The kings were content with the level of honour accorded them, the aristocracy with their dominance of the *gerousia*, and the people with their equal right to seek election to the Ephorate, together with their role as members of the Popular Assembly.[22]

But Spartan stability and internal unity were a product not just of social levelling and political balances. They were obviously also strengthened and sustained by the rigidly conformist, mind-conditioning educational regime. They were further supported by one other consequence of the reforms, the entrenchment of the rule of law. Sparta won fame throughout the Greek world for *eunomia*, the concept to which Hesiod gave prominence as a major force of social order alongside justice and peace. In classical Greece the term described the condition of a society that was well governed and where law and order and a law-abiding culture prevailed.

The Spartan concern with *eunomia* and their success in achieving it are well documented. Tyrtaeus devoted a whole poem to the topic, the remains of which show that it was a rallying cry for order and for obedience to the new god-ordained constitutional system. The prominence given to the poem is a good indication of the importance of the law-and-order theme in the reform agenda.

The Greek historians also highlight the Spartan dedication to the rule of law. Herodotus relates that in early times the Spartans were the worst governed of the Greeks, but that the laws of Lycurgus, with their military, social and political dimensions, changed all that and brought *eunomia*. Elsewhere, in a well-known passage, he reports a debate about the Spartans between the exiled Spartan king Demaratus and the Persian king Xerxes, in which Demaratus emphasises the strength the Spartans derive from the fact that law is their master, the one limitation on their freedom, and that whatever it commands, they do.

Thucydides paints a similar picture. He describes how Sparta, despite a long history of civil strife, achieved a government of law and order which kept tyrants out and enabled the Spartans to retain the same constitution for more than four hundred years, a stability that gave them power and an ability to settle the affairs of others. He provides another illustration of the high place of law and order in the Spartan system and psyche when he cites a speech of the Spartan king Archidamus in 432 urging caution about going to war with Athens. The king exalts the whole way of life and outlook of the Spartans and their prudent conservatism and the wisdom they derive from a well-ordered life and from the fact that they are not so well educated as to despise their laws, and are too well disciplined to be able to disobey them.

Xenophon, the Athenian aristocrat and Socratic disciple, who lived for a time at Sparta, was another admirer of Spartan *eunomia* and singles out, in his account of the Spartan constitution, obedience to law and unanimity about the sovereignty of law as particular Spartan characteristics. He describes how obedience was seen as the highest good in the state, in the army and in the home. The most powerful citizens gave the lead in showing obedience, priding themselves on bowing to authority. Magistrates were strictly bound to abide by the law, and could be called to account and subjected to severe penalties, even while in office, for any violation of the law. Even the kings had to affirm in the most public way their subordination to the law by going through a monthly ritual of swearing an oath to rule in accordance with the law, and they too could be called to account for breaches.[23]

Overall, the Spartan constitution is a notable phenomenon in the history of government, and it has commanded attention and won admirers in every age, though its shortcomings have also been well documented. But there were many attributes of the culture that, when considered in the abstract, had huge appeal – order, discipline, law-abidingness, service before self, heroism on the battlefield, an inclusive, innovative system of government – and were seen as contributing to lasting unity and stability. It was easy to idealise particular features, a trend that began in the latter part of the fifth century in Athens as disenchantment, especially among those of oligarchic leanings, and most notably among those who seized power in 404, with what was seen as the anarchic excesses of democracy took hold. The well-ordered, faction-free society of Sparta seemed ideal by comparison.

The Greek philosophers, especially Plato, who shows particular disillusionment with the selfish individualism he saw around him in Athens, were strongly attracted by Spartan *eunomia*, its culture of duty and communal responsibility, its mixed government and a public system of education that could instil civic virtue. Both Plato and Aristotle were, however, also well aware of Sparta's deficiencies, and Aristotle's criticisms were especially sharp.[24]

But while the ancient world had many laconisers, as they were known, the era of greatest Spartan adulation and influence came during the Renaissance and the Enlightenment, when there was a strong revival of interest in politics and political systems and, of course, in classical antiquity. Most of the great writers of these centuries, such as Machiavelli, More, Milton, Harrington, Montesquieu and Rousseau, fell in varying degrees under the Spartan spell. The later eighteenth century in France has been described as the great era of modern laconomania, the phenomenon led by Montesquieu, Rousseau, Helvetius and Mably. Lycurgus was the great hero, seen as the model par excellence of the ideal legislator.

In the nineteenth century the interest in Sparta seemed to shift to Leonidas and the legend of Thermopylae. The epic saga was commemorated widely in art and literature in many parts of Europe. There was also some interest in Sparta from the socialists, who found in Spartan attitudes towards equality and the distribution of land, the status of women and the social reforms of later revolutionary kings, such as Agis and Cleomenes, support for their own view of the world. A new body of admirers was soon to emerge with the rise of Nazism, which embraced Sparta as a great Nordic nation, a strong state controlled by an elite military caste with the invincibility and conquering spirit that were the marks of the superior Aryan race.[25]

The fascination with Sparta took many forms, was driven by widely varying motives and did not always focus on the more enduring aspects of the Spartan political legacy. That legacy was considerable and has some relevance to the evolution of democracy. Two aspects of the system stand out, which were to gain an important place in the history of democracy.

Sparta's commitment to a rule of law equally applied to all, the guarantor of freedom and the one limitation on freedom, made a strong impression on the Greek world. Many Greek states were, of course, pursuing this principle in the seventh century but, as noted earlier, the manner of Sparta's implementation of it attracted wide attention and admiration.[26] The rule of law would become a fundamental principle of Greek democracy and Roman republicanism, accepted as the indispensable safeguard of the common freedom, and regulator of every action of every person entrusted with power. Cicero gives eloquent expression to the concept in one of his speeches (*Cluent.* 146), where he says: 'Law is liberty's foundation . . . and we are all slaves of the law so that we may be free.' These sentiments were resurrected in the seventeenth century with the rise of liberal movements and constitutionalism. John Locke wrote: 'Where there is no law there is no freedom,' and James Harrington famously called for 'an empire of laws, not of men'. Law as liberty's foundation acquired new importance with the slow rebirth of democracy in the wake of the American and

French Revolutions, and it remains at the heart of the liberal democratic ideal. Sparta cannot, of course, be seen as the sole progenitor or primary transmitter of the principle of the rule of law, but it stood out as a shining exemplar when the idea was taking root in European political culture.

Sparta's blending in its constitution of monarchic, aristocratic and democratic features also had an important impact on subsequent political thought. Both Plato and Aristotle approved such blending of power between upper and lower classes. But it was Polybius, the Greek historian of the second century B.C., author of a history of Rome's rise to power, who bestowed the highest praise on the Spartan system and on Lycurgus and his foresight in realising that the simple forms of monarchy, aristocracy and democracy were all prone to perversion, leading to abuse of power and consequent revolution, and that upright and stable government could only be achieved by a balanced mixing of these elements which would prevent any achieving dominance and the power to oppress. Polybius believed Rome had found its way to the same result as Lycurgus, and he attributed Rome's success to the resulting constitution. Cicero followed the lead of Polybius in his political writings, the *De Republica* and *De Legibus*, presenting the republican constitution as a well-tempered mixed constitution and the ideal form of government.

Athens took a different route. Solon leaned towards a mixed system by giving the people a greater role, but the ideological leap by Cleisthenes to rule by the people, reinforced by the subsequent reforms of Ephialtes and Pericles, resulted in a democracy that was pure, with no semblance of monarchic or aristocratic dimensions, one of its most serious flaws in the eyes of its critics. But the theory of the mixed constitution as exemplified by Sparta and Rome, with its underlying concept of checks and balances, had appeal for the political theorists of the eighteenth century, notably Montesquieu, a great admirer of Sparta, Lycurgus and republican Rome and their constitutional models. The authors of the American Constitution were similarly interested in concepts of checks and balances in government, but the form of constitution that emerged in the USA and other modern democracies was concerned not with a balanced division of power between the social classes, but with a balanced division or separation of powers between the main branches of government, the executive, legislative and judicial. But both systems share the goal of splitting powers to prevent unchecked control and its corrupting influence, with the ancient model having the additional purpose of promoting harmony of the social orders.[27]

But the Spartan constitution, while it had features that impressed later political thinkers, including the democratically minded, had a darker side and massive flaws. Its citizen body was defined in exceedingly narrow terms. It was a military caste, a minority that lived off the labour of a majority, which consisted of fellow Greeks and was held in harsh subjugation, a brutal example of exploitative oppression that carried a constant risk of insurrection.

Sparta single-mindedly fostered a warrior culture that, as Aristotle remarked, was appropriate only to conditions of war, extolling martial powers and the art of war while ignoring the arts of peace. It turned its back on the new age of vibrant literary and artistic creativity and intellectual discovery that was sweeping across most of the rest of Greece.

Its concept of citizenship was, in the final analysis, seriously defective. It carried its control of the lives of citizens and the commitment to public service that it demanded to unacceptable extremes, stifling personal initiative and the development of personal aptitudes, eliminating all private rights and the human need for a private space and a sense of self, and what Aristotle called *philautia*, a regard for oneself as a separate human being. It put the state before the people, and where the power and glory of an institution, whether it be church or state or any social entity, are elevated above the well-being of the people it is intended to serve, there is an obvious perversion of purpose, and the means are made the end. Sparta was flagrantly guilty of that error.

The Spartan system ultimately failed, and the decline took hold within a few decades of its greatest victory, the triumph over Athens in 404 B.C.. Sparta used badly the ascendancy won by that victory. Falling numbers of citizens, a breakdown in the traditional discipline and austerity under the corruptive force of power and success, and mismanagement of the empire to which it now laid claim left it vulnerable, and in 371 B.C. it was decisively defeated by a Boeotian alliance led by Thebes. The Messenian helots were liberated, another major blow. Sparta went into permanent decline and ceased to be a major power in Greece.

Athens before 500 B.C.

The story of early Athens presents a striking contrast to that of Sparta. It emerged from the revolutionary era with a very different form of society and political culture, though it shared more common ground with Sparta in regard to many basic political ideas than is sometimes recognised. As in the case of most Greek states, there is virtually no evidence for the history of Athens before the later seventh century. The Athenians themselves claimed that they were autochthonous, and that the communities of Attica (an area of about 1,000 square miles or 2,590 square kilometres) had been united into a single state under Athens at an early date by the legendary Athenian king Theseus. There is certainly reason to believe that Attica was remarkably free of upheaval from Mycenaean times onwards and kept its Ionian links and character intact. The

Athenians played no role in the colonisation movement, but, judging by the high quality of their Protogeometric and Geometric pottery, they were relatively prosperous.

In the seventh century Athens was still firmly under the control of a narrow group of noble families known as *eupatridae* (well-born). There was an executive of three, annually elected: the archon, who was the civil head and judge in civil cases; the polemarch, who commanded the army and was the judge in cases involving foreigners; and the archon basileus, who had charge of the state religion. Later, six additional archons were created and became known as *thesmothetai*. They comprised a board responsible for recording the law and eventually for the administration of the jury courts. There was a Council known as the Areopagus whose members came from the nobility and held office for life. It formed a criminal court in cases of homicide and was, no doubt, in practice the real controlling power. A Popular Assembly (*ecclesia*) existed, but its powers are unknown.

The same factionalism and popular unrest evident in the rest of Greece in the seventh century also afflicted Athens, and in 632/1 B.C. there was an attempt by a nobleman, Cylon, to establish a tyranny. It failed, and he and his supporters were executed. But the unrest continued, and ten years later the ruling nobility resorted to the common expedient of struggling aristocracies in the period, the appointment of a lawgiver. His name was Draco, but all that is known of his laws is that they dealt largely with homicide and became notorious for their severity.[28]

Around the beginning of the sixth century there was a fresh upsurge of social unrest, which resulted once again in the appointment of a lawgiver. This time the choice was Solon, a well-known aristocrat who, though he belonged to the *eupatridae*, had taken a public position as a champion of the poor. He was elected archon in 594 B.C. with full powers to reform the legal and political system. Solon was a prolific writer and an intellectual who confronted at the level of principle the ethical and political issues of his time. In line with contemporary custom, he wrote in verse, using iambic and elegiac forms. Substantial fragments remain, providing unique first-hand evidence and analysis of the social turbulence that faced him and of the political and moral vision that inspired his reforms. He is an important figure in the history of Greek political thought and in the political evolution of the *polis*.[29]

Solon saw around him a failing and decadent ruling class that had lost its moral moorings and that was murdering the oldest of the Ionian states. He believed the moral decline derived from greed and a state of mind that had lost all sense of justice. He describes a chain of decadence. Leaders accumulate wealth (*olbos*) through misdeeds and a rule of crooked judgements, stealing without regard for the sacred or profane or the hallowed foundations of justice. They know no limit, and the result is excess (*koros*) which breeds insolence (*hybris*), which in turn is a spur to still more immoderate behaviour.

Solon believed that the ultimate consequence for such wrongdoers is delusion and ruin (*ate*), but he emphasises that the consequences for the whole state are equally ruinous. He spells out an inevitable chain of social disintegration that follows from leadership that is divorced from justice: factional strife, civil war, a slide into servitude, the poor driven from their homes, many enslaved and sold overseas because of debt. No one escapes. The evil is epidemic.

The corpus of Solonian fragments, and especially the lengthy elegy generally entitled *Eunomia*, not only presents a clear diagnosis of the problems of Athens, but universalises them and their causes and progression as paradigms of what he clearly believed were fixed laws governing the life of political communities. The corpus also contains the first statement of the famous chain of moral decline, extending from unlimited wealth to unrestrained excess to insolent pride to the delusion that brings ruin. It was soon to become proverbial, and to provide themes and inspiration for many of the greatest masterpieces of Greek tragedy, as they explored the frailties and complexities of the human psyche and its propensity to turn good fortune into disaster.

Solon's remedy for the moral and social decay of his time was a restoration of the way of justice (*dike*) and of the order and harmony (*eunomia*) that came with it. His vision for society is centred around these closely connected concepts and is strongly reminiscent of Hesiod, who first articulated the view that human beings are endowed by their nature with a particular social gift that fits them for communal life, namely the gift of justice, that shared sense of what is right and fair in human relationships.[30]

In Solon's political poems justice clearly emerges as the supreme civic virtue, the ethical bedrock on which all facets of society, its laws, institutions and social interactions, must be founded. Where justice is absent and a spirit of injustice (*adikos noos*) possesses the leaders, there is moral and social chaos (*dysnomia*); where justice is present, there is *eunomia*, which Solon presents as that orderly and perfect form of society that shackles the unjust, straightens crooked judgements, puts an end to excess, blunts the forces of insolence and delusion and their arrogant acts, and eliminates factionalism and strife.

The other ethical principle that runs through Solon's political poems is the idea of moderation, or the Mean. It is implicit in much of his political vocabulary and underlies many aspects of his concept of *eunomia*. The Attic orators and Aristotle associate him with images of moderation and temperance, and according to Plutarch he had been advised by the Delphic Oracle 'to sit in the middle of the boat'. He can fairly be seen as the pivotal figure in the evolution of two of the later Greek canon of cardinal virtues, namely justice and temperance.

Solon's reforms were driven by his highly developed sense of social ethics and the mechanisms of political life. He believed that he was dealing with an unjust society, heavily weighted in favour of an hereditary oligarchy, and he was determined to make the necessary changes to rectify that. But he was equally determined to do this without injustice to those who had wealth and power. He saw himself as a mediator or referee, standing in a no-man's-land, a barrier between the two colliding divisions in his society, the well-born (*agathoi*) and the lowly (*kakoi*). His task was to find the just balance between conflicting claims that would allow neither side to triumph unjustly over the other. He believed any other course would fail and would lead to large-scale bloodshed.[31]

His first concern was to eliminate the main injustices being inflicted on the poor, and he tackled this by a series of laws known as the *seisachtheia* (the shaking-off of burdens), which essentially cancelled debts. Indebtedness was the main source of hardship. The law allowed lending on the security of the person of the debtor, which meant that, in case of default, the debtor became the property of the creditor and could be enslaved. This law also affected a particular group of peasant farmers known as *hectemoroi*, who, for some unknown reason, were in a form of bondage, with an encumbrance on their land requiring them to pay a portion of their produce to their overlord. For them, too, default meant the possibility of enslavement.

Solon abolished lending on the security of the person, ended *hectemorage*, liberated those caught in that position and gave them back full ownership of their land. He also freed all who had been enslaved because of debt. He did not, however, yield to calls for a redistribution of land, which would have meant taking property from the rich. This went beyond his view of a balanced solution. He saw the demand as greed and the pursuit of excess, and he did not consider such enforced equality in the distribution of wealth as just or necessary. The cause of the poor could not be advanced through injustice to others.

Solon was well aware that large-scale inequality in the distribution of wealth was a barrier to civic harmony, and he railed against excess in the pursuit and accumulation of wealth. He may even have imposed a limit on the acquisition of land. He certainly had no hesitation about interfering in the market, and there are records of measures in his laws to control exports and protect against food shortages and high prices. But he did not attack private property that was justly secured, and he accepted economic disparity and the class divisions that went with it as part of the natural order. Justice did not entail equal shares of a country's wealth for all. But he was insistent that the rights of the lower classes to their property should be as fully protected as those of the nobility, and that their freedom should be inalienable, and he gave the important class of small farmers a secure place in Athenian society.

Solon also sought to entrench the ideal of justice by affirming equality for all before the law. He summed it up in one of his iambic poems: 'I wrote laws equally for the low-born and the well-born which offered upright justice for everyone.'[32]

He also made important changes in the administration of justice to curb abuse and extend access to justice to all who had been wronged. He gave a right of appeal to a court of the people. It is unclear whether this meant the Popular Assembly or some subset of the Assembly, which became known as the *Heliaia*, but in any case the right provided a popular check on the judicial powers of magistrates. Aristotle says that Solon also gave the people the right to call magistrates to account at the end of their term of office, which provided another means of checking political corruption. In another important innovation, he gave citizens the right to initiate judicial proceedings on behalf of anyone they felt had suffered a wrong, further broadening popular involvement in the administration of justice. Aristotle regarded these measures, along with the abolition of lending on security of the person, as the most democratic features of the Solonian constitution. They certainly meant a more secure place for justice in Athenian society.[33]

Solon's other constitutional reforms were also based on his concepts of justice and balance. The most fundamental change was the replacement of birth with wealth as the qualification for political office. The citizen body was divided into four classes on the basis of landed property and its produce. The highest office, the archonship, was confined to members of the two wealthiest classes, while the lower offices were open to members of the third class. The fourth class, known as thetes, who were essentially the landless labourers, were excluded from political office altogether, but were entitled to sit in the Popular Assembly, the *ecclesia*, and in the court of the people.

The Areopagus lost some of its dominance and exclusivity. It was no longer able to choose its own members or the state's magistrates and became instead a body of ex-archons, which gave it a timocratic rather than an aristocratic base. But its general influence would have remained strong, and it continued as the court for all cases of premeditated murder, and was given clearer powers as guardian of the laws and the constitution, with the right to impeach anyone suspected of conspiring against the constitution.

The role of the Popular Assembly was enhanced. It now included all citizens on an equal basis, and it was given the two crucial rights that Aristotle considered a necessary minimum of power for the people: the rights to elect magistrates and to call them to account. The extent of the Assembly's role and powers as a deliberative and decision-making body cannot be determined with any certainty, though it is likely that its consent was sought for major decisions. Solon clearly wanted a politically engaged and active citizenry, as is illustrated by one of his well-known laws which penalised citizens who failed to take a side in factional disputes.[34]

The Aristotelian account of the constitution of Athens says that Solon also introduced a new Council (*boule*) of four hundred members, consisting of a hundred representatives from each of the four Attic tribes. The account has often been doubted on the basis that there is no record of such a Council performing any function before the reforms of Cleisthenes, but it is difficult to reject such a clear statement on an argument from silence, and Solon may well have seen the need for such a Council to facilitate the work of the Assembly. According to Plutarch, its functions were probouleutic, and the Assembly could only consider what the Council brought before it.[35]

Solon failed in his immediate objective to end factionalism and social unrest in Athens, but the impact of his work and ideas on Athenian political culture and the evolution of democracy was of fundamental importance. His stature as a lawgiver soon rivalled that of Lycurgus, and he was included in the Seven Sages of Greece. In an age when the Ionian natural philosophers were coming to the fore, he emerged as the first political philosopher and the first statesman whose agenda was determined by reasoned ethical and political principles.

Some of his greatest achievements lie in his contribution to the concepts of justice and the rule of the law. He gave new prominence to the idea of justice as the basis of human fellowship and association, and as the supreme civic virtue and the only means to the order and harmony that are the essence of the ideal political community. In line with these beliefs, he sought to enshrine justice in a body of law that would give upright justice to all, would be equally applicable to all, and would be administered in a way that ensured equal treatment and gave protection against abuse. The goal was *eunomia*, a rule of law that was fair and equal, commanding consent and obedience, and leading on to order and harmony. These were ideas that, as emphasised earlier, the Spartans had developed as a cornerstone of their constitution, and that became embedded in Athenian, Roman and modern democratic thought. But the arguments for the rule of law and for the supremacy of the law over those who administer it have had few more fervent or effective advocates than Solon.

His work as a lawgiver also left behind a vision of the rights of the individual citizen that endured and paved the way for Athenian progress towards a fully democratic form of government. He vindicated the right of every citizen to personal liberty and to freedom from all forms of oppressive dependence.

He gave every citizen equality before the law and protection against arbitrary use of power and so-called crooked judgements by creating a broad written legal code, and by instituting a right of appeal and a system of accountability. On the positive side of freedom he recognised the right and need of all citizens to have a share in the management of the state sufficient to remove any sense of exclusion or alienation and ensure broad-based loyalty to the constitution, and he accordingly increased significantly the political powers of the mass of the people and gave them a more integral role in public affairs.

The democratic nature of these rights of the individual citizen was often stressed in antiquity, and they are essential features of any democratic system, but Solon was no democrat. He equated justice with equality in the sphere of law but not in the sphere of politics. His timocratic system swept aside the monopoly of political office by an exclusive, hereditary oligarchy, and broadened considerably the base of the ruling class and allowed for greater upward mobility. But the mass of citizens were still a long way from having a controlling power in political affairs. The Assembly had the power to elect magistrates and hold them to account, but apart from that, there is no evidence that it had power to dictate anything. Oligarchic factionalism and tyranny would be the dominant forces in Athenian politics for another eighty years.

Solon accepted the reality of political hierarchy just as he accepted the reality of a social hierarchy. He did not challenge the traditional aristocratic pretension that high birth and wealth gave not only a greater claim to power but a greater capacity for it. He used the standard morally loaded terminology of *agathoi* and *kakoi* to describe the upper and lower classes, with its implication that high-born meant high merit and low-born the opposite. He saw the mass of the people as followers, not leaders, and he believed they would be more willing followers if they had moderate political rights. Excess would only breed insolence. He maintained that he had given the people as much privilege as they needed, and as much as was due. He had found the just balance. Two quotations from his writings preserved in the Aristotelian *Constitution of Athens* encapsulate this view of the proper balance of power between mass and elite:

> To the people I gave as much privilege as was sufficient for them, neither reducing nor exceeding what was their due. Those who had power and were enviable for their wealth I took good care not to injure. I stood casting my strong shield around both parties, and allowed neither to triumph unjustly. . . . The people will follow their leaders best if they are neither too free nor too much restrained, for excess produces insolent behaviour when great wealth falls to men who lack sound judgment. (Arist. *Ath. Pol.* 12.1–2, trans. Jowett)

Solon's constitution sought a middle way. The narrow, exclusive oligarchy was no longer in full control. There was considerable widening at the top, with a bigger role for a growing middle class and readier upward mobility. The lower classes had been given a higher political status and a meaningful involvement in political life. The pyramid remained, but it was a good deal flatter, and offered a far more equal and just society.

The Solonian constitution was widely praised in antiquity, and seen as moderating the excesses to which radical democracy was prone, while also eliminating the dangers of unchecked oligarchy through protections for individual freedom and adequate public control of leaders. Aristotle described it as 'admirably tempered', and when he came to construct his own ideal polity, it contained many Solonian features, centred as it was around the idea of a society in which the gap between rich and poor would be the smallest possible and the predominant influence would be a large middle class of true equals predisposed neither to oligarchy nor democracy, but favouring the moderate features of both. This would produce a mean between the oligarchic and democratic extremes, leaving scope for merit, but also ensuring justice and moderate levels of political involvement for all. Many strands of Cicero's political thought and of conservative Roman republicanism as a whole also show affinity with Solon's ideals. He pointed the way to many of the concepts that have shaped republican and democratic theory down the ages.[36]

After completing his term as archon, Solon laid aside his powers and went abroad for ten years. His reforms did not have the desired effect, and within a few years factionalism and civil unrest reappeared. This time Athens succumbed to the fate that Solon had warned against, and that many Greek states had experienced as the outcome of internal feuding. A populist factional leader, Peisistratus, won enough public support to enable him to seize power by force in 561 and make himself tyrant. Solon died soon afterwards. Peisistratus held power for five years and was then expelled in a new eruption of violence. He was soon restored but quickly suffered a second expulsion, which lasted ten years, until 546, when he fought his way back with foreign help. This time, he secured his power by neutralising his opponents and maintaining a strong force of Thracian mercenaries, and his tyranny lasted until his death, in 527.[37]

There is general agreement in the tradition that Peisistratus was a benevolent despot, pursuing a policy of moderation and reconciliation. He made few changes to Solon's legislation, maintaining the semblance of constitutional rule and merely ensuring that the highest offices went to his supporters. He maintained peace and good relations with other states, which gave a fillip to Athenian trade. He also sought to boost agriculture and rural life in general, and was especially supportive of small farmers, making grants to those in difficulty. There was certainly a growth in the prosperity of Athens during his reign, and his era was remembered as an 'age of Cronus' – in other words, a golden age. Peisistratus added to prosperity and to his own popularity by embarking on a major programme of public works, a common morale-boosting stratagem of despots. It created employment and provided a symbol of well-being and a stimulus to national pride. Temples featured prominently in the building programme, and Peisistratus showed a particular interest in promoting state religion and the big religious festivals. He established a major new festival, the Great Dionysia, and extended the scale of others, notably the Panathenaea, the annual festival in honour of Athena, the patroness of Athens. He also had a broad interest in the arts, and he and his sons attracted to Athens many of the foremost literary figures of his day. It was during his reign that Greek tragedy made its first appearance with a production by Thespis in c. 534. Athens became a cultural hub under Peisistratus, and there can be little doubt that his cultural policy and broad patronage of the arts helped pave the way for the golden age of art, architecture, literary creativity and philosophical enquiry that flowered at Athens over the following century.[38]

The rule of Peisistratus also had other effects. It further undermined the already weakening dominance of the aristocracy. Some of its most powerful families, who had led the opposition to Peisistratus, had gone abroad or had been forced out. Others found it expedient to submit to the inevitable and cooperate. The long duration of the tyranny accustomed the people to look to the tyrant for their well-being, and broke down the earlier forms of dependency on which the influence of the local lords was based.

Furthermore, the middle and lower classes enjoyed a favoured place under Peisistratus. This was generally the case in Greek tyrannies, most of which were created by means of demagogic exploitation of popular grievances against the ruling aristocracy. Along with a measure of armed force, popular support provided their power-base. Peisistratus was especially assiduous in cultivating the support of the people, and without doubt he gave them a better life. They had the benefits of peace. The veneer of constitutional rule was carefully maintained, and the indications are that the Solonian reforms remained intact as far as the role of the *demos* was concerned. There is clear evidence of increased prosperity, and there was a richer life of entertainment and civic celebration. Peisistratus provided his own form of 'bread and circuses', and the whole manner of his rule, combined with Solon's reforms, left little possibility of a return to the old order of aristocratic ascendancy. To this extent he helped lay foundations not only for new cultural directions but also for new political directions in the century ahead.

On his death in 527, his eldest son, Hippias, took his place, assisted by his brother, Hipparchus. They continued their father's policies and ruled securely until 514, when a personal quarrel between Hipparchus and two of his friends, Harmodius and Aristogiton, led to an attempted coup and the murder of Hipparchus. Hippias reacted harshly and his rule degenerated into an oppressive purge of real or imagined enemies, which eventually encouraged some of the exiled noble families to organise an invasion to overthrow him. The enterprise was spearheaded by the Alcmaeonids, a formidable, activist family, who traditionally controlled a major aristocratic faction comprising the men of the Attic shoreline (the *Paralioi*), and who were led at this time by Cleisthenes, who had been archon under Hippias and whose sister had been married to Peisistratus. The initial attempt failed, but Cleisthenes, using the support of the Delphic Oracle, was then able to enlist the aid of the Spartans, who dispatched an army led by their king, Cleomenes, which resulted in the capitulation of Hippias and his departure into exile. Athens had been liberated and was soon to set out on a new political road that would lead to the world's first real democracy.[39]

Summary and Conclusions

The 250 years of Greek history between 750 and 500 B.C. produced revolutionary change in the structure and outlook of the *polis* and a remarkable body of ideas that is still at the heart of the continuing search for a political ideology that can move our civilisation towards just and stable political structures capable of bringing peace within and between nations and of protecting the dignity and well-being of every individual.

The change in the Greek world in this so-called Archaic Age was driven by many interconnected factors: the waves of colonisation that brought Greeks into contact with other lands and cultures; expanded economic opportunities that broke the monopoly of the aristocracy on wealth and gave rise to a larger, less dependent and more influential middle class; changing military requirements that further strengthened the place of the middle class; degeneration in aristocratic rule, bringing corruption, increased factional strife and alienation of the lower classes; a cultural revolution that ushered in an era of liberated creativity, in which individualism, rationalism and intellectual freedom came to the fore. All of these developments heightened political awareness and fed into a demand for social and political change. Initially the demand centred not on issues of power and its distribution, but on that most basic of personal rights, freedom from arbitrary domination by those in authority. The demand became more urgent as the ruling elites lost the trust of the people, and it crystallised around calls for justice and a rule of law.

The idea of justice as the god-given immanent human quality that was the source of human fellowship and sociability, and that distinguished human society from the brutal animal world governed by force and might, was well rooted in Greek culture by the early seventh century. Justice meant that human behaviour was directed by a higher principle, by a common innate sense of what was fair and due as reflected in established norms and traditions.

Hesiod was the first to give extended treatment to the theme of justice as the basis of society and the means to a well-ordered life for the individual and the *polis* alike. A century later Solon provided another eloquent testament to the power of justice to combat the destructive, anti-social forces of corruption and factious arrogance, and to open the way to order and harmony. Echoes of similar sentiments survive in the fragments of the Ionian literary tradition throughout the seventh and sixth centuries and in the work of the early philosophers.

The emphasis on justice was sparked by the behaviour of a decadent nobility, who were seen to be perverting it. It was accompanied by a demand that the unchecked and arbitrary control of rulers over the interpretation and administration of justice should be ended, and that the principles of justice should be defined and enshrined in a code of law. There followed the era of the lawgivers, trusted, authoritative leaders who were empowered to produce codes that would give certainty to the substance of the laws of the state and the manner of their administration.

Sparta and Athens provide the only substantial examples of these codes, but they show that the principle of the rule of law took firm root in Greece in the seventh and sixth centuries with all its important implications for the freedom and security of the individual. The law, clearly defined and in most cases written, now stood as the highest authority in the state, and every citizen, regardless of wealth, birth or political position, was equally subject to it. The condition of law and order became a cherished ideal. These are principles that remain pillars of every free society, that ensure equality for all before the law, and that protect the weak against domination by the strong and the individual against domination by the state.[40]

But the issue soon extended beyond the sphere of justice to the broader sphere of government. The remit of many lawgivers, as Aristotle records, went beyond producing legal codes to writing a constitution (*politeia*), which meant confronting the big constitutional issues, such as the political role of the citizen, the distribution of political power and the best form of government. The outcome of that reformist exercise brought into European political thought and practice some of the key components of our modern liberal-democratic heritage.

Freedom and equality, greatly strengthened by the codification of law, became established as core elements of the rights of citizenship. At Sparta the citizens were described as *eleutheroi*, the free, and at Athens, Solon took particular steps to ensure that the citizen's right to personal freedom would be inalienable. Equality was a key feature of the legal reforms and was an especially prominent element in the Spartan system, which went to extraordinary lengths to foster the concept of a citizen body of equals. In practice the concept proved limited outside the sphere of law, but both the Spartan and Athenian systems reflected a strong recognition that a cherished goal of the reforms, order and internal harmony, could only be achieved if a sufficient level of political equality existed to ensure broad loyalty to the constitution and what in modern terminology is called consent of the governed.

Both systems sought to achieve that level of equality by ending the monopoly of power by a narrow, hereditary nobility and by enhancing the political role of the ordinary citizen. The populace was given the right to choose its leaders, and the place of the popular assemblies in decision-making was enhanced. Sparta went further and opened its most powerful elective office to all its citizens, though its Council largely remained an aristocratic preserve. At Athens, Solon was content to widen the ranks of the ruling elite and facilitate upward mobility by changing the requirement for high office from birth to wealth. But he extended the power of the people in a different way by giving them a role in the administration of justice. Neither system accepted the principle of full equality of political rights for all citizens, instead holding on to the idea of political preferment and control for those of high birth and high wealth, with which superior merit was traditionally associated. But both recognised the need for significant popular participation in the business of government, a development that did not by any means entail inevitable progression to the democratic system, but that was nonetheless a necessary step on the road to it.

The form of government that resulted from the reforms at Sparta was classified in antiquity as a mixed constitution, a blend of monarchy, aristocracy and democracy. The constitution of Solon was seen as a variant of the mixed form, described by Aristotle as an admirable blend of oligarchic and democratic elements, replacing an excessively pure (*akraton*) oligarchic form. Both systems carefully circumscribed the role of the masses, limiting it to what was considered necessary to meet the public's need for political engagement. But they did create a genuine sharing of power between the classes sufficiently balanced to alter significantly the traditional power structure and dynamics of factional politics. The people were now a force to be reckoned with as never before, a factor that, when combined with other features such as annual terms of office and various forms of accountability, made accumulation and abuse of power considerably more difficult. The concept of a balanced distribution of power between classes was well established in the constitutional reforms at both Sparta and Athens.

The evolution of the rights of the citizen also brought into focus the duties that went with them. These were linked to the Greek concept of the *polis* as a community drawn together by a natural need and aptitude for human fellowship, and seeking not just the safety and material benefits of organised society but the more complete associative existence made possible by human interaction and participation in the communal life of a state.

These views were later given fullest expression by Plato and Aristotle, but the idea that the well-ordered state was the means to a good life is already apparent in Homer's portrait of the ideal *polis*, and in his contrasting description of the lawless brutality and isolation of the life of those who lacked its benefits. It also underlies the concept of justice and human sociability that emerged so prominently in the era from Hesiod to Solon, with its implications that communal life was the divinely ordained, natural order for human beings and therefore the way to true human fulfilment.

These were ideas that naturally favoured the collectivist vision of the state as a community in which all members work cooperatively as part of one whole, for the good of that whole, on which depends the ultimate good of each individual. The smallness and homogeneity of the *polis* also promoted a sense of communal solidarity, so there emerged the principle that the common good, the phrase first found in Tyrtaeus, is the end of political action and must take precedence over private advantage. Citizenship meant membership of this form of communal association, bound by shared political and ethical values expressed in laws, and committed to the promotion of the common welfare. It required respect for law and the rights of others and adherence to the spirit of law-abidingness represented by *eunomia*. It brought with it a right of participation in the management of the state – a right that also carried a duty to contribute to public needs and the common good, and to reject the socially destructive forces of injustice, greed and overweening personal ambition.

At Sparta this collectivist ethos developed into a totalitarian form of communitarianism, which established control by the *polis* over every sphere of life and demanded total subordination of private interests and aspirations to the purposes and requirements of the state. Elsewhere, especially in Ionian regions of Greece, a far stronger sense of individualism and personal liberty prevailed. In general, the early Greek *polis* was not preoccupied with sharp distinctions between public and private spheres or with modern Hegelian notions of divides between the state and civil society, but, outside Sparta, citizenship for the Greeks did not deny the individual a sense of self or a private domain, free from intervention by the state.

Overall, the history of the early *polis* provides a fascinating and informative case study of political evolution and integration. It was a journey from a primitive, loosely constituted form of community, dominated by an all-powerful, land-rich elite to a more equal, stable, orderly and structured form of political organisation. The broadening economic prosperity, the vibrant cultural and intellectual environment, and the sometimes inspired leadership that shaped this history resulted in a steady evolution towards new ideas of human dignity and individual autonomy, of the value of community and communal identity, and of the necessity for inclusive government that gave a voice to all citizens and was based on agreed principles of justice expressed in law. This was the era that laid the groundwork for the emergence of the democratic ideal. It represents a noteworthy first chapter in the history of European political thought.

CHAPTER 2

The Rise of Democracy

After the expulsion of Hippias in 510 B.C., Athens soon faced again the prospect of being mired in factional strife. Two main groups emerged, one led by Cleisthenes, who had spearheaded the overthrow of Hippias, the other by a nobleman named Isagoras, about whom little is known, but who clearly commanded significant noble support. Isagoras won the first round by gaining election to the archonship of 508/7. Cleisthenes reacted by rallying popular support with a set of radical proposals designed to extend the power of the people. Isagoras countered by inviting Cleomenes to intervene again, and the Spartan king returned to Athens with a small force. Cleisthenes was forced to leave the city, and seven hundred of his supporters were driven out by Cleomenes, who then attempted to dissolve the Council and install Isagoras in power with three hundred of his supporters. But the Council resisted and the *demos*, who wanted its champion Cleisthenes back, united in rebellion and besieged Cleomenes and Isagoras in the Acropolis. After two days Cleomenes and his men were allowed to leave the city under a truce. Isagoras escaped with him. Cleisthenes and his exiled supporters were able to return to pursue implementation of the programme of reform.[1]

Cleisthenes in effect enacted a new constitution for the state built on three main pillars. The first involved a totally new organisation of the citizen body at the local level. The old system was based on kinship and comprised a threefold structure of clan, phratry and tribe, in all of which membership was hereditary. The clan (*genos*) was an important part of the old pyramidal order. A clan consisted of a group of aristocratic houses that could claim descent from a common ancestor. They controlled a network of dependants who may not have been formally members of the clan but who undoubtedly formed part of its power-base. Clans were organised bodies with elected officials, and their regular activities included such matters as enrolling new members and celebrating the religious rites associated with the clan's tutelary deities.

The origin and role of phratries (brotherhoods) are much more obscure. They were broader groupings than the clan, and were presumably formed originally, as the term suggests, on some basis of kinship. But they became inclusive bodies and, before Cleisthenes, all citizens had to be members of a phratry, and membership was proof of citizenship. The only functions of phratries supported by the meagre evidence were religious and social, but the connection between membership and citizenship gave them a special importance.

The tribe (*phyle*) was the largest hereditary division of the Athenian citizen body. There were four of them, reflecting ancient ethnic distinctions. But, though the personal character of the tribes remained important and membership remained hereditary, it seems clear that they became, to a large extent, regional divisions. They were subdivided into units that had to function on a local basis. Each tribe was divided into three sections called *trittyes*, and there were twelve further subdivisions known as *naukraries*. The relationship between them is not entirely certain, but together they appear to have provided the main elements of the state's local government, and *naukraries* were especially important in regard to military organisation and matters related to taxation and finance.[2]

Cleisthenes replaced this social order, with its old kinship-linked networks so favourable to the ascendancy of an hereditary elite, with a system that laid the basis for popular sovereignty and a far greater level of political equality and opportunity. He took a very basic social unit, the local village or settlement, and reorganised the citizen body into these neighbourhood groupings, which were known as demes. They numbered 139 according to latest estimates. In Athens the demes were formed by dividing the city into wards. But while the demes were local units, membership once gained was retained regardless of residence and was passed on to male descendants.

Each deme had its own political structure with a high measure of popular control. There was a popular assembly which elected a chief officer (*demarch*) and other officials, and held them to account through a formal process of scrutiny (*euthuna*), a practice that now began to permeate every area of the Athenian political system. Cleisthenes also established new religious cults to increase the cohesion of the demes, and the priesthoods associated with these cults were open to all citizens, and the priests were chosen by lot. The effect was a further loosening of the local control of the nobility.

The deme had responsibility for its own local government and, according to Aristotle, took over the duties of the *naukraries*. Membership of a deme became the new criterion of citizenship, and it was the demes that maintained the official registers of citizens. It also became the practice that the name of the deme, the *demotikon*, was added as an official part of a member's name. The deme therefore had special significance in the life of every member.

The establishment of the local, self-governing system of demes, operating along the lines of the central democratic administration, was perhaps the most far-seeing and far-reaching of all the reforms of Cleisthenes. It created democratic cells in every local community, loosening the hold of local aristocracies, empowering ordinary citizens and embedding the ethos of self-rule on a basis of equality. Cohesion, stability and the spirit of participation were further enhanced by communal engagement in a busy religious life involving numerous cults and frequent festivals. Aristotle argued in the *Politics* that the stability of a political system could best be ensured by schooling citizens by habit and training in the particular ethos of their system. The participatory form of local government and communal life instituted in the demes by Cleisthenes followed such a course, imbuing at grassroots level the ethos of rule by the people.

But the demes became a building block of democracy in another important way. They were linked into a new tribal structure. A system of ten new tribes was created by a radical reordering of the regional divisions of Attica. The entire state was divided into three main regions: the City (*asty*), the Coast (*paralia*) and the Interior (*mesogaia*). Each region was further subdivided into ten districts, which were given the old title of *trittyes,* and the ten tribes were formed by combining one *trittys* chosen from each region.

The basis on which the *trittyes* were themselves formed and then combined into the new tribes has given rise to an ongoing debate about the purpose underlying the whole elaborate restructuring. But the most obvious explanation, and the one best supported by the evidence, is that Cleisthenes was seeking to create regional divisions roughly similar in size which would join together in their public capacities an aggregate of demes, geographically and socially diverse, and representative of a cross section of the state's social strata and occupations.

Aristotle states that the purpose was to give each tribe a share in every region so as to achieve a mixing together of citizens. He gives two reasons for the mixing: to break down old affiliations, and to enable more citizens to share in the political system. Both reasons seem entirely plausible, and indeed are interrelated. Cleisthenes was seeking to forge a new unity by creating a new alignment of citizens in groupings with a geographical and social diversity of membership that would cut across old loyalties centred around class issues and factional rivalries. He was also seeking to draw all of the demes, however remote, into a new political structure and thereby increase opportunity for greater political participation by all citizens. Unity, inclusiveness and participation were prominent themes in Greek political thought, seen as the foundations of consensus (*homonia*) and loyalty to the constitution, and the counterforce to *stasis*.

All of this fits well with the role envisaged for the tribes in the overall reforms. The tribal groupings were to have two main purposes. They would serve as the basis for the recruitment and organisation of the army, each tribe responsible for providing a hoplite regiment and a squadron of cavalry. Each tribe would also elect its own commander (*strategos*). This would result in a military organisation that fully exploited the national manpower and drew together in its main units soldiers from different areas and backgrounds and placed them under an elected commander. The new structure would obviously have an integrating effect and reduce risks of regional splits and social tensions within the military.[3]

But the most important function of the reformed tribes related to the second main pillar of Cleisthenes' constitution, a new national Council of five hundred members to replace the Solonian Council of four hundred. The structure and procedures of the new Council were closely linked to the new system of demes and tribes. Each tribe was given equal representation in the Council and contributed fifty members, who were chosen by the demes comprising the tribe, each deme assigned a quota of seats in proportion to its size. To increase the efficiency of the Council's operations, it was provided with a steering committee, which convened the Council, presided over it, set its agenda and had general responsibility for the management of its business. The committee comprised the fifty representatives of each tribe, serving on a rotating basis for one-tenth of the year, a division of the year known as a prytany. During their tenure they had the title of *prytaneis* (presidents), and lived and worked in a special building near the Agora.

The Council became what has rightly been termed the linchpin of the new constitution and eventually acquired extensive administrative, deliberative and judicial functions. Its initial responsibilities were undoubtedly more modest, but from the beginning it had control of important levers of power and was clearly designed to have a central role. It set the agenda of the Assembly and had a comprehensive probouleutic function to give prior consideration to all issues brought before the Assembly. This could result in a specific proposal (*probouleuma*) being placed before the Assembly, or in an open proposal that introduced an issue for debate without recommending a course of action. It became a firm principle that no decree could be enacted by the Assembly without benefit of some form of *probouleuma*, and issues not previously considered by the Council could only be raised and debated within the Assembly by the mechanism of first commissioning the Council to bring forward a *probouleuma* in regard to them. This ensured that the business of the Assembly was orderly and focused, and that debates and decisions had the benefit of a preliminary assessment of the issues by a representative and accountable steering committee.

This was a Council radically different from any contemporary *boule*, and reflected a new democratic spirit that was inclusive, equalitarian and intent on giving control to the people. The Council was democratically chosen at local level, an example of the so-called grassroots democracy introduced by the reform of the demes. It was inclusive, representative of every deme throughout the country. It was also inclusive in that the structure of the tribes protected against domination by the elite and guaranteed a geographical and social mix both in the Council as a whole and in its presidency.

It was equalitarian in several aspects. It gave representation to each local community on a proportional basis, the first known example of a democratically elected and evenly representative political body. It also gave each tribe equal representation within the Council, and rotated leadership of the Council between the tribal delegations on an equal basis. Membership was for one year and re-election was permitted only once, which meant rapid turnover and wider access, in line with the principle of rule and be ruled, which Aristotle presents as a primary characteristic of democratic equality. It appears that the rules of eligibility for membership also favoured broad access. The only known requirements were that members should be over thirty and of good character. This does not mean, of course, that birth, wealth and other traditional prejudices did not continue to favour the elite and limit participation by the lower classes, but these are factors that reduce equality of political opportunity in even the most egalitarian societies.

The new Council was in many ways a people's Council, which would have given it high popular standing and authority. It also drew significant power from its probouleutic and other leadership functions in regard to the Assembly. But its diversity of membership, short term of office and the rotation of its leadership were powerful checks to keep it from becoming an independent power bloc or usurping the powers of the Assembly. All indications are that its purpose was the opposite: to provide authoritative leadership for the Assembly that would give firmer control of the state to the people. It was an adjunct of the Assembly, not a rival.[4]

The interconnected institutions of deme, tribe and Council had several important effects on the character and vitality of Athenian democracy. The demes created a new political awareness and strong local popular rule, and opened a pathway for the engagement of citizens from every deme in Attica in the larger grouping of the tribe. Each tribe intermingled citizens of every social stratum and geographical region, and gave this diverse cross-section of the citizenry an opportunity to interact and work together in discharging two crucial public responsibilities: the defence of the state, and the work of a main pillar of central government, the Council. The effects were greater engagement of all citizens in political life at all levels, the strengthening of social cohesion and political solidarity by the interaction and collaboration of citizens from all backgrounds in dealing with high public responsibilities, and a greater level of political experience and understanding of public affairs throughout the population. It was a comprehensive, well-conceived programme of radical reform that laid strong foundations for a stable, effective democracy.[5]

The third, and central, pillar of the constitution of Cleisthenes was the Assembly (*ecclesia*), the one arena, inclusive of all citizens, where the voice of the people could be expressed and its will determined. The Aristotelian *Constitution of Athens* states that Cleisthenes had pledged to deliver the administration of the state to the mass (*to plethos*), and that required that the Assembly should be the state's highest decision-making body. The manner in which the Assembly functioned in the succeeding decades would show how dominant the position of the Assembly was following the reforms of Cleisthenes. As we shall see in more detail below, it quickly became the platform for ambitious aristocrats who no longer sought power through factions of their peers but through courting the confidence of the mass of citizens in the forum where decisions were now made. Themistocles provides the first great example. All the critical decisions of the 490s and 480s were made in the Assembly. The role of the Assembly was, of course, further extended by the reforms of Ephialtes in 462, but long before that it was determining the course of political affairs under the guidance of those of the elite whose stature and abilities had won them positions of leadership. Cleisthenes had kept his pledge to the *demos*.

There are other reasons for this conclusion. The level of internal harmony that prevailed in Athens in the decades after the uprising is indicative of broad popular satisfaction with the new order. Herodotus mentions of liberation and inspiration as the effects of the reforms. In a striking passage he talks about the energising effects of the reforms, which bestowed *isegoria*, the equal right to speak. Elsewhere, in a Persian constitutional debate, he has the advocate of the rule of the people describe it as having the most beautiful of names, *isonomia*, which denoted political equality. It seems likely that these terms became political catchwords of the new order, symbols of political equality with a corresponding power for the voice of the majority. In any event these were the terms that Herodotus used to characterise the new status of the people of Athens after Cleisthenes, and its effect on the people was, in his view, a sense that they had been set free, a sense that inspired and motivated them to strive for higher levels of personal achievement. Cleisthenes quite clearly had satisfied popular expectations.[6]

One further important indication that Cleisthenes was intent on entrenching the rule of the people was the introduction of the law of ostracism. The law created a mechanism by which the people could vote once a year to send a citizen, usually a prominent citizen whom, for some reason, they feared or distrusted, into exile for ten years. The banishment carried no loss of citizenship or property. Under the procedure the people were asked during the sixth presidency of the Council if an ostracism should be held. If they voted in favour, the ostracism itself took place soon afterwards. At a special meeting of the Assembly, at which a quorum of six thousand was required, each citizen wrote on a potsherd (*ostrakon*) the name of the person whom he wished to be ostracised. The person whose name appeared on the largest number of *ostraka* had to go into exile within ten days. The last known ostracism occurred in the years 417–415, and there is certain evidence for only nine ostracisms in total.

The ancient evidence relating to ostracism indicates that its purpose was to give the people the right to take pre-emptive action to avert a perceived public danger by removing individuals whose behaviour and level of power raised fears for the safety of the state or the constitution. Aristotle considered it an especially understandable feature of democracies because of their particular concern with equality, which made them uncomfortable with pre-eminence that was out of proportion. He believed that any such superiority that gave an individual a degree of power too great for the state or the ruling authority led to sedition and was likely to result in some form of oligarchy or autocracy. In such circumstances he considered ostracism an appropriate expedient which had a kind of political justice, though he conceded that it was not absolutely just, and could be and had been used for factional purposes rather than the preservation of the constitution.

To modern minds, ostracism has often seemed a crude political device open to abuse and manipulation, involving a gross violation of the rule of law and a serious denial of personal rights. But it has had its modern defenders too, prominent among them the notable nineteenth-century Greek historian George Grote, who saw it as a necessary defence of a nascent democracy before a sense of reverence and loyalty towards the constitution, which he describes as constitutional morality, had taken hold. Others have seen it as a valuable safety valve that helped keep Athens free of serious internal upheaval during most of the fifth century.

There are many aspects of ostracism that will always be controversial, but the institution does throw further light on the purposes that drove the reforms of Cleisthenes. Ostracism grew out of a history of factional strife that had set aside the key aspirations of Solon's constitution and had brought Athens under a prolonged, though benign, period of absolute rule, which was soon followed by further internal upheavals and threats of a return to domination by an oligarchic elite. The people had dramatically shown that they were no longer willing to accept such a prospect, but the risk of it must still have seemed high when Cleisthenes set out to fulfil his compact with them. The protection for the constitution that Solon had sought to create by empowering the Areopagus to impeach anyone suspected of plotting against it had failed utterly. Cleisthenes sought a new remedy to cope with an inveterate threat to unity and stability and the safety of the state's institutions.

The law of ostracism gave an exceptional power to the people to deal with an exceptional risk, and the number of recorded ostracisms shows that it was used exceptionally. It was in many respects analogous to the various forms of emergency provisions that can be found in many constitutional states that are committed to the rule of law, but that accept that extraordinary measures may be necessary when the normal processes of law are inadequate to guarantee the safety of the state. The Romans had the office of dictator to confront national emergencies, which was later largely replaced by the ultimate decree of the Senate, which authorised the executive to take any measures necessary to protect the public safety. Martial law and various forms of emergency powers are common modern expedients that suspend fundamental constitutional rights to allow the executive branch to bypass normal legal procedures and act with speed to protect national security. The justification is that the safety of the people is the highest law. What is different and significant about the law of ostracism is that it was a regular constitutional power rather than an emergency measure, and that it was vested not in any Council or executive arm of government, but in the people themselves. It was therefore a continuous power, a constant warning to the factious and the power-hungry that the *demos* was watching and guarding its liberty and its constitution. Whatever the flaws or merits of the law, it shows very clearly two persistent purposes that are visible in all the reforms of Cleisthenes, the elimination of potentially seditious power blocs from Athenian politics, and the concentration of important decision-making in the hands of the people as the main deliberative and legislative body of the state.[7]

While Cleisthenes was undoubtedly intent on entrenching popular rule, he did not seek to eliminate all vestiges of aristocratic privilege. He left intact the Council of the Areopagus, comprised of ex-archons, and the property qualifications for the highest political offices. But neither of these features of the constitution entailed roles or powers that could stem the democratic tide set in motion by the reforms, or limit significantly the capacity of the *demos* to control political events. The radical reordering of the political structures had left little real threat to popular rule.

The Achievements of Cleisthenes

The achievements of Cleisthenes and his place and importance in the history of Greek democracy have been variously viewed in both ancient and modern times. This has been partly due to the fact that he is a somewhat shadowy figure. He disappears from the history of Athenian politics after the events of 508/7, and, unlike Solon, he has left no writings to shed light on his views and purposes, and did not attract the attention of ancient biographers such as Plutarch.

The ancient view is chiefly represented by Herodotus and Aristotle, who are broadly in agreement. Herodotus clearly states that it was Cleisthenes who established democratic government at Athens. Aristotle gives Solon credit for introducing essential democratic features, but emphasises that they gave the people only the necessary minimum of power to keep them from servitude and rebellion. He considered the constitution of Cleisthenes more democratic (*demotikotera*) than that of Solon. Other ancient writers, however, such as Isocrates and Plutarch, reveal a different tradition which emphasised an aristo-cratic character to the system.[8]

The modern debate about the significance of the events of 508/7 and of the reforms of Cleisthenes only gathered momentum after publication of George Grote's voluminous history of Greece in the mid-nineteenth century. Grote acclaimed the constitution of Cleisthenes as 'the first Athenian democracy . . . a striking revolution . . . the grand and new idea of the sovereign people composed of free and equal citizens'. He believed it regenerated the Athenian people, creating loyalty to the constitution, a common bond of unity and fraternity, and a new energy in public and private life. He presented it as the best form of government. Grote's analyses, written at a time of strong anti-democratic senti-ment, by no means won full acceptance, but they were groundbreaking and have remained influential. The last quarter of the twentieth century brought a fresh upsurge of interest in the origins of democracy and the Athenian experience, as a fresh wave of democratisation swept across the world and was further acceler-ated by the collapse of communism in 1989. The 2,500th anniversary of the events of 508/7 in 1992/93 focused particular attention on Cleisthenes and his reforms. While he is seen as a significant figure at a significant turning point in Athenian political history, disagreement persists about many aspects of the man and his purposes, and about the question whether his constitution represented real democracy or was merely another step in a long progression towards it.[9]

Cleisthenes did not, of course, create the final form of Greek democracy, nor can he be regarded as democracy's inventor or discoverer (the *protos heuretes*). Greek democracy had no single progenitor. It evolved over two centuries which saw revolutionary change. Many movements and leaders contributed to it and set in place principles and structures that were essential prerequisites for the emergence of a fully democratic system.

But Cleisthenes holds a pre-eminent place in the list of statesmen who led Greece towards democratic governments. Before him many Greek states, including Athens, had moved towards political equality (*isonomia*) and greater popular involvement in government to the extent that they recognised that a just and stable society required a rule of law that treated all citizens equally, and also required a system of government that gave the people a meaningful role in public affairs. But the deep-rooted aristocratic conception that political power should follow birth and wealth, and that ultimate control of government should be vested in the elite, still lingered. It was Cleisthenes who made the definitive ideological leap beyond that to an opposing political ideal, which held that it was the whole body of citizens, not the privileged few, who had the right to political power and the right to control directly the course of political affairs. This was the vision that inspired the popular revolution against Cleomenes and Isagoras, and it was the vision that dictated the form of the new constitution.

The reforms of Cleisthenes were not a quick opportunistic response to popular sentiment, as is sometimes suggested. They were comprehensive, innovative and transformative, clearly the product of careful thought and planning by him or those around him. They had one grand design: to create a politically engaged and experienced body of citizens, habituated to involvement in public life at varying levels, and to interacting and cooperating on a basis of equality with fellow citizens of all social backgrounds. Citizens would bring the benefits of experience in many political fora to the highest forum of all, the Assembly, the supreme deliberative and legislative body to which all citizens belonged, and where every citizen had a voice (*isegoria*), and where each counted as one and no one counted as more than one.

It is hard to dispute that this elaborately conceived, well-integrated series of reforms – all directed towards achieving stable, effective popular rule on a basis of equality, including a high level of equality of opportunity – established the form of government that the Greeks called *demokratia*. The only contemporary definition of the term that survives is provided by Pericles in the Funeral Oration attributed to him by Thucydides, where he says that the Athenian model of government is called *demokratia* because 'its management is in the control, not of the few, but of the greater number': in other words, it gives power (*kratos*) to the mass (*demos*). This was precisely what the constitution of

Cleisthenes was designed to achieve, and subsequent decades would show how complete the control of the people under the new order proved to be. Further democratisation did take place in the fifth century, which continued to extend the control of the people, but these were extensions and adjustments rather than fundamental shifts in the distribution of power. The later democracy differed in degree, not in kind.[10]

The Democracy at War

Over the first four decades of its life the democracy was severely tested by almost continuous war and the trauma of the Persian invasions. They were pivotal years in the shaping and cementing of the new political order. The following section will review in some detail the events and their effects on the evolution of the nascent democracy. The first threat came from the Spartans. Cleomenes was intent on avenging his humiliation in 508, and in 506, together with Sparta's Peloponnesian allies, he led an attack on Attica from the south and persuaded the Boeotians and Chalcidians to attack from the north. But dissension among the Peloponnesian allies caused his expedition to collapse, and Athens subsequently defeated the Boeotians and Chalcidians in separate encounters. The Athenians seized a section of the land of Chalcis and established a new type of colony there known as a cleruchy, where the colonists remained full citizens and retained membership of their demes and tribes. The cleruchy was, in effect, an extension of the Athenian state.[11]

A far bigger threat soon emerged from the east. The central area of the west coast of Asia Minor, which became known as Ionia, had been colonised by Greeks from the mainland in a migration that began at the end of the Mycenaean era. Athens claimed to be the mother city of all Ionians, but it is clear that the Ionian Greeks had a more mixed pedigree. In the sixth century the region achieved a high level of prosperity, as they took to the sea and developed trade with Lydia and Egypt and with cities as far west as Sicily and southern Italy. Prosperity was accompanied by an extraordinary upsurge of cultural and intellectual creativity, centred in the city of Miletus, which, as noted earlier, marked the beginning of Greek science and rationalism and laid the foundations of the age of enlightenment that reached its peak in Athens in the fifth century.

But the Ionian states were slow to achieve any real political cohesion, and in the latter half of the sixth century they fell under the domination of the great powers of the hinterland, first the Lydians and then the Persians. The latter by the end of the sixth century, under two conquering kings, Cyrus and Darius, had extended Persian control over all of Asia Minor and Egypt and had gained a foothold across the Bosporus in Thrace.

In 499 the Ionian states, at the instigation of Miletus, revolted against Persian rule. They sought help from the Greeks of the mainland. Sparta refused to get involved, but Athens and Eretria agreed to send support. Athens sent a sizeable squadron of twenty ships, but their involvement was apparently half-hearted and they withdrew from the war after the first defeat of the Greeks in 498. The revolt was finally crushed by the middle of 493.[12]

But the Persian king Darius was intent on punishing the Greek states that had supported the Ionians, and in the summer of 490 an expedition was dispatched. Eretria was taken and sacked. The Persians then landed on the plain of Marathon. The Athenian Assembly decided to confront them in open battle and, led by Miltiades, a member of the leading Philaid family and an experienced military commander, the Athenian army won a famous victory against superior odds. They were helped only by a contingent from Plataea. The Spartans had promised support, but their troops were delayed by a religious festival and arrived too late.[13]

The Persians returned home after their defeat, but it was certain that they would be back. Persian preparations for a fresh invasion to conquer Greece gathered pace after Darius' son Xerxes ascended the throne in 486. By 481 it was clear that an attack on Greece was imminent. Sparta and Athens joined in summoning a congress of all Greek states committed to fighting Persia to plan a united defence of Greek freedom. Sparta was appointed to command the allied Greek forces, but the Athenians were always going to be prime movers in the initiative because of the prestige they had earned by their victory at Marathon and because, in the course of the 480s, they had acquired by far the largest fleet of any Greek state.

The development of Athens into a leading sea power was the work of a remarkable political leader, Themistocles, who came to the fore in the late 490s when he was elected archon. Themistocles undoubtedly had flaws of character – he was ruthlessly ambitious and unscrupulous – but he was an able politician and a gifted military strategist and commander who had the foresight to realise that it was only through naval power that Athens could withstand the threat from Persia, along with dangers at home from hostile neighbours such as Aegina. He won popular support for his policy and, with the help of additional public revenues that came from the discovery of a new vein of silver at the mines in Laurium, Athens managed to build the greatest fleet in Greece, possibly as many as two hundred triremes, by the late 480s. It was an extraordinary achievement to build for the first time so large a fleet of warships in so short a period. The task of procuring the raw materials, building the shipyards, assembling the skilled workforce and training the crews was enormous, a feat indicative of the adventurous, innovative drive that was to mark the young democracy.[14]

Xerxes launched his great invasion of Greece by land and sea early in 480. The Greek alliance decided to try to halt the Persian advance in central Greece at the pass of Thermopylae. The Spartan king Leonidas led a force of about seven thousand, of whom three hundred were Spartans, north to defend the pass. The Greek fleet, commanded by the Spartan Eurybiades, assembled nearby at Artemisium on the northern coast of Euboea.

The Persians reached Thermopylae in July and managed to gain control of a path through the mountains that would enable them to attack the Greeks from the rear. This made defence of the pass impossible, and most of the Greek forces withdrew. But Leonidas and his Spartans and a contingent of Thespians and Thebans decided to make a gallant last stand, and created an enduring legend that immortalised Spartan valour.

The fall of Thermopylae caused the Greek fleet to withdraw from Artemisium and reassemble at Salamis. It soon became clear that the Peloponnesians were not prepared to defend Boeotia and Attica, and were concerned only with fortifying the line of the Isthmus of Corinth and protecting the Peloponnese. In these circumstances Themistocles decided, with support from other Athenian leaders, that Athens could not be defended and that the entire population should be evacuated to neighbouring areas in Salamis, Aegina and Troezen. The Persians would have to be confronted by sea. It was a drastic solution, but Themistocles secured the consent of the Assembly, and the evacuation took place, with only small numbers remaining behind, entrenched on the Acropolis.

Around mid-September, Xerxes arrived at Athens and took the Acropolis and burned its temples. Over the following weeks Themistocles persuaded the Greek alliance to keep the fleet at Salamis and manoeuvred the Persians into fighting a decisive sea battle in late September in unfavourable conditions in the narrow Salaminian straits, where their superior numbers could not be effectively deployed. The result was a disastrous defeat for the Persian fleet, the remnants of which returned to Asia. Xerxes quickly followed over land.

Themistocles was the hero of the day, widely acclaimed throughout Greece as a wise leader. But the war was far from over. Xerxes left a major part of his army behind in Thessaly under the command of Mardonius, son-in-law of Darius. Mardonius tried to divide and conquer by offering Athens a favourable alliance. The offer was spurned, but when Sparta failed to send help and the Athenians had to face unaided the invading forces of Mardonius in early 479, they were forced once again to evacuate their families and property. Mardonius occupied the city and renewed his offer. It was spurned again. The Spartans were finally spurred to action and sent ten thousand of their own forces, who were joined by contingents from their Peloponnesian allies. The Athenians supplied eight thousand men, commanded by Aristides, an experienced general who had fought at Marathon and was famed for his integrity. The overall Greek forces were commanded by the Spartan Pausanias, nephew of Leonidas.

The two armies faced each other near Plataea in the late summer of 479. After weeks of skirmishing and manoeuvring they fought the greatest pitched battle of the Persian Wars, and once again the Greeks won a resounding victory. The brunt of the battle was borne by the Spartan hoplites who routed the main body of the elite Persian infantry. Mardonius was killed. The victory was total. The remainder of the Persian forces rapidly retreated back to Asia. Soon afterwards the Greek fleet, commanded by the Spartan king Leotychides, delivered a further blow to the might of Persia with a successful attack on the promontory of Mycale on the Ionian coast, where a Persian fleet had been beached and a large land force was stationed. The ships were burned and the defeated garrison was forced to withdraw inland.

The combined Greek fleet ended its operations after Mycale, but the Athenian contingent, led by Xanthippus, another prominent aristocrat who came to the fore during the Persian Wars, undertook a separate expedition to seize control of the Hellespont. Xanthippus succeeded in capturing the key Persian stronghold of Sestos, which controlled the vital trade route to the Black Sea, and near which Xerxes had built twin bridges over the Hellespont for his invasion of Greece.[15]

The *History* of Herodotus ends at this point, but Thucydides covers the period from the end of the Persian Wars to the start of the Peloponnesian War in a digression designed to provide an accurate account of events that brought a level of growth in Athenian power that instilled fear in the Spartans. This he believed was the real cause of the start of the Peloponnesian War. He sees the digression as telling the story of how the Athenian empire (*arche*) came into being.[16]

Thucydides records that in 478 the naval forces of the Greek alliance led by Pausanias, with Aristides commanding its Athenian contingent, again combined to launch a new offensive against Persia designed to secure the freedom of the Greeks in the eastern Aegean and Ionia. Athens was the chief proponent of this policy. Sparta, still predominantly a land power and wary of foreign military involvements, was a reluctant partner. But the offensive of 478 was highly successful and gained control of the strategic territories of Cyprus and Byzantium. Soon afterwards, increasingly autocratic behaviour by Pausanias and rumours of intrigue with Persia led to his recall to Sparta. The other allies asked Athens to take command and they rejected a new commander sent by Sparta to replace Pausanias. This brought to an end Peloponnesian involvement in the ongoing Persian conflict.

Athens assumed control of the allies in 478 under a new agreement that established the so-called Delian League. Aristides led the negotiations that created the new alliance. Each member of the League agreed either to contribute ships or make a financial contribution (*phoros*) towards the cost of the war. The Athenians assessed the level of the contributions and appointed treasurers to collect the payments. A central treasury for the League was established in Delos, where the allies also held their meetings. The League is estimated to have included as many as 150 states. While Athens was the undisputed leader (*hegemon*), the autonomy of each member was recognised by the creation of a central council which all states attended, including Athens, and which had responsibility for deciding policy, with each state having equal voting power.[17]

Over the next decade the League pursued the war against Persia with remarkable success. Aristides was soon replaced by Cimon, son of Miltiades, a popular, charismatic, well-connected politician and a brilliant military leader. He had a series of successes during the 470s, crowned by a famous victory c. 468 on land and sea at the river Eurymedon in Pamphylia, which routed the Persian army and destroyed an entire Phoenician fleet of two hundred triremes. The victory gave the Greeks full control of the Aegean and of the Asiatic coast and, for the time being, brought to an end the Persian threat to the freedom of the Greeks.

But the character of the Delian League began to change in the course of this period, as Athens increasingly imposed its will on its allies and its hegemony began to take the form of imperial rule. The structures of the alliance, which gave Athens an inordinate level of control and enabled its military power to grow, made this virtually inevitable. Athens controlled the leadership of the League and appointed the officials who managed the treasury. The agreement about tribute was with Athens, not with the League. Most of the allies gave money rather than ships, but the ships built with the money became part of the Athenian navy. As problems arose and states failed to meet their obligations, or attempted to leave the League, or when their interests clashed with those of Athens, force was used to impose the will of Athens, and they ended up as subjects rather than independent allies. The high-handedness of Athens in dealing with members of the League is well illustrated by its treatment of two major members, Naxos and Thasos, when they sought to secede in the first half of the 460s. Both were besieged, forced to surrender and lost their independence. Thucydides singles out these two instances to show how the established agreement governing the League was violated by the Athenians, and allies were reduced to subjects. The Athenians also did not hesitate, when it seemed expedient, to force states that had remained outside the League to join on terms dictated by the Athenian leadership. The power of Athens grew apace in this period, but at the cost of the autonomy of some of its fellow Greek states.[18]

The Democracy Consolidates

The Persian Wars imposed exceptional stress and hardship on the entire Athenian population. They had to cope not only with the military demands of successive wars, but with lost harvests, the ravages of two invasions, and the trauma of two evacuations and the abandonment of home and property. But they resolutely persisted in resisting the invader and provided the decisive leadership for the Greeks as a whole in the struggles against the Persians from Marathon to Plataea. After Plataea they returned to begin the work of restoration after the devastation left by Mardonius' occupation. At the urging of Themistocles they also built new walls around the city and completed the fortification of the harbours of the Piraeus which had been started by Themistocles about twelve years earlier. But none of these urgent domestic needs kept them from pressing for a more complete victory over the Persians and assuming the leadership of the new Delian League, which was to bring about a final elimination of Persian control in the Aegean and Ionia. It was a confident, assertive and militarily formidable Athens that emerged from the travails of the protracted Persian Wars.[19]

This remarkable performance of Athens in the most trying circumstances was a powerful vindication of the new democratic order. The political structures and dynamics of government set in place by Cleisthenes on the back of the demotic uprising of 508/7 held firm and provided the revolutionary energy, unity, strong leadership and military cohesion that were in evidence throughout the Persian Wars and brought successive victories against the odds. The high morale, which Herodotus believed was the cause of the first Athenian successes after the reforms of Cleisthenes and which he attributed to the new sense of freedom generated by these reforms, was still energising the Athenians. But there were signs already appearing that the self-belief and resolution of the *demos* that brought victory over the Persians and brought Athens to leadership of a major federation of Greek states might mutate into an exploitative imperialist mentality more concerned with Athenian power and prosperity than the general welfare of the federation.

The Persian Wars also had the effect of embedding in the new order a secure place for the traditional aristocracy. The great houses of the old nobility continued to play an outstanding role throughout the wars, but within the confines of the constitution of Cleisthenes. There is no sign of any effort to undermine the new order or take advantage of fear and crisis to restore oligarchic dominance or launch individual power plays. The consensus that allowed smooth passage for the reforms seemed to be holding. The aristocracy accommodated themselves to a new form of politics, and those with talent and ambition found ample opportunity within it to achieve power and position. The Persian Wars showed that democracy, like other forms of government, needed strong leaders, and that the *demos* was ready to give power to such leaders and to be led by them so long as they continued to command public confidence and showed they had the ability to advance the public good. Wealth and high birth brought great advantages in such circumstances and, while the Athenian elite may not have had the formal system of *clientela* that was such an important part of political influence in republican Rome, they did have various means of building a political base. Famous families had the usual benefits of status, reputation and extensive connections. Social clubs, known as *hetaireiai*, which were an important part of the social life of the Athenian upper class, provided a further means of gathering friends and like-minded political associates and using them as a corps of political supporters. Wealth could be used in various ways to woo the public through sponsorship of choruses and other forms of entertainment or through public benefactions or private philanthropy.

Political influence was also enhanced by the benefits of education. Talk and debate were central features of Athenian democracy, and speaking skills were an important political tool. The Assembly was not tolerant of fumbling, incoherent speakers, as is well attested by a variety of Greek authors. The ability to persuade was a vital element of leadership in a people's Assembly. It was obviously developed by the form of education available to the rich, and especially by training in rhetoric, which was a growing phenomenon in Athens from the mid-fifth century. Given the many factors favouring the elite, it is not surprising that the foremost leaders of the war generation – Miltiades, Themistocles, Aristides, Xanthippus, Cimon – all came from the heart of the aristocracy.[20]

A continuing expansion in the role and character of the office of general gave widening scope for the ablest among the aristocracy to rise to prominence. We know from Herodotus that, by the time of the battle of Marathon in 490, the ten generals formed a board of commanders of the national armed forces. In theory they had equal power but rotated the position of supreme commander between them on a daily basis. The Assembly might also award overall leadership of a particular assignment to one of the ten. They were elected by the Assembly, but it was normal that one be chosen from each tribe. The office was annual, but re-election without limit was permitted. This gave particular opportunity to those who proved their worth to acquire a high level of influence. Changes in the archonship, which will be discussed later, further increased the political importance of the generals, and, in the world of the fifth century, where war was the norm rather than peace, they assumed a critical role in shaping as well as implementing policy, and gradually emerged as the most important executive element of the government.[21]

All of these circumstances left room for a continuation of the traditional rivalries among the leading families, and these remained a feature of the politics of the early fifth century. Besides exploiting birth and wealth, they could increase influence and achieve success over rivals by supporting popular reforms, or bringing down competitors through prosecution in the courts, or manipulation of the device of ostracism. Themistocles is often seen as the master of factional politics in this era, and it is true that some of his main rivals were brought down during his period of greatest ascendancy in the 480s. But the web of political intrigue extended more widely. Miltiades, hero of Marathon, was convicted on a charge of deceiving the people brought by Xanthippus, an associate of the powerful Alcmaeonids. Xanthippus himself became a victim of ostracism in 484, as did Aristides a couple of years later. Themistocles can plausibly be seen as the prime mover in these two cases. But both men were recalled before Salamis to help confront the threat from Xerxes.

The influence of Themistocles declined in the 470s, and the anti-Spartan policy he was pursuing lost favour. He was eclipsed by the rising popularity of Cimon, who combined the influence derived from his outstanding military success with strong political connections, which included Aristides and the Alcmaeonid family. Cimon was a proponent of friendly relations with Sparta, and he was a firm opponent of Themistocles and his policies. He emerged the winner when the *demos* voted to ostracise Themistocles towards the end of the 470s.[22]

The Athenians showed their pragmatism in building one powerful executive element into the constitution in the area where ability, expertise and the power to act were most crucial. But the emphasis on demotic control, direct rule and minimal delegation of power, which underlay the constitution of Cleisthenes, remained, and the system was careful to create abundant checks on all magistrates, including generals, to ensure their power would not be abused or pose a threat to popular sovereignty. All offices, including that of general, were annual. While the re-election of generals was possible, they all had to pass the test of popular approval each year. There was also a vetting process (*dokimasia*) for all magistrates before entering office, and a formal scrutiny of their conduct (*euthyna*) at the end of their term. The threat of prosecution on a charge of treason, which, as we shall see later, covered a wide range of offences against the state, also hung over all magistrates, especially generals. In addition, if anyone did emerge who seemed able or likely to threaten the rule of the *demos*, ostracism was at hand to provide the ultimate remedy.[23]

There are many other indications that the Assembly and its adjunct, the Council, maintained a firm hold over key decision-making during the Persian Wars and their aftermath, and that the general trend of the constitutional developments in the period was towards greater democratisation. The phrase *edoxe toi demoi*, 'the people decided', the official formula that introduced resolutions passed by the Assembly, made its appearance early in the fifth century. It was a solemn declaration that the people had spoken, and shows the Assembly exercising its role as the sovereign voice of the people. There is direct evidence that the big decisions of the war era – to send ships to aid the Ionians against the Persians, to make Athens a major naval power, to evacuate the city before the battle of Salamis, to reject the overtures of Mardonius – were all made by the Assembly working with its Council.[24]

The continuing expansion of the fleet, which was manned by the poorest citizens, the thetes, further strengthened the status and authority of the Assembly. For the first time the lower classes, the largest element of the citizen body, formed a crucial part of the defence forces and assumed a new importance as citizens. The linkage between military service and political rights was pervasive in the ancient Greek and Roman world. Those who defended the *polis* were regarded as having the right to participate in its government. According to Aristotle, where the defence forces were based on cavalry and heavy infantry, the rule of the few was the natural outcome, because these were the forms of service in which only the wealthy could participate. But where light infantry and the navy predominated, democracy was strongly favoured, because these services drew their personnel from the masses. Athens had achieved democracy and had given the thetes an equal place in the Assembly before they acquired their military importance, but there can be no doubt that the inclusion of the lowest class in a significant way in the defence forces resulted in a more integrated and confident Assembly, with a stronger claim to its sovereignty.[25]

The constitutional developments from the period of the Persian Wars and the decades following continue to show a firmly rooted democracy reaching towards ever greater control for the Assembly and its Council. The developments centred around the two major remaining bastions of aristocratic privilege left untouched by Cleisthenes, the archonship and the Areopagus. In 487 a new method of selecting the archons, who had previously been elected by the Assembly, was adopted: a pool of five hundred candidates was elected by the demes, and from this pool the archons were selected by lot, one from each tribe. The reform had several effects, all of which had democratic overtones. It gave the grassroots democracy in the demes a further say in national politics; it ensured at least greater geographical diversity in the pool of candidates; and

the use of the lot, the favourite Athenian mode of selection when special expertise was not an issue, would further increase the possibility of new blood
entering national office.

But the most important effect by far was a reduction in the functions of the
chief archon and of the polemarch, which apparently accompanied the change
in the mode of selection. It is certain that the polemarch lost his military functions around the time of the reforms, and it seems a reasonable assumption
that the downgrading of the role of the chief archon, which later in the fifth
century was confined to preliminary legal proceedings, issues affecting property and regulation of certain religious festivals, occurred at the same time. The
Assembly and Council were now the centre of political decision-making, and
the concept of a controlling power for the *demos* was well embedded. A weak
executive was a corollary of that concept. Strong military leadership was
accepted out of necessity, though with abundant safeguards. But the traditionally powerful office of chief archon, monopolised by the upper classes, was not
acceptable and, if not in 487 then soon thereafter, it was reduced to insignifi-
cance as a political force.[26]

The dismantling of the powers of the Areopagus proved more contentious,
and showed that there was an abiding ideological rift in Athens surrounding
the place that the nobility, with its traditional claims to *arete* and political
preferment, should hold within a strengthening democracy. It would appear
that the influence of the Areopagus in political affairs had increased significantly during the Persian Wars, mainly as a result of the strong leadership that
it showed during the Salaminian crisis and of the support that it gave citizens
to help them cope with the trauma of the evacuation. There is no evidence that
the Council acquired new powers, and it is more likely that it used its added
auctoritas to stretch its judicial role and the control over magistrates inherent
in its position as guardian of the laws and the constitution.[27]

The attack on the position of the Areopagus came in 462 and was led by
Ephialtes, about whom little is known other than that he had a reputation for
honesty, was a strong proponent of democracy and an opponent of the more
aristocratically minded Cimon and of Cimon's pro-Spartan policies. The
timing of his reforms may have been linked to a decline in Cimon's popularity
and to his absence in 462 on an expedition to help the Spartans confront a
major revolt by helots which ended in embarrassment when the Spartans
rejected the proffered assistance.

In any event Ephialtes successfully carried his reforms in 462, which in
effect deprived the Areopagus of its role as guardian of the laws and the constitution. It lost its right to hear cases of treason (*eisangeliai*), which covered
serious offences against the state. It was also deprived of any role in the scrutiny

of magistrates before entering office (*dokimasia*) and in the accounting that magistrates were required to render at the end of their term (*euthyna*). All of these functions were placed in the hands of the Council and the Assembly, which, in its judicial role, acted as the Heliaia, the court of the people established by Solon. To meet its additional judicial responsibilities, the Heliaia soon had to be divided into a number of courts (*dikasteria*) manned by juries of ordinary citizens, who acted on behalf of the people. Jurors were drawn from a national panel of 6,000, recruited annually by lot from those who volunteered for service. There was no bar to repeated selection as a juror. In private cases jurors numbered 201 or 401 depending on the seriousness of the issue. In public prosecutions the number was normally 501, but there are examples of panels of 1,001, 1,501 and 2,001, and, in one instance, of the full national panel of 6,000 being used.[28]

The downgrading of the role of the Areopagus undoubtedly stirred major controversy and lasting resentment among elements of the upper classes. The Areopagus, comprised of ex-archons, who in this period came exclusively from these classes, had been given a lofty role as guardians of the law and the constitution by Solon. Its powers had been left untouched by Cleisthenes. According to Aristotle, it was seen as an oligarchic element that gave a necessary balance to the democratic constitution. Cimon, described in the Aristotelian *Constitution of Athens* as the leader of the well-to-do (*euporoi*), attempted on his return from Sparta to repeal the law, but failed. The *demos* exacted a price for his anti-democratic stance, and had him ostracised in 461. The division ran deep, and Ephialtes was assassinated later in the same year, an exceptional act of political violence in the evolution of the democracy. There was no further violent protest, but a segment of the aristocracy never accepted the reforms and looked back to the constitutions of Solon and Cleisthenes as representing the true, balanced form of Athenian democracy. They were a minority, however, and a strong consensus behind a greater realisation of the ideal of democracy was building across the body of citizens as a whole.[29]

CHAPTER 3

The Democracy's Drive for Power, Glory and Gain

The Ascendancy of Pericles

After the death of Ephialtes the course of Athenian politics and public policy was increasingly dominated by one man, Pericles, whom Thucydides described as 'the foremost Athenian of his time and the most powerful in speech and action'. Pericles brought many advantages and talents to political life. He belonged to the highest ranks of the nobility: his father was Xanthippus, a member of the leading house of the Buzygae, and his mother was Agariste, a niece of Cleisthenes. He had the benefit of an education that extended well beyond the traditional aristocratic curriculum centred around physical and moral development and artistic appreciation, enjoying a long-term association with two of the most famous intellectuals of his day, Damon, an Athenian, and Anaxagoras, an Ionian from Clazomenae. According to Plato, Damon was the most accomplished expert of his time in music but also 'in all other pursuits of value to young men'. Anaxagoras was one of the long line of great Ionian philosophers who set out to explain the natural world on a rational basis through the power of the mind and reason. Plutarch attributes many of the traits and abilities of Pericles to these teachers, and there can be little doubt that his intellectual bent and rational, visionary approach to politics were to some extent shaped by their influence. His rhetorical powers were also enhanced by the intellectual breadth and sophistication that he acquired from Anaxagoras in particular.[1]

But in the case of Pericles nurture was powerfully aided by nature. He had the full spectrum of talents required for political power-building in the conditions of fifth-century Athenian democracy. He had military talents and was a brave leader in the field who took particular care of the safety of his men and avoided unacceptable risks. He built up a strong record of military success and acquired a high reputation as a commander. In a world where war was the norm, his reliability as a general was a major asset in securing and retaining the confidence of the *demos*.

But it was in the political arena that his talents were most pronounced. Thucydides identified his intelligence, his ability to judge the right course of action, his well-known incorruptibility, and his capacity to control and persuade the people as his main virtues and the source of his unique influence. His rhetorical prowess was especially acclaimed in his time and throughout antiquity. Socrates refers to him in Plato's *Phaedrus* as probably the greatest of all the orators, who fully used his philosophical training to perfect his talent. Plutarch's account is closely similar. Cicero is particularly lavish in his praise. He describes Pericles as pre-eminent in every form of excellence, but especially in the art of eloquence, and he speaks of his erudition and wise judgement which gave substance to his oratory and which kept him at the head of civil and military affairs at Athens for forty years. His style he describes as having charm and appeal, but also the copious energy of the grand mode and a vitality and forcefulness that could strike terror into the hearts of his hearers and leave them with their ears stinging. The power to persuade was a formidable political weapon in democratic Athens, as in republican Rome, and no one could match Pericles in its use.

Even his general personality, which was in many ways forbidding, with little trace of the populism characteristic of champions of democracy, seems to have helped rather than hindered him. He was reserved and aloof, and always maintained a dignified composure. He entirely lacked the common touch and easy-going charm of someone like Cimon. His lifestyle was austere and he studiously avoided the social diversions of his peers. His opponents and the comic poets liked to portray all this as expressing arrogance, pomposity and scorn for the ordinary man. They styled him 'the Olympian', mocking both his oratory and his demeanour. But others saw his manner and way of life as reflective of the seriousness of a superior statesman. Most important of all, the mass of the people continued to see in him a man of impeccable character and the best leader they had, and they continued to turn to him in good times and bad. For the last fifteen years of his life he was elected general continuously. So great was his control of Athens that Thucydides described the government during the time he headed affairs as nominally a democracy but in reality the rule of its foremost man. His commanding position, which he held with the free consent of a sovereign *demos*, was a remarkable phenomenon, and provides a first and striking example of how in a democracy force of personality and moral power (*auctoritas*) can supplement legal power (*potestas*) to give de facto dominance to one person.[2]

The period of the ascendancy of Pericles brought transformative change to Athens and its democracy in three main, interconnected ways. The Athenian state continued its march towards a more complete form of democratic rule. It greatly increased its military strength, especially its naval power, and tightened its control over an extensive empire. In addition, it experienced a cultural and intellectual revolution that ushered in Europe's first age of enlightenment and showed another side of the democratic society, an eagerness for a cultural eminence that would enrich the lives of citizens and declare to the world the glories and the primacy of a divinely favoured people who excelled not only in military heroics and political organisation, but in the domains of the mind.

A number of significant constitutional changes were introduced in the decade following the reforms of Ephialtes to open further the government of Athens to the mass of the people and to increase their opportunities to participate in it. Not all of the measures are directly attributed by the sources to Pericles, but they all contributed to a common goal, and it is generally and reasonably assumed that Pericles was the driving force behind the package as a whole. He was, besides, a long-time political associate of Ephialtes, and the obvious leader to carry on his political agenda.[3]

In 457 the hoplite class, the *zeugitae*, were made eligible for the preliminary selection of the candidates from which the archons were chosen by lot. Although the archonship had lost most of its powers, the office still carried prestige, and admission of the *zeugitae* to it was another levelling move which would have the further effect of making the Areopagus a more broadly representative body. More important was a law, directly attributed to Pericles, that introduced pay for jurors. The idea of pay for discharging one's duty as a citizen was a radical innovation, but an essential one to ensure that the expanded system of jury courts, which made heavy demands on Athenian manpower, could function effectively and avail itself of the services of the lower classes. But the practice of pay for public service soon spread and was extended to those holding non-elective offices, to those serving in the army and navy, and to members of the Council. The Aristotelian *Constitution of Athens* put the numbers in receipt of public pay after these changes at twenty thousand.[4]

Another law, again attributed to Pericles and introduced in 451/0, provided a new definition of citizenship, limiting it to those whose parents were both Athenian citizens. The reason for the law is much debated, but the Aristotlian *Constitution of Athens* gives a plausible explanation, namely a bulge in the citizen population, which was probably a result of growing prosperity, greater interaction between Athens and its allies, and an increased level of intermarriage between Athenians and foreigners. In the *Politics*, Aristotle says that states are generous with citizenship when there is a drop in the citizen population and restrictive when there is an increase.

In any event the law illustrates a feature not just of Athens, but of Greek *poleis* in general, an exclusivity that was concerned not only with limiting size, but with preserving an ethnic core that formed the basis of a common identity with a common culture and traditions, including religious traditions. Athenians took great pride in the fact that they were an indigenous people, autochthonous, descended from ancestors who sprung from the soil of Athens. They gloried in an heroic past and in religious traditions that kept them in favour with the gods. There was no element of pluralism in their outlook. It was a culture that fostered strong feelings of national pride, loyalty, commitment and patriotism, intensified by a strengthening democratic system that empowered ordinary citizens and made them feel in charge of their destiny. They may have had no terms corresponding to the notions of 'nation' and 'nationalism' that emerged in the eighteenth century, but their view of themselves as a people with a common origin (*ethnos*), the indigenous inhabitants of Attica since time immemorial, sharing a common culture and religious practices, gave them a deep sense of nationhood. They also certainly understood and cherished the concept of nationalism and, as we shall see later, especially what modern idiom terms expansionist nationalism.[5]

Another important development of the Periclean era that helped shape the character of Athenian democracy was the adoption of selection by lot as the method for choosing all magistrates other than generals and those whose functions required special experience or professional expertise. Sortition would seem to have been used originally in the selection of religious officials. The date of its extension to the political sphere is disputed, the evidence tenuous and contradictory, but it is clear that it was only in the fifth century that its political use became widespread and that it became the established way of appointing jurors, members of the Council and members of all non-specialist executive boards.[6]

Selection by lot and pay for public service became cornerstones of Athenian democracy in its fullest form, and were important symbols of equal political rights and of equal opportunity. Aristotle regarded any system in which magistrates were not chosen by lot or paid as aristocratic. Several times he repeats that appointing magistrates by lot was the way of democracy. Herodotus expresses a similar view. Selection by lot was the great political leveller. It was a major step towards equalising political opportunity. But above all it was a powerful affirmation of the principle that most fundamentally underpins the ideal of political equality, the principle that no elite has a monopoly of political wisdom and that the judgement of ordinary citizens in political affairs is as trustworthy as any other, and collectively more likely to be right. It also brought to the fore a related Greek view, that justice among political equals meant equal shares in the offices of state, and justice in democracies therefore meant every citizen should have an equal right to office, which favoured rotation of office and the principle that everyone should rule and be ruled in turn.

The roots of these egalitarian views go back to Hesiod, who first aired the doctrine that all human beings have an innate, god-given sense of justice (*dike*) and of what is fair and right in social relationships and in the management of government. These social instincts made them political beings, capable of achieving a just, orderly, peaceful society.

These views reappear in more elaborate form in arguments attributed by Plato to Protagoras, the famous fifth-century Sophist from Thrace, who taught at Athens during the Periclean era. Protagoras uses myth to make his point that all human beings possess the basic social virtues of justice and restraint from which political excellence derives. He tells a novel version of the myth of Prometheus and the evolution of civilisation and an intervention by Zeus when he feared the human race would be destroyed because it lacked the art of politics. To remedy this, Zeus sent Hermes to bring justice and restraint to mortals so that order and friendship would unite societies. But unlike other skills, which were given to some but not to others, these basic social virtues were to be given to all, because otherwise states could not exist. Protagoras goes on to give this as the reason why the Athenians and others, though they are careful in other areas to consult the relevant professionals when they need expert advice, are willing in political debates to take advice from any citizen: they accept that the capacity for political wisdom is shared by all. Selection by lot carried this argument one step further by affirming that all citizens not only had an equal right to a voice and a vote in political debate, but also an equal right to participate directly in the executive and judicial spheres of government as councillors, non-specialist magistrates or jurors.[7]

Pay for public service was the further element required to enable the lower classes to avail of these opportunities. In Aristotle's view the need to make a living was the greatest obstacle to political participation by the masses. Pay for public service changed all that. It gave time and incentive to the poor to take advantage of their right to hold public office. Contemporary critics of democracy saw it as adding to the power of the masses to the dangerous extent of giving them sovereignty in the state and control of the constitution, with the risk of government being transformed into a despotism of the poor. But what Pericles and like-minded democrats were clearly aiming to do was to ensure that the vision of democracy as a constitution that gave management of the state not to the few but to the greater number was realised in practice by increasing the opportunities for the poor as well as the rich to gain access to that power in accordance with the cardinal democratic principle of political equality.[8]

The reforms of the Periclean era were the final significant step in the evolution of fifth-century democracy. They continued the consolidation of *kratos* in the hands of the *demos* and completed the conversion of the constitution into what critics saw as an extreme form of democracy. There are signs that the alienation of a segment of the aristocracy deepened further. The visceral aversion of hardline oligarchs to unchecked popular rule is well illustrated in a pamphlet written in the late 430s or early 420s by an anonymous author generally referred to as the Old Oligarch.[9] The very notion of a state governed by what he sees as the base, undisciplined, uncultured mass of the poor is anathema to him, manifestly unjust and perverse. There are other signs of greater polarisation of views about political forms and the role of the few and the many in the latter half of the fifth century. There was certainly open opposition in the Assembly to some of the designs of Pericles. This was led by Thucydides, son of Melesias, who, according to the Aristotelian *Constitution of Athens*, assumed the role of Cimon, to whom he was related, as the leader of conservative elements of the aristocracy. But, like Cimon, he eventually paid a price for opposing popular reforms and was ostracised in 444/3. The *demos* stood firmly behind Pericles, but disunity had taken root among the elite.[10]

The Periclean Vision of Democracy

Pericles not only made an important contribution to the development of the democratic constitution, but also, according to Thucydides, produced a memorable statement of the system's core principles and ideals and of the way of life and government that it represented. The statement occurs in the Funeral Oration (Thuc. 2.35–46), delivered in 431 in commemoration of those who had given their lives in the first year of the Peloponnesian War. If it is an authentic representation of what Pericles said, it is the only contemporary analysis of the character of the democracy by a proponent, and it has obvious importance coming from a significant architect of the system and an intellectual with the capacity to articulate its social and political foundations.

But the extent to which the speeches in Thucydides can be taken to represent accurately what was said on any given occasion is highly contentious. There is also a broader question concerning the reliability and objectivity of his *History* as a whole and the degree to which his account is coloured by a particular political or social bias. This issue will be discussed later. Thucydides' use of speeches, however, has been a source of particular debate, and needs to be considered here. He himself felt the need to raise the issue, and he set out his method near the start of his *History* (1.22.2):

> I have found it difficult to remember the precise words used in the speeches which I listened to myself, and my various informants have experienced the same difficulty; so my method has been, while keeping as closely as possible to the general sense of the words used, to make the speakers say what, in my opinion, was called for by each occasion. (Penguin Classics, trans. Rex Warner)

The statement has a level of ambiguity, but is not as opaque as is sometimes alleged. No verbatim records of the speeches were available to Thucydides, so he had their speakers say what he felt the occasion required while adhering as closely as possible to the general thrust of what they were known to have said. He therefore had to supply the words, and he fleshed out the gist of what was known to have been said into a fuller statement of points appropriate to the occasion and consistent with the speaker's position. The practice might not meet the canons of modern historiography, but for Thucydides it was an analytical tool and a vivid way of presenting a full picture of the case that could be made, and likely was made, by a particular side in a particular situation. More will be said about this below when analysing the speeches recorded by Thucydides at critical junctures in his narrative. The degree of invention in all these cases would have depended on how much was known about what the speakers actually said, but the purpose was always to present the line the speaker took but, as needed, fleshed out with the full appropriate arguments. The method did not involve any departure from his professed determination to give a true picture of what was at issue in any given situation.

In the case of the Funeral Oration, Thucydides was likely to have had more knowledge than usual of what was actually said. He may well have heard the speech, as he was in Athens around this time and fell victim to the plague, which hit the city shortly after it was delivered. Besides, it was a highly emotional occasion, and Pericles had the challenging task of boosting morale following the difficult first year of the Peloponnesian War, which had brought the invasion of Attica and the migration of most of the rural population to the city. Given the special situation, the speech of an orator who was a master of moulding the emotions of his audience would have been well remembered. Thucydides therefore had little reason for invention here, and there is little sign of it. The oration he records is a stirring, inspiring speech exalting a bold new vision of government and of a way of life that protected the freedom and dignity of every citizen and inspired men to greatness and a willingness to die in defence of their superior values. It perfectly fitted the occasion and the outlook of the man who had contributed so much to the evolution of the democracy. It fitted far less well the political outlook of Thucydides, whose view of democracy was at best ambivalent. It seems a safe assumption that the Funeral Oration is not expounding the views of Thucydides, but is a close approximation of the substance of what Pericles said.[11]

It departs from the convention of dwelling on the courage of the fallen, and for much of the time puts the emphasis instead on the form of government (*politeia*) and way of life (*tropoi*) that inspired the devotion (*epitedeusis*) that made Athens great (*megale*). Pericles saw the success of Athens as ultimately deriving from a new political order that produced a superior way of life and the will to protect it (2.36.4, 41.5).

He dwells on that newness. The system does not imitate the institutions of others, but provides a model for them. It is given the name *demokratia* because it gives power to the many. This adds a new dimension to the freedom of its citizens, a new form of equality, which not only gave equality to all before the law in the settlement of private disputes, but in public life allowed no discrimination on the basis of class or wealth, but gave opportunity to everyone on the basis of their merits and capacity to benefit the state (2.37.1). It was also a form of equality that meant the people themselves made the political decisions, or at least ensured they were properly debated, in the belief that deliberation brought greater understanding of risks and attractions, and greater courage and resolution in acting on decisions (2.40.2–3). The effect was a culture of political engagement and a caring spirit (*epimeleia*) about public as well as private affairs, and a belief, peculiar to Athenians, that those who took no part in politics not only had no political use, but no use at all (2.40.2).

A striking element of the Funeral Oration is the repeated stress laid by Pericles on the fact that democracy did not just create a form of government and a particular political ethos – it also created a way of life. It gave protection to citizens to allow them a private sphere where they were free to live their lives as they saw fit. He clearly distinguishes between a private domain (*ta idia*) and a public domain (*ta demosia*), and uses the same adverb *eleutheros*, meaning 'freely', to describe how life in Athens was conducted in both of them (2.37.2–3). In their private domain citizens were free from watchful suspicion, and could pursue whatever gave them pleasure without incurring the resentment of their neighbours. Private living was conducted in an atmosphere of tolerant ease (*anepacthos*). But in the public arena Athenians were careful to observe the law out of a reverent fear, and also to obey those in authority. They had a particular respect for laws that brought help to the oppressed, and for unwritten laws whose violation was seen as shameful.

Pericles stresses many other aspects of the culture of democratic Athens that gave Athenians freer and more fulfilling lives. They had time for relaxation and had many things to lift their spirits. There were public festivals and sacrifices throughout the year. They had the enjoyment of elegantly furnished homes. They had access to the products of all lands, which the greatness of their city brought flowing into it. They had a society that favoured a relaxed approach to life, free of excessive restrictions or harsh discipline. Unlike the Spartans, their military training and education were not based on endless toiling and harsh routines, but on the belief that courage came from ease of mind (*rhathumia*) and a stout heart (*eupsychia*). Pericles also mentions the Athenian taste for culture, aesthetic and intellectual, and a spirit of fellowship and liberality that cements friendship. He sums it all up in the statement that the whole *polis* is the school of Greece (2.38–41).

The Funeral Oration is, of course, a highly idealised portrait, replete with the patriotic embellishment appropriate to a commemoration of fallen heroes, but it clearly identifies the core principles of Athenian democracy: freedom; equality before the law; a new form of political equality that put decision-making in the hands of the people themselves, and allocated political responsibility purely on the basis of merit; a reverence for the rule of law, including unwritten laws that were seen as inviolable; a respect for authority; a caring public-spiritedness that brought engagement with political affairs and active participation.

But the leitmotif is freedom, not only the freedom that bestowed legal and political equality, but a freedom that permeated the entire life of citizens, public and private. It was a freedom that respected a right to a private space and private possessions, that ensured leisure enlivened by communal celebrations and entertainment, that did not impose harsh regimens in its military and educational systems, that allowed, alongside dedication to public service and political participation, a personal life that had a free and easy quality (*rhathumia*) and was lived free of troublesome intrusions (*anepachthōs*).

There is a striking ethos of liberalism in the Funeral Oration that contrasted strongly, and was intended to contrast, with the extreme communitarianism of the Spartan system, which recognised no private sphere and subordinated all individual needs to the communal interest. Athens, of course, also had a strong communitarian ethos, which is reflected in the Oration, but Pericles gives a prominent place to individual liberty, and strikes a balance between the authoritarianism of the Spartans and the modern form of individualism and the intense preoccupation with personal liberty that would mark the liberal movements that emerged from the seventeenth century onwards. His picture of Athenian life under the democracy shows that, while the community mattered, the individual and personal freedom mattered too, and that a contented citizenry stimulated the most dedicated commitment to serving and defending the community (*koinonia*) of citizens which comprised the state.

There are many other references in the sources that show that Pericles' view was not merely embroidered rhetoric for an emotional occasion, but represented the general perceptions of freedom under the democracy. Thucydides (7.69.2) records a speech of Nicias in the final stages of the doomed Sicilian expedition exhorting his trierarchs to remember that they had a fatherland that gave them the highest level of freedom and unrestricted control of their way of life. There are frequent references in the fourth-century orators to the unique freedoms enjoyed by Athenians. Freedom of speech was often cited in illustration. In comparing Athenian democracy and Spartan oligarchy, Demosthenes used the example that Athenians were free to praise the Spartan constitution and way of life if they wished, but in Sparta it was forbidden to praise any system other than the Spartan.

The right of free speech had two aspects, represented by the terms *parrhesia* and *isegoria*. Both were deeply embedded democratic ideals. The word *parrhesia* implied the right to say anything. It came with freedom (*eleutheria*), and the two words are frequent companions in our sources. It belonged only to the citizen. Euripides tells us: 'the foreigner had a bondsman's tongue.' *Isegoria* had a similar status as a symbol of freedom. Herodotus, as noted earlier, saw it as a liberation that transformed the spirit and created the will to achieve. It applied especially to the equal right of all citizens to speak in the Assembly, and reflected the fundamental democratic belief that debate was a prerequisite for good decision-making, that the view of every individual could contribute something and that the collective judgement of the many was most likely to be right.[12]

The vehemence with which the critics of democracy attacked the level of personal freedom under the system further illustrates how prominent a feature of the democratic ideal it was seen to be. Plato is the most scathing critic, alleging that the democratic way (*tropos*) turns morality on its head and creates a city brimful of freedom and outspokenness (*parrhesia*), where everyone has licence to do whatever he wishes, and where leaders are chosen because they favour the masses. Isocrates uses similar language to describe the radical democracy, which he saw as a far cry from the constitution of Solon and Cleisthenes. Aristotle also had misgivings about a view of freedom that contained the notion of living as one wished. He was a fervent advocate of the rule of law, and believed that an excessive emphasis on personal freedom was at variance with constitutional loyalty. But opposed though he was to many aspects of radical democracy, Aristotle did recognise the importance of personal freedom, and accepted that the individual must be allowed a private sphere where his life was his own, and he especially defended the right to private property.[13]

The surviving evidence also shows that the freedom of the individual from oppressive action by the powerful or the institutions of government was well protected in law or popular decrees (which in the fifth century had the same force in practice as laws). Laws could not be applied retrospectively or directed against an individual. There were laws forbidding torture of citizens or execution without trial. There was a law of *hybris*, which is dealt with in detail in Demosthenes' speech against Meidias, and which provided for public prosecution by any qualified citizen of anyone who physically assaulted any child, woman or man, free or slave. The right to private property was reaffirmed annually, when, on entering office, the archon proclaimed security of property for everyone during his year in office. There was also probably a law, or at least an unwritten law, against invasion of the privacy of the home without a warrant.[14]

There are other features of the democracy that show a desire to maximise personal freedom and a reluctance to resort to compulsion. Robert Wallace has recently pointed out the absence of laws regulating most aspects of private life or activities that did not threaten other individuals or the public interest. The evidence of the orators is emphatic that the law was not much concerned with private morality or lifestyles or the behaviour of those pursuing their private affairs, but was mostly directed towards those who might have done harm to the state in their public life.[15]

In regard to the obligations of citizenship, the emphasis was on volunteering rather than compulsion: military service and service as arbitrators for a year after reaching the end of the liability for military service were the only legally required duties. Otherwise a citizen could stand aloof from political involvement. Even jury service was not obligatory, as it is in many modern democracies.

The system of taxation was also loose and limited, and volunteering was again a prominent feature. The system of liturgies provided the funds for dramatic productions and athletic contests at the festivals, and the equipping of warships. The wealthier citizens were obliged to undertake liturgies, but the amount spent was discretionary, and the number of imposed liturgies was greatly reduced by the fact that the wealthy and ambitious volunteered to take on more than was required, in an effort to court popular favour. There were high political rewards for good citizenship under the democracy.

The only other form of direct taxation was a war tax (*eisphora*) based on capital valuation of all assets. It was not used in the fifth century until the start of the Peloponnesian War, but it was a regular feature in the fourth century after the revenues from the empire had been lost. It was resented, however, evasion was common and the amounts raised often fell far short of military needs. There was a great reluctance, nonetheless, to impose higher levies, and the *demos* finally resorted in 357 to a device known as the *epidosis*, which was a special appeal by the Assembly for voluntary contributions to meet a special need, and a challenge to the public-spiritedness of the upper class. It was an expedient commonly used in the fourth century, a striking example of the preference of the democracy for a culture of voluntary commitment to public service and the common good driven by a spirit of patriotic dedication rather than the compulsion of laws.[16]

Even in the area of religion the intrusion on personal freedoms was minimal. The supervision of religion and the safeguarding of the state's relationship with the gods to ensure their continuing goodwill was seen as a primary responsibility of the state, and there was tight public regulation of the administration of religious cults and festivals. But there was no body of dogma to which the individual had to subscribe, and no dogmatic moral code directing how individuals had to conduct their lives. All that was required was a respectful attitude towards traditional beliefs and practices. The only offences against religion that we know of related to violations or profanation of cultic rules or rituals, and offences arising from a decree proposed by a religious devotee, Diopeithes, in the early 430s, which made failure 'to pay customary respect to the divine or teach doctrines about celestial phenomena' a crime of impiety (*asebeia*). The decree was directed against Anaxagoras, the friend of Pericles, and his ilk. It was not directed against ordinary Athenians. Prosecutions for *asebeia* were rare. The two most notorious cases were the trials of those implicated in the affair of the herms, and the trial of Socrates. Both will be discussed in more detail later.[17]

The strong libertarian ethos proclaimed by Pericles and backed up by other evidence presented above has not, in general, been given due weight in modern analyses of the Athenian concept of freedom. George Grote, the nineteenth-century historian and Utilitarian, argued the truth of the liberal vision presented in the Funeral Oration and rejected the common assertion in his day that 'ancient societies sacrificed the individual to the state'. Benjamin Constant, an influential political writer of the same period, agreed that the Athenian view of freedom closely resembled the modern in its emphasis on individual freedom, but insisted that the Greeks in general were chiefly concerned with a freedom that gave strong political rights to participate in political decision-making, but were otherwise willing to accept the complete subjection of the individual to the authority of the community. This contrast drawn by Constant between political and individual freedom evolved, largely as a result of the work of

Isaiah Berlin, into a trend of dividing freedom into two elements, positive and negative, the positive element signifying freedom to participate in government, the negative signifying freedom from undue intrusion by government. The prevailing view has been that Athenians were chiefly concerned with their positive freedoms and the authority of the *demos*, and that this left little room for consideration of individual freedoms. It is also commonly held that the Athenians had no developed sense of the modern concept of rights, had no word to denote a right, and in particular had no concept of universal or human rights deriving from the dignity, worth or natural needs of human beings and therefore inalienable and beyond the power of the state to breach.[18]

It seems impossible to reconcile these views of Athenian personal freedom with the evidence discussed above from the Funeral Oration and other contemporary sources, and from the general evidence of the Athenian way of life and the functioning of the democratic government. It is also questionable to assert that the Athenians had no sense of the modern concept of rights. It is true that they had no word that corresponds exactly to the modern term 'rights'. They thought more in terms of freedoms. But the freedoms they recognised gave entitlements that were confirmed in laws, or in decrees of the Assembly (which, as stated above, in the fifth century had the same force as laws). These entitlements are exactly analogous to the legal rights bestowed by the laws of modern states, and there can be no objection to calling them rights, since the word accurately describes what they were.

The evidence also does not support the idea that the Greeks had no concept of universal human rights deriving from the nature and needs of human beings. Greek political thought is built around the nature of man (*anthropeia physis*), its singleness, constancy, and the instincts and needs immanent in it. Thucydides wrote his *History* to be a possession for all time, its lessons everlasting because, he believed, human nature being what it is, history is almost certain to repeat itself. In an analysis of a revolution in Corcyra in 427, he speaks again of *anthropeia physis* as single and constant, prone to behave in similar ways in similar circumstances, its qualities of justice, self-control (*sophrosyne*) and goodness of spirit (*euethes*) apparent in good times, all forms of depravity breaking out in bad.

In the opening chapter I discussed early Greek ideas, especially evident in the writings of Hesiod and Solon, about the state as a community bonded by a natural, universal, divinely inspired sense of justice, the great civic virtue that ensures each his due. Law and the rule of law are products of this natural justice, and so therefore are the rights and duties defined by the law. The laws are expressions of universal, natural human rights derived from a universal, innate human sense of the just (*to dikaion*).

Aristotle further illuminates the point. He saw the state as the outcome of a natural impulse, a human need. Man is a political animal who needs the fellowship of other human beings and is endowed by nature with gifts that suit him for life in society. Justice is foremost among these gifts. It is the sense or judgement of what is right that brings order to the political community, and is the foundation of its laws. He has a further important passage in the *Politics*, briefly mentioned earlier, where he attacks extreme aspects of Plato's communitarianism which proposed not only community of property, but community of wives and children. He maintains that human traits that are universal – such as a form of self-love that treasures what is one's own (*ta idia*) – must be seen as natural and having a purpose, since nature does nothing in vain, and the laws of the state should not go against nature and suppress such traits, as Plato was proposing to do. Aristotle is here giving a very clear example of a universal, natural, inviolable human right.[19]

These ideas led to the development by the Stoics at the end of the fourth century of the theory of natural law, which was given its most articulate expression by Cicero in the *De Republica*: 'true law is right reason, in accord with nature, a possession of all people, unchanging and eternal. It summons to duty by its commands and deters from wrongdoing by its prohibitions.' Cicero elaborates on the definition in his two further theoretical works, the *De Legibus* and *De Officiis*, driving home the message that all human beings share a common nature commanded by a common gift of reason which identifies the true natural instincts of human beings and translates them into principles of what is just and morally right (*honestum*). These principles are not based on opinion but on the common nature of all mankind. Cicero repeatedly emphasises that there is no difference in kind between humans. There is only one human species. One definition covers all, and if depraved practices and false beliefs did not twist weaker minds no one would be more like himself than all people would be like each other. The principles of the just and the right deriving from this one nature, and discernible by the common gift of reason, are therefore universal and unchanging. All must live in accordance with nature (*secundum naturam*), and the laws of individual states must accord with nature's law. It is not morally permissible to alter or repeal this law, and it can never be entirely abolished.

Cicero is also insistent that nature's law does not allow different moral standards to apply within or between states. Nature's law is one and the same in all circumstances. What it requires in relations between fellow citizens, it also requires in relations between states. Nature's law is a law of nations (*ius gentium*) and essential to protect the universal brotherhood of the human species (*communis humani generis societas*).

Cicero's theoretical political writings, which draw heavily on the work of the historian Polybius and the Stoic philosopher Panaetius, combined with the other evidence presented above, show how fully Greek political thought, and Cicero's elaboration of it, understood and accepted the concept that all human beings share a common nature, a common rational faculty, and a common natural sense of the right and just, which together give all a moral equality and entitlement to the basic rights that derive from their shared nature and shared sense of justice.[20]

It is therefore misleading to claim that the concept of universal human rights is a modern contribution to a more enlightened view of humanity and of human relationships within and between states. What is new in the modern world is a much sharper focus on such rights, and on the need for international agreement about what they are, and for international treaties to ensure their protection. This focus was given particular impetus by the atrocities of the Second World War, which inspired the creation of new agreements and institutions to promote peace and the protection of human dignity. There resulted the creation of the United Nations in 1945, along with an International Court of Justice to help settle international legal disputes and enforce international law. In 1950 came the European Convention on Human Rights and Freedom, which also provided for a court, the European Court of Human Rights, that would allow individuals to appeal to it against governments. The Athenians had no such concerns about promoting human rights beyond their borders, or indeed for promoting peace, but in other respects their view of human nature and human rights did not differ greatly from the modern one.

But to what extent did practice conform to theory? In political affairs there is generally a considerable gap between aspiration and reality. Cicero warns that one of the greatest mistakes is to assume that the laws of all states accord with the universal principles of justice. The first obvious example of a lack of accord in Athens was the acceptance of slavery and unequal rights for women. These deficiencies in Athenian democracy will be discussed in more detail later. It is sufficient to say here that these were social phenomena that proved to be too deeply embedded in the social and economic fabric of the state to allow any theorist or statesman, or even a thinker of the calibre of Aristotle, to conceive of changing them. The same dilemma confronted the leaders of the American and French revolutions, and they similarly ignored the problem as they proclaimed their new liberal and more democratic political visions. The Athenian failure to deal with social issues that defied resolution by church or state for a further twenty-two centuries should be viewed in its historical context and should not obscure what they did achieve in the areas of political and legal rights.[21]

Athenian practice also often failed to match theory in its foreign policy. There was certainly a recognition in the Greek world that there must be rules governing relations between states, and justice was often invoked as the guiding principle that should prevail in such relations. Before the Peloponnesian War the Athenians went to considerable lengths to show the merit of their international record, the justice of their empire and their adherence to accepted international conventions. But the exigencies of war brought an end to Athenian pretensions to justice in their treatment of their allies or their conduct of the war, and they embraced instead the cynical doctrine, well illustrated in the Mytilenian debate and the Melian dialogue, that justice is whatever serves the interests of the stronger. They uncoupled power from justice, an attitude Isocrates would later roundly condemn. But that has been the pattern of imperial rule in all eras. Altruism wanes, and the welfare of the ruled takes second place to the interests of the rulers. It is also easy to find examples of modern states, including leading democracies, that are willing to violate international law if they believe it serves their national interest or security.[22]

But in the domestic sphere theory and practice were in accord at Athens when it came to the rule of law and the rights of citizens. Solon had proclaimed the doctrine that the rule of law, based on the god-given sense of justice innate in all human beings, was the saving bond of society. The democracy embraced that ethos. Pericles extolled the law-abiding spirit of the Athenians as a particular strength of the democracy. The law was seen as the voice of justice, the great leveller, protecting the weak against the strong, and the state against subversion. Euripides wrote in the *Suppliants*: 'where there are written laws the weak and wealthy get equal justice ... the small man who has right on his side defeats the big man.' The enforcement of the law was in the hands of the *demos* itself, operating through the jury courts, with elaborate precautions against corruption. Jurors swore never to take bribes or vote for tyranny or oligarchy, and to make their judgements in accordance with the laws and decrees of the *demos* and the Council, and, where the laws did not reach, in accordance with their sense of what was most just.[23]

But how fixed and stable was the body of established law, and to what extent did the *demos*, acting through the Assembly, have the right to override, abrogate or change it? There was no Bill of Rights or written constitution with higher authority than statutory law. Was there no limit therefore, as is sometimes asserted, to the power of the *demos*, through decisions validly taken in the Assembly, to alter the law and its reach into the lives of citizens? There were in fact various forms of constraint on the legislative power of the *demos* once the constitution reached a settled state, which can be said to have happened after the reforms of Ephialtes and Pericles. A powerful de facto barrier to legal change was a cultural aversion to altering long-established traditions or legal provisions properly agreed. This is reflected in a strong attachment to the *agraphoi nomoi*, unwritten laws based on use and wont, the analogue of English common law. Pericles emphasised and commended that attachment in the Funeral Oration. There was a similar attachment to the body of written law, whose core had been created by Solon to protect the mass against the injustice of the elite. As the democracy evolved, the laws gave expression to its spirit and ideals, what Demosthenes called the *tropoi*, the ways of the community. To preserve the integrity of the laws, a new law (the *graphe paranomon*) was enacted during the Peloponnesian War that provided for the indictment of anyone who proposed and secured passage of a measure that was contrary to existing law or not in the public interest. It was extensively used over the following century to guard against tampering with the body of established law. Other enactments in the reforms following the overthrow of the Thirty Tyrants in 403 provided further protection against ill-considered legal change. The Assembly neither had nor sought the right to rule as it pleased. Its concern was the permanent protection in law of the democratic ideals so definitively proclaimed by Pericles in the Funeral Oration.[24]

Athens Builds an Empire

Athenian foreign policy and military operations in the decades after the reforms of Ephialtes were other factors that significantly affected the character of Athenian democracy and society. Throughout the period Athens consistently pursued aggressive, interventionist, militaristic policies, which continued the confident, assertive and ambitious character of its behaviour during the Persian Wars and in the takeover of the leadership of the Delian League. An energised *demos*, with its control of political affairs steadily increasing, was embarked on a drive for dominance within the Greek world, and a position of security against the other two big powers in the region, Sparta with its Peloponnesian allies, and Persia.

Sparta's rebuff of the expedition led by Cimon in 462 to help in the revolt of the helots, and Cimon's subsequent ostracism, ended any pro-Spartan sentiment at Athens, which promptly formed alliances with old Spartan foes Argos and Thessaly. When Megara, strategically located on the Isthmus of Corinth, broke with Corinth in 459 and sought help from Athens, it readily responded. The Argive and Megarian alliances constituted interference in the Spartan sphere of influence and led to war with Corinth and the beginning of what is commonly known as the First Peloponnesian War, which was to drag on sporadically until 446.

Athens was initially successful on all fronts. A naval victory over the fleets of Corinth and its allies, the Aeginetans, in 458 gave Athens possession of Aegina and secure control of the Saronic Gulf. When the Spartans led an army into Boeotia in 457 and took up position on the border of Attica at Tanagra, the Athenians promptly marched to confront them. The Spartans were able to claim victory, but their losses were so heavy that they returned home. Soon afterwards the Athenians invaded Boeotia, won a decisive victory and became masters of central Greece. Over the following years Athens continued to press its advantage and to use its naval supremacy to attack coastal areas of the Peloponnesus and the Corinthian Gulf. Alongside the military operations, the Athenians also embarked early in the decade on a massive defensive project to build the so-called Long Walls to link Athens to the Piraeus, its port four miles south-west of the city. The walls would secure access to the sea and safe harbours for its fleets. It was the clearest possible signal of the aggressive intentions of Athens, and was so regarded by its enemies.[25]

But Athenian ambition overreached itself when a decision was taken to support a revolt in Egypt against Persia in 459. The expedition ended in catastrophe in 454 with large losses of ships and men. It brought a sudden halt to Athenian attacks on the Peloponnesus, and no further military action is recorded for the remainder of the decade. Athens needed a break from war, and when Cimon returned in 451, after his period of ostracism, a five-year peace with Sparta was negotiated with his help. Athens had to end its alliance with Argos as a condition of the peace. Peace with Persia soon followed, negotiated by Callias, brother-in-law of Cimon. Persia agreed to keep its ships out of the Aegean and to leave the Ionian Greeks free and exempt from tribute. Athens agreed not to attack Cyprus or Egypt. The so-called Peace of Callias is not mentioned by Thucydides, and many have rejected it, but the arguments for accepting it seem conclusive.

The early part of the 440s brought further difficulties for Athens. Boeotia revolted and inflicted a humiliating defeat on an Athenian army at Coroneia in 447. Athens had to abandon central Greece. Megara defected soon afterwards and was lost. Euboea revolted about the same time, but was eventually subdued. The extent of the threat facing Athens was further highlighted when, in the midst of the Euboean revolt, a Spartan army invaded Attica, though it quickly withdrew after ravaging border areas.

Athens was now ready for a more lasting peace with Sparta. Its ambition to acquire an empire on the mainland in addition to its hegemony over the maritime Delian League had proved unsustainable. Pericles, who had played a major part in the expansionist drive of the 450s, was by now reaching the height of his ascendancy. He was a confirmed imperialist, as his subsequent policies would further demonstrate, but he had evolved a more realistic view of the type and scale of empire Athens could control and defend, and for the moment at least, his vision no longer included contesting with Sparta its dominant position on the Greek mainland.

An end to the conflicts on the mainland was apparently the wish of all sides in 446, and a Thirty Years' Peace was agreed which saw Athens relinquish the footholds won in the Peloponnesus and essentially concede hegemony on the mainland to Sparta. But it retained Aegina and had control of a far-flung empire throughout the Aegean and its surrounding territories.[26]

Athens was now free to concentrate on two main goals that formed the cornerstone of the foreign policy of Pericles after 446: the strengthening of its navy and consolidation of its control over its maritime empire. He had unwavering support from the *demos* behind him. The number of ships was gradually increased to three hundred. These were manned mostly by citizens from the lowest economic class, the thetes, with an admixture of metics and, in emergencies, slaves. A large navy therefore enabled the state to use its total able-bodied population to fullest military effect, rather than being dependent solely on those who had the property rating required for hoplite service.

Pericles saw the navy as the key to Athenian military superiority and security. He believed that Athens had amassed the skills and experience in seamanship to create a navy that none of its rivals could match, and that would enable it to control the seas and sail anywhere in the world that it wished. He saw its fleets as the true base of the power of Athens and the guarantee of its dominance. He was later to urge the Athenians to think of themselves as islanders who must avoid confronting the superior infantry of the Peloponnesians and, if necessary, abandon land and homes to protect the lives of their soldiers and safeguard the city and the sea. The Long Walls to the Piraeus, built in the early 450s, made such a strategy possible. A third Long Wall was begun in 445 in continuation of the strategy, and at the urging of Pericles.[27]

Extending imperial rule over the allies was an equally critical objective. Pericles saw empire as the ultimate basis of Athenian power, the means of securing the resources that would sustain the war machine that would give Athens mastery of the seas and military supremacy. It would also keep the many strategically important and powerful states in the Aegean from any possibility of alliance with the enemies of Athens. But the control required meant ruling rather than leading and brooking no resistance, and that was very much the course followed by Athens in the late 450s and the 440s.

Extensive epigraphic evidence that has come to light over the past seventy years has greatly increased our information about the relationship between Athens and the Delian League that evolved during the ascendancy of Pericles.

After 462 public decisions and public accounts began to be published on stone, bronze and wood at Athens on a regular and extensive scale. The public recording of political action for all to see was a sudden development at Athens and was obviously the result of an upsurge of political transparency linked to the latest wave of democratisation initiated by Ephialtes. The inscriptions that have been uncovered include decrees that provide information, otherwise unknown, about disputes and revolts and Athenian methods of control. They also provide new information about the list of tribute-paying states and the amount of the tribute.

A particulary well-preserved inscription which gives the text of an oath of allegiance that all adult citizens of Chalchis in Euboea had to swear provides a good insight into the nature of the relationship between Athens and its allies in the Periclean era:

> I shall not revolt against the people of the Athenians either by guile or trick of any kind, either by word or deed. Nor shall I follow anyone in revolt, and if anyone does revolt, I shall denounce him to the Athenians. I shall pay the Athenians the tribute which I persuade them (to assess), and as an ally I shall be the best and truest possible. I shall help the people of the Athenians and defend them if anyone does injury to the people of the Athenians, and I shall obey the people of the Athenians. (ML 52.21–32. Trans. Fox, *The Classical World*, 125)

This wealth of epigraphic data combined with the literary evidence presents a picture of a hegemonic power openly intent on imposing its will. Most states retained a form of home rule, but they gradually lost any say in foreign policy or in the use of the resources of the League. They were dragged into the Athenian wars on the mainland in the 450s, which showed that the original purpose of the League – to defend Greeks against the Persians – had been replaced by a require-ment to defend Athens against all its enemies. Only three states, Samos, Chios and Lesbos, retained any real autonomy and had their own fleets. At least 160 others paid an annual tribute, the amount of which was fixed at Athens in a process conducted by the Council assisted by a board of assessors.

In 454 the treasury of the League was transferred from the Temple of Apollo in Delos to the Temple of Athena on the Acropolis and came under full Athenian control. From then on it became the practice that the tributary states would send their delegations to Athens at the time of the City Dionysia in March/April to present the tribute and participate in the festivities. At some point they were also required to attend the Great Panathenaea, which was held every fourth year in July/August, and to present an offering of a cow and a suit of armour (*panoplia*). Failure to do so incurred penalties. All the provisions were set out in peremptory terms in an inscription known as the decree of Clinias, which is now generally dated to 447. The subservience of the allies and the sovereignty of Athens were being affirmed in the bluntest fashion.[28]

The high-handedness of Athens was shown again when, around 450, the Assembly passed a decree proposed by Pericles to use money from a reserve built up from the tribute of the allies to help fund a new programme of public building. This programme, which will be discussed more fully later, was part of a grand design of Pericles to give Athens a physical splendour and an artistic and cultural eminence that would bring it fame and overawe its enemies, and confirm the belief of its citizens in the superiority of their state and its way of life. It would also provide large-scale employment and bring a new prosperity to the lower classes.

Pericles faced strong criticism from his political opponents for this use of the tribute. The attack was led by Thucydides of Melesias, who was related to Cimon by marriage, an able orator who, as mentioned earlier, headed the conservative aristocratic opposition to the designs of Pericles. Thucydides accused him of bringing dishonour on Athens by diverting money, given by the allies to fight a war, to fund extravagant adornment of the city. Pericles was unapologetic, declaring that once Athens had fulfilled its obligations to protect the allies, it was entitled to use the money for its own important national purposes. One can safely assume that many of the allies, especially those struggling to pay the tribute, did not agree with that sentiment.[29]

Other measures were introduced that continued to erode the autonomy of the allies and to increase their dependence on Athens. Fragments of a decree, traditionally dated to the early 440s, though arguments have recently been made for the 420s, show that the allied states were forced to adopt Athenian silver coinage and weights and measures. Autonomy was further breached by a requirement, well established in the Periclean era, that the allies must bring major judicial cases to Athens for settlement by Athenian courts. The evidence for the evolution of this practice and for the precise types of cases that had to be referred to Athens is scattered and hard to interpret, but it seems clear that the volume was large, and included not only cases involving Athenian imperial interests or Athenian citizens but all the most serious cases. The Athenians in justification argued the value to the allies of fair and uniform justice, but the loss of control of their judicial proceedings was deeply resented by the allies and was an additional proof of their subjugation.[30]

It is not surprising that there was discontent, which showed itself in disputes about the tribute and occasionally led to outright revolt. The Athenians spared no effort in imposing their will and bringing the rebellious to heel. The manner in which they dealt with a major revolt in 440 by Samos, which was ruled by an oligarchy and was one of the most powerful of the allied states, with its own fleet, shows their determination to brook no opposition. Samos became embroiled in a dispute with Miletus, another allied state. Miletus appealed for help to Athens. Samos refused to accept Athenian intervention. Pericles responded with speed and led an expedition of forty ships to Samos, imposed a democratic government and left a small garrison. But the oligarchs regained control. Pericles returned and launched an all-out blockade, but it took a nine-month siege to force the surrender of the Samians in early 439. Pericles exacted a savage retribution. There were brutal executions. The Samians had to tear down their walls, surrender their fleet, pay a war indemnity of about 1,500 talents, and accept a democratic government sworn to loyalty to Athens and its allies. Samos thereafter remained loyal, its democrats firmly in control.

Some of the same methods of control were used in other circumstances. Garrisons and commissioners became a common method of restoring order in troubled states. Another means of containing sedition was the founding of cleruchies in strategic areas, which not only offered a better life to some of the landless poor of Athens, but provided Athenian outposts to guard against unrest. The capacity of Athenian fleets, which regularly patrolled the Aegean, to respond rapidly to any crisis was a further deterrent to rebellion.

Military muscle was supplemented by political intervention. The Athenians did not hesitate, where expedient, to impose what in modern terms would be called a regime change and set up puppet democratic governments sworn to loyalty to Athens. In general they shrewdly used a policy of divide and conquer by favouring the lower classes and reining in the wealthy oligarchic elements. They also tried to soften the image of the oppressor by leaving it to the courts at Athens to decide the outcome of disputes with allies, and they boasted that, unlike other imperial powers, they substituted the rule of law for the rule of force.[31]

Athenian rule undoubtedly brought benefits to the allies. It brought freedom from Persian domination to the Ionian cities and a higher level of peace and security to the Aegean region as a whole. It brought safer seas for commerce. It brought greater equality to the political life of many states through its support for the lower classes, who tended to see Athens as their protector against oppression by their own oligarchic elites.

But whatever the benevolent and beneficial aspects of Athenian rule, both the literary and epigraphic evidence show that, by the 430s, the Delian League had moved from being an alliance of free states (*summachia*) to an empire (*arche*), and ultimately to a manner of rule by Athens that Pericles admitted could be called a *tyrannis*.[32]

Thucydides as an Historical Source

Before examining in more detail the character of the empire that had evolved by the 430s, and its consequences for the character of democracy, it is necessary to look more closely at the reliability of our main political source from this period, Thucydides. He was an historian with a particular fascination with power and its use, and his *History* provides a wealth of information about the genesis, character and contemporary perceptions of Athenian imperialism, and about the ethos and mentality of the democratic society that built an empire and was determined to retain it. He was long regarded as an impeccable source – informed, objective, intellectually gifted, preoccupied with finding and recording the truth – but, as mentioned above, serious questions have been raised over the past half-century about his general reliability. I have already discussed his use of speeches and the problems of interpretation that they raise. But broader questions have arisen about his objectivity, and the degree to which aristocratic political biases may have coloured his account of both Athenian politics and Athenian imperialism. The issue is complicated by the fact that there is no contemporary source beyond the dubious evidence provided by drama against which to test his accuracy or impartiality. The growing body of inscriptional evidence, while it has increased our knowledge of how Athens governed its empire, remains a limited source, and it does not throw much light on the Thucydidean question.

The evidence for his life and political beliefs is also meagre. It is clear that he had aristocratic roots. He tells us that his father was Olorus, which was also the name of the Thracian king whose daughter was married to Miltiades. The family of Thucydides had property and standing in Thrace, and it is a fair assumption that his father belonged to the same Thracian clan as the wife of Miltiades and mother of Cimon. His intellectual sophistication indicates that he was well educated, a product of the new learning that came with the Sophists. There is general agreement that he was born around 460 or soon thereafter on the basis of his statement that he lived through the entirety of the Peloponnesian War and was of an age to comprehend what was happening, and the fact that he was a general in 424, an office that was almost certainly restricted to those over thirty. He served in the northern Aegean, and was exiled for twenty years for a failure to prevent the capture of Amphipolis by Brasidas in 424. He returned to Athens at the end of the war in 404, but apparently died soon afterwards.[33]

He provides only scattered indications of his political leanings, and their import is too uncertain to allow definite conclusions about his political convictions or loyalties. He certainly had reservations about the capacity of the *demos* for good government unless it was well led, but he nowhere criticises democracy as a form of government in the manner of Plato, Aristotle or the Old Oligarch.

There are in fact signs that he was attracted by aspects of the system. He expresses admiration for the resolve and discipline of the *demos* after the catastrophic defeat in Sicily, a response that he says was typical of the spirit of a democracy in times of adversity. He clearly admired Pericles and the manner in which the democracy functioned in the Periclean era. It was a democracy where one man dominated, but Thucydides makes clear that it was a de facto ascendancy. The *demos* freely chose to use the exceptional talents of a leader who had its full trust and to give him effective control of political affairs. It was a control based on his reputation (*axiosis*), on his sound judgement (*gnome*) and on the fact that he showed himself completely incorruptible (*adorotatos*). It was also a control that was exercised with respect for the liberties of the *demos*. It lasted only so long as Pericles retained the trust that underlay it, and when things went awry after the plague and the early setbacks in the war, the *demos* quickly reasserted itself, removed Pericles from office, and had him tried and fined. He was soon reinstated, but only after the *demos* realised he was still the best leader available.

The democracy was not dormant under Pericles. It was still in control, but was sensibly using the wisdom and integrity of a remarkable leader. Thucydides emphasises that it failed only when its leadership failed, and when those who sought to lead after Pericles proved more concerned with their own power than the welfare of the state and resorted to demagoguery and intrigues in pursuit of their own ends.[34]

The Funeral Oration can also be seen as a further indication that Thucydides sympathised with many of the democracy's basic ideals. While I believe that it represents the views of Pericles rather than Thucydides, the memorable language in which it is expressed, and which is almost certainly the creation of Thucydides, shows a deep appreciation of the appeal and lofty aspirations of the system.

His disapproval of the leaders who followed Pericles, and his particular disdain for Cleon, whom he presents as the archetypal demagogue, are sometimes taken as indications of an aversion to democracy that caused him to malign its most ardent champions. But Thucydides includes all political leaders after Pericles, with the exception of Nicias, in his censure. The high-born Alcibiades, who once described democracy as madness, fares no better than Cleon and his ilk. Neither does Diodotus, a member of the intellectual elite and Cleon's adversary in the Mytilenian debate in 427, who is portrayed by Thucydides as just as unprincipled and devoid of moral scruple as Cleon.[35]

Only once does Thucydides praise a particular constitutional form in a manner that suggests it may represent his ideal form of government. He records that in 411, following internal disturbances in Athens and a revolt in Euboea that spread panic in the city, a meeting of the Assembly was held, which deposed the Council of Four Hundred that had taken power a few months earlier, and voted to hand over control of political affairs (*ta pragmata*) to a body of five thousand drawn from those of hoplite status. It also abolished pay for all public offices. Thucydides gives no further details of the new constitution, nor does any other source. But he does offer a comment in praise of the new system. Though it is couched in language that is notoriously difficult to decipher, its gist seems clear enough. He is saying that, for the first time in his lifetime, the Athenians seemed to have a good form of government, because a balanced blend (*metria synkrisis*) had been created with respect to the few and the many, which lifted the state out of the dire circumstances that had arisen.

The decision of the Assembly was not a new departure. It merely represented the implementation, though with significant modification, of what it had voted four months earlier, when the Council of Four Hundred was created in a time of crisis to rule as they thought best, aided by a body of five thousand drawn from those best able to defend the state by their possessions and persons. The Four Hundred had quickly introduced a rule of force and refused to appoint the Five Thousand, and it was this, combined with a fresh crisis, that led to their removal and the installation of the Five Thousand to take charge of public affairs with magistrates who would no longer receive pay.

This was the arrangement that Thucydides saw as a balanced mix of the few and the many. The many comprised the large segment of the citizenry who had hoplite status, and who would provide the membership of a powerful Council that was large enough in the view of the Four Hundred to create an outright democracy (*antikrus demos*). The few comprised the office-holders, who would necessarily be chosen from the wealthier elements who could afford to hold office without pay. The model had a definite oligarchic cast, excluding the lowest and largest class, the thetes, but it could be seen as a middle ground, giving a high level of control to the upper classes, but still involving the broad spectrum of social categories of hoplite rank that made up the population. It was the model championed in this period by the proponents of the so-called *patrios politeia*, the ancestral constitution associated with Solon and Cleisthenes. It was also the model promoted by the orator Isocrates in the fourth century, and it had the fusion of democratic and oligarchic features so strongly commended by Aristotle.[36]

Thucydides would appear to have shared this centrist position. He could admire radical democracy when it was led by Pericles, though his remarks after the latter's death show that he did not favour handing unguided political control to the full *demos*. But he was no oligarch. His account of the events leading to the establishment of the Four Hundred presents the full ugly picture of violence, intimidation and intrigue that brought them to power. He admired the intellectual power of the masterminds behind the revolution, but he shows no sympathy with their aims and methods. It is hard to put a label on his political views, but there is nothing in what he reveals about them that would warrant the conclusion that he was a foe of the concept of democracy or a biased witness of the functioning and achievements of the Athenian system.[37]

It is equally difficult to show any pronounced bias in his treatment of Athenian imperialism. In his digression recounting the rise of the Athenian empire he makes no criticism of the behaviour of Athens, its harsh treatment of rebellious allies or its insistence on obligations being met.[38] He puts the blame for the increasing domination of Athens on the allies themselves and their reluctance to fight or contribute ships, and their preference to pay money rather than bear the burden of active service. He makes no criticism of the imperialist policies of Pericles, who glories in the triumphs of Athenian arms in the Funeral Oration, and in the daring that achieved entry by Athens into every land and sea. Even the costly Egyptian adventure is recounted without a hint of disapproval. The speeches that he attributes to the Athenian envoys who spoke at a debate in 432 in Sparta, at which the Corinthians were urging Sparta to go to war against Athens, are cogent defences of the empire based on the principle, grounded in human nature, that the strong rule the weak and to their own advantage, though the Athenians boast that they treat their allies with greater justice than is required of them. Similar arguments in defence of their empire were made by the Athenians at Camerina in Sicily in 415/14.[39]

The empire and its management represented *Realpolitik*, natural forces at work in interstate relations. Thucydides does not question it. He is a realist, his purpose didactic, harvesting the true lessons of how states use power and for what reasons. He is a moralist only when it comes to the domestic mores of states. He is insistent that justice, morality and obedience to law have to govern internal relations between citizens, but he offers no criticism of the doctrine that expediency prevails, by the laws of human nature, in the international sphere. He only criticised Athenian foreign policy when it was directed not by what was expedient for the state but by reckless adventurism and personal ambition on the part of politicians, ultimately destructive to the state. There will be further discussion of these issues below, in chapter 5.[40]

One aspect of his treatment of Athenian imperialism has come under particular scrutiny and criticism – the persistent impression that he creates, either by direct comment or through the speeches of key figures, that the Athenian empire inspired hatred of Athens among the allies as a whole. He says that, at the start of the Peloponnesian War, the goodwill of Greeks generally lay with the Spartans, especially as they proclaimed that their purpose in going to war was the liberation of Greece. There was so much anger against Athens that everyone wanted to assist the Spartans, some because of the hope of deliverance from Athenian rule, others because of fear of falling under it. He writes in similar terms about sentiment in Greece after the Athenian defeat in Sicily. In the speeches we find both Pericles and Cleon describing the empire as a tyranny, ruled by superior power rather than goodwill. The Athenian envoys in the debate in Sparta in 432 freely admit that the allies find Athenian rule hard to bear. Other speeches equate Athenian rule with slavery.[41]

The accuracy and objectivity of this view of the empire and allied attitudes have been strongly challenged, in particular by the distinguished Greek historian G.E.M. de Ste Croix, who argues that the Athenian policy of encouraging and protecting democracy in allied states created strong support for Athens in many cities, and that Thucydides presents a distorted picture because of his natural inclination as an aristocrat to identify with the upper classes, who represented the real opposition to Athens. These are bold, controversial claims, much debated, with varying conclusions.[42]

It is true that Thucydides' general statements about the relationship between Athens and its allies ignore the complexity of the political environment in many of the states, the rivalry between democratic and oligarchic factions, and the varying attitudes towards Athenian rule. But that does not invalidate the abundant evidence both in Thucydides and elsewhere that what mattered most to any Greek *polis* as a collective, whatever its internal divisions, was, alongside security, freedom from external control and the right of self-government under its own laws (*autonomia*).

Spartan propaganda in relation to the war illustrates the point. The Spartans repeatedly claimed both before and during the war that their purpose in going to war was to liberate Greeks from subjection to Athens, obviously believing this would have a telling effect. Their king, Archidamus, when trying to win over Plataea in 429, based his case on the fact that his goal was to liberate those under the yoke of Athens, and he urged the Plataeans to recover their *autonomia* and join with Sparta in helping other Greeks to do likewise. In his Thracian campaign in 424/3 the Spartan commander Brasidas sounded the same theme: he came as a liberator, not seeking empire, but guaranteeing *autonomia* to all who joined him. His pledges struck a chord, and he had remarkable success in winning over Athenian allies. But it is Phrynichus, the Athenian oligarch, who provides the clearest statement of what freedom and self-rule meant to Greeks. A leading member of the Four Hundred, which seized power in Athens in 411, he said the form of government in Athens would have no effect on the loyalties of the allies, since 'they were more interested in being free under whatever kind of government they happened to have than in being slaves, whether under an oligarchy or a democracy' (trans. Warner, Penguin Thucydides).[43]

As for the idea that Thucydides distorted the relationship between Athens and its allies because of his natural affinity as an aristocrat with the sentiments of the upper classes in the allied cities who represented the real opposition to Athens, that is an assumption, not a demonstrable fact. It is far more in keeping with his purposes that his general statements were seeking to identify another fundamental reality in interstate relations: that imperial rule, depriving those subjected to it of the most cherished features of life in a *polis*, inevitably bred hatred in the ruled against the rulers.

It is, in fact, his purposes and method in writing his *History*, repeatedly and emphatically stated, that provide the most compelling argument for caution in challenging his objectivity, or rejecting his evidence. In the opening sentence of the first book he says that

> He, Thucydides, an Athenian, wrote the history of the war between the Peloponnesians and the Athenians, starting from the very beginning of the war in the expectation that it would be largescale and worthy beyond any of the previous wars of being recorded, judging by the fact that both sides were at the height of their power and readiness, and that the rest of the Greek world was in league with one side or the other.

He sets out his method later in the first book (1.22). He explains how he dealt with the speeches that were made just before the war began or during it, and goes on to describe how he ascertained the facts of what happened:

> With regard to my factual reporting of the events of the war I have made it a principle not to write down the first story that came my way, and not even to be guided by my own general impressions; either I was present myself at the events which I have described or else I heard them from eyewitnesses whose reports I have checked with as much thoroughness as possible. Not that even so the truth was easy to discover: different eyewitnesses gave different accounts of the same events, speaking out of partiality for one side or the other, or else from imperfect memories. And it may well be that my history will seem less easy to read because of the absence in it of a romantic element. It will be enough for me, however, if these words of mine are judged useful by those who want to understand clearly the events which happened in the past and which, human nature being what it is, will at some time or other, and in much the same ways, be repeated in the future. My work is not a piece of writing designed to meet the taste of an immediate public, but was done to last forever. (Trans. Warner, Penguin Thucydides)

He returns once more to his purpose and method in the fifth book (5.26). He says that he lived through the whole of the war and was of an age to understand what was happening, so he applied his mind to getting an accurate grasp of it. He refers to his banishment for twenty years, which enabled him to see what was being done on both sides, particularly by the Peloponnesians, and his leisure allowed him to achieve a better perception of it.

Throughout these statements the word 'accuracy' (*akribeia or akribes*) is prominent. He was proud of the thoroughness with which he tested the truth of what he heard and read, distrustful of tradition and of earlier historians, and he felt that the reader could confidently accept that what he wrote represented as closely as possible what actually happened. As Moses Finley has pointed out, he set himself a standard of accuracy unknown among historians before him or in his time and, according to Finley, not to be found in the historians, Greek or Roman, who came after him. His passion for finding the truth and accurately recording it was driven, as Finley again emphasises, by the fact that his ultimate purpose was not the mere accumulation of information. Rather, it was probing that information to extract the lessons it could impart about human nature and the springs of human behaviour. Thucydides believed that human nature and its motivation were constants, making it likely that history would repeat itself. It was that fact that would make his history of enduring value, a possession for ever.[44]

No historian can be totally objective or free from the risk of error, and Thucydides must be read critically like any other source, but his passion for the truth and his rigorous pursuit of it, fuelled by his conviction that in historical truth there were enduring lessons for the future, make him an exceptionally credible source, unique among other contemporary sources, and undeniably our best witness of the events of his era.

The Character of Athenian Imperialism

Athenian imperial policies and the morality of imperial rule by Greeks over Greeks became a subject of extensive debate not only among Greeks in general but within Athens itself. Power and its role and legitimate uses in human relationships became prominent themes in the broader discourse on ethics and politics that opened up with the advent of the Sophists, about whom more will be said later. The justification for imperial rule and the manner in which it should be conducted became part of that discourse, and increasingly so during the prelude to the Peloponnesian War and in the course of the war itself.

Thucydides devotes a lot of attention to the issue, and makes particular use of the speeches of key figures to show how *arche* was viewed by the Athenians, by certain of the allies, and by the rivals and enemies of Athens. Six major speeches and one famous dialogue deal with the subject. In the first of these speeches an Athenian delegation, speaking before a Spartan Assembly in 432, gave their version of the reasons for the growth of the empire. They claimed that it began with the request from the allies in 478 to lead them in finishing the war against Persia and developed into its present form largely at first because of fear (*deos*), but later because of honour (*time*) and profit (*ophelia*).

The evidence strongly supports this frank assertion of the motivations underlying Athenian imperial policy. The fear was initially fear of Persia, which had still not been decisively defeated. That threat receded after Cimon's victory at the Eurymedon c. 467, but it was replaced by fear of Sparta's intentions following a deterioration in relations between Athens and Sparta in the 450s and a revival of the inveterate hostility of the Athenians towards the Dorians of the Peloponnesus. 'Ionians are always the enemies of the Dorians,' an Athenian envoy, Euphemus, told a Sicilian audience at Camerina in 415, and he repeated the familiar claim that Athens built its empire to protect itself against domination by the Peloponnesians by acquiring the strength needed to match them. In the Athenian view the empire was a strategic necessity, essential to the security of Athens. It was a case of rule or be ruled, and the Athenians resolutely chose the former.[45]

The expansionist drive of the 450s showed the massive scale of their initial ambition to dominate the Greek mainland as well as the Aegean. When it became clear that this objective was beyond their reach, they agreed to the Thirty Years' Peace. But all this achieved was to establish a classic cold-war situation in which two traditionally hostile powers coexisted in a climate of high tension and suspicion.

The continuing power-building of Athens after the peace agreement ensured the tension and suspicion did not diminish. The expansion of the fleet into a force of three hundred battle-ready triremes, the building of a third Long Wall to the Piraeus, which began only one year after the signing of the peace, and the relentless progression of the Delian League towards total subservience to Athens seriously upset the balance of power in Greece and understandably alarmed the Spartans. But the Athenians did not feel they had to justify their behaviour. Euphemus summarised their attitude when he told the Camarinaeans that no one could be reproached for protecting their own safety.

Safety and defence against enemies are worries of all states, yet they rarely lead to pursuit of empire as the remedy in place of creating defensive alliances, such as NATO. The power-building of Athens after the conclusion of the Thirty Years' Peace was not paralleled elsewhere in Greece, nor was there any unusual imminent threat that would have warranted its imperial policy and consequent expansion of its military capabilities. Its behaviour suggests that the other two reasons for its foreign policy listed by Thucydides, honour (*time*) and profit (*ophelia*), played the greater role in determining its decisions.

The concept of *time* had a special place in Greek culture. *Time* was the honour and renown that came from recognition of superior merit (*arete*) as expressed especially in deeds of martial valour. Such deeds were the proof of excellence, and achieving that excellence was the consuming ambition of the epic hero, who had one surpassing goal instilled from youth: 'always to be best and distinguished above others'. In a memorable passage in the *Symposium*, Plato presents the love of honour as a pervasive and seemingly irrational force in human behaviour which drives people, like the heroes of old, to endure extremes of hardship and suffering, and even death, in the pursuit of fame. He explains it as the longing of a mortal nature for immortality. All people are in love with immortality, and survival through the eternal memory of great virtue was a means to it.

The Homeric hero's preoccupation with *time* was concerned above all with his own status and reputation. But as the city-state evolved and ideas of community (*koinonia*), fatherland (*patris*) and serving the common good (*xunon esthlon*) came to the fore, *time* became more closely linked to patriotism and achievements that brought glory and benefit to the fatherland.

It was the honour of the nation that came to matter most. National pride and the glory of the fatherland became the great motivator of those whose *arete* drove them to strive for great achievements, and the greatest personal honour came from heroism in the nation's cause. The Spartans most of all exalted service to country and selfless bravery in its defence as the true *arete* which deserved the highest *time*. Tyrtaeus gave the ideal its most memorable expression. Thermopylae provided the supreme example.[46]

But the Spartan way did not lead to any ambition to achieve dominion in Greece. Sparta's rigidly disciplined and controlled social and political structures made change difficult and discouraged adventurous new directions in foreign policy. In foreign relations the Spartans tended to be reactive and defensive rather than pre-emptive and aggressive. The Corinthians accused them in 432 of slowness and procrastination, of being prisoners of their old-fashioned ways and unable to adapt to new circumstances.

The Athenians of the post-Cleisthenian era presented a striking contrast. Their aggressive foreign policy, described earlier and guided by a series of great leaders from Themistocles to Pericles, shows all the marks of a people who were ready for new undertakings, who were driven by a sense of national pride and a high confidence in their abilities, and who were determined to prove their *arete* and capacity to be first and best.

This activist ethos surfaced soon after the reforms of Cleisthenes, and there can be little doubt that the impetus for it came largely from the new political order which was made possible by a demotic uprising and which increasingly engaged and energised the *demos*. As mentioned earlier, Herodotus noted the coincidence and linked the remarkable military victories of Athens in the aftermath of the reforms to the political equality that they brought and that liberated and inspired the Athenians and transformed them from a mediocre military power into a conquering force.

But it was the successes in the Persian Wars that most of all lifted the national pride of Athens and generated the ambition and the will to become the foremost power in Greece. They had no doubts about their worthiness. The speech of the Athenian envoys at Sparta in 432 set out their credentials. They claimed they stood alone at Marathon and bore the brunt of the first attack of the barbarian. Later they risked all by evacuating their city to confront the enemy by sea. They provided most of the ships at Salamis and the leadership of Themistocles, who saved the day. They continued to resist and refused to come to terms with the Persians, even when Sparta was slow to come to their aid. Without their courage and determination, the Persians would have achieved all that they wished.

The Athenians therefore saw themselves as the saviours of Greece. They had proven their *arete* and they wanted the *time* appropriate to their superior merits. They chafed at taking orders from Sparta, and bided their time until the Persian threat was over and the Spartan commander, Pausanias, had lost favour. Then they moved quickly to assume command of the allies in what Herodotus saw as an opportunistic takeover. Before long they were not just leading but ruling the allies.

It is a story of extraordinary enterprise, courage and resolution from a people brimming with self-belief and in pursuit of power and glory. It is also a story of achievement not by the few but by the greater number. The Athenians had democratised *arete*. It was no longer the preserve of the elite, though the *demos* was led by a succession of exceptional aristocrats who found more room to excel under the democracy than would have been the case in the peer culture of an oligarchy.

The Corinthians gave a revealing summary in a speech in 432 of how opponents viewed the Athenians. They saw them as revolutionary, daring, risk-taking, quick to decide and act, reckless of their personal safety, always hungering for the next achievement, a restless people who found idleness more onerous than activity and were destined neither to have a quiet life themselves nor to allow others to have one.[47]

The description is half-admiring, half-denigrating, seeking as it does to magnify the threat from the Athenians and heighten the contrast between their energy and Spartan inertia. It does, however, capture the essence of the drive and ambition that directed Athenian foreign policy in the mid-fifth century.

But the clearest insight into the character and imperial attitudes of the Athenians in this era comes from three speeches of Pericles, delivered between 432 and 430. The most famous is, of course, the Funeral Oration, most of which concentrates on the character of Athenian democracy as described above. But while Pericles believed that it was the democratic way of life and government that inspired the *arete* of its citizens, for him the crowning glory of Athens had to do with how that *arete* was displayed, and resulted in power greater than had ever been attained before, in an empire that gave Athens control over more Greeks than any other Greek state, in mastery of the seas, and in deeds that excited wonder and gave it a name that was the greatest in the world and that would live forever.

This was what made Athens truly great (*megale*). It was the work of men of steel, doers of great deeds who despised those who sought the quiet life (*apragmones*), who followed the path of fame (*doxa*), not fear (*deos*), and believed the greatest honours came from the greatest dangers. They exulted in the glory that came from empire and believed that they were worthy to rule.[48] The Oration is, of course, replete with the high-flown rhetoric and patriotic fervour appropriate to a commemoration of fallen heroes, but it is also a true reflection of the initiative and driving ambition visible in Athenian foreign policy since the first Persian invasion and freely acknowledged in the speech of the Corinthians.

The other motives for empire advanced by the Athenians, security and profit, are not to the fore in the Periclean speeches, but he does use security as an important argument for not relinquishing the empire. The material gain, which will be considered in more detail later, he also regarded as a mainstay of Athenian power.[49] But the extent of the financial benefits would only have become clear after the empire was established, so it was another reason for retaining it rather than seeking it. The balance of the evidence from both the historical events and the literary sources points clearly to an imperial policy that was motivated above all by the collective pride and energy of a people invigorated by a sense of liberation and by real involvement in deciding their own affairs. The success in the Persian Wars further raised their confidence and ambition. The result was, in Nietzsche's famous phrase, 'the will to power' or, in the Greek epic tradition, a determination 'always to be best and distinguished above others'.

The Athenians were frank and open about their motivations in pursuing empire but, as mentioned at the start of this chapter, there was not total unity about imperial policy. The stance of Thucydides, son of Melesias, in regard to the use of the tribute has been discussed earlier, but there are other signs of broader concerns about Athenian militarism and the politics of power, and clearly there were some who questioned Athenian aggressive expansionism. Pericles described them as 'do-nothings' (*apragmones*), kept safe by the doers (*drasterioi*), and the Athenians overall took the line of Pericles and were proud of their primacy and imperial might. They felt that they had earned their supremacy and had a natural right to rule, and that their security required it. They found further justification in the fact that their rule was benign, was law-based and brought benefits to the ruled. But the character of Athenian imperialism, rooted in the character of the democracy, and marked by the restless ambition and a daring beyond strength so memorably described by the Corinthians, had an adventurist edge that justifiably concerned the more cautious, and that would eventually expose a serious fault line in the system of rule by the people.[50]

The Effects of Empire

The consolidation of its rule over the allies had profound effects on the politics and life of Athens, and created the conditions for a further strengthening of the institutions of democracy and of popular sovereignty. The most basic effect of the growth of empire was the high level of revenue that Athens derived from it on an annual basis, mostly in the form of the tribute levied on each ally, with additional sums coming from other forms of imposition. According to Thucydides, these imperial revenues came to 600 talents a year, considerably more than the domestic revenues, which, according to our best evidence, amounted to about 400 talents. In the view of Pericles, the return that Athens had to make to the allies for these revenues was to provide the defences necessary to protect them against the barbarian. The empire therefore provided a justification for a military build-up, especially expansion of the fleet, and a means of achieving it without imposing new burdens of domestic taxation.

The expansion of its sea power was Athenian policy from the 480s, when the Assembly diverted funds from new finds of silver at Laurium to building ships. By the time of the battle of Salamis in 480, Athens was able to put 180 triremes into action against the Persians. The expansion continued after the formation of the Delian League, and received fresh impetus from the emphasis of Pericles on mastery of the seas. In 431, as war with the Peloponnesians was looming, Pericles was able to announce to the Assembly that there were three hundred triremes in the Piraeus ready to sail. That, however, may not have been the total number of the fleet. Plutarch tells us that Pericles kept sixty ships on patrol in the Aegean for eight months of the year on training and policing duties, which may have been additional to the number berthed in the dockyards.

The size of the land forces had increased also. At the same meeting of the Assembly, Pericles listed 13,000 heavy-armed hoplites and an additional 16,000 drawn from the younger and older citizens who had the task of manning the walls of the city and the defences along the walls extending to the Piraeus. In addition there were 1,200 cavalry, including the mounted archers, and 1,600 bowmen. In 490 Athens had mustered only 9,000 hoplites at Marathon, and 8,000 at Plataea in 479.[51]

The military build-up, especially the expansion of the navy, had a major economic and social impact, injecting large sums of money into the economy on a regular basis, and creating employment on a grand scale. It cost one to two talents to build a trireme. Each ship had a crew of two hundred, of whom 170 were rowers. Their pay for a month of active service around the time of the Peloponnesian War came to about one talent, or a drachma each per day. Occasionally triremes also carried a number of hoplites and they too were each paid a drachma a day. Unlike land campaigns, which tended to be seasonal and intermittent, naval operations were generally of much longer duration, and training to maintain skills was continuous.

But building, repairing and maintaining a fleet of three hundred or more warships would also have required an elaborate industrial infrastructure and a host of skilled craftsmen and labourers. The numbers employed at the shipyards at the Piraeus are nowhere quoted, but it is estimated that the fourth-century fleet, which at one point had about four hundred ships, would have required a shipbuilding workforce of twenty thousand. Even half that number would have transformed the economic situation of the working class at Athens in the fifth century.

The expansion of the land forces would also have meant extra expenditure by the state and extra earning power for those of hoplite status, the *zeugitae*, who comprised the upper tier of the so-called poor, the *penetes*. They, like the sailors, each received a drachma a day when on active service. They received a further drachma a day for an attendant, who carried their supplies. But the main beneficiaries of the increased military spending were undoubtedly the lowest social stratum, the thetes. They supplied the bulk of the crews and formed the backbone of the workforce needed in the shipyards. Slaves certainly supplied some of the labour, but references in our sources to industrial slaves suggest that they were mainly concentrated in the mining industry and craftshops, and we hear nothing of their use in the shipyards. But we do hear about the mass of ordinary citizens, who earned a living by their labour and built the ships and did the metalwork, and provided the bricklayers, carpenters, day labourers, tanners, shoemakers, tailors, shopkeepers and seamen. These were the people on whom Athenian naval power chiefly depended.[52]

But imperial revenues did more than fund the enlargement and recurring costs of the military machine. It seems certain that the introduction of pay for public service was made possible, or at least made easier, by the large inflows of money from the allied states. It began with pay for jurors, which was probably occasioned by the increased workload of the courts after the allies were required to refer all major cases to Athens. It was therefore to a degree a cost of empire. But the practice quickly spread to the armed forces and the Council and all non-elective offices. The empire involved substantial expenditure which, if not met from the tribute, would have required substantial new taxation, of which there is no sign whatever.

The imperial revenues also enabled Athens to accumulate a large reserve of cash, which at one point amounted to 9,700 talents. This reserve was clearly intended to provide insurance that Athens could further increase its military capability, if needed. But neither Pericles nor the Assembly hesitated to use the fund for non-military purposes as well. The ambitious building programme mentioned earlier is the most notable example. The scale of that programme provided another major stimulus for the economy and further jobs for the lower classes. Plutarch describes the benefits the programme brought to the urban poor and the desire of Pericles that the civilian population of the lower orders, 'the banausic throng', should have their share of the public wealth as well as those serving in the armed forces.[53]

The empire also brought other economic benefits unrelated to the tribute or military spending. The founding of colonies and cleruchies on land confiscated from recalcitrant allies had important economic and social benefits. The available list of these settlements indicates that up to ten thousand of the city's poor were given the chance of a new life and a decent livelihood as small landowners. Their allotments almost certainly qualified them for zeugite status, which meant the cleruchs were liable for military service as hoplites. The colonists would be expected to serve as part of allied contingents. All the settlements would further act, in effect, as local garrisons to keep watch on restive allies. Athens had found another way, aside from naval service, to make greater military use of all strata of its manpower while reducing the levels of poverty in the state.[54]

The other notable economic impact of empire was the impetus that it gave to trade and commerce by opening up new markets, stimulating greater consumer spending by a more affluent population, creating new needs for imports and making the seas safer for sailing. Athens became a market for the world. In the Funeral Oration, Pericles says, 'the greatness of the city draws in all the produce of the earth.' The Piraeus became the great emporium. Athens had particular need for grain and other foodstuffs, as well as raw materials for shipbuilding and armaments. We know little about its exports other than olive oil and pottery, but the fact that many of its imports related to public expenditures paid for with the imperial revenues would have eased problems with the balance of payments.[55]

Significant numbers of Athenian merchants and shipowners must have prospered as a result of the boom in trade. We know that metics were particularly prominent in this area, but hardly to the exclusion of Athenian entrepreneurs. It is not believable that the Athenians were so lacking in enterprise that they failed to take their share of the benefits of the large trading opportunities of empire.

Athens also gained economically and earned additional foreign revenue from its status as the imperial capital, which brought an influx of overseas visitors – ambassadors, officials of the allied states, the many citizens of these states who had to deal with the Athenian courts, businessmen of all sorts. It was also a magnet for artists, intellectuals and the general tourist.[56]

A clear indication of the scale of the economic benefits that flowed from the empire is the rapid rise in population that took place in the half-century between 480 and 430, obviously a response to enhanced prosperity and opportunity. Once again, figures are scarce and modern estimates vary considerably, but the archaeological and literary evidence, together with deductions from the numbers of hoplites and sailors that Athens was able to muster at different times, suggest that the numbers of adult male citizens rose from about thirty thousand at the time of the Persian Wars to over fifty thousand in 430. That was a dramatic increase, and could only have been sustained by large-scale expansion of the economy and of the employment opportunities for the mass of the people. The often-discussed 'balance sheet of empire', weighing the gains and losses of Athenian imperial rule, comes down firmly on the side of the gains.[57]

Political Effects

The economic and military effects of empire were accompanied by political effects that further extended the role and broadened the participation of the mass of citizens in government. The growth of empire and of the Athenian state increased the scale of government, expanding in particular the executive branch. Administrative functions multiplied, and the number of office-holders or magistrates grew accordingly. The Aristotelian *Constitution of Athens* states that after the consolidation of the empire the number of magistrates expanded to seven hundred, with as many more officials serving abroad in the allied states. Magistrates in Athens mostly operated in boards of ten and had specific functions ranging over the military and financial areas, religious affairs, judicial affairs, supervision of markets and the physical infrastructure. With the exception of the military and financial areas, they were chosen by lot from eligible candidates who put their names forward, held office for a year and could not be reappointed to the same post, though they could hold a variety of different posts. The role of the magistrates was strictly confined to implementing the decisions of the Assembly – though, as we shall see, generals in particular had the potential to exert a decisive influence on the outcome of the Assembly's deliberations.[58]

The executive role of the Council also expanded. It evolved as the executive arm of the Assembly in addition to maintaining its important probouleutic role. The Assembly was too unwieldy to act as an executive body, and besides, it met irregularly in the fifth century, with probably no more than ten mandatory meetings a year. The Council met every day, except holidays, and was the obvious means of providing the Assembly with an overall administrative authority that could ensure decisions of the Assembly were implemented, that routine decisions were taken expeditiously and that the work of the various public offices was properly supervised.

The Council had an especially important role in the management of the state's finances. It also acquired significant judicial powers in areas for which it had particular responsibility, and it could act as a court of first instance in cases involving crimes against the state (*eisangeliai*). But its managerial mandate extended into most areas of public administration. It oversaw the building and equipping of ships authorised by the Assembly. It had involvement in the public building programmes, in religious festivals, in matters of diplomacy and relations with other states, in the systems of scrutiny (*dokimasia*) and accountability (*euthuna*) for magistrates. It provided, in effect, a single, comprehensive managerial authority for an increasingly complex state.

But even at the height of its powers, it never posed a threat to the sovereignty and control of the *demos*. As noted earlier, the initial checks on its power, which came from mixing regions and classes in its membership and from procedures that changed the leadership every month and the entire membership every year, and allowed reappointment only once, never altered or weakened. The continuity and common interests necessary to build an independent, ongoing power-base were totally absent.[59]

These changes in the executive arm of government greatly expanded the incentives and opportunities for ordinary citizens to participate in government, not just at the deliberative level but at important executive levels. The introduction of pay for public office and selection by lot, annual rotation and the bar on re-election to the same office helped ensure that participation in the executive offices was broad and inclusive. These features were the great levellers, the defining symbols of full equality and true democracy. They extended the meaning of political equality to include not just the equal right to rule but the equal opportunity to do so.

Membership of the Council now became a realistic option for those who had to earn a living by their labour. The annual turnover of the entire membership of the Council made appointment sooner or later very likely for those who sought it. It is estimated that one in every two or three Athenian citizens who reached the qualifying age of thirty served at least once as a Councillor. This year of service on the body that exercised such broad control over the management of public affairs meant high responsibility and total immersion in all dimensions of government. It also meant a better-informed citizenry. Jury service drew a further six thousand citizens each year into another crucial branch of government where important political issues and the fate of prominent statesmen and prominent allies were often decided. The incentive of pay also applied to this service.[60]

This was participatory democracy in a fuller form, providing easier access to high executive levels of government and to service in the judicial system for the mass of ordinary citizens. But the most important participation by the *demos* continued to take place in the Assembly, where every citizen had permanent membership and full equality, and where the people as a whole had the power to control the course of public affairs.

Empire had no impact on the constitutional position of the Assembly. It remained the highest governing authority in the state, subject only to the restriction that it act in accordance with established law, a restriction that was made explicit in a law of the late fifth century that made it an indictable offence for anyone to propose a law or decree that contradicted existing law (*graphe paranomon*).[61]

All the main sources for the fifth-century constitution agree that the *demos*, acting through the Assembly, controlled all major matters of public policy. It elected the most important magistrates, the generals, and held them to account. It also elected the other holders of the electoral offices. It decided matters of war and peace and all issues relating to foreign policy. It alone had the power to make laws or to pass administrative decrees, which in the fifth century had the same legal standing as laws. It was in these sweeping deliberative and decision-making powers of the Assembly that the *kratos* of the *demos* found its fullest expression. The level of participation in the Assembly and the social composition of those attending will be discussed in more detail later in the chapter. Suffice to say here that there is no hard evidence or reason to believe that the normal composition of the Assembly did not broadly represent the overall body of citizens.

The Contemporary Critics of the Democracy

Many of the main contemporary or near-contemporary sources for the fifth-century constitution strongly disapproved of the trend towards greater democratisation in the course of the century and the concentration of power in the hands of the mass of citizens. In particular, the essay of the Old Oligarch and the writings of Plato and Aristotle illustrate the breadth and depth of the objections to democracy that flowed from class prejudices and philosophical theorising. They also provide a valuable insight into the character of ongoing political debate in Athens about political roles and systems and controversial aspects of the democratic ideal, and it is obviously important in any study of Athenian democracy to examine the views of the major critics of the system and the validity of their analyses.

The essay of the Old Oligarch has been referred to already, but it has particular interest as the only analysis, aside from the rare and sparing comments of Thucydides, of the constitution in the age of Pericles, and so deserves a closer look. It is also a unique view of an unabashed, intellectually unsophisticated bigot, who parades his elitist class prejudices without inhibition.

The writer is implacably opposed to the very idea of democracy, which he sees as favouring the worthless (*poneroi*) over the worthy (*chrestoi*). It gives power over the aristocracy, who alone have an inbred sense of virtue and goodness, to the knavish, impoverished, disorderly, ignorant and uncultured *demos*, who by birth and circumstances are incapable of moral behaviour or orderly government. He uses the term *demos*, as was the practice of writers of elitist persuasion, to describe, not the full body of citizens, but the mass of ordinary people, the great body of the so-called poor (*penetes*), which included all who had to earn a living by their labour, as distinct from the small elite of the well-born and the rich (the *gennaioi* or *gnorimoi* and the *plousioi),* who lived off their wealth.[62]

But the main purpose of the essay is not to expose the evil perversity of this form of government, but to show how such a system arose and how the *demos* has managed to entrench it so firmly that resistance seems futile. He bases the ascendancy of the masses over the noble and the good on the fact that it is the ordinary people who man the ships and thereby confer far greater power on Athens than the hoplites or high-born. It is this that has made it seem right that everyone should share in public office and that everyone should have the right to stand forth and speak on public affairs. He then goes on to list the main practices and policies introduced by the *demos* into the life and government of Athens and the empire, which puzzle and outrage the right-minded, but which are carefully calculated to serve the interests of the masses and preserve their freedom and control of government. He concludes that, in these circumstances, reforming or overthrowing the system would be difficult and would require more than a few to achieve it. He does not believe that the numbers of the disaffected are sufficient to pose any danger to democracy. The essay offers a revealing glimpse into the unrelenting mentality of a die-hard oligarch, but also an indication of how solidly the democratic structures were entrenched.[63]

The analyses of democracy by Plato and Aristotle present a stark contrast to the crudities of style and reasoning of the Old Oligarch, but behind the intellectual brilliance and well-argued ideas of both philosophers some similar views are evident, and they provide an equally damning indictment of the character and composition of the Athenian *demos* and of its fitness to rule. Reference has been made earlier to the particular concerns of Plato and Aristotle about the level of personal freedom under the democracy, but their objections to the system were far more wide-ranging and fundamental.

Plato, an Athenian of distinguished lineage, was born around 428/7. He experienced the turbulence of the Peloponnesian War and witnessed the failings of the democracy in that period. Not long afterwards, he saw his teacher, friend and idol, Socrates, condemned to death under that same democracy. These events may have helped shape his thinking, but his objections to democracy went far deeper, and his writings memorably got to the root of the deep-seated antipathy to full-blown democracy that has been evident in many political leaders and thinkers down to modern times.[64]

Plato's vision of the ideal form of government, most fully presented in the *Republic*, proceeded from the premise that statesmanship was an art (*techne*) that required knowledge of a special kind, knowledge of what was good for the individual and for the state. He believed such knowledge was attainable, but only by those who had superior intellectual powers perfected by a rigorous education. Those who could aspire to this level of political excellence would be few and would have to be carefully selected as the future rulers or guardians of the state. Some of those chosen would fail to achieve the highest level and would be assigned a subordinate role as auxiliary guardians. They would form the military arm of the state. A third social division comprising the mass of ordinary citizens would serve the state and each other as specialist providers of the society's needs.

Those who achieved the pinnacle of wisdom would become the rulers, physicians of the state, their mission the betterment of the body politic. Their rule would be totalitarian, their wisdom making law dispensable. They would shape and regulate the other components of the society, just as the rational mind in the well-ordered, disciplined individual controls and moderates the spirited and appetitive aspects of the human psyche. The result would be a society in which all individuals had their place and their due in accordance with their aptitudes and abilities, a society guided by expert knowledge (*episteme*), unified and harmonious, and characterised by wisdom, courage, moderation and justice.[65]

Later in his life Plato acknowledged the utopian character of this vision, and in his final work, the *Laws*, he turned to considering more practical models. He replaced the rule of wisdom with the rule of law, but attempted to ensure the state would still be guided to the greatest extent possible by wisdom. The law would be enshrined in a written code and based on the wisdom of the ages, use and wont, its principles affirmed as representing true right by the best and oldest citizens drawing on their experience. It would be designed to serve the good of all, and would be supreme. Magistrates and all governing authorities would be its servant.

But the law should not be seen as an oppressive master. Plato is always conscious of the need for consensus and a friendly spirit of community. The law should therefore persuade rather than compel. It must be shown to be for the good of all, and every individual law should have a preamble to explain its purpose and encourage acceptance. Laws should promote freedom, unity and wisdom.[66]

Plato concluded that the form of constitution most likely to incorporate all his stipulations for good government – the sovereignty of law, rationality (*nous*), freedom subject to the constraints of law, order, consensus, friendship and fellowship – was a mixed system rather than any of the conventional types that gave power to the one, the few or the many. Unchecked power to one person or one social division was certain to degenerate into oppression and corruption and to consider its own rather than the common interest. Monarchy and democracy he considered the two mother constitutions, and he saw a blend of the best of both as the means of achieving order without coercion, and freedom without licence. But the complicated blend that he finally proposed was far more oligarchic than democratic, its chief concern being to ensure the rule of the best, while offering a modest electoral role to the people that was heavily weighted in favour of the better-off.[67]

Plato's democratic instincts were minimal, and when he turned his critical eye on Athenian democracy in its developed form, his verdict was scathing. He saw it as a perversion of the moderate, law-abiding democracy that preceded the Persian Wars, which was characterised by a restraint (*aidos*) that fostered acceptance of authority and by a strong sense of friendly solidarity (*philia*) reinforced by fear of the Persian threat. But later that fear disappeared, confidence grew, and with it came insolence (*thrasos*) and a belief that everyone was wise in all matters and knew what should be done. The leaders, such as

Themistocles, Cimon and Pericles, instead of directing the people towards better ways, pandered to their wishes and corrupted them with an excess of freedom, and filled the city with harbours, docks, walls and tribute rather than fostering justice and restraint.

The constitution that resulted failed every canon of good government prescribed by Plato. It rejected the principle of the sovereignty of law. It gave control to one of the major social divisions of the state, the poor, with unchecked power to rule in its own interest and oppress the rich. It exalted freedom to the point where it was absolute (*panteles*) and became licence, giving everyone the right to do what he pleased. The consequence was a society that lacked the true foundations of a state – order and respect for authority, and the solidarity, consensus and restraint essential for unity. There was no place for *aidos* or *sophrosyne*, which were replaced by *hybris* and indulgence.

But the most fatal flaw in the Athenian brand of democracy in Plato's view was its concept of political equality, which, as in the case of freedom, it took to extremes, and gave equal political rights to the equal and unequal alike, going so far as to assign office mostly by lot. This meant the ascendancy of the lower classes, since they formed the majority. But they were the farthest removed from knowledge and wisdom. They were characterised instead by ignorance (*amathia*) and a lack of rational capacity (*anoia*), and these were the greatest destroyers of great states. Plato equated the masses in the state with the appetitive element in the individual soul, and they similarly needed to be led and moderated by reason and the certain knowledge (*episteme*) derived from it. There could be no justice or moderation in a state governed by the unlettered, unreasoning multitude, and the only end he could see for such a state was a slide into tyranny.[68]

Aristotle is a fourth-century writer, but he has much to say about the fifth-century constitution. He provides a more specific and down-to-earth analysis of the developed Athenian democracy than Plato, but his conclusions are, in several major respects, similar. Born in 384 in Stagira in Chalcidice, he spent twenty years at Plato's Academy, between 367 and 347, as student and scholar, and though he later disagreed with many aspects of Platonic doctrine, his debt to the seminal ethical and political views of his teacher is clearly evident.

But Aristotle was not a die-hard opponent of democracy in the mould of Plato. His views in fact provide a surprisingly strong endorsement of many of the central tenets of the democratic ideal. He far preferred it as a form of government to oligarchy, the only real alternative in the Greece of his day. Oligarchy he defined as the rule of the wealthy few, as distinct from the meritorious few, and he considered it divisive in its exclusiveness, misguided in its view that those superior in wealth should be superior in everything, and prone to corruption, instability, factional strife and a continuing concentration of greater power in fewer hands.

Democracy he defines as the rule of the mass of citizens, which, he emphasises, meant in effect the rule of the poor, since everywhere the poor are in the majority. He considered democracy a close neighbour of his own ideal form, the polity, which he saw as inclining towards democracy, deviating only slightly from it. Both forms stood for the rule of the majority, which Aristotle strongly favoured. He fully approved the democratic emphasis on freedom and described the state as an association of the free, devoid of any despotic element. His only qualification was that freedom must be subject to the prescriptions of the law, and must see that living by the constitution is not servitude but salvation. He liked the principle of rule and be ruled, which prevented a build-up of power by individuals. He saw democracy as less prone to corruption, infighting and factional strife, and the most likely to command the loyalty and support of the majority of citizens, always easier to secure when the majority itself was involved in ruling. This high level of political consensus (*homonoia*) and commitment to a constitution he considered the most essential requirement for stable government.

Aristotle also advanced an interesting argument in favour of the rule of the many, sometimes called the summation theory. He suggested that while each individual among the many might not be outstanding, everyone has a share in virtue and common sense and can add something, and the sum of the collective contributions of the many may well be better than the judgement of the more expert few.[69]

But everything depended on the character of the many and the extent to which they controlled unchecked the overall apparatus of government (the *politeuma*). It was here that Aristotle saw fatal flaws in the democracy of both the fifth and fourth centuries. His ideal system envisaged a population in which the majority comprised citizens of moderate means, neither rich nor poor but in the middle (*hoi mesoi*), predominantly small landholders, who formed the hoplite core of the state, the fighting men who defended the nation. They might not have the broad excellence that could come with high birth and high wealth, but they had the excellence of the warrior (*polemike arete*), which is found in the many and which entitled them to political rights. Just as virtue lies in the mean, the middle form of life (*mesos bios*), such as is attainable by all, is best. Those who pursue such a life are more likely to be contented, committed to their work, least covetous of the property of others or of political power, and least given to factionalism. In other words they had the capacity to provide the basis for a stable government.[70]

Aristotle considered the citizen population that evolved in the wake of the Persian Wars and the rise of the empire as a far cry from this model. He shared the view of the Old Oligarch that the emergence of Athens as a great sea power transformed the political landscape of the Athenian state. He saw Salamis as the decisive turning point. The victory was won by the common people who manned the ships, and it led on to the acquisition of an empire based on naval power. This created in Athens a throng of naval oarsmen, an element always determinedly democratic, and the result was a strengthening of the democracy. The *demos*, buoyed by their maritime supremacy, became presumptuous and sought greater power, and, despite opposition from the better elements, found demagogic leaders to support them. Ephialtes and Pericles introduced the critical changes by curtailing the powers of the Areopagus and introducing pay for public office.[71]

Aristotle classified the constitution that followed as the most extreme form of democracy (*teleutaia demokratia*). It corresponded to what he presents as the fourth and worst democratic constitution in his various discussions of types of democracy in the *Politics*, and it was the farthest removed from his ideal system. It reached its peak as Athens grew and prospered and the public revenues increased, which resulted in the population of landed *mesoi* being outnumbered by the urban commercial and industrial classes. The citizen population now consisted mainly of inferior types, a proletariat of artisans, traders and labourers wedded to the political status they enjoyed in the democracy as a core element of Athenian naval power.

Aristotle's contempt for this motley proletariat fully equals that of Plato. Their lives gave no scope for the development of excellence or any capacity to contribute to political life. Their preponderance in the population created the risk of a deviation from constitutional government and a domination of the lowliest elements governing in their own interest, creating in effect a collective tyranny of the poor.[72]

Aristotle also found serious fault with radical democracy's view of both freedom and equality. He identified freedom as the fundamental principle (*hypothesis*) on which democracy is based. He distinguished two aspects, one that held that, since all citizens were equal in freedom, they were equal in all respects, and therefore had the right to an equal share in political power, which ensured that the multitude (*plethos*) was supreme and the decisions of the majority had to be seen as final and just. He considered this a false theory of equality, which was at variance with justice and the end (*telos*) for which the state existed.

He saw the ultimate end of the state as extending beyond security or material necessities, or the accumulation of wealth, or a social contract to prevent injustice, to a higher form of living based on friendship (*philia*), communal fellowship or partnership (*koinonia*), goodness (*to kalon*) and the happiness (*eudaimonia*) that derived from it. This was the form of the common good (*koinon sumpheron*) whose advancement must be the ultimate aim of all good government. It followed that those who had the greater capacity to contribute to this aim should be given the greater share of political power. Justice in the distribution of power therefore required that it be apportioned on the basis of ability to advance the raison d'être of the state, not on the basis of mere numbers.[73]

Aristotle had still stronger objections to the second aspect of freedom found in extreme democracy: the idea of living as one wishes, preferably not being ruled by anybody or, failing that, living by a system of rule by turns. He considered this a debased idea of freedom, since salvation lies in living in accordance with the provisions of the constitution.[74]

Aristotle's view that equality should be proportionate to ability to contribute to the true purpose of the state led him to believe that in theory participation in government should be confined to the landed classes, where political capacity was more likely to reside. But he was conscious that exclusion bred division, and in sections of the *Politics* he seems willing to consider ways by which all classes could have a role in the deliberative arm of government, but in a manner that would keep the poor from having a controlling say.

When it came to the major political offices, however, he saw no place whatever for the proletariat. Here the overriding consideration must be merit. These offices should be elective, should be unpaid and should require a property qualification – the higher the office, the higher the qualification. For Aristotle, this was the best form of democracy, placing the most capable and distinguished in office with the consent of the *demos*. In this way the ambition of the upper classes was satisfied without diminishing the rights of the people, who retained the power to elect and to hold the elected accountable in the people's court.[75]

Aristotle also favoured giving magistrates an independent role in decision-making to moderate the unrestricted control of public affairs by the Assembly and provide more balance in the constitution. He did not accept the principle that what concerns all must be decided by all, and maintained that some blending of the best features of oligarchy with the democratic ideal was essential for the stability of the constitution and its protection against perversion.[76]

The vulnerability of constitutions to perversion was a particular concern for Aristotle. He believed the only defence against it was the stability that came from a broad consensus (*homonoia*) derived from a constitution that commanded the firm loyalty of a majority of citizens who had the will to ensure its continuance.

To maintain this loyalty and ensure durability, a constitution had to have as its ultimate purpose the promotion of the public interest and the good life for all citizens. It also had to create, in conjunction with its associated laws, an apparatus of government (*politeuma*) and rules for the behaviour of citizens and their relations with one another that were suited to the character of the particular society and that embodied its values, political beliefs and expectations. For Aristotle, the state was a partnership (*koinonia*) of citizens in a particular type of constitution that represented the particular way of life and form of government desired by that state. At one point he says the partnership consists in the constitution.

Similar views of the constitution and its associated laws were expressed by other leading figures of the fourth century. Isocrates calls the constitution the soul (*psyche*) of the state, controlling the state as the mind does the body. Demosthenes presents the laws as an expression of the ways (*tropoi*) or manner of life of a society.

Changing a constitution therefore had profound implications, and Aristotle was of the view that, once a constitution had been created by wise lawgivers according to just principles that promoted the common good and had been agreed and adopted by the *koinonia* of citizens, it should be virtually unchangeable. He argued that altering a constitution meant altering the innermost character and very identity of a state, a development that could seriously threaten consensus and sow the seeds of instability. It should therefore only be contemplated in circumstances where the people could be readily persuaded to accept the change and adapt to it.

But Aristotle was very conscious that changing social conditions and the power of special interests were a constant threat to constitutions. He saw two forms of protection. Citizens must be schooled by the political culture and educational structures in the spirit of the constitution and be attuned to its values and beliefs. But above all the constitution itself must have a power structure that gave protection against the rise to dominance of any social class or faction that was more likely to pursue its own interests than the common good, and to place itself above the law and adjust the constitution to serve its selfish ends. He saw no such protection in radical democracy. It could only be provided by a constitution that had a balanced mix of democratic and oligarchic features along the lines of the constitution that he called the polity. He could not believe that a system controlled by a popular Assembly that saw itself as supreme (*kyrios*) and that was dominated by the least worthy was capable of just and stable government.[77]

The views of Plato and Aristotle do not fit well with what is otherwise known of the structure, functioning and outlook of Athenian democracy in this era. They both had profound, principled objections to the notion of radical democracy. They found its underlying principles irrational, unjust and anarchic. They did not fit their theoretical formulations of how society should be organised and governed, and if they did not work in theory, they could not accept that they would work in practice.

The fears of Plato and Aristotle of a lawless tyranny of the poor were never borne out in Athens. The democracy never threatened to overthrow the rule of law or oppress the rich. The evidence presented earlier in this chapter shows how jealously the *demos* guarded the integrity of the body of established law, which was the guarantor of the personal and public rights of the mass of citizens. There was no more highly valued or carefully protected principle in Athenian democracy than the sovereignty of law.[78]

The contention, particularly explicit in Aristotle, that the Assembly and political decision-making were dominated by an urban proletariat is also a misrepresentation of the dynamics of Athenian politics in the later fifth century. The huge expansion of the navy and the vital role in the state's defences that it gave to the lowest economic class, the thetes, undoubtedly raised their status and strengthened their influence in political life. It is clear that their numbers also grew significantly as a result of the gains of empire. But it is also clear that, despite these developments, the thetes did not achieve anything approaching a controlling influence in the Assembly. The voice of the *demos* was never just the voice of the thetes.

The reasons were many. The numbers of the lower classes available to attend the Assembly were diminished by several factors. It is estimated that the Athenians kept about sixty triremes at sea on a regular basis for most of the year. That meant, at a conservative estimate, that six thousand thetes were away on naval duty at any one time. Colonies and cleruchies drained off another ten thousand during the consolidation of the empire. Employment among the lower classes was dramatically increased by the many economic gains of empire. As a result fewer had the leisure to attend the Assembly without sacrificing pay, and there was no compensating financial reward for attendance in the fifth century.[79]

The impact on the thetes as a political force would have been further affected by upward mobility, which must have been considerable in an age of prosperity such as the Periclean era. Hard evidence in this area is extremely limited, but we do know that the citizens continued to be classified in accordance with the Solonian system, and since the classes were the basis of military recruitment, a census must have been held at fairly regular intervals. The Solonian classes were originally based on landed wealth only, but as other forms of wealth developed it has to be assumed that the criteria were widened to include all forms of capital worth. This was the system used in assessing liability for the war tax (*eisphora*) which was levied on citizens in emergencies. Upward mobility would therefore have followed growth in capital wealth, as was the case with the *ordo equester* in Rome.

The opportunities for those with skills and enterprise to increase their wealth were numerous in the booming economic conditions of the mid-fifth century. State contracts would have proliferated in areas such as shipbuilding, mining and the public building programme. There is evidence of a large-scale trade in industrial slaves. Manufacturing, commerce, property rental and moneylending were other occupations that could yield high profits. Aristotle makes the remarkable statement in the *Politics* that the majority of *banausoi* (artisans) became rich. We know of one instance where a citizen went directly from the ranks of the thetes to the class of the *hippeis*. There are also many examples of politicians, such as Nicias and Cleon, who belonged to the rich, but whose wealth went back no further than a generation or two, and came from commercial and industrial sources.

These several factors undoubtedly lessened the political impact of the thetes, but their greatest weakness as a political force was not any lack of numbers, but a lack of organisation and leadership, and the fact that the other two social divisions of the *demos*, the hoplite class and the wealthy elite, were much better placed to control decisions of the Assembly.[80]

The hoplite class, the Solonian *zeugitae*, whose capital worth made them liable for service in the land army, formed the more prosperous wing of the broad division of the population commonly described as the poor (*penetes*). They were a numerous class in the latter half of the fifth century. When the war with Sparta and its allies was looming in 431, Pericles gave the Assembly a list of all the armed forces available to Athens. The number he gave for the hoplites was 29,000. The figure included six thousand metics and presumably those elevated from the thetic class to zeugite status. But the bulk of the hoplite class and hoplite forces would have continued to come from the farming communities throughout Attica.

Thucydides (2.15–16) has interesting things to say about this rural population. He presents the rural life as especially characteristic of the Athenian people, who originally lived in their separate communities and managed their own affairs under their own magistrates. He goes on to describe the unification of Attica under Theseus, who centred all institutions of government in the one city. But he stresses that, even after the union, the majority of the Athenians and their descendants, because of their attachment to their rural traditions, continued down to the start of the Peloponnesian War to live with their entire households in the country.

This ancient rural core of the citizens of the Athenian state, and the backbone of its hoplite class, was a powerful force in the evolution of the democracy, and there is no evidence to suggest that its members ever relinquished their influence. As the only well-armed, experienced infantry the Athenians had, the hoplites must have played a central role in the defeat of Isagoras and Cleomenes in 508/7, which opened the way for the introduction of the reforms of Cleisthenes. It was the hoplites, energised according to Herodotus by a new sense of liberation, who preserved the new order in 506 by causing a Peloponnesian invasion force to disperse, and then went on to defeat the Boeotians and Chalcidians in separate battles on the same day. Even more significantly, it was the hoplites, unaided by the rest of Greece except for a small contingent from Plataea, who won the glorious victory at Marathon.

This same spirit of daring and activism continued to inspire Athenian policy and actions over the next half-century. The Athenian character is a frequent theme in Thucydides, most memorably described, as noted earlier, in the speech attributed to the Corinthians in 431 and in the Funeral Oration of Pericles. Qualities normally associated with Homeric heroes and the nobility – the thirst for fame, willingness to endure hardship and danger for glory and country, contempt for the life of ease and inaction – all of these are attributed to the Athenian people as a whole, and would be especially associated with the sturdy yeomen who supplied the majority of its hoplite power.

The political engagement of this population would have been especially stimulated and extended by the reforms of Cleisthenes. These reforms had reinvigorated the political life of the rural communities and laid the ground-work for strong hoplite engagement at both the local and the national level. The demes, as emphasised earlier, became important centres of local government, which restored the cherished tradition of local control referred to by Thucydides. The hold of the aristocratic elite was loosened and grassroots democracy was given room to flourish. The hoplite class would have been well placed to take a leading political role as a result.

The reform of local government had implications for national government as well. The demes effectively selected the members of the powerful Council of Five Hundred, which had such an important role in the functioning of the Assembly. The decline in aristocratic control of local politics would have enabled the hoplite class to secure strong representation on the Council, and the annual rotation of the Council's membership would have created the opportunity for greater numbers to acquire broad experience of the issues and workings of the national government. All of these factors would have given the hoplite class a significant influence in the affairs of the Assembly.

I can find no basis for any assumption that they failed to exercise that influence at any period in the fifth century or that they were outnumbered or over-shadowed in the Assembly by the thetes. There is an image of the Athenian farmer as politically inactive (*apragmon*), ill at ease in the city, focused, in Hesiodic style, on making ends meet, which appears in the writings of some of the philosophers and Aristophanes, but it is sharply at odds with the mainstream evidence. Other arguments discounting hoplite political influence are also questionable. There were undoubtedly obstacles to attendance at the Assembly for rural residents due to military duties, pressures of work and distance from the city, but these can be easily exaggerated. Hoplites were far less likely to be away on military service than thetes. Their work as farmers was seasonal, and they had more flexibility than those who worked for an employer to manage their time so as to enable them to attend the Assembly. They also had many reasons of buying and selling to visit the city, and could time such visits to coincide with meetings of the Assembly. Those serving on the Council, or in any other national office, would in any event be present in the city most of the time during their term. It is entirely likely that citizens from the farthest reaches of Attica and many subsistence farmers struggling for survival had difficulties participating on a regular basis in public bodies in the city, but there is no likelihood that the culture of participation so carefully nurtured by the interconnected system of demes, *trittyes*, tribes and Council did not result in high rural participation.[81]

The third main social division of the Athenian people, the nobility (*gennaioi*) and the rich (*plousioi*), also continued to wield major influence over Athenian policy and decision-making. I have alluded earlier, in reviewing the role of the aristocracy in the Persian Wars, to the remarkable balance and resultant stability achieved by the democratic constitution, which gave powerful positions of leadership to members of the upper class while ensuring the preservation of popular sovereignty. This situation did not change during what is often called the *pentekontaetia*, the fifty-year interval from the end of the Persian Wars to the beginning of the Peloponnesian War. The critical elective senior military commands continued to go to those who proved their worth and won the trust of the public. This in practice meant members of the wealthy elite, who alone had the status, education, leisure and resources to devote themselves to public life and win the support and reputation required. We know of no thetes or *zeugitae* who achieved high military or political prominence at any time during the fifth century.

This monopoly of the most important executive offices gave the upper class an ongoing leading place in Athenian politics, a fact that is seriously understated or ignored in the analyses of the democracy in Plato and Aristotle. The office of general in particular, to which re-election was unlimited, brought an opportunity to acquire lasting prominence and moral authority. With the decline of the archonship it became the most prestigious and powerful executive office in the state. The Assembly relied on its generals for advice on all matters of war and peace and foreign policy, and there is evidence that, at least in times of war, generals enjoyed special privileges with regard to summoning the Assembly and making proposals to it. The procedures of Council and Assembly also gave those with high moral authority and the capacity to persuade a powerful influence on decisions. It was from his position as general that Pericles was able to use these platforms and his great range of skills and powers of persuasion to win repeated re-election and achieve his unique position of pre-eminence. Political decision-making was never in practice dominated by the lower classes in the period between the Persian and the Peloponnesian wars.[82]

The Athenian democracy therefore continued throughout the Periclean era to be led by a largely hereditary elite. The *demos* saw no paradox in this situation. The Old Oligarch explains their attitude: 'The people do not seek to share in those offices which, if administered well, bring benefit to all, but, if administered badly, bring danger. They recognise that it is more beneficial for them not to hold these offices but to leave them to the superior class.'[83]

Where did this leave the Athenian concept of equality? Athenian democracy was based on the closely related principles of freedom and equality. It held that all citizens were free and equal members of their state, equal in their freedom, equal before the law and entitled to share on an equal basis in what was equally the concern of all – the management of the state.

The democratic constitution went to extraordinary lengths to make this form of equality work in practice. It is worth rehearsing the array of equalising features. There was an Assembly of all citizens which formed the deliberative element with supreme authority in all matters, limited only by the rule of law. All members had an equal right to express their views (*isegoria*) and an equal vote (*isopsephia*). The will of the majority determined the decisions.

The judicial system was controlled by ordinary citizens through a series of people's courts in which juries were chosen by lot from an annually changing panel, which was also chosen by lot from whatever group of citizens offered themselves for service. To encourage participation in the judicial process across the widest range of the population, pay was introduced for jury service. Local government was also democratised and appointment to the Council became feasible for all citizens.

In the executive sphere all offices were opened to all, and a range of measures was taken to increase equality of opportunity and spread participation across the social classes. The majority of posts were filled by lot to give those who sought them an equal chance. Pay was introduced to enable poorer citizens to participate. Annual rotation of the membership of offices extended as widely as possible the numbers who could hold an executive post and highlighted the principle of rule and be ruled.

But when it came to the most critical executive positions, principally the senior financial and military posts, which required special skills and experience, the idea of access for all and random selection had to be abandoned, and these offices remained elective, a practice generally seen as oligarchic. But political preferment on the basis of merit in cases where particular abilities were required was prudently and readily accepted as compatible with justice and equality, and Pericles hailed it as one of the glories of Athenian democracy. The difficulty with it in relation to equality was that, under the social structure prevailing in Athens, it had the effect of confining the highest positions of leadership to the narrow elite of birth and wealth, who had unequalled opportunity to acquire the abilities and reputation needed to win high office. Equality of opportunity for anyone outside this privileged circle was absent, without which the right of participation was largely meaningless.

Athenian democracy made no attempt to change this situation. Economic and social reform were outside its agenda. It did not even take modest steps by creating a career path or supporting a system of patronage that might nurture young talent from outside the ranks of the elite. The Athenians were content to live with their social heritage and use talent where they found it. The circle remained largely closed. Nouveaux riches might gain grudging acceptance into the upper class after a generation or two, but no one resembling the Roman Marius, who rose from a modest middle-class background in a rural town to the pinnacle of military and political fame in Rome, emerged in democratic Athens.[84]

But the *demos* did maintain tight control over those it placed in power. It held them strictly to account and was quick to punish failure or behaviours that seemed contrary to the interests of the democracy. It also exacted a price from the wealthy for their privileged position. The latter were expected – and, in the fourth century, compelled – to prop up the public finances by undertaking certain functions (liturgies). The most frequently mentioned are equipping a trireme or funding choruses and athletic contests at the festivals. But the wealthy were also expected to be public-minded in other ways and to show themselves to be generous benefactors of their society (*euergetes*). The people saw this as an appropriate way of reducing the gap between rich and poor.

The Old Oligarch considered that the system represented a good deal for the *demos*. In any event it was a deal that brought a high level of social harmony during a high point in the history of the democracy and enabled Athens to build an empire and rise to become the greatest power in Greece. It moved a long way towards absolute political equality, but stopped well short of the social and economic reforms required to produce a reasonable level of equality of opportunity in regard to the highest offices. It was not the extreme democracy depicted by the philosophers, nor was it ever dominated by the urban prole-tariat or the wider poor. What emerged, though at some cost to ideological purity, was a balanced modus vivendi between the social classes that offered no threat to wealth and that gave a de facto monopoly of the most important offices to the elite while maintaining the ultimate control of the *demos* over leaders and the broad course of public affairs.[85]

CHAPTER 4

An Age of Enlightenment

The strengthening of Athenian democracy and imperial rule coincided with one of the most memorable eras in the artistic and intellectual history of Europe. The connection between cultural progress and political environment has an abiding interest, and the coincidence between the maturing of the democracy and the emergence of a golden era of artistic and intellectual accomplishment does raise the question of the extent to which the ethos and aspirations of democracy inspired and nurtured this cultural upsurge. The subject has received much attention, but without much agreement. The question is obviously relevant to the story of the democracy, and this chapter will review the scale and character of the cultural achievement and the extent of its debt to the democratic society that produced it.[1]

The phenomenon was extraordinary in its range, quantity and quality. It encompassed the visual arts of sculpture, painting and monumental architecture. It produced literary masterpieces in drama, historiography and oratory. It brought a general intellectual awakening which prompted intensified activity in philosophy, and especially in ethical and political thought.

Some of its greatest figures came from outside Athens, which shows that the creative power behind it was a Greek rather than an Athenian phenomenon. But Athens was the hub and the midwife of this great revolution, and was also the begetter of some of its greatest legacies. Athens had emerged as a cultural centre in the age of Peisistratus and his sons, who were strong patrons of the arts and attracted to Athens leading literary figures such as Lasus of Hermione, Simonides of Ceos and Anacreon of Teos. Peisistratus also promoted the state religion, especially the worship of Athena and Dionysus. He restored and extended a temple of Athena on the Acropolis, on the site of the later Erechtheum, and added to the festival of the Great Panathenaea a competition involving recitals of passages of Homer. A more significant addition to Athenian cultural life was a new temple of Dionysus on the southern slope of the Acropolis, and a new festival in honour of the god, the City Dionysia. The latter included a competition between choruses dressed as satyrs, who danced and performed songs, known as dithyrambs, on themes related to Dionysus. Lasus and Simonides were prolific authors of dithyrambic choral songs.

Out of this form developed satyr plays, with plots that leaned towards burlesque and the more obscene features of Dionysiac celebrations, and tragedy, with plots that explored, through the tribulations of great figures caught in great predicaments, the relationship between the human and the divine and the vulnerability to tragic suffering and calamity inherent in the human condition. The transition to drama meant telling the story by enacting rather than narrating it, which required the introduction of an actor separate from the chorus, who could impersonate the characters in the plot and advance the action through dialogue with the chorus. Thespis, a poet and playwright from Ikaria in Attica, is credited with this innovation, and he presented the first tragedy at the City Dionysia around 535. A new form, which ranks among the most important of all literary creations, had been born in Athens.

Democracy and the Visual Arts

The cultural advance of Athens continued after the fall of the Peisistratids, though slowed by the trauma of the Persian Wars. Drama became quickly entrenched as a regular feature of Athenian life. Tragedy was well on its way towards its peak early in the fifth century when Aeschylus began to present his plays. Sophocles was competing by the early 470s. Yet another form of drama, comedy, made its appearance in the early decades of the century. It was a complete contrast to tragedy, with loose, fantastical plots built around topical events, and with dialogue laced with ribald humour and unrestrained ridicule of prominent figures. By the early 480s it had been added to the entertainment at the City Dionysia.[2]

Painting and monumental art were also coming to the fore. A famous example was a colonnade in the Agora known as the Stoa Poikile, which was adorned with wall paintings commemorating both mythical and recent military victories involving Athens. Marathon was prominent, linked with such legendary events as the victory of Theseus over the Amazons and the Fall of Troy. The painters were Polygnotus of Thasos and Micon of Athens, and the sponsors were Cimon and his friends.[3]

But the crowning achievements of Athens in the visual arts came after the consolidation of the Delian League and the transfer of the treasury at Delos to the Acropolis in 454. The building programme, initiated by Pericles and funded, at least in part, from this treasury, has been referred to already. The most famous element of the programme, the monumental buildings and statuary of the Acropolis, an area laid waste by the Persians, produced architecture and sculpture that had a majesty and quality of execution that astonished the Greek world, and that have provoked admiration and imitation in all ages.

The beautiful Doric temple that came to be known as the Parthenon was begun in 447. The monumental entrance to the Acropolis, the Propylaea, was begun in 437 and completed in 432. The elegant temple of Athena Nike, on the bastion at the southwestern rim of the Acropolis, was planned at the same time, but its construction was delayed until the late 420s. The other great temple on the Acropolis, the Erechtheum, which housed cults of Athena, Erechtheus and Poseidon, was built on the site of an earlier temple of Athens. It was begun in the 420s, but war delayed its completion until early in the final decade of the century. Another notable building, the Odeum, a music hall, was constructed on the southern slope of the Acropolis in the 440s. According to Plutarch, Pericles personally supervised the project, and introduced musical contests there as part of the celebration of the Panathenaea.

A great number of artists must have shared in the creation of these masterpieces, and many must have come from abroad, but two of the protagonists were Athenian: Ictinus, one of the main architects of the Parthenon; and Pheidias, friend of Pericles, the foremost name in Greek sculpture and the mastermind behind the entire building programme. Pheidias also contributed two celebrated statues of Athens, both sadly lost. One was a bronze statue of Athena Promachus, the warrior goddess, which stood 30 feet (91 metres) tall inside the entrance to the Acropolis. The other was a still larger statue of Athena Parthenos finished in gold and ivory. It was set up in the Parthenon and dedicated in 438.

The wave of monumental building and sculpture extended beyond the Acropolis to other areas of Athens and Attica. An imposing temple to Hephaestus and Athena was built on the hill of Colonus overlooking the Agora, the civic centre and political heart of Athens. In the Agora itself a statue group representing the Eponymous Heroes, the legendary heroes chosen by the Delphic Oracle as the names for the ten tribes established by Cleisthenes, was set up not far from an earlier statue group of the tyrannicides Harmodius and Aristogeiton. These two monuments had a clear political purpose: to commemorate at the centre of political life the downfall of tyranny and the rise of a democratic order that embraced and linked the entire body of citizens to an heroic past.

In Attica new temples erased other traces of Persian pillaging. Among the most notable were temples of Poseidon on the promontory of Sunium and of

Nemesis at Rhamnus. At Eleusis the shrine of Demeter and Persephone, ravaged by the Persians, was restored with the construction of the new Hall of Initiation (*telesterion*), designed by Ictinus. Other areas of the Greek world had monumental buildings that showed that artistic and architectural brilliance were not confined to Athens, but there was nothing to match the concentration of excellence produced in Athens and Attica by the building programme initiated by Pericles.[4]

Many explanations can be offered for the emergence of this phenomenal era in the history of the visual arts. Most of them are related to national pride and driving ambition. The Greeks were well aware of the power of striking architecture and monumental art as a means of laying claim to greatness and perpetuating the memory of great achievements. Herodotus tells of the impact the monuments of Egypt had on him. He calls them 'wonders', 'beyond words', and they moved him to write at length about the country and its culture. According to Isocrates, who was born in 436 when the building programme was still very much in progress, the physical splendour of Athens made visitors feel it was worthy to rule the world. Thucydides warns against the dangers of using such physical evidence as a measure of greatness, but he accepts that this in reality is what tends to happen. Plutarch, writing more than five centuries after Thucydides, had no doubt that splendid monuments and artistic brilliance betokened greatness. For him, the Periclean programme, which he says delighted Athenians and astonished all others, confirmed that the tale of its power and prosperity was not false.

Demosthenes provides the most explicit evidence that the Athenians believed there was glory and prestige in dazzling the world with monumental public buildings and artistic virtuosity that exalted their achievements and capabilities. He says that they spent their wealth for the love of honour (*philotimia*), and passed on eternal possessions in the memory of their deeds and the beauty of their memorials. The same motivation is repeated in Plutarch's account of the Periclean building programme where he says that Pericles told the people that, once adequate military provision had been made, it was fitting that they should use their affluence for projects that would bring them eternal glory.[5]

But there were also other influences at work. Religion played a major role. Religion was a powerful force and a very public affair in the Greek world, as in other ancient societies. It differed markedly from modern religions in that there was no body of dogma or sacred texts, but there was a deep-seated belief that supernatural beings existed, and that their goodwill and support required veneration and the avoidance of behaviour offensive to them. The details of the rituals of worship were left to priests and priestesses, but the regulation of religion and provision for proper worship of the gods to ensure their goodwill was a fundamental state responsibility.

The great bulk of Athenian monumental art was related to religion, and the initial motivation for the building programme undoubtedly had a religious basis. Not long after Athens negotiated a peace with Persia around 450, Pericles had proposed to the Greek states that a Panhellenic Congress be held to deal with three issues: the temples destroyed by the Persians; the sacrifices vowed to the gods during the Persian Wars; and the security of the seas. The initiative failed to get a response, but a few years later work began on the Parthenon. Pericles was determined that Athens would restore its ruined temples and fulfil its obligations to the gods irrespective of what happened in the rest of Greece. The fruits of empire and access to the tribute from the allies made a grander scale of building possible, and the *demos* was supportive despite the protestations of the political opponents of Pericles. The purpose now extended beyond the religious. The deities most clearly associated with Athens would have their temples back, but they would be the finest in the world, and honour to the gods would be combined with glorification of the achievements and might of Athens through monumental art of unparalleled splendour.

The majesty of the architecture and sculpture was combined with sculptural decoration that provided vignettes that wove a story of an ancient, autochthonous people of superior character, distinguished by an heroic past and by a favoured relationship with great Greek deities. The relationship between Athens and Athena naturally received special emphasis. The Acropolis was dominated by her temples and by the massive statue of the warrior goddess inside the entrance. Her attributes and high place among the gods and the maternal closeness of her relationship to Athens were highlighted in all these monuments, most memorably in the decoration of the Parthenon.

Athena was the favourite daughter of Zeus, born from his brow full-grown and in full armour. The tale of her miraculous birth was portrayed on the eastern pediment of the Parthenon. The closeness of her association with Athens was given prominence on the western pediment, which dealt with the contest in which she vied with Poseidon for the patronage of Athens, and won. Her centrality in the religious life of Athens was illustrated in the elaborate frieze, which portrayed the procession that formed part of the Panathenaic festival. This was the greatest civic and religious event in the Athenian calendar. The procession involved a broad spectrum of the population, who made their way through the city from the Ceramicus to the Acropolis to pay homage to the city's divine protectress with offerings and large-scale sacrifice of animals. It was an inclusive event, a lavish affair and a unifying, morale-boosting celebration of a great deity for whom Athenians were her chosen people. It was a fitting subject for the frieze of Athena's greatest temple.[6]

But the closest bond linking Athena to Athens was the ancient tradition that she had acted as virtual foster mother to one of the earliest kings of Athens, Erechtheus/Erichthonios, who was revered as the father of all Athenians. Erechtheus was fathered by Hephaestus, conceived and born on the Acropolis, where Earth rose up and delivered the child to the care of Athena. According to Homer, Athena nurtured him and gave him a place in her temple on the Acropolis, where the sons of the Athenians propitiate him with sacrifices. The story was a common motif in vase painting of the fifth century, and the construction of the new Erechtheum on the site where a cult of Athena and Erechtheus had existed from early times represented another use of the monumental building programme to revive a legend that presented the Athenians as a people apart in their origin and their links to the divine.

The other side of Athena given prominence in the monuments was her role as the warrior goddess. The manner of her birth as well as both of the Pheidian statues accentuated her association with war and victory. The Nike temple was specifically designed to celebrate her as the war goddess who symbolised victory and brought it to those she favoured. In this case the victories in question were primarily those in the Persian Wars and in subsequent decades against foes of Athens in Greece itself. The frieze was devoted to these recent triumphs, but they were linked in the decoration of the pediments with heroic tales of past glories. The parapet has a fascinating scene of a victory celebration, with Athena seated on a rock surrounded by figures of Victory erecting trophies and offering sacrifice. The triumphs of Athens past and present were being given the patron deity's seal of approval.[7]

Other major deities, Poseidon and Hephaestus in particular, were also given high prominence in the building programme and claimed as protectors of Athens. Poseidon emerged in the fifth century as the father of Theseus, another revered early king of Athens. Poseidon's portrayal on the western pediment of the Parthenon in competition with Athena for the patronage of Athens proclaimed his high regard for the city. His striking temple of Parian marble, built around the same time as the Parthenon near the edge of the cliff on the highest point of the promontory of Sunium, was another indication of the importance he had assumed in Athenian religion. Perhaps most significant of all was the inclusion of his cult in the Erechtheum alongside Athens and Erechtheus. The god of the sea was being conspicuously cultivated by the Greek world's greatest sea power, and was being linked to it as the father of one of its legendary founders.

Hephaestus, of course, held a special place in Athenian tradition as the father of Erechtheus. His cult was given a more elevated status in the Periclean era. A new or extended festival was created in his honour. His new temple is dated to 449 and was probably the first building constructed in the Periclean programme. It was shared with Athena, and had grandeur and prominence in its key location overlooking the Agora. The nerve centre of Athenian political life was overlooked by the two deities with the closest ties to the city.[8]

The representation in the decoration of the monuments of an heroic mytho-logical past was the other means by which the building programme promoted the glorification of Athens and its history. The most common subjects of these patriotic myths were epic struggles against barbaric forces threatening the Greek world, especially the battles against the Giants, the Centaurs, the Amazons and Troy. As mentioned earlier, some of these themes appear in the murals of the Stoa Poikile and in the Nike temple, combined in these cases with stories of modern triumphs. But they were ubiquitous in the fifth-century monuments. The battle against the Centaurs adorned the shield of Athena Promachus. The metopes of the Parthenon portrayed all four myths mentioned above. There are traces of the Centaurs in the western pediment of the Hephaesteion, and of the Centaurs and Giants in the frieze of the temple of Poseidon at Sunium. The Theseion, the shrine of Theseus, built in the Cimonian era, had paintings of the Amazons attacking Athens and of the conflict with the Centaurs.

Theseus was the main hero in almost all of these patriotic myths. He led the Athenian contingent at Troy. He joined with the Lapiths and defeated the Centaurs. He saved Athens from the Amazons and drove them from Attica. His Cretan adventures, during which he slew the Minotaur, which freed Athens from the gruesome tribute of seven youths and seven maidens whom the city was forced to send annually to Minos to be fed to the Minotaur, were included in the paintings in the Theseion, and were popular subjects of Greek art from the end of the sixth century.

The popularity of Theseus as the great national hero was boosted further when Cimon claimed to have found his bones on the island of Skyros and brought them back to Athens in the 470s. But in addition to his heroic role as warrior and protector, Theseus also had high status as a statesman. Thucydides credits him with unifying Attica into a single state. In tragedy he appears as a champion of the rights of the people and the principles of democracy. His story, like so much of the art of the fifth century, presented Athens as a state rooted in heroic traditions, set apart by its divine associations, and continuing to manifest the greatness destined for it from its origins.[9]

How much of all of this can be said to have been caused by the rise and character of the democracy? At first glance the links may seem tenuous. Clearly it was wealth that made possible the scale of the building programme and helped gather in the best talent. The wealth came mainly from empire, and it can be argued that the motives that typically give rise to empires – security, power, glory and profit – are products of human nature rather than democracy or any particular form of government. Similarly, it can be argued that the motives behind the building programme had little direct connection with democracy, but were linked to national pride and ambition and a desire, typical of great powers in every age, to build monuments to symbolise the greatness of the nation and to enshrine in stone the glories of the past.

It is clear, and clearly attested, that the main purpose of the building programme was to enshrine in memorable visual form the greatness of Athens. But the links between the democracy and this ambition and the manner of its accomplishment are more numerous and fundamental than might first appear. There are many monuments, especially in key public areas, that relate directly to democracy. The Agora, which had such a central place in the political life of Athenians, had many reminders of what democracy had brought and signified. The statues of the tyrannicides, Harmodius and Aristogeiton, were an imposing symbol of the liberation of the people. Nearby, the statue group of the Eponymous Heroes, generally dated to the Periclean era, celebrated the ten tribes of the isonomic reorganisation of the *demos* under the constitution of Cleisthenes. In the Stoa Poikile on the north side of the Agora, large frescoes commemorated the first great victory of the democracy over the Persians at Marathon, and joined it with scenes of legendary Athenian heroism.

Religion and legend did have a prominent place in the monuments and their decoration, but there is often a political subtext reflecting current Athenian eminence. Athena has a dominant place as the patron and guardian of Athens, but the way she is portrayed, the decoration of her temples and the form of the festivals associated with her worship all had political overtones linking the daughter of Zeus to the triumphs of the democracy. Her role as the warrior goddess and the goddess of victory is highlighted, a fitting image for the patron of a state that had proved its martial prowess. The Nike temple was designed to enshrine that image, and its frieze was devoted to portrayals of the Persian and more recent victories of Athens under the democracy, again blended with heroic tales of the past. Athena's annual festival, the Panathenaea, united all elements of the population in a grand procession and elaborate festivities, but there was a still grander and more pointedly political celebration every fourth year, when the Great Panathenaea took place and all the allied states were required to send representatives to join in paying homage to the warrior guardian deity of Athens. The event was a political statement, an affirmation of the divinely sanctioned Athenian ascendancy and right to rule. There were also political overtones in the prominence given to Poseidon and his links to Athens. The *demos* was laying claim to the favour of the god of the sea, the sea over which Athens ruled supreme with a superior navy manned by thetes and hoplites, the backbone of the democracy.

The legendary themes reinforced the general image of Athenians in the monumental art as a divinely favoured, superior people who had been saviours of Greece since time immemorial and who were worthy to rule. But here too there was a democratic subtext. The central figure in most of the legendary tales was Theseus, whose cult had been given new life with the building of the Theseion. As noted earlier, Theseus emerged in the fifth century as an enlightened ruler who had unified the people of Attica. He was presented, especially in tragedy, as the ultimate champion of the rule of law and the rights of the people and democratic values. He was a national hero and a founding father, and, in commemorating him, Athens was commemorating a symbol of the qualities and values that had led it to its current greatness.

But the democracy was responsible for the revolution in the visual arts in a more fundamental way. The resources to fund the programme, the successes that gave credibility to its claims to greatness and the will to carry it to completion all ultimately sprang from the character and achievements of the democracy. Before the revolution of 508/7 Athens had modest claims to greatness. Herodotus makes the point concisely. He says that, before the advent of what he terms *isegoria* (equality of speech), 'the Athenians were no better in war than any of their neighbours but, after they were set free from despotism, they became the foremost by far'. He goes on to say: 'while they were held down, their spirit was cowardly, but once freed, each individually had a zeal to achieve'. It was this activist trait that caused the Corinthians to describe the Athenians in 432 as a people always ready for new ventures, daring beyond their strength, constantly seeking more, and to contrast their vitality with the lethargic dithering character of the Spartan oligarchy.

But it is Pericles who most powerfully makes the connection between the great achievements of Athens and the democratic system. As emphasised earlier, the main theme of the Funeral Oration is that the greatness of Athens reflected the greatness of its form of government and way of life. Instead of eulogising the dead, he eulogises the system that inspired in them a devotion to their country and its mores that made them determined to defend it, and to be first and best.[10]

The revolution of 508/7 did, beyond doubt, have a permanent transformative effect on the people of Athens. There was a revolutionary energy and a strong self-confidence and ambition driving the Athenian decisions and behaviour that brought the victories in the Persian Wars and eventually a powerful empire. These were triumphs of the democracy. The new order was the catalytic force underlying all the achievements of this remarkable era. It was the people who took the big decisions and the big risks, and made the sacrifices that resulted in power and wealth, and it was the people who decided to spend a sizeable portion of that wealth on art and architecture and the glorification of their city and its gods. It was a choice wholly in keeping with the attitudes and goals that had inspired them since the seismic events of 508/7. They were led in all of this by a succession of notable aristocrats, but it was they who chose them, and they retained them only as long as they successfully led them where they wanted to go. Pericles was the greatest of them all, and the prime mover behind the building programme. Much of the credit for the upsurge in the visual arts must go to him. But the people strongly supported him and brushed aside the opposition of a group of prominent aristocrats. Pericles was leading a people eager to follow. In the Funeral Oration he had commended their love of beauty and things of the mind, and their delight in elegant living. For many reasons democratic Athens was a receptive environment for the arts in the fifth century.

Democracy and the Literary Revolution

The impact of the democracy on the literary and intellectual dimensions of the cultural revolution was perhaps even more direct and decisive than in the case of the visual arts. The literary output of the period was prodigious. Its originality and quality were remarkable, and its impact has been enduring. The Greeks were great verbalisers. Their strong tradition of epic and the continuous flow of new forms of poetic expression, much of it personal and outspoken, that emerged in the Greek world from the seventh century are testimony to a rare ability to exploit the possibilities of language.

Drama, oratory and historiography were the forms that especially flourished in the fifth century, and they have left us the masterpieces of Aeschylus, Sophocles, Euripides, Aristophanes, Herodotus and Thucydides, all Athenians with the exception of Herodotus, who came from the Ionian city of Halicarnassus.

Dramatic productions were a central part of the publicly organised recreational life of Athens, and were linked to festivals and public holidays. In the Funeral Oration, Pericles described these periods as a rest from labours for the mind. He considered them part of the cultured and relaxed way of life that characterised the democracy, and that banished mental stress and produced a manly spirit that was real rather than enforced.

The Athenians were certainly devoted to their festivals and all that went with them. The Old Oligarch, in his usual tendentious and cynical way, claims they had more festivals than any other Greek state. He describes how the *demos* took advantage of the free meat from the sacrifices and enjoyed the entertainment paid for by the wealthy. He also says the *demos* realised that the festivals gave them luxuries they could never themselves afford, and they believed this was fitting so that they might have more and the rich less.[11]

The beginnings of tragedy and the production of plays predated the democracy, but the rise of the dramatic art to the pinnacle achieved in the fifth century was fostered in significant ways by the important place given to it in the celebration of public festivals, and by a supportive political environment and generous patronage from the state and the wealthy elite.

Dramatic productions were concentrated in the festivals associated with the worship of Dionysus. The most important of these was the City or Great Dionysia, which was held in March/April and lasted at least five days. Tragedies, comedies and dithyrambs were all performed, but tragedies predominated. A second large Dionysiac festival, the Lenaea, took place a month earlier, with a greater emphasis on comedy. There was also a Rural Dionysia in December/January, when the demes celebrated Dionysus and enjoyed plays performed by travelling companies of actors.

Plays in Athens took place in the theatre of Dionysus on the southern slope of the Acropolis. It was big enough to accommodate a large proportion of the entire population, as many as thirty thousand according to Plato, though the archaeological evidence indicates about seventeen thousand. Theatrical performances were seen as a major civic event, an affair of state involving the whole community. There were no known restrictions on attendance. Women and children, even metics, visiting foreigners and slaves were admitted. After a charge for admission was introduced, a special fund (*theorikon*) was established to provide grants to encourage poorer citizens to attend.[12]

A certain amount of pomp and ceremony added to the sense of occasion. There were special seats at the front for the celebrities – the state's highest officials and foreign dignitaries and others whom the state especially wished to recognise. The proceedings began with the ten generals pouring a libation. There was a ceremony to announce awards to those deserving of special honours. The annual tribute from the allies was displayed in the orchestra. War orphans received special recognition.

All dramatic presentations were organised as competitions, reflecting the Greek love of a contest (*agon*). Tragedians had to compete by providing a trilogy of tragedies and a satyr play. All contestants submitted their entries to the chief archon, who selected three tragedians and five comedians, and awarded each a chorus and a *choregus*. The job of *choregus* was one of the major liturgies that wealthy citizens were called on to undertake. It involved supervising and funding the training of the chorus and everything related to the choral performances. It was a job that was taken seriously. For the winning *choregus*, the political gains could be substantial in terms of reputation and popular favour. As a result the amounts of money expended were often lavish. Other costs associated with mounting plays, such as prizes, pay for writers and actors, were borne by the state. Winners were selected by judges chosen by lot from lists submitted by the tribes and approved by the Council. The engagement of the state with every facet of theatrical presentations could hardly have been more total.[13]

The themes and messages of Attic drama also tended to have a political focus. Comedy was almost wholly preoccupied with current events, issues and personalities. Its lifeblood was unrestrained caricature and ridicule of leading politicians and well-known figures, and of new trends and ideas that lent themselves to comic distortion. Comedy of the fifth century, or Old Comedy as it is now known, had a character, vitality and brilliance all its own, and that was, partly at least, a result of the richness of the material provided by democratic politics, and of the appetite of a politically minded audience for political satire.

Tragedy had an opposite character and a very different appeal, and was less directly connected to contemporary events. It was the successor to epic, featuring the great figures of myth, but in circumstances that were painfully difficult and often overwhelmingly tragic, and that graphically illustrated the vulnerability of human beings to error and calamity arising from their own nature and the workings of fate and the divine order.

Tragedy also had an important reflective side, as Aristotle emphasised. It not only told the story, but drove home the general truths behind the story, and with a powerful emotional impact that especially stirred pity and fear. Since the plots of tragedy were mostly concerned with political, social and religious issues, so were its lessons and messages. This has given rise to endless debate about the purposes of tragedy and its relationship to contemporary politics, and to a frequent overemphasis on the tragic poets as political commentators or moral teachers, preoccupied with espousing, challenging or seeking to shape the political and religious thinking of their time. Evidence can be found in the plays to support these contentions, but none of them represents the heart and purpose of tragedy. The tragic poets certainly drew inspiration from contemporary events and ideas, and used them when it suited their dramatic purposes, and many of the themes and messages of tragedy may well have had an educative effect. But the tragic art had a wider scope and a loftier purpose. Its domain was the dark side of human experience, and its dramatic power and enduring appeal as theatre derive from the fact that its characters, language, tragic dilemmas and outcomes create suspenseful, absorbing drama that is ultimately divorced from time and place. When the Athenian public thronged the theatre of Dionysus and sat through long days of theatrical presentations, it is a fair assumption that they were there, not looking for moral improvement or political enlightenment or indoctrination, but for excitement and the entertainment of watching moving representations of famous figures grappling with some of the painful predicaments and awful calamities that haunt human existence.

Tragedy, like comedy, owed a great deal to the vitality of the political and intellectual milieu of democratic Athens, and to the Athenian fondness for communal celebration and recreation centred on contests and the performing arts. It owed even more to the generous patronage of the state and of the wealthy, and to the fulsome support of a captivated public, all of which gave a succession of extraordinarily talented writers room to flourish. But its debts to the democratic society that helped nurture it did not mean that tragedy was the servant of democracy or a platform for the promotion of any particular set of political or religious beliefs. It was above all else a new art presenting the old epic tales and their significance in a vivid, multidimensional form which included music, dance and spectacle and which sought to exploit all the dramatic possibilities of live re-enactment.[14]

There was one other feature of Athenian democracy that contributed to the rise of both tragedy and comedy – freedom of speech. This aspect of democratic freedom has been mentioned earlier. It was wide-ranging in its scope, though there were some limits. Libel laws gave protection against false accusations of crimes that the Greeks considered especially heinous. Those who used their right to speak in the Assembly ran the risk of heckling and abuse if their speaking skills fell short or their advice seemed foolish. They ran a far greater risk if their advice was taken and turned out to be harmful to the state. The Athenians blamed wrong decisions, not on the *demos* itself, but on those who gave the wrong advice. It was they who were accountable under the law. Outside the political sphere there was also risk for anyone whose views were seen as having harmed, or as likely to harm, the safety of the state or its institutions.

But despite these limitations the freedom to speak one's mind and air one's views remained a real and cherished aspect of the Athenian concept of *eleutheria*, and Athenians were proud of it. The limits of free speech tolerated in Athens were especially wide when it came to personal attacks on enemies, opponents or rivals. The Greeks had a taste for invective, which had emerged as a literary form in the seventh century. Long before Aristophanes, the master of comedy and of virulent lampoon, the Athenians were familiar with the art of ridicule and personal vilification (*loidoria*). The remedy was retaliation in kind, not legal action. Demosthenes says the law was not concerned with personal smears, but with wrongs against the state, a view that is echoed by other Greek orators.

But even in the realm of public affairs and debates involving sensitive areas of politics and religion, the overall evidence indicates that freedom of speech was largely respected. The number of prosecutions involving offences related to speech that can be reliably documented are few. The democratic aura surrounding free speech would have protected it against efforts to repress it. The people's courts would not have been quick to curtail such a basic democratic right.

It is also indicative of the overall liberal attitude towards free speech under the democracy that the oligarchs who seized power for brief intervals in 411 and 404 moved quickly to repress it. They could not live with the level of free speech tolerated by the democracy. While freedom of speech may not have been seen as an inalienable right in the modern sense under the democracy, in practice it was encouraged as a necessary part of democratic decision-making and was treated with a high degree of tolerance in other areas of life.

Comedy and tragedy were obvious beneficiaries of the culture of free speech. The comic, often cruel ingenuity of Aristophanes in ridiculing the leading figures of his day required such a culture and stretched it to its limits. But there is no sign that the public was shocked or offended. The Old Oligarch says the *demos* relished the humbling of the high and mighty, the rich, the well-born and the powerful, as he described the main targets of comedy. The most vitriolic of all the plays of Aristophanes, the *Knights*, which attacked the powerful populist leader Cleon, won first prize. At some stage Cleon did launch an action against Aristophanes on the grounds that he was harming the state, but it failed. Clearly there was no appetite for imposing restrictions on a very popular form of entertainment.

There seem to have been few restrictions on tragedy either, though it often confronted political and moral dilemmas in ways that challenged popular beliefs. Euripides in particular, who was immersed in the new intellectual movements of his time and injected rationalism and realism into his telling of the myths, ran the risk of seriously offending conservative sensibilities. But he enjoyed a long and prolific career as a dramatist. There is a report that he was once prosecuted for impiety, but the source is unreliable, and he was certainly not convicted. It must also be remembered that all plays staged in the competitions were preselected by the chief archon, and the fact that so many that might have been seen as subversive, heretical or unacceptably slanderous passed the scrutiny of successive archons down the years is another indication of the liberality of Athenian attitudes towards the content of drama. Attic dramatists had little reason to feel inhibited by any risk of censorship or legal retribution. Overall, the range of supports and protections given to drama under the democracy was so extensive that it must be seen as a major factor in the genre's rise to such high eminence. In a real sense Athenian democracy was the foster mother of Greek drama.[15]

Democracy, the Sophists and New Intellectual Movements

The systems and the milieu of openness and *parrhesia* and cultural awareness that democracy engendered also helped promote the rise of the other main elements of the cultural revolution – oratory, historiography and philosophical enquiry. By the mid-fifth century Athens was ready for a broader engagement with the world of the mind and with the new intellectual movements and forms of learning already developing elsewhere in Greece. I referred earlier to Pericles' allusion to the relaxed, tolerant, culturally receptive way of life of Athenians under the democracy, their love of elegance, beauty and the pursuit of knowledge, and their sociability and generosity towards each other, all of which taken together made Athens an educational model for Greece. Aristotle more explicitly highlights a turning towards culture by the Athenians after affluence and military success gave them greater leisure and a more high-minded view of *arete*, and a presumptuous eagerness for all forms of learning.

There was a particular eagerness for speaking skills, a direct consequence of a system of government that made debate central to decision-making, and whose structures of Assembly, Council and courts made the power to persuade a vital ingredient of political success. Pericles, whose own ascendancy depended largely on his formidable rhetorical skills, once told the Athenians that knowing what must be done but failing to explain it clearly was the same as not knowing. Under the democracy, the art of speaking well assumed a new overriding importance. It was the new *arete*.[16]

The Athenians, or at least those who constituted the wealthier classes, soon had ample opportunity to pursue their educational goals and intellectual interests. Around the middle of the century an assortment of teachers and intellectuals began to gravitate towards Athens, lured by the attractions and opportunities of the imperial capital. Athens had, of course, attracted writers, thinkers and artists long before 450, but these newcomers were a different breed. They became known as the Sophists, a term that developed derogatory connotations in the fourth century, but in the fifth century was used to describe those who had a special expertise that offered a benefit to society.[17]

The Sophists did not constitute a school or movement advocating a particular set of beliefs. They were individualists, but they did have several things in common. They were mostly itinerant professional teachers who charged significant fees for their services. They saw themselves as educators with a common practical purpose: to provide the knowledge and skills required for political success in a democratic society. They regarded the power of the word as the supreme weapon of the politician, and they focused their teaching on the art of rhetoric, the discipline that aimed to bestow eloquence and the power of persuasion, and the skills required for verbal combat (*agon logon*) and winning arguments, what Plato called the eristic art (*eristike techne*).

But the development of rhetorical skills required broad intellectual development as well, and exposure to the world of literature and ideas, and it is clear that the interests of the Sophists and the intellectual range of what they taught extended widely. The study and criticism of poetry are well attested as part of their curriculum. Some Sophists included subjects such as mathematics, astronomy and music. The big questions relating to ethics and politics were certainly very much to the fore. They could hardly claim to train politicians and not give those subjects prominence. Even Gorgias, the eminent rhetorician from Leontini in Sicily, who made a huge impact when he visited Athens on an embassy in 427, and who liked to insist that his job was to make clever speakers, accepted that he had a broader mission to give his students the capacity to govern and to manage the affairs of the state well. He conceded that there was a moral dimension to the training of an orator, who must use his skills, like the master of any craft, for just purposes. If anyone therefore came to him who was ignorant of what was just and good, he would teach him about these things.[18]

Protagoras from Abdera in Thrace, who was one of the earliest and most famous of the Sophists, a frequent visitor to Athens and a friend of Pericles, is more explicit about the scope and character of the learning that his profession sought to impart. Protagoras saw his task as teaching his students good judgement (*euboulia*), both with respect to the management of their private affairs and to enable them to have maximum influence in affairs of state through speech and action. He accepted that this meant teaching the art of politics (*politike techne*) and good citizenship, and that this had a moral dimension. To illustrate what this teaching entailed and to prove that what he professed to teach was teachable, he gave his famous mythical account of the origins of society described earlier. The moral of the story was that all human beings have a need for life in society and are suited to it because they have an inbred instinct for justice and restraint, the civic virtues that can produce the harmony and order essential for society's survival. But, while all share in the virtue of justice, it does not emerge naturally or spontaneously, but has to be taught and nurtured.

But Protagoras does not claim that what the Sophists taught was unchanging, universal truth about the principles of the just and the honourable. Instead he maintains that no such permanent moral absolutes exist. The principles of justice that do exist are those that society at any given time judges to be just and honourable. Some of those judgements may be flawed, however, and it is the task of the wise leader to convince the people to replace a flawed convention with a better one. It was the job of the Sophist, therefore, with his superior expertise in the craft of politics to provide political leaders with the good judgement (*euboulia*) to recognise the better course and with the skills to convince the public through the power of words.[19]

The views of Protagoras may not have been typical of the Sophists as a whole, but there is abundant evidence, especially in Plato, that as a group they were broadly learned, and that, in addition to their focus on rhetoric, they were in the vanguard of philosophical debate in Athens and of a new humanism that stirred fresh controversies about such fundamental questions as the nature of man and society and the basis of law, morality and religion. Some of these debates and their impact on the democracy will be considered further in the following chapter.

The Sophists did not confine their activities to private instruction of students or to lectures and seminars in private settings. They also regularly paraded their skills and ideas and breadth of learning in public. They were eager public performers, ready to discourse on any subject. The Athenians developed a fondness for such displays, and rhetorical competitions (*agon logon*) were introduced into the festivals. The populist politician Cleon upraided the *demos* for their fascination with such contests and beguilement by the cleverness of Sophists. Rhetorical contests became a feature of Panhellenic festivals as well. Hippias of Elis, one of the younger Sophists active in Athens and a noted polymath, was a regular contestant at the Olympic Games and boasted that he never lost. Gorgias also performed at Olympia and delivered an oration on *harmonia*, concord or consensus, a key democratic concept. Most Sophists were also writers, producing an array of handbooks on rhetoric, and, in some cases, general works on social and ethical subjects.

They were visible in many aspects of Athenian life, and their impact was lasting and far-reaching. They were broadly welcomed in Athens. The best known easily found patronage from the rich and powerful. They were treated as celebrities and their services were in high demand. The younger generation of the elite was captivated by the new skills and ideas that they offered. The general public relished their rhetorical virtuosity and intellectual ingenuity. It is clear that they offended some conservative sensibilities, and the extent of the hostility towards them in certain quarters is well illustrated in comedy, especially the *Clouds* of Aristophanes, and in many of Plato's dialogues. But on the whole they were given the freedom and opportunity to ply their trade and air their often unconventional views without restriction.[20]

Their legacy was of several kinds. They made development of the intellect and of the mental skills of speech, reasoning, analysis and argumentation the main objective in the education of those who aspired to be leaders. This was a sharp contrast to the traditional aristocratic ideal of political *arete* represented in the term *kalokagathia*, which stood for physical prowess, courage, honour and duty, and was seen as the preserve of the high-born. What the Sophists offered as the essence of the new political *arete* was brain-power and word-power, and the capacity these gave to see the right course and persuade the people to follow it. This was a capacity that could be taught and was divorced from class. It was a new educational ideal that was to leave a permanent imprint on the European educational tradition.[21]

The Sophists obviously have a central place in the history of rhetoric. The art of persuasion had its origins, not in Athens, but in far-flung areas of the Greek world, but it was the Sophists who frequented Athens in the latter half of the fifth century who embedded it in the consciousness of the public and established it as a key instrument of power in democratic politics. This led on to the use of the word *rhetor* as a virtual synonym for political leader, and to the masterpieces of oratory produced by the Attic orators of the fourth century, who were virtually all politicians, and to the seminal works on rhetorical theory by philosophers such as Aristotle.

The influence of the Sophists is also visible in the work of Thucydides, whose history of the Peloponnesian War raised historiography to such a high level. His purposes and methods were discussed earlier, in chapter 3. His strict rationalism, his empirical approach to the search for truth, his view of historical causation as a product of human nature and human behaviour, with some element of chance (*tyche*) but no element of supernatural influence – all of these attributes of his history reflect the spirit of his age and the intellectual realism fostered by the Sophists. His accounts of major political debates during the Peloponnesian War show even more clearly his immersion in the philosophical controversies led by prominent Sophists that were current in his day.

The big topical, moral and political questions relating to the nature of the law (*nomos*) and the nature of man (*physis*), the meaning of justice, the role of self-interest and expediency in human behaviour, and the morality governing the use of power all feature or are subtexts in the discussions regarding such key issues as the fate of Mytilene and the Sicilian expedition. They are especially prominent in the famous Melian dialogue. These debates are also full of arguments that reappear in the mouths of Sophists in dialogues of Plato.

In his structuring of these key debates Thucydides shows a further debt to the Sophists by adopting one of their favourite rhetorical techniques, the so-called antilogy, or antithetical mode of argument, which placed side by side the opposing arguments that could be built around any issue. Thucydides uses the form very effectively to crystallise the issues at stake in a debate, and the motivations and outlook that were driving policy at a particular time. The brilliance of the work of Thucydides was undoubtedly the product of a strong intellect and an exceptional literary talent, but it was shaped in important ways by the new rhetoric and the new intellectual currents that came with the era of the Sophists.[22]

In a more general way the Sophists made Athens the intellectual centre of Greece, 'the capital of wisdom', as Hippias called it. They have left no groundbreaking philosophical writings, but, in important ways, they set the agenda that led to the seminal philosophical breakthroughs that came a generation later. They made philosophy man-centred, a practical discipline concerned with issues of morality, politics and political leadership. Their views and methods started controversies that acted as a springboard for an era of intense philosophical enquiry and progress led by Socrates and Plato, and continued by Aristotle.

Socrates and Plato objected strongly to the amoral approach of the Sophists to teaching rhetorical and political skills without adequately providing the moral foundations that should govern their use. They objected even more fundamentally to their moral relativism, and to an empiricism that held that the rational pursuit of knowledge must rely primarily on experience and sense-data, with the corollary that, since these sources were to a degree fallible, absolute truth was unattainable. It was in the process of refuting these views and seeking a more secure basis for knowledge, morality and responsible politics that Socrates and Plato evolved a whole new theoretical framework that underpinned new conceptions of epistemology, education, the nature of man, the absolute universal character of moral principles, the origin, nature and purpose of the state, and the structuring of society and government.

The Sophists had started debates that transformed philosophy forever. There are some scholars who go so far as to argue that there could not have been a Socrates or a Plato without the Sophists. Whatever the truth of that, the Sophists, often maligned and dismissed as clever charlatans, deserve, at the least, to be recognised as an educative and catalytic force who contributed in a lasting and significant way to the Athenian cultural revolution. Their role was made possible, however, only by the fact that they found in Athens a democratic society that was eager for the skills they brought, but was also attracted by things of the mind and was liberal in its attitude to intellectual speculation and debate.

The general question about the connection between democracy and the so-called era of enlightenment at Athens has been largely dealt with in the review of the various elements of the phenomenon, but a summary might be useful.

The connection is perhaps least obvious, though undoubtedly fundamental, in the case of the visual arts, which could not have developed as they did without the wealth that came mainly from empire, and without the desire, born of national pride and a passion for glory and primacy, to create an imperial capital that would symbolise by its physical splendour the greatness of Athens and memorably commemorate its gods, its heroes and its achievements. Pericles was also a decisive influence.

But all these factors were themselves rooted in the birth of democracy and in its transformative effects on the character of political life and on the outlook and aspirations of the whole body politic. The same revolutionary energy and ambition dictated all the big decisions of the *demos* during the first half of the fifth century, and its decision to divert large sums of public money to make Athens a symbol and a shrine of Athenian achievement and superiority was fully in keeping with this drive to be first and best. Pericles did play a pivotal role, but it was also the *demos* who gave him his position of high power, and they did so because they trusted his ability, and because his goals and politics were in tune with their own. The spirit of Athenian democracy deserves to be recognised as a primary influence in the generation of the great legacy of Athenian art and architecture.

The debt of the literary and intellectual movements to democracy is even greater. They were first of all boosted by the power and wealth of Athens which attracted talent to the imperial capital and helped make Athens a cultural hub. But many aspects of life under the democracy created a climate favourable to literary and intellectual advances. There was a need for new directions in education to provide the skills required for success in a democracy. The culture of free speech gave scope for literary innovation and intellectual speculation. In a city where leisure was growing and there was a fondness for festivals and entertainment, the theatre became a central feature of recreational life.

In general there was a higher cultural awareness, reflected in the emphasis in the Funeral Oration on Athenian appreciation of elegance, beauty and things of the mind. Aristotle more expressly affirms the trend when he states that, after wealth and military success had been achieved, there was a turning towards the intellectual. By the mid-fifth century the Athenians had found a new outlet for their restless energy and ambition. They wanted to crown their prosperity and military superiority with cultural eminence. In that they were also spectacularly successful.

CHAPTER 5

The Democracy Falters

The decades between 460 and 430, which were the subject of the two previous chapters, represent one of the most fascinating episodes in European history, and one of the most far-reaching in its impact. It is a story of the coming of age of a form of government whose political ideals remain the bedrock of democracy, of the creation of a powerful empire, and of the emergence of a golden age of cultural genius. But these remarkable achievements were soon followed by a tragic reversal of fortune, as war, plague and a gradual breakdown of political stability in the final decades of the fifth century brought untold suffering, a humiliating military defeat and eventually internal strife resulting in a temporary overthrow of democracy. These events and the aspects of Athenian democracy that contributed to them form the subject of this chapter. They show the negative side of demotic rule when driven by overconfidence and hegemonic ambition, and guided by leaders who, in differing degrees, were intent on imperial dominance.

The Democracy's Penchant for Brinkmanship

The clouds of war had begun to gather in Greece by the middle of the 430s. The reasons for this have been endlessly debated, but Thucydides was in no doubt.[1] The real cause for him was the drive for primacy that led Athens to greatness, and the fear it generated in the Peloponnesians. The history of the relationship between Athens and Sparta in the decades between the Persian and Peloponnesian wars supports this analysis. Some of the main events of this period have been recounted earlier, but a brief review here will illustrate the inveterate suspicion, fear and rivalry, overlain with an ingrained ethnic hostility, that divided the Ionian Athenians and the Dorian Peloponnesians, and presented fundamental barriers to peaceful coexistence. They regarded themselves as different races and perpetual enemies, and each lived in constant fear of domination by the other.

That fear showed itself the moment the Persians retreated from Greece. The Athenians immediately set about rebuilding the city and its walls. The Spartans, urged on by their Peloponnesian allies, who were alarmed by the size of the now enlarged Athenian fleet and the daring they had shown during the Persian conflict, attempted to dissuade them from building fortifications. But Themistocles, while pretending to negotiate, got the walls around Athens completed and went on to fortify the Piraeus to secure further the position of Athens as a great sea power.

There followed the Athenian takeover from the Spartans of the leadership of the allies and the creation of the Delian League, which led to another major expansion of the Athenian fleet, as more of the allies began to contribute money rather than ships to the alliance and the Athenians used that money to extend their own navy. The anxieties of the Peloponnesians naturally increased. Thucydides says the Spartans were aware of what was happening, but failed to act because of their aversion to war and their own domestic troubles. The Corinthians were later to upbraid them in trenchant terms for their repeated failure to take pre-emptive action to curb the rise of Athens.

There was a measure of rapprochement between Athens and Sparta in the 460s when Cimon, who was at the height of his influence in Athens, promoted a policy of friendship with Sparta. But the détente abruptly foundered towards the end of the 460s when Sparta asked Athens for help against the helots who were entrenched on Mount Ithome. The request sparked a debate that brought familiar prejudices to the surface once more. Cimon supported the request, but it was strongly opposed by Ephialtes, the influential reformist democrat, who argued that 'they should not prop up a state that was an enemy, but should allow its arrogance to lie prone and be trampled under foot'. But Cimon won the day and led an expedition to Sparta in 462. The Spartans, however, had a quick change of heart and sent the expedition home because they feared, according to Thucydides, the daring, revolutionary spirit of the Athenians, and furthermore considered them a different race who might end up supporting the rebels. It was an extraordinary decision, showing a distrust verging on paranoia, and the whole affair was a stark example of the intractable hostility dividing Sparta and Athens in this era.[2]

The rejection of the Athenian offer of help by Sparta caused outrage at Athens and abruptly ended any further pretence of friendly relations. The Athenians quickly formed alliances with traditional Spartan foes, Argos and Thessaly, and soon afterwards with Megara, which had left the Peloponnesian League because of a dispute with Corinth. The Megarian decision brought

Athens into direct conflict with Corinth, and this led on to the wider so-called First Peloponnesian War, involving not only Sparta and Athens but the allies on both sides.

It was a war about primacy on the mainland. Sparta had long been regarded as having hegemonic status in Greece itself, and had been elected leader of the Hellenic League formed in 480 to fight the Persians. But even then the Athenians felt they had a claim to the leadership, and Thucydides makes clear that after the Persian Wars they were no longer willing to accept that Sparta had any right to give them orders. The goal was to break away from Spartan hegemony and build the power that would guarantee their security against the threat from the Dorian foe. At the heart of their power-building strategy was expansion of the navy, and soon after the break with Sparta they began the building of the Long Walls to the Piraeus and Phalerum to protect their access to the sea and their shipbuilding operations. It was a massive project of major strategic signifi-cance, and was later singled out by the Corinthians as a key development in the Athenian rise to power that the Spartans had failed to prevent. But the war did not otherwise enhance Athenian dominance on the mainland. It developed into something of a stalemate, and by 446 both sides needed a respite and signed the Thirty Years' Peace.

But none of the underlying barriers to a stable peace had gone away and, in particular, the energy and ambition of the Athenian *demos* and of its now dominant leader, Pericles, had not diminished. Pericles, the patriotic, committed democrat, who believed that Athenian democracy was a superior form of government that offered its citizens a superior way of life and a superior culture, and gave them a superior capacity for high achievement, wanted Athens to be the greatest power in Greece. He saw two ways to achieve that: mastery of the seas and mastery of the allies. Naval supremacy would make Athens invincible, and the empire would provide the resources to sustain the naval war machine and the reserves of money that would enable Athens to cope with even a protracted war.

Pericles vigorously pursued both goals in the decade after the signing of the Peace, and the power of Athens grew relentlessly during this period. In the first year of the Peace, Pericles persuaded the Assembly to build another Long Wall, the so-called Middle Wall, to strengthen further the links to the all-important Piraeus. The fleet grew to three hundred battle-ready ships. Reserves of money were built up. The grip on the allies was tightened and resistance ruthlessly suppressed. In the city the *demos* saw all around them monumental symbols of Athenian greatness, valour and divine favour.[3]

This was not a culture of peace. It exuded an air of superiority, of militarism and of determination to be first and best. The daring and revolutionary spirit of the Athenian democracy, so feared by the Peloponnesians and sharpened by leaders like Themistocles and Pericles, made peaceful coexistence between the great rivals, which required preserving a balance of power, a fragile hope. The Peloponnesians naturally saw the continuing growth of Athenian power after the Peace as a threat, but the Spartans, as noted earlier, were slow to react, to the great frustration of the Corinthians. Sooner or later an incident was bound to occur that would turn tension into war.

That incident was a dispute that broke out in the mid-430s between Corinth and Corcyra and soon involved Athens. Corcyra was a colony of Corinth but was not part of any alliance. In 433 a Corcyraean delegation came to Athens to seek an alliance and help in the quarrel with Corinth. It was a tempting opportunity for the Athenians to add to their allies a state that had one of the largest fleets in Greece. They were also by now convinced that war with the Peloponnesians was inevitable, and they did not want the Corinthians gaining control of the Corcyraean fleet. The Assembly debated the request for two days in autumn 433 and finally decided to offer Corcyra a defensive alliance, which meant helping each other only if either were attacked. They believed this did not violate the Thirty Years' Peace. But the Corinthians saw it differently. It was certainly a provocative act of brinkmanship, in line with the Peloponnesian view of the aggressive, power-seeking pattern of Athenian behaviour.

It quickly resulted in direct military conflict between Athens and Corinth, when a squadron of Athenian ships got involved in a major naval battle between Corcyra and Corinth off the island of Sybota in the latter part of 433. The intervention saved Corcyra from a major defeat. Thucydides says the incident gave Corinth its first grounds for war with Athens.[4]

Soon it had other grounds. After the encounter at Sybota the Athenians sparked a new incident in the winter of 433 involving the city of Potidaea, which was in the unusual position of being a tributary ally of Athens as well as a colony of Corinth which still received its annual magistrates from the mother city. Potidaea was strategically important, located on the western edge of the peninsula of Chalcidice, which bordered Thrace and Macedonia. The Athenians were afraid that the Corinthians would persuade the Potidaeans to revolt, and that the neighbouring cities and Macedonia, whose king, Perdiccas, was at the time hostile to Athens, might come to their aid. In an attempt to pre-empt such a development, the Athenians ordered the Potidaeans to pull down their walls, provide hostages and end their practice of receiving their magistrates from Corinth.

The Potidaeans responded by sending envoys to Athens to negotiate and to Sparta to seek help. Sparta promised help if Athens attacked. The Athenians offered no concessions and the Potidaeans revolted and were supported by other cities in the region and by Perdiccas. The Corinthians and other Peloponnesians also sent help. Athens sent an expedition against Potidaea. It was now at war with significant elements of the Peloponnesian League.

At some stage Athens also issued a decree barring Megara, which had fought with Corinth at Sybota, from the harbours of the Athenian empire and from the Athenian Agora. The exact date and purpose of the decree are uncertain, but it would seem to have been an effort to warn of the cost of going to war with Athens. But it was seen, of course, as another hostile act against a Spartan ally.[5]

These events were followed by the great debate in the Spartan Assembly in the middle of 432 to which all Sparta's allies and others who had complaints against Athens were invited. Thucydides reports the event in detail, and records the Corinthian speech advocating war. Envoys from Athens were allowed to speak in defence of Athenian behaviour. When the visitors had had their say they withdrew, and the Spartan Assembly began its own deliberations. The Spartan king, Archidamus, urged caution and warned the Assembly that the Spartans were no match for the Athenians in ships and money. They should not rush to war but send envoys while they built up their resources and sought more allies. If the envoys succeeded, that would be best; if not, they would go to war better prepared. One of the Ephors, Stheneleides, took a tougher stand, urging immediate action to avenge the wrongs to their allies and to prevent further wrongs.

The Assembly decided by a large majority that the treaty had been broken, and that they should go to war. They announced that a full convocation of the allies would be summoned so they could formally vote on the issue. Thucydides emphasises again that the decision was based on fear of Athens rather than the complaints of the allies, and by the realisation at last by Sparta that Athenian power had reached a point where it had to be crushed. The convocation was duly held and the majority voted for war.

But it was almost a year before hostilities began. Sparta sent a succession of delegations to Athens seeking redress for its grievances in order, according to Thucydides, to have the best grounds for going to war if Athens refused to heed them. But Pericles was adamantly opposed to any concessions. His advice was that the Athenians should tell the Spartans that they were willing to submit to arbitration in accordance with the treaty and would not start a war, but would repel those who did. He was convinced that Sparta, in any case, was now bent on war and had been previously, and that war rather than yielding to demands was the best course for the Athenians. He was confident that their superiority in ships and money would give them the advantage, and he had a strategy for victory. They would not engage the superior land forces of the enemy, but would gather their property, leave their homes and land, and retire behind the city's defences. Preserving lives was more important than preserving property. They would make it a war of attrition, which they were better equipped to sustain than the enemy. They would rely on their superior naval power and on secure control of their allies. If the enemy marched against Athenian territory, the Athenians would sail against theirs, and devastation of areas of the Peloponnesus would be more damaging than devastation of Attica, since Athens had land all around the Aegean. The only risk he saw was that Athenian ambition might lead them to try to extend their empire while they were at war and take on endless dangers.

Pericles had no fear of this war and no interest in preventing it. He had prepared for such a conflict almost from the day Athens signed the Thirty Years' Peace. His distrust of the Spartans was total. In a strong statement Thucydides says he was opposed to them in all things, would allow no concessions to them and kept urging the Athenians to war. He was fully confident of victory, and victory would achieve his greatest aim of security and supremacy for Athens. There would be only one superpower in Greece.

Though there were speakers against going to war, the Athenian Assembly accepted the advice of Pericles and rejected all Spartan demands, but agreed to submit to arbitration in accordance with the treaty. Informal contacts between the two sides continued, but to no effect. An unsuccessful attempt by Thebans, allies of Sparta, to gain control of Plataea, an ally of Athens, in early 431 speeded up the preparations for war on both sides. Finally, in late May 431, Archidamus invaded Attica and the greatest war in Greek history began.[6]

I have described the events leading to this war in some detail because they provide perhaps the most telling example of the imperialist culture that gripped the democracy in this era and generated an almost compulsive urge to grasp opportunities for greater dominance and to take risks in the name of power and glory. The Athenians were careful not to start the war, but took decisions likely to provoke it. They certainly made no effort to avert it. Confident of victory, they clung to their goal of primacy through power, and preferred confrontation to the policy of peaceful coexistence and a share in the leadership of Greece in alliance with Sparta advocated by leaders like Cimon and Nicias. Pericles was the architect of this policy, and must bear the main responsibility for the breakdown in the relationship between Athens and the Peloponnesian League that culminated in all-out war. He had launched Athens on a perilous path that left little goodwill towards it in any part of Greece. According to Thucydides, at the start of the war the majority of Greeks, both those who wanted to be liberated from Athenian domination and those who feared they would fall under it, were so enraged against Athens that they were eager to help the Spartans in every possible way. In defence of Pericles, however, it must be said that he had built the military resources and a strategy likely to deliver victory and, while he bears a responsibility for the start of the war, he was not responsible for its calamitous outcome.[7]

As soon as Archidamus invaded, Pericles' plan was put into action. The rural population of Attica, which still represented the majority of Athenians, gathered their possessions and took refuge in the city. The uprooting was painful in the extreme, and the large influx caused major problems of over-crowding. Only a few of the new arrivals had accommodation, or friends or relatives with whom they could live, so they had to occupy empty spaces in the city or shrines. Gradually they spread along the walls as far as the Piraeus.

Archidamus failed to entice the Athenians to come out against him, though many in Athens wanted to do so. Instead Pericles stuck to his plan and Archidamus had to be content with ravaging the countryside. He led his army back to the Peloponnesus after spending less than forty days in Attica. The Athenians for their part had taken over Aegina and sent a fleet to ravage parts of the western coast of the Peloponnesus.

The same pattern was repeated in the summer of 430, but soon after the campaigning season began Athens was suddenly hit by a deadly plague. Thucydides, who caught the disease himself but recovered, gives a memorably vivid description of the symptoms and the suffering, and the havoc it especially caused among those from the country who had no proper homes. Doctors were helpless. No art or science could assist. Athens suffered most, while the Peloponnesus was virtually untouched. It lasted two years and recurred again in the winter of 427/6, though with less virulence. The losses in the army were 4,400 hoplites and three hundred cavalry. The numbers in the general popula-tion who died were never determined.[8]

Despite the ravages of the plague, the Athenians kept the war effort going, but morale was now at a low point. Thucydides records the scale of the disil-lusionment. They had seen their lands ravaged twice. The upper class had lost their beautiful estates and homes in the country, and ordinary people had lost the little that they had. The plague was destroying both those on active service and those in the city. The war was not going well. In their desperation the Athenians even sent envoys to Sparta seeking peace, but without success. They then turned their anger on Pericles, blaming him for having persuaded them to go to war and for their general misfortunes. But he rallied them with a rousing defence, and once again they listened to his political advice and determined to continue the war. But their grief at their private misfortunes was so great that in their anger they were not satisfied until they had punished him with a fine – before soon afterwards electing him general again, because they realised he was their most valuable political leader. But within a year Pericles was dead, a victim of the plague, a further setback for Athens, and a tragic end to the life of one of the truly remarkable figures of classical antiquity.[9]

The death of Pericles left a major political vacuum and a dearth of leadership, and marks a turning point in the character of democratic politics and policy. There was no successor of comparable stature in sight. He had held sway for a long time, had overshadowed rivals and had groomed no successors. Athens had competent generals during the Peloponnesian War, but none in the Periclean mould. Nicias, wealthy, though not a member of the old aristocracy, came closest – a loyal democrat, honest, patriotic, well regarded by both the public and the upper classes. He was elected general, with only one short break, from 427 to 413, and was prominent in debates in the Assembly, but he lacked the vision, strength of personality and eloquence to be a decisive, authoritative leader.

I have stressed before the high dependency of the democracy on talented leaders, and the dilemma of reconciling the need to delegate power to individuals with the principle of collective government on a basis of equality. While the constitution was painstakingly designed to ensure that ultimate control of important decisions was retained in the hands of the people, and that the mass of citizens had ample opportunity to become actively engaged in and fully conversant with political affairs and the workings of government at both local and national level, there were crucial areas of decision-making, notably those concerning war and peace and foreign relations, where expertise and professional experience beyond the reach of ordinary citizens were required. A mass Assembly needed to have experienced and responsible political leadership to guide its decisions in such areas.

But political leadership was a curiously unstructured feature of Athenian democracy. The concern to keep *kratos* with the *demos* through a sovereign Assembly was at variance with the idea of a strong executive. There was nothing at Athens resembling the executive branches of modern parliamentary or presidential systems, which have responsibility for leading the process of identifying priorities, formulating policy and overseeing the implementation of measures approved by the legislature. There were executive officials or magistrates at Athens, but their function was to implement policy, not to make it. Generals had some special prerogatives in time of war regarding access to the Council, the summoning of Assemblies and the making of proposals, but even in their case their primary function was to command the military forces assigned to them and to accomplish their military missions.

The Council did, of course, fulfil many of the functions of a modern executive branch. It managed the routine day-to-day business of government, and had a broad managerial mandate in regard to all the operations of the state. It also organised the business of the Assembly, summoned meetings, fixed the agenda and made preliminary proposals (*probouleumata*) with regard to each issue that specified the action that the Council believed should be taken, or set out what needed to be debated and decided, but without recommendation. But while its control over administrative officials and departments was substantial and crucial to coordinated and efficient administration of the state, and its input into policy was important, it did not make policy and did not have the capacity to steer its recommendations through the Assembly. Even the *probouleumata* that specified the action to be taken could be rejected or amended, or an alternative proposal from the Assembly could be accepted in preference. The Assembly could also direct the Council to put items on the Assembly's agenda. The Council's annually changing membership and the use of the lot in selecting its members were further checks on its influence, depriving it of continuity and of any assurance of ability or expertise in its ranks that would give it claims to a commanding role.

The Assembly tightly guarded in the fifth century its sovereign right to make all important political decisions, and in the Assembly there were no gradations of rank. No one had any official mandate to lead. Everyone in theory had an equal right to be heard. In practice, however, leaders did emerge and acquire huge influence, but on the basis of credibility and authority derived from reputation, achievement or sheer powers of persuasion. Generals had a clear advantage through most of the fifth century when war and empire were so prominent on the agenda, and, as I have noted before, Athens at its peak was led in both the military and political spheres by a succession of notable military figures who also had the political skills to achieve a leading place in the Assembly and forge consensus behind dynamic policies that brought Athens great success. The people were eager to use talent and readily listened to and gave power to those who had their trust, though under the tight rein of their strict regime of accountability.

But there remained a haphazard quality about leadership in the Assembly which left a lot to chance. The system gave a pathway to power to anyone with the force of personality and skills in persuasion to bend the *demos* to his purposes. But good statesmanship required more, as Thucydides was at pains to point out – foresight, judgement, integrity, devotion to state more than self. When the leadership lacked such qualities, there was a risk that the process of mass decision-making could become wayward and prone to error. This was the situation that began to emerge in the aftermath of the death of Pericles. He was the last in the line of the distinguished leaders of the first eighty years of the democracy, and was the most gifted and influential. He was a fine military strategist, a visionary, a patriot, a committed democrat, and an imperialist who saw limits to expansion, and who had the authoritative personality and power of eloquence to control the energy and exuberance of the *demos*. The people recognised his abilities and willingly gave him a commanding authority. He is the supreme example of the willingness of the *demos* to accept the ascendancy of those whose wisdom and integrity promised success.[10]

The Rise of the So-Called Demagogues

Thucydides believed that it was under Pericles that Athens was at its greatest. His death left a vacuum at the top and brought a change in the character of Athenian politics and its leadership. Thucydides describes the change in a pithy overview of Pericles' successors: 'Those who came after him were more on a par with one another and, with each striving to achieve primacy, they resorted to surrendering control even of public affairs to the whims of the *demos*.' Thucydides saw this scramble for leadership of the people (*demou prostasia*) as the cause of many mistakes that blunted the conduct of the war and brought civil dissension in the state for the first time.

The Aristotelian *Constitution of Athens* also highlights the change after the death of Pericles, emphasising the emergence of Cleon as the leader of the people, the first leader who did not come from the ranks of the upper class (the *epineikeis*), and did not have their approval. Previously those leading the people (*demagogountes*) had always come from this class. The writer goes on to mention another leader of the people, Cleophon, who came to prominence after the overthrow of the Four Hundred in 411, and he is similarly portrayed in an unfavourable light, as are those who held the leadership of the people (*demagogia*) after him, all of them bent on brazenness and pleasing the masses. Isocrates also notes the change after Pericles, whom he calls a *demagogos*, but an honest, responsible one. Those who came after him, however, he describes as a different breed of 'worthless *rhetores* and *demagogoi*'.[11]

There are difficulties in determining the role and impact of the new breed of politician that emerged in the post-Periclean democracy. We have information about only a small number of them and, with the exception of Cleon, the available information is meagre in the extreme. The main ancient sources are, as indicated above, strongly biased against them, and they have also tradition-ally been labelled demagogues by modern historians, a word that, since the seventeenth century, has carried the derogatory meaning of a rabble-rouser pandering to the wishes of the masses.

Moses Finley, in a forcefully argued and influential article in 1962, attempted to provide a corrective to this biased tradition. He downplays the change after

Pericles, and the difference between the leaders who came after him and those who had gone before. He argues that all leaders, of whatever stamp, who took it upon themselves to address the Assembly, an open-air, mass meeting on the Pnyx of whatever segment of the *demos* assembled on any given day, faced the same exacting and often risky challenge of persuading the gathering to their point of view. They were all demagogues in the neutral sense of the term, regardless of class or point of view, and they were a structural element in a system that could not function without them. Finley insists they should only be called demagogues in the pejorative sense if they made false promises to the people to serve their own interests.

Many of Finley's points are valid and needed stating. It is true that all political leaders faced the same formidable task of persuading a gathering whose composition they could not know ahead of time, and they doubtless used every skill and rhetorical stratagem at their disposal to do it. The leaders were indeed a crucial element in a direct democracy where the *demos* needed a variety of information and expert guidance to help them make decisions. It was the responsibility of the leader to inform and guide. There is a revealing passage in the *Memorabilia* of Xenophon that emphasises that fame and admiration in public life require thorough knowledge of what needs to be done. It gives a taste of what those addressing the Assembly had to master – the condition of the state's revenues and the sources of those revenues, the level of its expenditures, its military resources, the military resources of its enemies, the condition of its defences and garrisons, the adequacy of the food supply. Aristotle's *Rhetoric* has an even more daunting list of the topics that political leaders might have to confront. Men like Cleon could not have maintained a leading position without intense engagement with all the many-sided dimensions of administering the Athenian state and its extensive empire, and there is evidence from inscriptions and fragments that these new politicians were involved in the nuts and bolts of governing as well as in the big issues. They were playing their part in making the democracy work.[12]

But that it not the whole story. Finley may have overcorrected the traditional view of the so-called demagogues and their significance. It is hard to ignore the evidence that the emergence of Cleon in a position of high influence was a shock to the political system, and brought a new divisiveness in Athenian politics and a new meaning to the words *demagogos* and *demagogia*. The passage from the Aristotelian *Constitution of Athens* about the change in Athenian politics after Pericles cited above describes as *demagogoi* all those who, from the start, led the drive for greater justice and political equality for the *demos*. The word *demos* is used here, as often, to denote the mass of ordinary citizens (the *hoi polloi* or *to plethos*), as distinct from the high-born, wealthy elite, variously called in this passage *epieikeis* (upper class), *gnorimoi* (distinguished), *euporoi* (wealthy) and *epiphanes* (notable). These *demagogoi* are listed as Solon, Peisistratus before he established a tyranny, Cleisthenes, Xanthippus, Themistocles, Ephialtes and Pericles. They all came from the aristocratic elite, and were acceptable to it. They were *demagogoi* in the word's literal, neutral sense. There is no hint that the word as applied to them had any of the pejorative connotations that it later acquired.[13]

But Cleon came from a lower class and did not enjoy the favour of the elite. More alarming for the aristocracy, he rose to a position of unrivalled influence with the *demos*, and did it with an abrasive style and new methods of power-building that presented him as a man of the people, devoted to the people (*philodemos*), in contrast to an arrogant, highfalutin upper class, He was a wholly different type of *demagogos*, and he brought a new divisiveness into the political arena that threatened the position of the aristocratic establishment and the high level of political consensus and stability that marked the earlier democracy.[14] A review of his background and career will illustrate his impact on the course of the democracy and the dynamics of its political life.

Cleon belonged to a new social class, the nouveaux riches, what Aristophanes called the *neoploutoi*, entrepreneurs who had become wealthy by exploiting the commercial opportunities that arose from the growth of empire. He was the son of a tanner who had become rich enough to undertake expensive liturgies. His education was modest, judging by the comments of his detractors and his own scorn for culture and learning. There is no indication that he had any significant military experience or distinction. The fact that he was not in favour with the upper class meant he would face an uphill struggle to reach a position of any influence by attempting to compete with established aristocratic families on their own ground or using their methods, so he embarked on a new populist route to power.

His goal was winning the support of the masses. That, of course, had been a goal of all the leaders of the democracy since Cleisthenes had made the *demos* his *hetaireia*, but Cleon pursued the favour of the *demos* by new methods. He was not relying on a famous name, or on the benefits of advanced education or of military expertise and distinction, or on networks of influential friends, or on public philanthropy to build political muscle and popular appeal. Instead he made a virtue of his low birth and lack of high culture or learning, and presented himself as a plain man of the people, one of them, their champion and the watchdog of their welfare. He ranged himself in opposition to the better bred and better educated and their brand of statesmanship. Thucydides records a speech that Cleon made in the Assembly in 427 following a revolt by an important ally, Mytilene, which provides a sample of the rhetoric he employed against the high and mighty of the upper classes. He warns the people not to be misled by clever speech, and drives home the point that the unlettered common sense of ordinary citizens, who are modest enough to show restraint and be respectful of the law, more often produces better government than the undisciplined cleverness of the smart set who love to dominate all debate and to show off their intelligence and appear wiser than the law. It was a clear, crowd-pleasing message exalting the instinctive wisdom of the masses above the specious cleverness of intellectuals.

Cleon drove home his messages in a new, forceful, flamboyant style of oratory. Thucydides described him as a very violent figure. The aggression showed itself in his mode of delivery. According to Aristotle, he was the first to shout when addressing the people, and to use abusive language, and to speak with his cloak tucked up. He was also the first to use extravagant gestures. His style may have shocked some, but it was effective and the great oratorical fora of Athenian democracy, the Assembly, Council and courts, became the main platforms for the exercise of his political influence.[15]

Thucydides repeatedly mentions Cleon's dominance in the Assembly between 427 and his death in 422, and twice states that he had by far the greatest influence of any politician over the *demos*. He served the maximum two terms on the Council and also used that body to launch prosecutions for alleged crimes against the state. But it was the jury courts that presented him with the greatest opportunity to harass the powerful, especially generals, and to show himself as the people's watchdog and the scourge of those who conspired against the state or betrayed the people's trust by failure or malfeasance in office.

Any citizen was entitled in Athenian law to bring charges of a crime against the state (*eisangelia*), or charges arising from the detailed accounting (*euthuna*) required of all magistrates at the end of their term of office. Allies could also be indicted by ordinary citizens in Athenian courts on a variety of charges. There were rewards for successful prosecutions or information leading to conviction. This inevitably gave rise to abuse and led to the emergence of so-called *sycophantai*, prosecutors or informers motivated by money or malice. There is abundant evidence, though it comes mainly from comedy, that demagogues used the courts extensively for political purposes and personal gain, and Cleon was prominent in the emergence of that trend in the late fifth century.[16]

Cleon's popular appeal was also enhanced by his militaristic, jingoistic attitude towards the war and foreign policy generally. His uncompromising rhetoric was congenial to a long-suffering public hungry for victory, accustomed to victory, and characteristically aggressive in matters of war and the assertion of power. He quickly rose to a leading position after the death of Pericles. The

Athenians soon recovered from the plague and kept the war effort going, as Pericles had urged them to do. But in 428 they faced a serious threat from the revolt of Mytilene, mentioned above, which also involved most of the rest of the island of Lesbos. This was crushed by 427, but the Athenians were in angry mood and, on the motion of Cleon, decided on the ultimate punishment for Mytilene, the execution of the adult male population and the enslavement of the women and children. They had a sudden change of heart, however, and next day held another debate to reconsider the decision. Cleon was again to the fore, arguing that the decision taken must stand. Thucydides, deeply interested as he was in issues of power and empire, chose the occasion for detailed treatment, obviously seeing it as an example of the attitudes now beginning to drive Athenian foreign policy. In his usual manner he presents a speech from two opponents in the debate, in this case Cleon and an otherwise unknown figure, Diodotus.

Cleon's attack on the clever rhetoric of the upper-class intelligentsia has been mentioned already, but the bulk of the speech represented a hardline doctrine of *Machtpolitik* that he would continue to pursue in the years ahead. He argued that the Athenians must accept that the empire is a tyranny, imposed by superior strength on unwilling subjects. There is no room in it for pity. To show softness is to court danger. It is strength, not goodwill, that will maintain it, together with speedy, fitting punishments for those who resist it.

The people must not therefore be led by pity, beguiling words or a sense of equity, the three things most damaging to dominion. If they want to hold on to their empire they must instead be led by expediency, regardless of the rights and wrongs of it. Otherwise they should give up their rule and retire to doing good deeds in safety. The speech is an unvarnished, cynical view of empire as the strong-arm rule of a superior power over unwilling subjects for the benefit of the ruler. Self-interest alone, not the good of the subjects, must direct its management. Moral scruples are its greatest enemy.

The response came from Diodotus, about whom virtually nothing is known, but he clearly represented the well-bred, well-educated, rhetorically able politician whom Cleon professed to despise. He had also been the main speaker against the motion in the previous day's debate. His speech defends the importance of debate as the means to informed action, but its most striking aspect is its full acceptance of Cleon's contention that expediency alone, not compassion or concerns of morality, must determine the decision of the Assembly. He maintains, however, that self-interest in this case demands not extreme punishments, which are never an effective deterrent given the ingrained impulses of human nature, but a moderation that does not penalise or alienate those well disposed to Athens, and that will not foment future revolts.

The arguments of Diodotus narrowly won the day, but Cleon succeeded in getting the execution of more than a thousand Mytilenians who were deemed most responsible for the revolt. The debate overall clearly showed that Athenian imperialism had now taken a harsher turn. The Athenians had never been slow to admit that their empire was based on selfish motives, but they had done their best in earlier days to counter criticism by claiming that power had been thrust upon them and used to save Greece from the barbarian, and that their supremacy was earned, fair and beneficial. Such protestations were obviously no longer a concern. The advantage of the ruler was now the guiding principle, and the extreme form of that doctrine was being given powerful voice by a radically new breed of populist politician.[17]

Cleon retained his prominent place in Athenian politics until his death in 422. He achieved his greatest success in 425, when an Athenian fleet, on its way to reinforce an Athenian squadron that had been sent to Sicily in 427 to protect Ionian allies against Syracuse, had to put into a harbour inside the promontory of Pylos in the western Peloponnesus because of bad weather. Demosthenes, one of the most able and enterprising commanders to emerge in the war, managed to get a fortification built on the promontory while the fleet waited for better weather. He remained behind with six ships to defend it.

The development proved to be a turning point in a war that had become a virtual stalemate. The Peloponnesians had continued to invade Attica in five of the first seven years of the war, but the Athenians continued the strategy of Pericles and refused to engage them, and they achieved little. The occupation of Spartan land by an Athenian force was, however, deeply disturbing to the Spartans, and they immediately dispatched their fleet to Pylos and occupied a neighbouring island, Sphacteria. But their fleet was defeated and Sphacteria blockaded by the Sicilian-bound Athenian fleet which had returned to help Demosthenes. The Spartans sought a truce to give an opportunity to negotiate an end to the war. The Athenians now had a chance to negotiate a favourable settlement, but their confidence and ambition were back and, egged on by an increasingly influential Cleon, they made demands that Sparta could not accept. The war resumed. Cleon was given command of a fresh expedition and, with help from Demosthenes, he captured Sphacteria and brought almost three hundred Spartan prisoners back to Athens. The Athenians threatened to kill them if Sparta invaded Attica again.

The victory made a big impression on the Greek world and gave the Athenians the advantage. But that soon changed. They suffered a serious setback at Delium in Boeotia in 424, and soon afterwards faced a new threat when a highly able Spartan commander, Brasidas, invaded Chalcidice and besieged the important Athenian colony of Amphipolis. The historian Thucydides, a general in 424, commanded a squadron nearby and was dispatched to help, but Brasidas had negotiated the surrender of Amphipolis before he arrived. Thucydides was exiled for twenty years for his failure to save the city.

The loss of Amphipolis, which commanded the trade routes to the Hellespont and was itself an important supplier of silver and timber to Athens, was a severe blow, and caused Athens to agree to a one-year truce with Sparta in 423. But the truce did not hold in Chalcidice, where two cities, Mende and Scione, revolted and opened their gates to Brasidas. The Athenians were outraged and sent an expedition of fifty ships to attack the rebel cities. Mende was quickly recovered, but Scione held out until 421. In accordance with a decree, proposed by Cleon when Scione defected, the adult males were executed and the women and children enslaved in an act of brutality that became infamous in Greece.

When the truce ended in 422, Cleon persuaded the Assembly to move to recover the Thracian territories, and he was given command of a large expedition. But he proved no match for Brasidas, and his army was routed at the first encounter. Both he and Brasidas were killed. Both sides were now ready for peace, and in 421 the Peace of Nicias, named after its main architect, was signed. It was agreed that it should be binding for fifty years, and that each side should return areas seized during the war.[18]

Cleon's period in the forefront of Athenian politics had a significant impact on the character of the political life of the democracy during the remainder of the fifth century. As mentioned earlier, he was a wholly different kind of *demagogos* from any that preceded him, different in his social background, in his education, in his style of politics and in the way he presented himself to the *demos* and portrayed and related to the aristocracy. He and the politicians of similar mode who came after him were a polarising force, questioning the role and judgement of the aristocracy, asserting the sovereign control of the *demos* itself, thus sharpening tensions between the masses and the elite which, as we shall see later, in conjunction with other polarising forces in the final decades of the fifth century, brought the civil discord mentioned by Thucydides (2.65.11) and helped pave the way for revolution. Their extreme militarism and callous brand of imperialism were also an impediment to a peaceful resolution of the war.

The final legacy of Cleon was to change for good the benign meaning of the term *demagogos*. After he came to prominence the term seems to have taken on a strongly negative connotation, and we now only find it used to describe a leader of whom the user disapproved. Thucydides uses the word *demagogos* only once, and that was to describe Cleon himself, whom he heartily despised. He also used *demagogia* only once, in relation to another prominent populist leader, Androcles, whose *demagogia*, he says, brought his assassination at the hands of oligarchic sympathisers in 411. The *Knights* of Aristophanes, produced in 424, which provides a scathing caricature of Cleon as a boorish, low-bred, fawning populist, carries the message that *demagogia* is no longer for the cultured or the respectable, but for the ignorant and the obnoxious. Aristophanes asserts that the tools necessary for leading the people (*demagogica*) have now become a disgusting voice, low birth and marketplace manners. Fourth-century writers such as Aristotle and Isocrates would confirm the place of *demagogos* in the political vocabulary as a designation for flatterers, sycophants and all who court the favour of the people in an effort to build their personal power.[19]

The death of Cleon blunted somewhat the impact of populist militarism on Athenian politics, but he had supporters and imitators, and *demagogoi* in the same mould continued to emerge off and on into the fourth century. Their role will be noted at the relevant points. Though the number of influential demagogues appears to have been small and mostly confined to the era of the war, they seriously upset the balance in the democratic constitution between the sovereignty of the *demos* and the place of the old aristocracy in leading and controlling the course of politics. More will be said about that later. In terms of the war, their behaviour had seriously detrimental effects. They exploited the most negative side of the dynamic energy and ambition that had brought the democracy such remarkable success, inciting an aggressive militarism and a harsh imperialism pursued with whatever brutality and ruthlessness expediency required. They succeeded, as we shall see, in blocking offers of peace on three occasions when notable victories gave Athens the advantage and the chance of a favourable agreement. They bear considerable responsibility for the cruelty that marred Athenian behaviour in the war and left Athens friendless, with the exception of Samos, at the end of the war, and that might well have led to the city's destruction were it not for Sparta's generous decision to save the one-time saviour of Greece.[20]

But there were also other forces shaping, with negative results, the mentality and decision-making of the Athenians during the war. Allowance must be made for the brutalising effects of the conflict and the exceptional suffering which the Athenians had to endure in its first seven years. They were suddenly afflicted by the horrors of a devastating plague for which they knew no remedy. They saw their armed forces seriously depleted by the plague and no prospect of the quick victory for which they had hoped. Instead they had their territory invaded by Archidamus in five of these first seven years of the war. In each of these years they had to abandon their homes and lands and helplessly watch them being repeatedly ravaged while they lived in confinement in primitive, overcrowded conditions behind the city walls for periods of up to forty days. There were no significant victories to compensate for these hardships.

Thucydides has left some compelling analyses of the effects of such experiences on the human psyche. He describes how the suffering and despair caused by the plague brought a breakdown of restraint and of regard for what was normally considered noble and good. Whatever seemed to serve people's selfish interests and pleasures became the honourable. Thucydides saw this as the beginning of a greater disregard for law (*anomia*) in Athens.[21]

He gives a still more graphic account of the psychological trauma of war in his record of a civil conflict in Corcyra in 427–425. He describes war as a brutal schoolmaster whose deprivations robbed people of their better instincts and lowered their mental disposition to match their circumstances. It brought extreme savagery. It turned morality on its head. The normal meaning of words became perverted to make vice seem commendable and virtue a fault.

He saw love of power, inspired by greed and ambition and intensified by passionate rivalry, as the root of the evils unleashed by war, and civil war especially. The result was every form of evil practice. Simple good-heartedness, the main ingredient of a noble nature, became a laughing stock and vanished. Human nature, prone to wrongdoing even when law prevails, now found itself triumphant over law and delighted in showing that its impulses (*orge*) were beyond control, were stronger than justice and were the enemy of any authority.

Thucydides obviously saw these effects as most extreme in civil wars, but when he refers to war as a brutal schoolmaster he clearly means all wars. He emphasises that hardship was an inevitable consequence of war in general, and that, while human nature remains what it is, people will react in proportion to their sufferings by abandoning their higher nature and giving free rein to their rawest instincts. As noted earlier, he attributed some similar effects to the plague. He clearly saw hardship and desperation as the enemies of any civilised, law-abiding society with a high sense of morality.[22]

The Young Radicals

There was one other phenomenon that began to show itself in the late 420s that further extended the political and cultural divides emerging in Athens, and that had perhaps the greatest impact of all on the outcome of the war and the near-overthrow of the democracy. A new generation of young aristocrats was coming to the fore in Athenian politics. They had grown up in the 440s and 430s at the height of Athenian power and prosperity, and had experienced the new education and the full influence of the intellectual revolution that came with the Sophists. Their lifestyle soon attracted the attention of the writers of comedy, who ridiculed their penchant for long hair, extravagant, foppish dress, addiction to drink, horses and sexual diversions, and their general lack of seriousness, discipline and commitment to duty. These were criticisms common in societies where changing times gave rise to marked generation gaps. Cicero made similar complaints about the youth of his day (the *iuventus*).[23]

But a more sinister feature of the young aristocrats in Athens was the pronounced militarism and political radicalism spreading among them. They were ambitious in the extreme, with new ideas of power and its uses and benefits. In the *Suppliants* of Euripides, produced about 420 and set in the age of Theseus, but with contemporary themes and messages, the young are described as hungry for honour and war and command and power and wealth, with no thought for morality or the welfare of citizens. The same image of this generation of aristocrats emerges from Thucydides. They were at odds with the older generation of leaders, such as Laches and Nicias, who were cautious and averse to unnecessary risks. But while the radical young aristocrats may have matched the warmongering and hard-headed imperialism of the demagogues, they otherwise despised them and were contemptuous of the democracy in general, though they were willing to work within it so long as there was no feasible alternative.[24]

The *Nomos/Physis* Controversy

There can be no doubt that many of the new generation of aristocrats were heavily influenced by some of the more extreme ideas emanating from the milieu of political speculation that evolved with the coming of the Sophists. The most radical of these ideas centred around the basis and function of law (*nomos*) and its relationship to the true nature of man (*physis*). The early Greek tradition in Hesiod, Solon, the tragedians and fragments of some of the philosophers identified law with justice (*dike*), the divinely inspired sense of right inbred in human nature which, aided by other social gifts, such as restraint (*sophrosyne)* and consideration for others (*aidos*), gave human beings a natural predilection for fairness and fellowship and a capacity for an orderly and harmonious life in society under a rule of law based on just principles. Justice therefore had a divine origin and was a divine gift to mankind. It was a universal trait of human nature, a guide to just human relationships and the single source of the immutable principles of human law.

The impact of these beliefs was still strong in Greece in the later fifth century, as is illustrated by the high respect that continued to be given to unwritten laws (*agraphoi nomoi*). These were traditional norms of right conduct that had wide acceptance and were seen as immutable principles that had superior, or even divine, authority. In the *Antigone* of Sophocles, the heroine appeals to such a law as justification for violating a decree of Creon, who, as king of Thebes, had the right to make law. This conflict between unwritten law, which claimed divine sanction, and a human law not founded on such authority forms the centrepiece of the tragedy. Perhaps the strongest indication of the continuing importance of unwritten law occurs in the Funeral Oration, where Pericles raises unwritten laws above the written and says that violation of them brought shame by common consent.[25]

But the idea that human law was the product of a natural justice of divine origin and immanent in the nature of all human beings was undermined by expanding knowledge of the laws and customs of other societies, which showed vast differences in the practices of different peoples. This seemed incompatible with the idea that law had any single source or any universal or immutable character. It suggested instead that laws, while essential to the order and stability of the state, were merely whatever conventions a given people at a given time decided to adopt as the legally binding rules of their society. The connection between *nomos* and *physis* was being broken. Popular consensus rather than immutable natural instincts was now seen as the basis of the moral and legal rules prevailing in any society. Plato associates Protagoras in particular with this relativistic approach and interprets his famous statement that 'Man is the measure of all things' to mean in the political context that whatever any *polis* considered just and right was just and right in that *polis* for as long as that opinion prevailed.

This is very much in line with a definition of law ascribed to Pericles by Xenophon. When asked by his young ward Alcibiades to teach him what a law was, Pericles responded that laws were the things considered and recorded by the assembled mass of the people prescribing what should and should not be done. When asked about laws passed by a minority, as happens in oligarchies, he replied that whatever the sovereign power in a state prescribes is called a law. But he later qualified this by saying that, where a minority rules, their enactments must carry public agreement through persuasion and must not be imposed by force. In other words, popular consensus should remain the arbiter of the rules of behaviour that govern a society.[26]

But there were some among the broad ranks of the Sophists who had more radical views about law and nature and the relationship between them. They started from the premise that the only true laws were the laws that accorded with the true natural instincts of human beings. These laws were more powerful than man-made law and were the dominant forces in human behaviour. But they had a radically new view of what the true natural instincts of human beings were, insisting that there was nothing in them to suggest that human nature was fundamentally altruistic or directed by any innate sense of fairness, fellowship or consideration for others. On the contrary, all evidence indicated that human beings were innately egotistic and selfish, driven by their nature to seek their self-interest (*to sumpheron*). They maintained that this truth of nature was impossible to deny or alter. It carried the power of necessity. It was illustrated in the animal world, and in the practices of whole states and peoples.

What this doctrine meant in political and moral terms was that the strong properly rule the weak and take the greater share. Under the law of nature the just is the advantage of the stronger. Might is right, and those who have the power will dominate those who do not, and will pursue their natural desires to the degree they deem expedient and achievable with impunity.

Laws emerged as part of the advance of civilisation, as it became clear that a world of brutish disorder based on strength carried for most people a risk of suffering wrong that outweighed the benefit of being able to inflict it. This made it seem expedient for communities to come together to agree compacts expressed in laws that would prevent people from either suffering or doing wrong, and would serve as a guarantee of mutual rights.

But such laws had no basis in nature and were in fact fetters on nature, mere conventions that formed a social contract of expediency designed to keep citizens from harm, and to protect especially the weaker majority against the natural right of the more powerful to dominance and a greater share.

These agreed conventions were considered to represent justice, but it was a justice that was entirely artificial, something honoured in the absence of power to inflict injustice. It was based on no natural universal standard but varied widely from place to place and was constantly changing, and was practised reluctantly as a necessity rather than a real good.

The more moderate advocates of these views, such as Antiphon, one of the earlier Sophists, accepted that it was expedient to live in a society that had order and harmony (*harmonia*) and gave protection against harm, and that therefore the laws and conventions of the society in which one lived should as a rule be accepted and obeyed since the alternative was likely to be worse. In the end, however, the touchstone in decisions to obey or disobey the law was self-interest.

But the more extreme form of the argument, as represented most notably by Callicles in Plato's *Gorgias*, denied any legitimacy to the whole structure of man-made covenants, which hold down and enslave the truly great. The man of real worth will trample on these constraints like the noble Hercules. The justice of nature will shine forth and he will ruthlessly give rein to his ambitions and desires and achieve his rightful destiny of supreme power. Nothing could be more virulently anti-democratic, or more at odds with the entire religious, political, social and ethical tradition of the *polis*. The whole debate surrounding *nomos* and *physis* is a good illustration of the intensity and audacity of the new intellectual movements at Athens centred around the nature of human beings and their political and ethical relationships.[27]

The evidence of Euripides, Aristophanes and Thucydides clearly shows that these speculations about human motivations and social and political relationships were not just idle musings of the intelligentsia confined to lecture halls or gatherings at symposia. They were ideas well known to the public at large. Arguments from *physis* to explain, justify or criticise human behaviour abound in Euripides. The first clear reference to the *nomos/physis* antithesis occurs in the *Clouds* of Aristophanes, produced in 423. Drama was aimed at the general public, and comedy in particular, which was based on topical satire, could not succeed if the audience were not familiar with the subject of the ridicule. In Thucydides we find that the rhetoric of politics from the late 430s onwards was laced with language and arguments that reflected current theories about the springs of human behaviour and issues surrounding law and morality, power and empire.

This is not to imply that all of these ideas found favour with the general public or with all of the upper classes. The Sophists and the new rhetoric and new thinking that came with them were always viewed with suspicion in Athens, especially by the demagogues and the more conservative elements of the society as a whole. The views of Cleon and of conservative democrats such as Anytus, the prosecutor of Socrates, and the scathing satire of Aristophanes provide ample illustration of this. The democratic ideal was based on essentially altruistic foundations of justice, equality, fellowship, communal solidarity and high civic participation, patriotism and devotion to the common good. It was the antithesis of the Calliclean view of society, which pointed towards lawless tyranny or oligarchy, moral nihilism and the destruction of all social boundaries.[28]

But the Athenians came to favour a wholly different set of values when it came to foreign relations. The restless ambition and expansionist urge of the fifth-century democracy disposed it to the view that a superior nation with a will to power had a natural entitlement to lead others and reap the benefits of its primacy. Ideas that argued the natural rights of the strong and the legitimacy of putting self-interest ahead of morality in international relations found fertile ground in Athens.

It was, however, a gradual process. Before the war the Athenians did their best to put a moral face on what their opponents charged was an enslavement of Greeks. Within Athens itself the place of morality in foreign policy was still a live issue. The enemies of Pericles deployed moral arguments against his use of part of the tribute from the allies to build his monuments. Pericles himself admitted the acquisition of the empire could be seen as unjust. The calls of men like Cleon to put aside all considerations of the right and the just in dealing with the allies showed such considerations still had influence and needed to be undermined.

But as the war progressed the mood hardened. The moral began to give way to the expedient under the influence of a more ruthless militarism promoted by the demagogues, but more especially under the influence of the new, amoral but alluring rhetoric of imperialism that came from the new breed of radical aristocrats, and that was shaped by Sophistic doctrines of the nature of power and the rights of the powerful.

Thucydides records in detail the change in the moral climate in a series of speeches relating to the period 430–415. The number and length of the speeches show the importance he attributes to the shift in thinking that was now determining foreign policy. He also records in detail another shift in the moral climate in his extended analyses of the effects of the plague and of the wave of civil conflicts that swept through Greece in the 420s. The substance of these analyses has been outlined earlier. He believed both the plague and the revolutions had a negative moral impact on Greece, the first initiating at Athens a breakdown in respect for law, the second bringing to Greece as a whole the rise of all forms of evil behaviour.

In the course of these analyses he gives an interesting insight into his personal views of the core issues involved in the *nomos/physis* antithesis. He did not subscribe to the view that human nature was fundamentally selfish, motivated by self-interest and a natural instinct to put the expedient before all else. But he did recognise that there was a dark side to the human psyche, which inclines people towards wrongdoing at the best of times, and which surfaces especially in times of hardship and tumult when life is thrown into confusion. In such circumstances the good-hearted, nobler side of human nature is suppressed and there emerges a human nature (*physis anthropeia*) that revels in the triumph of passion (*orge*) over law, justice and all authority. It is only when the raw instincts of *physis anthropeia* gain the upper hand that people throw off restraint and moderation, destroy the common standards of humanity, abandon righteousness and put gain before justice.

In summary Thucydides held to the view that human beings have a higher nature that values good-hearted fellowship, trust and a society of laws that fosters discipline and moderation and is based on common human standards of the right and the just. He saw a destructive decline in these values in Greece, including Athens, starting with the plague and intensifying with the civil conflicts of the 420s.

These analyses are, of course, primarily concerned with the values that should govern domestic rather than international relations, although Thucydides saw a connection between the two. There is no sign that he believed that the same values should govern both, and it is safe to assume that he accepted that states would resolutely pursue their self-interest in dealings with other states and would be guided by what they considered strategic necessities. He never hints that Athens was not justified in acquiring its empire and he never criticises the Periclean brand of imperialism.

But he emphatically disapproved of the military and imperial policies that followed the Periclean era. In his epitaph for Pericles he attacked his successors not only for ignoring his advice, but for a succession of blunders culminating in the Sicilian expedition. Thucydides links the bad decisions directly to moral flaws, and in language that points at the demagogues and Alcibiades and his like. The patriotism and incorruptible dedication to the common good that marked men like Pericles were replaced in the leaders that followed him by a populism that pandered to the whims of the *demos* and by egotism, selfish ambition, greed and factiousness. He believed the moral decline infecting Athenian life and its leadership had spilled over into foreign relations and led to decisions that, when they succeeded, benefited only individuals and, when they failed, damaged the state and the conduct of the war.[29]

Thucydides shows no sympathy for the new politics of the demagogues or for the new thinking and aspirations of the warlike young aristocrats, but he gave a clear airing to their views to provide a full understanding of the tenor of the public discourse in Athens in the period, and of the arguments that inspired decisions that he saw as ruinous.

The first speech in the series dealing with power and empire was the one delivered by Athenian envoys at the Spartan Assembly in 432. It has been mentioned several times already. The envoys were conciliatory, arguing the reasonableness and unsurprising nature of the actions of Athens in establishing the empire. But the language already shows the impact of Sophistic theorising about power and its workings in international relations. They claimed that their achievements made them worthy to rule, and that they behaved in the natural human way, impelled by three of the most important human motivators: honour, fear and profit. They went on to argue that it had always been an established rule that the weaker should be controlled by the stronger. Considerations of justice had never kept the strong from seizing an advantage.

On that occasion they did attempt, however, to show that, while they yielded to the natural human impulse (*physis anthropeia*) to rule others, they retained a concern for justice and treated the allies as equals and gave them equal status under Athenian law, going far beyond what they needed to do.[30]

By the time of the Mytilenian debate the tone had changed. Cleon presented the crude, hardline message that imperial rule had no place for compassion or moral concerns. The law in all its severity must be applied. But the opposing speech of the cultured Diodotus is just as chillingly amoral, accepting that the Athenians must make their decision on grounds of expediency, not on grounds of right and wrong. He differs from Cleon only in his view of what is expedient in this case, arguing that it is not always expedient to resort to the full rigour of the law because there is a force in human affairs more powerful than the law: the impulses of human nature (*physis anthropeia*). These cannot be controlled by use of law or terror and require more subtle management. The goal and mentality of both speakers are the same – the expedient unhindered by moral constraint. But Diodotus was asserting the Sophistic view that an understanding and acceptance of the realities of human nature provided a more accurate guide to the expedient than the law. Sophistic dogma was beginning to show itself in political discourse.[31]

But it is only after the Peace of Nicias, when the young nobility began to reach high office, that the more extreme elements of Sophistic thought get fully aired in Thucydides and become tools of the young radicals in reviving the traditional zest of the *demos* for war and dominion. The most gifted, influential and unscrupulous of the new breed of younger aristocrats was Alcibiades. He came from the highest nobility and had become a ward of Pericles and lived at his home for thirteen years following the death of his father at Coroneia in 447/6. He had striking good looks and was known as Alcibiades the Beautiful, and he became notorious for his profligate lifestyle and love of women and horses. He also had a brilliant intellect and was fully immersed in the intellectual movements of his day, and was well known as an associate of leading members of the intelligentsia. He was, in his early years at least, a pupil and friend of Socrates, but later, along with his close friend Critias, he seems to have come under the spell of the more extreme facets of Sophistic speculation. He had built his early career in a traditional way in the military and had won distinction by his actions at Potidaea and Delium.

Thucydides, who was only slightly older and similarly immersed in a successful political career until the disaster at Amphipolis, must have known Alcibiades well, and his verdict is far from favourable. He acknowledges his exceptional ability in public affairs and as a military commander, but highlights an excessive personal ambition in love with success and directed at conquests, glory and wealth. His later career was to show him as an unprincipled, single-minded egotist, with no sense of patriotism and no loyalty to the democracy that he once described as acknowledged folly (*anoia*). He claimed he worked with it only because it was the system in place, and he did not think it safe to change it while the war with Sparta continued.

Alcibiades became a key figure in the events that led to a breakdown of the Peace of Nicias in the years after 421. Thucydides describes him as the leader of those in Athens who wanted to destroy the Peace, and an enemy of Nicias and Laches, who were its chief advocates, because he felt they treated him as a mere youth and did not pay him the respect he thought he was due. He was elected general in 420 and immediately began leading Athens back to the way of aggression and brinkmanship. He started to intrigue to weaken Sparta in its own sphere of influence, the Peloponnesus, and to rekindle the war. By unofficial personal diplomacy, deceit and false promises he succeeded, over the opposition of Nicias, in forging an alliance between Athens and Argos and its allies, which was concluded in 420. When a war broke out in 419 between Argos and an ally of Sparta, Epidaurus, Sparta came to the latter's aid. A major battle ensued at Mantinea in 418 between a Spartan army and the forces of the Argive alliance, which included an Athenian contingent. Sparta won a decisive victory. The Argive coalition crumbled and with it the Peace of Nicias, though neither side formally declared it at an end.

But the failure of the Argive initiative did not damage Alcibiades for long, and he was later to boast of the strength of the coalition he had forged against Sparta in the Peloponnesus. He was general again in 416, as was Nicias, and at the beginning of the summer he was back again in the Peloponnesus, leading an expedition in support of a democratic faction in Argos that had gained control in 417 and had broken with Sparta. He transferred three hundred Spartan sympathisers to nearby islands controlled by Athens, and sought to rouse as much opposition to Sparta as he could.[32]

Alcibiades and Nicias were now the two most influential leaders in Athens and had directly opposite agendas – Nicias was the champion of peace, Alcibiades was intent on aggressive military expansionism to maintain the primacy of Athens in Greece. The rivalry between them became such an issue that a prominent demagogue, Hyperbolus, whom Thucydides later described as a scoundrel and a disgrace to the city, proposed that one or other of them be ostracised to end division and let the people decide which policy they favoured. According to Plutarch, both Nicias and Alcibiades felt threatened and, in an interesting example of the political dynamics of the Assembly, they united their supporters to procure the banishment of Hyperbolus. Afterwards there was regret that ostracism had been used against such an unworthy target rather than a person of dangerous pre-eminence, which was its purpose. Aristotle later condemned factious use of ostracism, which the ostracism of Hyperbolus clearly was. The law was never employed again.[33]

Imperialism without Rules or Limits

The policies of Alcibiades firmly emerged in the course of 416 as the preferred option of the *demos*. A decision was made for reasons of strategic expediency in the summer of 416 to take control of the island of Melos in the south Aegean. It was a colony of Sparta, but had stayed neutral in the war until Athens made an unsuccessful attempt to take it over in 426. Thucydides does not associate Alcibiades directly with the expedition, but it fitted his policy perfectly, and one of the commanders was his friend Teisias, another radical young aristocrat who later became one of the Thirty Tyrants.

The Athenians first tried negotiation, and the exchanges between them and the Melian leaders have been immortalised in the famous account in Thucydides. He records the exchanges in the form of a dialogue, the only time he uses this eristic form of disputation, which was taught by the early Sophists and was, of course, favoured by Plato as a superior method of debate to set speeches, being more conducive to close, analytical discussion.

His unique use of this form and the abstract nature of the arguments have convinced many that the Melian dialogue is pure invention on the part of Thucydides to highlight his own reflections about power and empire. That seems an overstatement. The rhetorical form and elements of style and language are almost certainly creations of Thucydides, but to suggest that the substance does not represent the issues discussed and the sentiments expressed on the day is to call into question Thucydides' avowed commitment to truth and accuracy, and his clear statement that his speeches reproduced as closely as possible the general sense of what was actually said.

But how much could he have known about what was said at these closed negotiations? The Assembly must have been kept well informed about what was happening in that theatre of the war in 416. There was at least one debate on Melos, which followed its takeover, and after which it was voted to execute all adult males and enslave the women and children. Alcibiades was the chief advocate of that decision. No doubt, like Cleon in the Mytilenian debate, he rehearsed all the reasons why the Melians deserved the ultimate penalty, which would naturally have included reference to the negotiations and their refusal to accept the opportunity offered them by the Athenian negotiators to save their city. Thucydides was a diligent researcher who was gathering information about the events of the war as they happened, and it is reasonable to assume that a person of his background had a network of good sources. He could have known a great deal about all aspects of the Melian incident.

Why did he go to such lengths to provide such a detailed account in such an elaborate form of a negotiation concerning a relatively minor incident in the context of this great war? The answer would seem to be that he saw this unprovoked attack on a small island and its brutal outcome as a landmark event in the history of Athenian imperialism and a dramatic illustration of new influences and a new rhetoric that were leading Athens into a dangerously unrestrained form of imperialist doctrine without rules or limits. He was pursuing a general purpose of all the speeches to crystallise the thinking and influences that were dictating public policy and actions at a particular time.

In the dialogue the Athenian envoys quickly got to the nub of the matter by removing issues of justice from the debate and insisting that both sides must face the inescapable fact that the strong do whatever they have the power to do and the weak accept what they have to accept. They tried to show that it was expedient for both sides that Melos should come under Athenian rule. For Athens to leave Melos independent would be seen as a sign of weakness and would encourage others to think they could have independence too. The benefit to Melos of Athenian rule would be the preservation of the state.

The Melians, who had made no ground with a plea to the Athenians that they should not abolish the principles of justice and fairness in case they were themselves defeated and needed to appeal to them, had to fall back on the argument that they could trust in the gods since their cause was just, and in the Spartans, who were their kinsmen.

The Athenians dismissed both hopes. They maintained that their behaviour was not at odds with what men believe about the divine order. It was their opinion about the gods, and their firm belief about men, that both, in all circumstances, under the compulsion of the law of nature, ruled wherever they had the power. Athens did not make this law. It was eternal. As for the Melian hope of Spartan support, they mocked their naïveté, and assured them that the Spartans behaved virtuously with respect to their internal laws and relationships, but in dealing with others they, more than anyone, considered that what pleased them was honourable and that what was expedient for them was just. They urged the Melians not to be led astray by these false hopes or by any misguided sense of honour. There was no shame in yielding to the greatest state in Greece.

The dialogue is a stark and brutal statement of what the Athenians insisted was an inescapable truth, that *Realpolitik* is *Machtpolitik*. Power dictates everything. There is a compelling unchanging law, ingrained in the nature of gods and men, that those who have power will use it for their advantage, and those who do not have it will, if wise, accept what they cannot change.

The Melians refused to be persuaded and were overrun in 415. The Assembly voted for the ultimate penalty, the execution of adult males and the enslavement of women and children. According to Plutarch, Alcibiades was mainly responsible for the Assembly's decree. It was another act of savagery, this time against a small independent state whose only offence was that it did not want to be ruled by Athens. A colony was planted on the island. Athenian imperialism had taken on a true Calliclean cast.[34]

The following year the Athenians embarked on a far more ambitious and fateful venture, a large-scale expedition to Sicily. The pretext was a request for help from an ally, Egesta, which was in conflict with the Dorian stronghold of Syracuse. Athens had had involvements in Sicily since 427, designed to curb the power of Syracuse and prevent it being a resource for Sparta. But in 415 talk of conquest was in the air, and the size of the expedition and the excitement it generated in Athens indicate its goals went far beyond helping an ally. Thucydides reports that the Athenians had no difficulty assembling the large armament of about 150 ships and five thousand hoplites. They had recovered from the plague and the war. A younger generation had grown to manhood. Reserves from the tribute had built up again. Allies and metics were available to form a large part of the expedition. Once again Alcibiades was the main proponent of a proposal for war. His goal, according to Thucydides, was to gain the command, go on to conquer Sicily and Carthage, and achieve the power and wealth that would follow. Nicias, as so often, provided his main opposition, arguing strongly against the expedition.

The debate between them highlighted again the growing division in Athenian politics between the older conservative elements opposed to war and the young radicals bent on extending dominance for Athens and achieving power and wealth for themselves. Nicias warned, in Periclean fashion, of the dangers of undertaking risky new ventures far away, when Athens had so many enemies nearer home who were waiting for an opportunity to renew the war. He made a personal attack on Alcibiades and his lifestyle, accusing him of seeking war to fund his extravagant habits. He extended the attack to his like-minded young associates, who apparently had gathered in significant numbers on this occasion, summoned, according to Nicias, to support Alcibiades and put pressure on the Assembly to vote for war. He urged the older generation not to yield to this younger set who were besotted with empty fantasies, when what was needed was not passion but foresight. But he acknowledged the activist militarism of the *demos* itself by admitting that no speech of his was likely to alter its character or persuade it to protect what it had rather than endanger it for uncertain future hopes.

It was precisely to that character that Alcibiades appealed in his response. He defended his private life with typical swagger and boasted of the splendour of his achievements at the Olympic Games and in sponsoring choruses. He accepted that brilliance bred resentment, but he was intent nonetheless on being a doer of great deeds. It is a sign of strength.

He urged a similar attitude on his audience. Their empire was won, as were all empires, by vigorously responding to all those who sought help, and by pre-emptive action to forestall danger. They cannot now set a limit to the extent of their empire. They must rule or be ruled. Neither can they seek the quiet life, as others do, unless they want to become like them and totally change their habits. Acting together as of old, they must aim to make the city greater. It is only through conflict that they can maintain their skills and add to their experience. A state committed to action will be destroyed by inaction. They must live in accordance with their natural traits and traditions.

It was a powerful rallying call, appealing to every sense of patriotic pride and every instinct to be first and best, with no acceptance of any limit to the greatness of a superior nation. Echoes of the Calliclean superman claiming his rightful place at the top are unmistakeable.

The speech was greeted with high enthusiasm, and when Nicias, in the hope that he might still dissuade its members, asked for huge resources, the Assembly became even more captivated by the grandeur of the venture. The older citizens thought it would succeed or at least suffer no harm. The young were excited by the glamour of faraway places; the masses were confident that it would bring material benefits, and that an expanded empire would bring secure employment for the future.

Thucydides describes the departure of the expedition in midsummer. It was the most costly and splendidly equipped armada ever sent out by a single Greek state, and left in a carnival atmosphere, with crowds on the shore and elaborate ceremonies and songs dispatching the fleet with the highest hopes on the longest voyage ever made by an Athenian expedition. The description shows that Athenian imperialist ambitions had reached new and dangerous heights. The *demos* had fallen under the spell of a charismatic leader who had fully embraced the Sophistic doctrine of the natural rights of the strong.[35]

The Mutilation of the Herms

The debate over Sicily was a contest between the new wave of expansionist young aristocrats, led by Alcibiades, and a more cautious older generation represented by Nicias. There were still active politicians in the mould of Cleon but, especially after the ostracism of Hyperbolus, they were eclipsed by the rising influence of Alcibiades and his associates in foreign policy. The *demos*, as Nicias expected, was beguiled by the prospect of new conquests and sources of wealth, and was not disposed to listen to the counsels of caution. Support for the expedition was overwhelming.

But domestically Athens was becoming a more troubled society, increasingly fractured and unsettled. I have already highlighted aspects of the polarisation in discussions of the rise of the demagogues and the emergence of a new generation of aristocrats steeped in the new learning and political ideas that came with the era of the Sophists. The dramatists, especially Aristophanes and Euripides, provide abundant indications of the unsettling effects of both the demagogues and young radicals and the friction between them.[36]

Some weeks before the Sicilian expedition departed an incident occurred that illustrates the degree to which the mass of citizens were losing trust in the new generation of the aristocracy. A large number of herms – small bronze or marble pillars with a bust of Hermes on top, commonly placed in doorways of houses and shrines – were defaced in a single night. There were also allegations of mock celebrations of the Eleusinian Mysteries in private houses. Alcibiades was alleged to have been involved in the profanation of the Mysteries.

These were sacrilegious acts of shocking proportions to a religious people who considered themselves favourites of the gods and who were committed to their worship and to retaining their goodwill. But they were quickly built into something bigger and seen both as a bad omen for the Sicilian expedition and as evidence of revolutionary forces at work and intent on overthrowing the democracy. Suspicion naturally fell on the young radicals with their wanton lifestyles and newfangled ideas.

The fear and suspicion of the public were exploited by populist politicians, in particular two well-known demagogues, Peisander and Androcles, who saw an opportunity to bring down their enemy and rival, Alcibiades. They magnified the conspiracy theory and the role of Alcibiades, dwelling on his lifestyle and disregard for the social code of ordinary people. Alcibiades denied the charges and called for an immediate trial, but his enemies – afraid that, if he were tried at once, he would have the support of the army and popular goodwill – argued that the expedition should not be delayed, and he was allowed to sail with the fleet.

But there was a general mood of anger and suspicion, and fear that a plot was afoot to establish an oligarchy or a tyranny. A commission of inquiry was immediately established; Peisander was a member. Rewards of 100 minae were offered for information. Informers quickly came forward. Every piece of information was acted upon, regardless of source, to ensure that no one who might possibly be guilty could escape. Thucydides says large numbers of notable citizens were thrown into prison, and every day brought greater savagery and a greater number of arrests. He describes the mood as harsh and angry, born of fear that the oppression of the last days of the tyranny of Peisistratus and his sons might return. The level of fear is also reflected in the fact that the Council and Assembly met several times within a few days, and the generals were ordered to arm and assemble the citizens who were resident in Athens and between the Long Walls and in the Piraeus. The Knights (the upper-class cavalry) were also marshalled.

The tension only eased when a leading suspect, Andocides, a young noble well known for his oligarchic leanings, was persuaded by his cousin, who was imprisoned with him, to turn informer and save himself and his family. In return for immunity Andocides admitted his guilt in the affair of the herms and named the others involved. His story was believed, and the people felt they now had the truth. Those named who were already in custody or who failed to flee were tried and executed, those who managed to flee were condemned in their absence and had a price placed on their heads. Some at least had their property confiscated. The people were at last persuaded that Alcibiades was implicated. He was recalled from Sicily but escaped to Sparta, where he advised the Spartans about how to win the war.

We know from the surviving speech of Andocides, *On the Mysteries*, that at least forty-nine people were tried on a charge of impiety (*asebeia*), though there were allegations that three hundred were involved. There is enough information about more than half of those who were definitely indicted to provide a good indication of the social background and political persuasions of those behind the religious offences. Those named by Andocides himself were his friends and drinking companions, presumably club mates or members of associated clubs. Andocides was a young noble, branded as a *misodemos* with strongly oligarchic views. His friends are likely to have been from a similar background with similar political sympathies. There is other evidence about twenty-seven of the forty-nine that shows that they were all members of the upper class and were predominantly young, many of them products of the new intellectual movements, students of leading Sophists. At least seven, most notably Alcibiades and Critias, had links to Socrates. Various forms of connection between Alcibiades and the group can also be established. A further indication of their political affiliations is the reappearance of several of the group in the upheavals of 411 and 404/3. It is a safe conclusion that the cluster of sacrilegious acts in 415 was the work of the radical anti-democratic elements of the younger nobility.[37]

The purpose behind these acts is less clear. They represented an egregious religious outrage, but almost certainly did not have the revolutionary intent alleged by the demagogues and believed by the people. Thucydides considered the public response an overreaction caused by popular anxieties inflamed by demagogic rhetoric. The timing argues against any form of revolutionary move by the young oligarchs that might halt the imminent departure of the Sicilian expedition, which had such high importance for them. It is also difficult to see how they could have hoped that acts of impiety, though certain to stir outrage, could advance a conspiracy to overthrow the democracy.

It seems far more likely that the mutilations of statues and mockery of the Mysteries were escapades of the kind favoured by a high-living, hard-drinking, sophisticated, young elite, who got kicks from profaning religious beliefs and practices that they scorned. Andocides says the idea to deface the herms arose at a drinking party. He excuses his own involvement as youthful folly that gave way to a moment of madness. Other alleged defacements of statues were attributed to drunken vandalism. The conspiracy theory, as Thucydides suggests, was a mixture of public paranoia and demagogic opportunism.[38]

But whatever lay behind it, the affair of the herms and the Mysteries had major political consequences and left Athens in a seriously divided and unsettled state. The people believed they had come through a dangerous threat of revolution from elements of the new generation of the nobility to whom they would normally be looking for future leadership. Populist politicians used it to heighten further the popular fear and suspicion of the young nobility. It brought the recall of Alcibiades, a decision that arguably cost Athens victory in the Sicilian War, and made him a valuable resource for Sparta and a more resolute opponent of the democracy. It widened the gap between the people and the aristocracy as a whole, who saw the masses launch a savage witch-hunt that resulted in the execution or exile of large numbers of young nobles, and in some cases the confiscation of their property. The wounds from such a class-based civil upheaval inevitably damaged the traditional consensus between *demos* and elite.

The recall of Alcibiades left Nicias and Lamachus in charge of Sicily, and neither had the military talent required for such a formidable mission. They had some initial successes but, after the arrival of a Spartan general, Gylippus, with reinforcements in late 414, the tide turned. Nicias sent a letter to Athens in the winter of 414/13 clearly indicating that the situation was hopeless. But, instead of cutting their losses and withdrawing, the Athenians sent a second expedition of seventy-three triremes and five thousand hoplites under the command of Demosthenes and Eurymedon.

It all ended in defeat and eventual surrender. Nicias and Demosthenes were executed. Thucydides wrote about Nicias: 'of all the Greeks of my time, he least deserved to come to such a level of misfortune because of his lifelong devotion to the cultivation of virtue'. The prisoners were kept in terrible conditions in stone quarries for seventy days, and those who survived were then sold into slavery.

Thucydides memorably summarises the expedition and its outcome:

> this was the greatest action of the war, and in my view the greatest of all recorded Hellenic events. It was the most glorious for the victors and the most disastrous for the vanquished, who were utterly defeated on every front and whose suffering in every respect was largescale. It was utter destruction for the army, the navy and everything else. Only a few out of many made their way home.[39]

The Sicilian expedition represented the climax of an increasingly ruthless brand of *Machtpolitik* that emerged in Athens in the course of the Peloponnesian War. It was partly a consequence of the exigencies and brutalising effects of war emphasised by Thucydides, but was also crucially shaped by the two new brands of leadership that appeared in the post-Periclean era. An extreme form of ruthless militarism and amoral imperialism was fomented by the populist chauvinism of the demagogues. A still more cynical and cogent appeal to the activist, power-hungry instincts of the *demos* came from the charismatic Alcibiades, who was backed by a like-minded, radical elite who, like him, had grown up in the heady years of the 440s and 430s when Athenian power and affluence were at their height. They were eager for military success and all that came with it, and had absorbed the radical new thinking of an intellectually vibrant era about power and the natural forces that drive human beings in its pursuit and use. Their influence is evident in the foreign policy of the years after the Peace of Nicias, and it was they, rallying behind Alcibiades, who created the popular excitement that led to the deployment of so large a proportion of the resources of the state on a military adventure far away from the real threats to the safety of Athens within Greece itself. The high ambition that drove Athenian imperialism from its beginnings had finally overreached itself under the influence of demagogic jingoism, and the egotism and unrestrained aspirations of elements of a new generation of the elite fired by alluring new concepts of power and supremacy as the natural prerogative of the bold and the strong. The democracy had shown its vulnerable side.

The Descent into Civil Strife

News of the final defeat caused disbelief and consternation in Athens. The people realised they had too few ships in the dockyards, no crews to man them, no money in the treasury, no way of replacing the loss of so many of their prime fighting men. They expected to be attacked from all sides.

They had good reason for their disquiet. Thucydides says that, in the winter of 413/12, all of Greece wanted to rise against Athens. The Spartans under the command of King Agis had already invaded Attica in the spring of 413 and built a fortification at Decelea, which became permanent and cut off Athens from the silver mines at Laurium and from its agricultural produce. Thucydides highlighted the devastation and economic damage caused by the occupation, which effectively put Athens under siege, forced to man the city's battlements day and night. But the most far-reaching effect of the disaster was a further weakening of the long tradition of internal unity and stability that had been a mainstay of the democracy. The upper class had particular reason to feel aggrieved in the wake of the defeat. The costs of rebuilding the city's military resources fell mainly on them. So did the losses and hardships resulting from the continuous occupation of Decelea. But the blunders that caused these problems were ultimately blunders of the democracy, as Thucydides points out. It was the *demos* who ignored the advice of their more conservative advisors and decided to send the expedition. It was the *demos* who recalled Alcibiades, the one leader who might have made the venture a success, and it was the *demos* who decided to send a second expedition in 413, when it was clear from the dispatches from Nicias that the situation was beyond rescue.

Thucydides dwells particularly on what he saw as the incredible nature of this last decision, the sending of a second major expedition to besiege a city almost the size of Athens, at a time when Athens, already worn out by war, was itself besieged by the forces occupying Decelea. It showed an indomitable spirit, but it was folly, and its calamitous end gave reason to question the fitness of the *demos* to govern, and provided opponents with the right conditions for a move to overthrow the democracy.

Initially the concern of all parties was to secure the state against the threats that were erupting on every side. An effort was made to lessen apprehensions by the agreement of the Assembly to appoint ten older citizens (*probouloi*) to give preliminary advice as needed on immediate issues. They had authority to summon the Council and Assembly. Aristotle saw the office as an oligarchic feature, a check on the full Council.[40]

The main military threat arose in the eastern Aegean where the island of Chios revolted along with other allies on the Asiatic coast, including Mytilene and Miletus. The war now became largely centred in Ionia. The Spartans decided to equip a fleet of a hundred ships to send to the aid of the rebel Ionian cities. The satrap of Sardis, Tissaphernes, also got involved and made an alliance with Sparta, hoping to restore Persian control over the Asiatic coast. Alcibiades, whose relations with the Spartans deteriorated suddenly in 412, fled to Sardis and was welcomed by Tissaphernes, becoming his close advisor.

But Athenian forces coped well with the military challenges of 412. They retained control of the critical area of the Hellespont and blunted the impact of the Ionian revolt by recovering Mytilene and Lesbos and inflicting heavy defeats on the Chians. They supported a popular rising in Samos against the upper class, formally granted the island independence and won a loyal supporter for the remainder of the war. Samos became the main base for the Athenian fleet.

The Athenian recovery was helped by the general ineptitude of the Spartans in naval warfare and in the management of their new allies. The expected help from Tissaphernes also did not materialise. Alcibiades, whose ambition now was to get recalled to Athens, advised him to let both sides weaken each other and thereby give himself the superior position. He also argued that Athens would be a more suitable partner for him than Sparta.[41]

But despite the fact that Athens held its own against the odds in the aftermath of Sicily, a long war still loomed, and the strains were increasing the disillusionment with the rule of the *demos*. By the end of 412 moves were under way to overthrow the democracy, largely driven, according to Thucydides, by resentment of the burden the war was imposing on the upper class, and the belief of the conspirators that they could gain control of public affairs at Athens and win the war with Persian help.

Alcibiades was a prime mover in triggering a coup in the first half of 411. He sent word to the most influential Athenians at the base in Samos that, if an oligarchy were established, he was ready to return and secure the friendship of Tissaphernes for Athens. The trierarchs (warship commanders) and the other leading Athenians at Samos were already contemplating removing the democracy and readily responded to the offer. A delegation was sent to talk to him, and after they returned, a group of sworn conspirators was formed. They drew their friends into the plot along with most of the club fraternity (*to hetairikon*). They told the troops the King of Persia would be their friend and paymaster if Alcibiades were restored and democracy abolished. There was some disquiet about the proposals, but the prospect of pay from the King silenced dissent. The conspiracy was now broad-based, extending across the upper tiers of the large concentration of military forces at Samos.

The effort to involve the club fraternity is especially noteworthy, and was to have a decisive impact. The clubs and their political role have been mentioned earlier. They were largely the preserve of the younger nobility. They provided social diversions for the younger elite, but they were also an important means by which politicians could build a network of friends and create a grouping of political supporters. Membership of more than one club was possible, which meant a talented, charismatic politician could amass a formidable following of friends through this route.

There is plenty of evidence that friendship (*philia*) had great importance in the Athenian mind and in Athenian politics, just as *amicitia* had in republican Rome. Aristotle calls a friend another self. Xenophon says true friends will never fail each other whether the need is financial or political. Help your friend was a sacred principle. There were various ways of acquiring friends, including family ties, clan loyalties, marriage alliances and favours of different kinds. But the clubs widened the possibilities greatly, and the indications are that membership of them was the norm for the elite.

The importance of friends in the dynamics of Athenian politics is well documented. Plutarch describes them as the living, thinking tools of politicians. The clubs, which regularly brought together people steeped in politics, provided an obvious, ready-made mechanism by which friendships could be translated into political cooperation in pursuit of personal objectives. It is therefore not surprising that the activities of the clubs had always extended beyond the social to the political. Thucydides indicates such groups traditionally existed to help each other in lawsuits and in the pursuit of public office. Plutarch emphasises the power and protection Themistocles derived from membership of a *hetaireia*. He records that Aristides, who was renowned for his integrity, refused to join clubs because of their political character and the risk that the friendships involved and the power deriving from them could lead to wrongdoing. Plutarch also has the story that Cleon broke away from his friends at the start of his political career on the grounds that such friendships might divert him from the right political policies. Plutarch believed, however, that in this case Cleon was merely trying to get rid of his respectable *hetairoi* so he could pander to the wishes of the masses. Like Cleisthenes, his *hetaireia* was to be the *demos*.[42]

The evidence that the clubs were central in the creation and operations of political alliances and factions is also substantial. Thucydides actually uses the words *hetaireia* and *to hetairikon* to describe the factions in the Corcyraean Civil War. Herodotus also uses *hetaireia* in the sense of a political faction. The coalition of conservative politicians that grew up around Thucydides, son of Melesias, in the 440s to curtail the rising power of a democratically minded Pericles is called a *hetaireia* by Plutarch. A speech against Alcibiades, wrongly ascribed in the tradition to Andocides, though probably from the same era, attributes the ostracism of Hyperbolus in 416/15 to the fact that his opponents, who were Alcibiades, Nicias and possibly Phaeax, an aristocratic contemporary of Alcibiades, had *hetairoi* and *sunomosiai* (confederates and fellow conspirators). Plutarch uses both *hetaireia* and *stasis*, the common word for faction, to describe these coteries of opponents of Hyperbolus. The blurring of the distinction between clubs and factions indicates a growing politicisation of clubs in the fifth century and a tendency to view them as primarily political action groups.

It is likely that the politicisation accelerated from the late 420s onwards. The clubs were now dominated and given greater unity of political purpose by a very different generation of younger nobles with their new lifestyle, new learning, new views of politics and power, and new ambition to turn foreign and domestic politics in new directions. They also needed to coalesce to counter the hostility of the demagogues who harassed them in the courts and accused them of subversion.

Alcibiades was by far the most flamboyant and successful figure among the radical elements of the younger nobility, and it is clear that his *hetairoi* were an important element of his power-base. Their role in the ostracism of Hyperbolus is a good illustration. Not long afterwards, in the crucial debate on the Sicilian expedition, they were out again in force to support him in the Assembly. Nicias expressed his alarm at the sight of these young men with their dangerous delusions, who had been summoned by Alcibiades and were gathered around him, and he urged the older members of the Assembly not to be intimidated by them. The subjugation of Melos and its brutal aftermath also bear the hallmarks of the ambition and mentality of the young radicals, and we know that one of the leaders in that episode was a close friend of Alcibiades, and that it was Alcibiades who took the leading role in the Assembly's cruel treatment of the island.

The affair of the herms was undoubtedly the work of the clubs, and while it almost certainly did not have the subversive purpose alleged by the demagogues and believed by the people, it showed their capacity for well-organised, concerted action. The executions and banishments that followed the affair may have temporarily weakened that capacity, but may also have further radicalised them, and the particular effort made by the Samian conspirators to involve them in the plot shows that they were seen as a distinct and important political component likely to be sympathetic to an oligarchic conspiracy.[43]

The response of the club fraternity was clearly favourable, as subsequent events were to show. A delegation of the conspirators, headed by Peisander, the demagogue turned oligarch, arrived in Athens in early 411. Its chief mission was to persuade the Assembly that the only way to save the state was to adopt a different form of democracy and accept the return of Alcibiades, who could win them the help of Persia. Peisander got a reluctant consent, but then made the rounds of the clubs, urging them to unite and work for a far more radical course, the complete overthrow of democracy.

The clubs responded quickly and violently. The young radicals, the *neoteroi*, as Thucydides called them, were back in action, and this time intent on revolution.

They launched a covert campaign of violence, which started with the murder of Androcles, the demagogue believed to have been chiefly responsible for the banishment of Alcibiades. The club fraternity was still loyal to an old *hetairos*. Others whom they considered obstacles they similarly did away with in secret. They spread fear throughout the population, who did not know how widespread the conspiracy was or whom they could trust. The Assembly and Council were still convened, but were dominated by the young conspirators, who had previously proposed openly that only those on active service should receive pay, and that only five thousand, comprising those best able to help the state by their wealth and persons, should share in government.

When Peisander and his delegation returned to Athens in mid-411, they found a *demos* thoroughly cowed, and they had no difficulty in achieving their goals. At a meeting of the Assembly at Colonus, a little over a mile from Athens, about the middle of 411, Peisander proposed that a new Council of four hundred should be appointed with full powers to rule as they thought best. A wider body of five thousand was to be selected from those best able to serve the state by their possessions and persons. There was no opposition to the proposal.

The extent to which the *demos* proved helpless in the face of the violent tactics of the clubs is revealing. This time there was no demotic uprising similar to the one that had thwarted the efforts of Cleomenes and Isagoras in 508. Nor was there a reaction of the kind that followed the mutilation of the herms, when the Council and Assembly met repeatedly and ordered the generals to arm the citizens and marshal the Knights. The machinery of popular rule, the Council and Assembly, was seemingly leaderless, and the people demoralised. The proponents of oligarchy had taken firm hold of affairs in the city. Their brutality and terror tactics were at the extreme end of the scale.[44]

It was Peisander who pushed through the measures to establish the main elements of a new constitution. But it was the radical younger nobility, organised through the clubs, who provided the terror tactics that silenced opposition and, according to Thucydides, it was a group of intellectually sophisticated aristocrats who conceived the ideology behind the new order and designed its systems. He gives some details of three of these prime movers: Antiphon, Phrynichus and Theramenes.

He considered Antiphon the chief architect of the new constitution and the person who had given most thought to its design. He describes him as second to none in ability, and an outstanding thinker and speaker. The details of Antiphon's life are obscure and disputed, but what is certain is that he was an exceptional orator with an exceptional intellect, and an oligarchic ideologue who had a central place in the new educational and intellectual movements that emerged with the Sophists.

Thucydides calls Phrynichus the most fervent of all the supporters of oligarchy. He was a general at Samos and was one of the conspirators there, though a strong opponent of Alcibiades whom he totally distrusted. He got involved in intrigues with the Spartan commander Astyochus in an attempt to discredit Alcibiades, which led to his removal from office early in 411. He returned to Athens. As in the case of Antiphon, Thucydides stresses his reputation for intelligence, and in Aristophanes he is linked with a group of high-living aristocrats, which included Antiphon and others associated with the new culture of the era of the Sophists.

Theramenes is also singled out by Thucydides for his rhetorical and intellectual capacities. He came from a distinguished family, the son of Hagnon, a prominent, respected general in the 430s and 420s. He was educated by one of the most famous of the Sophists, Prodicus of Ceos. Thucydides says he was in the forefront of those conspiring to overthrow the democracy. All in all it is clear that the main players in both the conception and implementation of the system that emerged with the Four Hundred belonged to circles linked to the Sophists and to intellectual movements that came with the Sophists.[45]

The first indication of the character of the change being brought by the conspirators came from the young radicals who were leading the drive for revolution in the early months of 411. It centred on the principle that participation in government should be limited to those best able to help the state by their possessions and persons. This, as Thucydides explains, meant those who had, at the least, the wealth required for hoplite status. This principle became a prominent theme in the subsequent debates leading to the establishment of the new constitution. It was joined with an argument that the democratic reforms of the mid-fifth century had perverted, with disastrous results, the ancestral constitution (*patrios politeia*) as conceived by Solon and Cleisthenes. There was a division, however, among the revolutionaries about what the *patrios politeia* really meant. One element favoured broad participation by the propertied classes, but a more hard-core oligarchic faction was committed to the absolute rule of the few. Antiphon held fast to the latter view, while Theramenes favoured the former.

The accounts of Thucydides and Aristotle indicate that both views were, on the surface, taken into account in the decisions made at Colonus to establish both a Council of Five Thousand and a Council of Four Hundred. But the outcome was heavily weighted in favour of the oligarchic extremists, who secured the immediate appointment of the Four Hundred with absolute powers. It was also left to them to decide when the body of the Five Thousand should be established and how it should be used. Athens was in the grip of an absolute dictatorship of the few.[46]

The Four Hundred moved quickly to cement their position and instituted a rule of force. They got rid of potential opponents by executing a few and imprisoning or banishing others. They sent envoys to Samos to win over the soldiers, but in this they failed. The rank and file showed their loyalty to the democracy, and even before the envoys arrived, the army at Samos had taken matters into its own hands. The firm democrats among the generals at Samos, Leon and Diomedes, combined with two other democratic adherents, a trier-arch, Thrasybulus, and Thrasyllus, who is simply described as a hoplite, to thwart an oligarchic coup in Samos itself. This led on to a pact, initiated by Thrasybulus and Thrasyllus, between Samian democrats and the rank and file of the Athenian forces to work in harmony to preserve democracy. The troops immediately called an Assembly, deposed the existing generals and elected others, among them Thrasybulus and Thrasyllus. They felt they had in Samos a state that was not weak, since they had the entire fleet in their control and could compel the other states under Athenian rule to pay tribute to them, not Athens. They still believed that Alcibiades, if recalled from exile, could win them an alliance with the king, and they accordingly recalled him. He came to Samos and had a beneficial effect in that he kept the troops focused on the war rather than on the politics at Athens.[47]

Meanwhile the Council of Four Hundred was beginning to disintegrate. Increasing disunity, which Thucydides describes as typical of oligarchies; fear of the army at Samos and the power of Alcibiades; the autocratic behaviour of the more extreme elements of the Four Hundred, who began to negotiate with Sparta and refused to nominate and activate the Council of Five Thousand as demanded by members such as Theramenes and Aristocrates, another prominent moderate – all of these factors undermined the confidence and stability of the regime. Increasing interventions by disillusioned hoplites stationed in the Piraeus posed a further threat. Matters came to a head in September, when a Spartan fleet moved against Euboea, defeated an Athenian squadron hurriedly mustered and caused all of Euboea to revolt. There was panic in Athens. An Assembly was called, meeting in its traditional location, the Pnyx, which deposed the Four Hundred and voted to give control of public affairs to the body of Five Thousand drawn from those of hoplite status. Pay for all in public office was abolished.

At further meetings Alcibiades and other exiles were recalled. Envoys were sent to Alcibiades and the army at Samos to invite their participation. Most of the extreme oligarchs fled to Decelea. Others were prosecuted, though under due process of law. Among them was Antiphon, who was convicted of treason and executed.

Theramenes and Aristocrates get the main credit in the sources for the deci-sions made at the Assembly, and it was presumably they who took the initiative in convening it. There was apparently no attempt at this point to restore full democracy. The perilous state in which the city found itself and the role of the moderates in ending the regime of the Four Hundred provided enough reason to accept, at least for the moment, a modification of the constitution that would give control of affairs (*ta pragmata*) to a body of Five Thousand drawn from those who were able to contribute most to the state's security.

Apart from this substitution of the sovereignty of the Five Thousand for the sovereignty of the full *demos*, little is known about the other constitutional elements of the new regime. Thucydides mentions that a number of meetings were held after the Five Thousand took office that appointed lawgivers (*nomothetai*) and dealt with other constitutional matters. The reference to lawgivers presumably means that a commission was appointed to pursue an objective of the moderates which, as already mentioned, first surfaced in 411 – to create a constitution based on the principles of the ancestral constitution (*patrios politeia*) that evolved with the laws of Solon and Cleisthenes. There is also evidence that the traditional Council of Five Hundred was restored and that senior officials were elected, presumably by the Five Thousand. All else is uncertain.

Thucydides' view of the new constitution has been discussed earlier in some detail. He considered it a measured blend of the few and the many that gave Athens good government and its first lift out of the awful plight that had befallen it. But it lasted less than a year, giving way in the middle of 410 to a restoration of full democracy. The *History* of Thucydides ends abruptly in 411, and no details are given in our sources of the circumstances surrounding the demise of the Five Thousand. Aristotle simply says that the *demos* deprived the Five Thousand of its control of government. But the likeliest reason for it was a series of victories by the Athenian fleet in the Aegean in 411/10, which largely removed the justification for the limitations on democracy that the Five Thousand imposed. It was probably always intended that the regime would be a temporary arrangement, a form of crisis management to see Athens through the war and at the same time update and clarify its laws and constitutional practices.[48]

The performance of the restored democracy over the following five years was an extraordinary mixture of successes and blunders. The Athenian fleet, commanded by Alcibiades, Thrasybulus and Theramenes, virtually destroyed the Peloponnesian navy in an encounter at Cyzicus in spring 410. The victory brought an offer of peace from Sparta on the basis that each should hold on to what it already had, but the Athenians, urged on by Cleophon, a new, forceful, populist warmonger in the mould of Cleon, rashly rejected the offer. More success followed in 409/8, largely due to the military skills of Alcibiades. He finally returned to Athens in 407 after an eight-year absence and was fully reconciled with the *demos*. He was given absolute powers to direct the war.

Some of the actions that quickly followed illustrate the intensity of the commitment to the democratic ideal that still persisted. Within a month of the restoration of full democracy a law was introduced by one of the commission of lawgivers, Demophantus, which stated that anyone who attempted to overthrow the democracy or took office after such an overthrow would be considered a public enemy and could be killed with impunity and have his property confiscated. Another law prescribed that Councillors be allotted seats and should not sit elsewhere, a measure clearly intended to end the tactic of massing supporters to sway meetings, a tactic which we know was used in the Assembly and also presumably in the Council. Severe action against those involved with the Four Hundred continued. A sign of the extent of the vindictiveness is contained in a plea for amnesty in the parabasis of the *Frogs* of Aristophanes, which was produced in 405. The restored democracy was affirming its control with determination.[49]

The military situation took a fresh turn when, in 407, Sparta appointed a new brand of commander, Lysander – ruthless, ambitious, a brilliant military strategist with strong diplomatic skills. He won the firm support of Cyrus, son of the Persian king, and now satrap of Sardis in place of Tissaphernes. He became an invaluable ally of Sparta, providing the money needed for ships and professional crews.

Early in 406 Lysander defeated an Athenian squadron at Notium. Alcibiades was not present, but he took the blame, and a fickle, impulsive *demos* replaced him and most of his fellow generals and appointed a new board. Cleophon, like all demagogues a bitter opponent of Alcibiades, was again a primary influence in the decision. He also secured the banishment of Critias, a loyal friend of Alcibiades who had proposed his recall in 407. Alcibiades retired to Thrace. He was replaced by Conon, an aristocrat with a strong record of service to democracy. Lysander's successor made further advances in the late spring of 406, and Conon found himself blockaded in Mytilene.

There was an air of crisis in Athens once more. The *demos* responded with another all-out effort and managed to send another 110 ships to the Aegean by the middle of 406. Allied ships raised the number to 150. The greatest naval battle of the war took place at Arginusae, south of Lesbos, in late 406, and the Athenians scored another resounding victory. But they lost twenty-five ships and five thousand men, many of whom died in the water when rescue efforts failed in bad weather. There was a huge reaction to the deaths in Athens and the eight generals involved in Arginusae were recalled and charged before the Assembly as a group, and condemned in a single vote in a process of questionable legality. The

1. The Acropolis, the imposing citadel of Athens, site of some of the most splendid architectural masterpieces of the Periclean building programme of the 440s and 430s, notably the majestic Doric temple to Athena, the Parthenon, and the monumental entrance to the Acropolis, the Propylaea.

2. The Pynx was a gently sloping hill south-west of the Agora and was the meeting place of the Assembly from c. 460 B.C. onwards. Previously the Assembly had normally met in the Agora. The site was radically reconstructed c. 400 B.C., creating a fully enclosed and enlarged theatre-shaped space with seating for about 6,000. Citizens could sit where they wished: all had equal status.

10. Aristotle (384–322 B.C.) was a native of Stagira in Chalcidice. He came to Athens in 367 as a student in Plato's Academy and remained there as student and scholar until Plato's death in 347. Later he was tutor to Alexander the Great, but returned to Athens in 335 to found his own school, the Lyceum. He was a polymath, scientist as well as philosopher, an empiricist who relied on hard evidence rather than solely theoretical speculation. His influence has been pervasive, extending to Islamic as well as Christian thought. After Alexander's death in 323, anti-Macedonian feeling in Athens caused him to leave the city. He died a year later in Chalcis.

11. Throwing the discus and javelin were major features of Greek athletic contests, along with running, wrestling and chariot-racing. These contests were the centrepiece of the four great Panhellenic Festivals – the Olympian, Pythian, Isthmian and Nemean Games – when panhellenism temporarily took hold, all hostilities were suspended, and Greeks joined together in celebrating athletic prowess.

12. The symposium was a drinking party following a meal, a common feature of the social life of the male upper classes. It took place in a separate room of the house known as the andron, the men's quarter. Wives were excluded, but it was common to have female entertainment, musical or sexual, provided by courtesans.

13. Spinning and weaving were part of the household duties of Athenian women. In Xenophon's dialogue on household management, the Oeconomicus, turning wool into clothing is listed as one of the responsibilities of the wife. In wealthier families, slaves likely did the work under the supervision of the mistress of the household. There was also a cloth-manufacturing industry that would have provided some of the needs of the wealthy.

14. It is difficult to determine the level of literacy in classical Athens, especially among women. The sources are largely silent about the education of women, but the general attitude towards them and their role in society suggests few received any significant amount of formal education. But the evidence of vase painting, such as this one, indicates that at least some upper-class women were literate.

15. Many Athenian houses had wells or cisterns in the courtyard for collecting rainwater. But water, presumably for drinking, was also collected from fountain houses. It was a standard task of women, one of the few occasions when they got out of the house and could enjoy female company. The south-east fountain house in the Agora was a major infrastructural development of the era of Peisistratus, giving the city piped potable water for the first time.

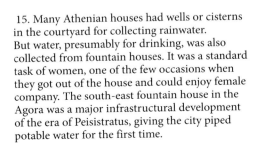

six who had actually returned were executed, including Thrasyllus and the son of Pericles. Xenophon records that there were some speakers who argued in the debate that this procedure was contrary to the law, but they were answered by shouts from the body of the Assembly that it was a terrible thing if the *demos* was not allowed to do whatever it wished. Socrates, a member of the *prytaneis*, the presiding officers of the Assembly, showed his objection by refusing to join his colleagues in putting the motion for a single vote on the fate of all eight generals. But all objections were ignored and the vote was taken. The Athenians compounded this error by rejecting yet another peace offer from Sparta, persuaded once again by the warmongers led by Cleophon. These were actions that displayed a level of volatility and misjudgement that brought further discredit on the concept of popular rule.[50]

Lysander was back in command in 405 and, with aid from Cyrus, assembled an armada of two hundred ships and moved to the Hellespont where he captured Lampsacus. Conon with 180 ships confronted him at Aegospotami, almost directly opposite. Alcibiades came from Thrace to warn about the dangers of the location, but Conon chose to ignore him. For days Lysander refused to fight, then suddenly attacked when most of the Athenians were foraging ashore. The entire Athenian fleet was captured, except for nine ships that escaped with Conon. The Spartan allies, remembering the cruelties Athens had perpetrated in the war, demanded the execution of the prisoners, and three thousand were put to death. The victory was total. By the end of 405 Lysander was blockading the Piraeus and the Spartan king, Pausanias, was besieging the city by land. The strategy was to starve the city into surrender. The Athenians were determined to hold out, but as famine took hold they sought negotiations, which were led by Theramenes. Again the Spartan allies wanted the extreme penalty that Athens had meted out to cities such as Scione and Melos, but the Spartans refused to enslave the city that had protected Greek liberty in the Persian Wars, and offered relatively lenient terms in the circumstances. Athens had to pull down the Long Walls and the fortifications at the Piraeus, abandon the empire, surrender all but twelve triremes and recall all exiles. It was allowed to retain its domestic autonomy on condition that it was governed in accordance with the ancestral constitution, but in foreign affairs it was required to follow the lead of Sparta. Lysander accepted the surrender of Athens in late March 404.[51]

Athens was left with domestic autonomy, but that did not restore unity or stability to Athenian politics. The democracy had less credibility and acceptability than ever, though it still had many vigorous proponents intent on preserving it. The moderate oligarchs who had supported the Five Thousand were still wedded to their vision of the ancestral constitution. The more extreme oligarchs, strengthened by the return of the exiles under the provisions of the peace, were another powerful force, and were aided by the radicals of the political clubs who were again organising, and were now seeking to create a Spartan-style constitution. They had signalled their intentions by appointing five Ephors to lead their efforts.

In the late summer of 404 action was finally taken by the oligarchic elements to establish a new political order. They invited Lysander to return to Athens to help them achieve their goal. He attended a meeting of the Assembly and supplied the necessary pressure to secure approval of a proposal by the oligarch Dracontides to establish a group of thirty to write a constitution based on the ancestral constitution, and in the meantime to manage all the affairs of the state. The main leaders were Theramenes and Critias.

The reign of the Thirty began moderately, but no real effort was made to produce a constitution in line with the *patrios politeia*. The extreme elements, led by Critias, were intent on a different model more in line with the Spartan tradition. There soon began a purge of likely opponents. As many as 1,500 were executed and a great many more were banished. A list of three thousand was compiled, who alone would have full citizen rights, which meant the regime was to be a narrow oligarchy headed by an all-powerful executive of thirty. The later disarming of all others, further expulsions and the subjugation of all, other than the Three Thousand, to the will of the Thirty without legal protections meant that the much-feared tyranny to which Thucydides referred in his account of the affair of the herms had become a reality for the majority.

The similarities with the Spartan system have often been noted, though the regime of the Thirty was far more absolute and extreme. The Thirty, who held supreme authority, bore a resemblance to the Spartan *gerousia*, which also numbered thirty. The body of the Three Thousand, who formed an elite group of full citizens, was analogous to the select group of full citizens at Sparta, the so-called *homoioi*, and the lesser citizens and metics had a status similar in many respects to that of the class of dependants in Laconia known as *perioikoi*.[52]

The driving force behind the regime and the methods used to impose it was Critias, a noted Laconophile and an ardent oligarchic ideologue. He belonged to the high nobility and was closely associated with the new learning and new thinking of the Sophistic era. He had a range of intellectual talents, and was a prolific writer, a one-time pupil of Socrates and a bosom friend of the other famous Socratic protégé, Alcibiades. Plato lists him among those who flocked around great Sophistic figures such as Protagoras, and he used him as an interlocutor of Socrates in several dialogues.

Not much is known about his early political views or activities, but he certainly had links to the club fraternity and was implicated in the affair of the herms. His association with the *hetaireiai* is evidenced by his selection as one of the Ephors appointed by the clubs to lead their cause in 404. There is no reason to believe that he was prominent in the revolution of the Four Hundred but, following his return in 404 from the exile imposed on him in the backlash against Alcibiades after the defeat at Notium, he emerged as a foremost activist in the movement to overthrow the democracy. His role in shaping and directing the regime of the Thirty was pivotal.[53]

The increasing extremism alienated the moderates led by Theramenes. It also caused some of the exiles to come together to resist the regime. Thrasybulus provided the leadership. In the winter of 404/3 a band of seventy seized Pyle, a stronghold near the border with Boeotia. Military efforts by the Thirty failed to dislodge them. The Thirty reacted to the threat with further steps to protect their power. They sought help from Sparta, and seven hundred troops were sent and stationed on the Acropolis. All citizens other than the Three Thousand were disarmed and large numbers were excluded from the city and forced to move to the Piraeus. Metics also became targets of the Thirty. The Council ratified a measure to give the Thirty powers of life and death over any citizen not a member of the Three Thousand. Another measure deprived all who had opposed the earlier Four Hundred of their rights as citizens. This may have been specifically directed at Theramenes, who was executed soon afterwards. The level of repression and brutality increased.

By late April 403 Thrasybulus had a force of seven hundred and succeeded in seizing the Piraeus, where the citizens excluded from the city naturally rallied to his cause. He established a camp on the hill of Munychia. The Thirty led their forces against him, but were heavily defeated and Critias was killed. The victory swelled the forces of Thrasybulus still further.

The oligarchs were now in disarray and hopelessly divided. There was a meeting of the Three Thousand, which deposed the Thirty and appointed in their place a body of ten with full powers to bring the war to an end. The surviving members of the Thirty fled to Eleusis, which they had earlier seized with their cavalry as an additional stronghold.

The Ten made no progress against the rebels in the Piraeus and had to appeal to Sparta for more help. They were deposed and a second board of Ten of more moderate views was appointed. Lysander was sent with forty ships and blockaded the Piraeus. But soon afterwards the Spartan king, Pausanias, was dispatched with an army to take control. He quickly concluded that the best option for Sparta was to seek to reconcile the warring parties, the democrats in the Piraeus and the oligarchs in the city. With the help of the delegation of mediators from Sparta and strong cooperation from the democrats in the Piraeus and the second Ten, Pausanias succeeded about September 403 in concluding an agreement that brought peace and reconciliation, and eventually the restoration of democracy in all its essential aspects.[54]

Summary and Conclusions

The last thirty years of the fifth century were the most turbulent, traumatic period in the history of the democracy, and tell a good deal about both its flaws and its merits. It was the one period when the stability and high level of consensus (*homonoia*) that were the hallmarks of the democracy from its inception broke down, precipitating major civil upheaval. It is worth reviewing the strong foundations on which that stability rested, before summarising conclusions about the factors that caused its collapse with such drastic consequences.

The democracy grew out of a popular uprising in support of a member of the high nobility and his pledge to give power to the people. The thoroughness with which that pledge was carried out generated in the people a sense of engagement and a broad loyalty to the constitution, and a new energy based on the belief that, in working for the state, they were working for themselves. The system of demes, tribes, Council, Assembly and courts embedded the democratic ideal at grassroots level and ensured ultimate popular control of decision-making. It also opened an opportunity for all citizens to participate in public affairs, both locally and nationally and at the deliberative and executive levels. The culture of participation was also promoted by maximising equal opportunities to hold public offices, outside those requiring special expertise, through annual rotation, use of the lot and the introduction of pay. The system was in accord with Aristotle's later thesis that citizens must be groomed in the spirit of the constitution and attuned by force of habit to its temper and to an understanding of how to preserve it. Aristotle believed there was no better means of ensuring the permanence of constitutions.

The integration of the lowest class, the thetes, into the political system was of particular importance. This happened mainly as a result of the decision to make Athens a major sea power. The thetes provided the naval skills and became the most important element of the military forces. The Old Oligarch concisely described the political effects when he wrote that it seemed right to everyone that those who manned the ships and, more than anyone else, gave the state its power should have a share in public office and the right to speak on public affairs. The thetes also benefited from the prosperity that came with empire as the opportunities for employment and enterprise multiplied. There was no idle, alienated urban proletariat in fifth-century Athens such as existed, with destructive effect, in the last generation of the Roman Republic. The thetes were later to show that they were the staunchest defenders of the democracy, in line with Aristotle's statement that wherever there was a strong navy, there was a strong democracy.

The greatest challenge facing the emergent democracy was, of course, the threat that such transformative political change would bring social division and face resistance from the traditional nobility, long accustomed to rule and imbued with the belief that only the high-born had the inbred *arete* required for political leadership. But that threat never materialised at Athens. The democracy was not the outcome of class conflict or mass popular agitation for power, or the work of a messianic leader from the lower classes. There is no denying that the mass of citizens were eager for a greater say in political affairs, and that the reforms of Solon and the cultivation of the masses by Peisistratus had accustomed them to a political role, but the evolution of the radical form of democracy that took root in Athens was, from the beginning, led by high-born aristocrats, most of them *eupatridai*, the highest tier of the nobility. It was they who shaped the democratic ideal. Whether they acted from opportunism and the conviction that the people were the best *hetaireia* they could have, or from the conviction, certainly held by Pericles, that the rule of the people posed no threat to the upper classes and was the best route to a successful society, is a matter of debate. But what is certain is that from the start the *demos* recognised the need for ability and expertise at the head of the most critical areas of government, and they found the necessary talents mostly among the elite. The offices that controlled the most important functions remained electoral and the *demos* consistently elected to them members of the high nobility who won their trust. The Old Oligarch admired their pragmatism in accepting that the wealthy and the well-born were best qualified to lead them in areas where the stakes were highest.

The result was that the Athenian state in the fifth century continued to be led for the most part by able aristocrats, and to such an extent that Plato (*Menex.* 238c–d) has Socrates recite a speech that he says he learned from Aspasia, the mistress of Pericles, in which he suggests that the constitution was an aristocracy with the consent of the majority. That was certainly an overstatement, but the reality was that the traditional aristocracy continued to have a meaningful political role and the opportunity to compete for power and to wield decisive influence when they had the skills to command public confidence. Pericles, of course, provides the greatest example. The reconciliation of the aristocracy to the notion of popular government was also helped by the fact that threats to the prosperity of the wealthy elite, commonly alleged to be a feature of democracies, never materialised at Athens. Solon had decisively dealt with this issue, rejecting calls for a redistribution of wealth and arguing that justice did not entail equal shares for all in a country's wealth. He maintained that the cause of the poor could not be advanced through injustice to others. The Athenians never departed from that prescription. The rich made public contributions through the system of liturgies which supported religious festivals and covered some of the costs of the navy, and there was a general culture of 'euergetism' (*euergesia*) which expected and politically rewarded voluntary giving by the wealthy to meet public needs. A special tax (*eisphora*) was also levied in times of emergency, but there is no evidence that it was excessively burdensome. The main assets of the rich were never at risk from the *demos*. The developed democratic constitution had managed to create conditions for a high level of harmony between the classes and a high level of political consensus.

But, not surprisingly, it was never a total consensus. There remained a core of aristocratic dissenters who never accepted that there was sense or justice in entrusting the safety and well-being of the state to the lowly multitude. They could accept the Solonian constitution and many revered it as the true ancestral constitution of Athens, and saw it as representing a fair balance that gave a significant say to all citizens, but reserved leadership and control for the upper classes, where the greatest merit resided. But absolute equality, which inevitably meant the sovereignty of those whom they regarded as least worthy, was a step too far. The Old Oligarch has left us the starkest statement of this view, but the poems of Theognis and Pindar, sections of Thucydides and Isocrates, and, most especially, the writings of Plato and Aristotle show how deep-rooted, if limited, the anti-democratic bias was.

But as the Old Oligarch emphasises, there was little opportunity for the dissenters to act on their beliefs. The democracy was well safeguarded against revolution. While the *demos* were willing to delegate power, they never lost control over those on whom they conferred it. The term of annual office and the requirement of re-election for any extension, combined with a rigorous, almost constant system of accountability, left little scope for the accumulation of power, and meant that even a Pericles could face immediate dismissal and retribution for any perceived failure or malfeasance.

Other features of the system also guarded against the emergence of dangerously powerful individuals or groups. After the dismantling of the powers of the Areopagus there was no permanent forum, such as was provided, for example, by the Roman Senate, that would allow an elite to build a commanding influence on public affairs. There was no excluded, impoverished lower class or system of clientage of the Roman variety to enable the ambitious to build a base of power through patronage. The structure and character of the armed forces also left little scope for the emergence of a strong man able to command military backing. The thetes and hoplites were the heart of the military power of

Athens, as the Old Oligarch testifies. They were a part-time militia with a civilian life and a central place in political decision-making. They were the most loyal of democrats and the least likely to support the ambitions of would-be dictators or oligarchic factions and welcome back an age of tyrants or faction-ridden politics. As a final safeguard against threats to the democracy, Cleisthenes had put in place the extreme expedient of ostracism for use against those whose power, or hunger for power, or potential for disruption, seemed to pose a danger to the state.

The breakdown of the stability of this well-hedged constitution began in the 420s. The hardships of war and plague helped create the conditions for it. Thucydides believed the cruelties of war undermined the moral fibre of society, and he traced a trend towards greater lawlessness (*anomia*) in Athens to the hardships inflicted by the plague. A prudent but frustrating strategy of war that meant Athenians had to endure repeated invasions and devastations of their homeland – forcing the rural population to abandon home and property and live virtually under siege for lengthy periods in an overcrowded city – undoubtedly generated dissatisfaction and social and political strains. But the greatest destabilising factors were the emergence of two new political forces, represented by the demagogues and the radical elements of the younger nobility. The dearth of eminent, authoritative, aristocratic leaders, loyal to the democracy in the decades following the death of Pericles, gave scope for both to acquire political influence. They came from opposite ends of the upper-class social scale, the demagogues from the nouveaux riches, the radical aristocrats from the upper reaches of the nobility. They were bitter political opponents and had opposite views of democracy. But both helped foment the militarism and the imperialist drive that characterised Athenian behaviour throughout most of the war and proved major obstacles to peace, though it was the young radicals, with Alcibiades in the lead, who were chiefly responsible for the breakdown of the Peace of Nicias and for the Sicilian adventure, which proved so destructive.

The political methods and behaviour of both were highly divisive, generating suspicion and apprehension among the body politic. The demagogues pursued the politics of division and confrontation, seeking advantage over better-placed aristocratic rivals by exploiting the instinctive prejudices and resentments of the lower classes against a privileged, leisured, well-educated elite. In contrast, they presented themselves as people of the masses, devoted to the interests of the masses, pitting mass popularity against the advantages of social privilege and social networks. A new political rhetoric dividing politicians into those who loved democracy and those who hated democracy began to appear in the late 420s, the demagogues laying claim to being the true devotees of the rule of the people. They used the courts to extend popular suspicion of the elite, exploiting the rigorous system of accountability to pursue allegations of incompetence or malfeasance. The new politics will have exacerbated the alienation of those elements of the aristocracy, typified by the Old Oligarch, who were implacably opposed to the concept of radical democracy, and will have widened the ranks of the more moderate oligarchs who yearned for the constitution of Solon. Consensus was breaking down. The machinations surrounding the ostracism of Hyperbolus in 416 or early 415 show how fractious Athenian politics had become by the time of the Sicilian expedition.

The destabilising impact of the young radicals, however, was to prove far more decisive than that of the demagogues. They were a striking new phenomenon in Athenian politics, schooled not in the spirit of the constitution, as Aristotle advised, but in the radical thinking of the new intellectual movements that raised visions of power and forms of rule that were the antithesis of the democratic ideal.

The young radicals were divisive in several ways. They were not only at loggerheads with the demagogues, but with the more conservative elements of the aristocracy as a whole. The speech of Nicias on the Sicilian expedition illustrates the extent of the gap that had opened between the older and younger members of the political elite. The gap was cultural as well as political. The extravagant lifestyle of the new generations of the nobility and their obvious disregard for conventional mores made them suspect to the general public, though there remained a certain admiration for their flair and for the new rhetorical skills they brought to public life. These had a natural appeal for a people who relished debate and admired all forms of verbal artistry. The flamboyance and bravado of an Alcibiades certainly appealed to the activist, adventurist side of the Athenian character, as evidenced by his repeated military commands. Aristophanes later described the love/hate relationship the *demos* had with him. He and his kind stirred feelings of admiration and fascination, but these were heavily tinged with suspicions of revolutionary design. The young radicals were an unsettling phenomenon for the *demos*.

The demagogues did their best to reinforce popular suspicions of the younger nobility. As early as the 420s Cleon was accusing them of conspiracy against the *demos*. They were presented as the prime example of the *misodemoi*, haters of the people and a threat to the democracy. There is no evidence to support the allegations of Cleon, but the frequency of references to conspirators and conspiracy in the plays of Aristophanes, such as the *Knights* and the *Wasps*, from the later 420s indicates that, even allowing for the hyperbole of comedy, conspiracy was in the air and alarming the public.

The degree of that alarm was to be illustrated in dramatic fashion in the events surrounding the mutilation of the herms. The popular reaction was extreme, radicalising further a powerful social segment already out of sympathy with democratic values. But the negative influence of the demagogues and the radical aristocrats was not confined to damage done to political consensus and social cohesion. It also contributed to a series of blunders that eventually brought defeat and large-scale civil strife. The demagogues and the radicals both impeded peace and promoted aggressive policies of naked imperialism that culminated in the ill-fated Sicilian expedition. It was the scale of that disaster and the burdens that it placed on the upper class that provided the trigger for the overthrow of the democracy in 411. The democracy staged a quick recovery, but no lessons were learned. The warmongers continued to hold sway, and offers of peace from Sparta were scorned on two occasions, after the victories at Cyzicus in 410 and Arginusae in 406. These were the last opportunities Athens had for a favourable settlement. A year later Lysander was blockading the Piraeus, and Athens had to negotiate a surrender.

But the flaws in Athenian conduct of the war and in the general tenor of its foreign policy cannot be blamed entirely on the waywardness of its leaders. Weaknesses were also revealed in the democracy at the level of the *demos* itself. It gave its sanction through the Assembly to every major decision taken in the war, and it bore ultimate responsibility for those decisions, despite the tendency to blame mistakes on its advisors.

The very essence of Athenian democracy was that it gave direct power to the people, a concept that drew its legitimacy from the belief that the members of a state constituted a community of free and equal citizens, all entitled to an equal say in deciding the common interests of all. It also presupposed that ordinary citizens had the capacity to make sensible decisions about what their best interests were, and that their collective judgement was the proper determinant of the common good. Even Aristotle saw merit in that view, and conceded that the collective judgement of the many, with each adding something of value, was on the whole more likely to be right than the judgement of the expert few. In the popular Assembly there was ample scope for such experts to give their advice and attempt to influence outcomes, but decisions taken represented the collective judgement of the mass, and responsibility for them rested with the mass.

In the course of the Peloponnesian War, that judgement too often proved defective. The fault lay in the readiness with which the *demos* succumbed to the allurements of the chauvinistic militarism of the demagogues and the heady supremacism of the young radicals, and in its refusal to heed the advice of long-trusted moderates such as Nicias. The *arete* of the early democracy, characterised by the self-belief and courageous energetic pursuit of high achievement and glory that brought Athens victory in the Persian Wars and mastery of the sea and an empire, had degenerated into a harsher imperialism and lust for dominion that was devoid of any noble attribute or moral sensibility, and that was certainly unconcerned with the justice and restraint that Solon had propounded as the cornerstones of a healthy society.

The *demos* increasingly absorbed the extremist new philosophy of the rights of the strong. The hubris that Solon had warned was the forerunner of delusion and destruction (*ate*) was coming more into evidence. The 'will to power' was prevailing over prudence and morality. The brutal takeover of Melos epitomised the new ethos. It was soon followed by enthusiastic acceptance of the rallying call of Alcibiades to invade Sicily, to set no limits to the Athenian empire, to keep alive its activist spirit and lead the city on to still greater power as the current generation's ancestors had done. Nicias acknowledged in the debate that any effort of his to change the temper of his audience or persuade them to put safety before risk would have no effect. Half a century later Isocrates wrote in strong terms about the follies of this era and the indiscipline (*akolasia*), hubris and obsession with empire that led to them.

The mistakes multiplied. The recall of Alcibiades from the Sicilian command and the extreme reaction to the affair of the herms contributed to defeat and division and led on to the revolution of 411. The revolution was quickly overturned, but the flaws in the behaviour of the *demos* continued. No lessons had been learned. The rejection of the peace offer from Sparta after the victory at Cyzicus in 410; the dismissal of Alcibiades from his command for the second time, along with most of his fellow generals after the setback at Notium in 407/6; the rejection of a further peace offer after the victory at Arginusae in late 406; and the decision to condemn to death all eight generals who had achieved the victory because of a failure to rescue shipwrecked sailors owing to a storm – all of these decisions showed the *demos* at its most erratic and capricious.

The condemnation of the generals en masse by a single vote had far-reaching implications. It was a clear violation of the law, and the debate revealed a disposition among the mass of the Assembly to challenge any limitation on the right of the *demos* to decide whatever it wished. The one check on the power of the people under the democracy was the requirement to abide by the rule of law as the safeguard of all citizens against any form of abuse of power. In the Funeral Oration, Pericles identified reverence for law and authority as one of the strengths of democracy. The requirement to govern in accordance with the law had been made explicit by the introducion of the *graphe paranomon*, which made anyone who introduced a proposal contrary to established law in the Assembly liable to prosecution. The emotional disregard of this fundamental bulwark of orderly stable government in the wake of the battle of Arginusae revealed a democracy that was dangerously lurching towards ochlocracy. Soon afterwards came the calamity at Aegospotami, which quickly brought the blockade of Athens and forced a surrender. There followed what Athenians feared most, a lawless tyranny.

But while the war revealed fault lines in the system, it also highlighted some notable enduring strengths. The survival of the democracy through almost three decades of gruelling warfare and a series of setbacks and catastrophic errors culminating in total defeat and a tyrannical oligarchy demonstrated an exceptional resilience and determination to overcome adversity among the population at large, and a level of commitment to the democratic ideal that was not matched by the resolution of those who sought to destroy it. The resilience was evident in the quick recovery from the plague and determination to continue the war. But it showed itself especially after the Sicilian disaster. Thucydides, though he roundly condemned the sending of the expedition and its management, could not help but admire the fact that, despite the loss of their army and most of their fleet, and the increased range of enemies whom they faced after the defeat – which included the Sicilians, most of the allies and Cyrus, the Persian commander in Asia Minor who sided with the Peloponnesians – the Athenians held out for a further ten years and were only brought down by their own private quarrels.[55]

Athens lost forty thousand men from its own forces and those of the allies, and more than two hundred ships in Sicily. The scale of the losses caused understandable consternation, but this was accompanied by a resolute, focused effort by the Athenians to rebuild a fleet. Thucydides remarked that 'in the fear of the moment they were ready, in a manner characteristic of the *demos*, to do everything in a disciplined way'. They procured timber and money from every available source, and reduced public expenditure wherever possible. They dealt carefully with the allies to maintain the loyalty of as many as possible. During 412 they kept the Peloponnesian forces at bay in the eastern Aegean, and won Samos as a firm ally and headquarters for their Aegean forces. They overcame the revolution of the Four Hundred and by the end of 411, with Alcibiades back in a position of leadership, they were gaining the upper hand in the eastern Aegean. The major victory over the Spartans at Cyzicus took place in early 410, and between then and 406 Athens had reached a point where it was reasonable to expect it could win the war. It was an astonishing comeback. The subsequent victory at Arginusae in the autumn of 406 could have brought a favourable peace, or even led to an outright victory in the war, if emotion and arrogance had not caused the Assembly to execute the victorious generals because of failed efforts to rescue shipwrecked sailors. The decision deprived the state of some of its best commanders and demoralised the forces they had so successfully led. The benefits of the heroic recovery had been squandered.

But the quality that never faltered, and that ultimately saved the democracy, was the deep-seated loyalty among the mass of the citizenry, and especially among the rank and file of the armed forces, to the democratic way of life and form of government. The systems in the city proved unable to prevent the first oligarchic coup in 411, but the armed forces at Samos, dominated by hoplites and sailors, always the most solid democratic loyalists, quickly launched a counter-revolution under the leadership of two generals along with two committed democrats, the trierarch Thrasybulus and a hoplite soldier, Thrasyllus. This paved the way for the quick demise of the Four Hundred, and brought Alcibiades back into a position of leadership in the eastern Aegean.

The takeover by the Thirty Tyrants in 404 similarly generated a democratic resistance movement outside Athens, and Thrasybulus was again the prime mover. The movement was initially centred in Phyle, a deme in northern Attica, and consisted mainly of exiles. But by the middle of 403 it had a stronghold on the hill of Munychia in the Piraeus and its forces had been greatly expanded by support from the citizens who had been excluded from the city. It was now a struggle between the *demos* and the oligarchs. The victory at the battle of Munychia soon followed and the *demos* had the upper hand. By September 403 Pausanias had negotiated the reconciliation agreement that provided a semi-autonomous political haven at Eleusis for the extremists, and left democrats and moderates to work together to restore the democratic order.

There are many similarities between the coups of 411 and 404. Both were triggered by mistakes of the *demos* that had disastrous consequences and shattered confidence in popular rule. Both were shaped and effectively took place at the instigation of able, intellectually sophisticated and politically radical aristocrats, who were part of that new generation of the nobility whose exposure to the life and capacities of the mind and to supremacist ideas of power made the concept of giving control of the state to the lowly, unlettered multitude seem absurd and repugnant. Both had strong support from like-minded younger upper-class aristocrats operating through the network of political clubs. There was also support from others less driven by ideological dogma who favoured change out of traditional class prejudices, or because they believed the democracy lacked the capacity to govern effectively.

These revolutions were initiated therefore by broad coalitions of those who, in varying degrees, were opposed to the democracy. But in spite of that they failed in both 411 and 404/3 to establish a sustainable power-base. The reasons were in many ways similar in both instances. Thucydides described the proneness of all oligarchies to factionalism and selfish ambition, and these phenomena quickly showed themselves in both the Four Hundred and the Thirty. There were also wide variations in their motivations and political convictions. The ideological extremism of an Antiphon, or more especially of a Critias, was unlikely to win wide acceptance even among elitist aristocrats, and the jockeying for power between moderates and extremists soon fragmented the coalitions. In the case of the Thirty the brutal repression to cement control amounted to a reign of terror that endangered anyone who was seen to pose a threat or was outside the chosen elite.

Neither the Four Hundred nor the Thirty ever had any real unity of purpose or political outlook or the military muscle sufficient to sustain dictatorial rule. Ranged against them was a public strongly united in its political beliefs, and enough capable, democratically minded leaders emerged to ensure that the rule of the *demos* would ultimately prevail. In the end the spirit of democracy was more broadly and deeply embedded in the Athenian psyche than the spirit of oligarchy.

Lessons were finally learned from the recurring civil strife. It was accepted that action was needed to rebuild harmony and stability, and that a safe, just and orderly society would require a reaffirmation of the principle of the rule of law and a long-sought revision and codification of the existing body of law. The story of these developments, and of the emergence of a more mature and complete form of democracy in the fourth century, forms the subject of the next three chapters.

CHAPTER 6

Reconciliation and Reform

The restoration of the control of the *demos* in October 403, and the constitutional modifications that accompanied it and set Athens on course for another eighty years of stable government, form another remarkable chapter in the story of Athenian democracy. For almost a year Athens had experienced increasingly brutal civil strife reminiscent of the *stasis* that had gripped Corcyra in the 420s. But the outcome in Athens differed markedly from the consequences of the Corcyraean and other Greek civil wars so memorably described by Thucydides. The victors were more intent on peace and unity than on vengeance, and the covenant (*syntheke*) concluded around the end of September 403 under the auspices of Pausanias and his team of Spartan mediators was focused on a lasting reconciliation, which both sides solemnly swore to uphold.

The terms are well documented. Everyone was allowed to return to their homes and possessions with the exception of the Thirty, the Eleven who had had charge of prisons and executions, and the Ten who had governed the Piraeus. Eleusis, which the Thirty had seized after their defeat at Phyle, was constituted as a semi-autonomous enclave for those afraid to stay in Athens. No access between the two cities was allowed except in relation to the celebration of the Mysteries. Those wishing to settle in Eleusis had to register within ten days of the swearing of the reconciliation oaths and leave within twenty. No one living in Eleusis could hold office at Athens without formally moving residence back to the city.

Trials for homicide in the case of those who had killed or wounded someone with their own hands could proceed under the ancestral laws, but otherwise an amnesty for all past actions was declared for all with the exception of the Thirty, the Eleven and the Ten governors of the Piraeus. Even they would be immune from prosecution if they submitted to the regular *euthyna*. After the agreement was completed, Pausanias withdrew, and that ended Spartan involvement in the internal affairs of Athens.

The generosity and statesmanship shown by the victors are widely commended in the sources. The Aristotelian *Constitution of Athens* says that they handled the matter as well as any had ever done in such situations, and contrasts their actions with what happened in other states. It emphasises the priority given to restoring unity and harmony.

Andocides writes in a similar vein. The men from the Piraeus had the opportunity for revenge, but considered the safety of the state more important than personal vengeance. They decided to let bygones be bygones, and bound themselves by oath not to bring up past evils except in relation to the Thirty, the Eleven and the Ten who had governed the Piraeus.

A speech by Thrasybulus, recorded by Xenophon, which was delivered at an Assembly after the men from the Piraeus entered the city, demonstrates the extent of the grievances felt by the democrats, but also their willingness to overcome them. The speech was directed at the oligarchs, and Thrasybulus advises them to ask themselves what grounds they had for the arrogance that made them seek to rule over the people. On the score of justice, the *demos*, though poorer, had never done them any wrong for the sake of money, while they had done many disgraceful things for gain. On the score of courage, the way both had conducted the war was the best measure of superiority. On the score of intelligence, despite having walls, weapons, money and Peloponnesian allies, they were beaten by men who had none of these. Even their allies abandoned them and delivered them to the *demos* they had wronged. He ended by saying that in spite of all that he expected them to abide by the oaths they had sworn and assured them they had no need to be fearful, but did need to adhere to the traditional legal order.

The speech, even if not an exact record of what was said, can be taken to represent the general feeling of the *demos*. It shows how wronged the public felt by a regime that lacked any semblance of the personal and civic virtues so prominent in the democratic ethos and so memorably articulated in the Funeral Oration of Pericles. The pretensions of the oligarchs to the right to rule had been thoroughly discredited, and the superiority of the rule of the people reaffirmed. But the speech ended on a conciliatory note. The adherents of the oligarchic movement represented a large and vital component of the Athenian state, and reconciliation with them and their reintegration into the democratic system was obviously essential.[1]

The covenant that sought to achieve that reconciliation was rightly singled out for praise in antiquity. It was a high-minded, forward-looking attempt to bury the past, heal wounds and re-establish a united, stable society. The sweeping amnesty clause showed statesmanship of the highest order, as Aristotle observed. The requirement that every citizen swear an oath to uphold the agreement gave it a special status and helped rally a broad consensus behind it. There was a realistic acceptance that there was an element that could not readily be integrated into the body politic, and elaborate provision was made to allow them to live in an insulated enclave where they would have control of their own affairs.

A number of factors contributed to the successful outcome of the negotiations in 403. The drive for reconciliation was coming from both sides. As the situation worsened for the people in the city, the moderates began to come to the fore. The appointment of the second Ten was a turning point. According to Aristotle, they were men of the highest reputation. He names the leaders as Rhinon and Phaullus, and says they had initiated negotiations with the leaders in the Piraeus even before the arrival of Pausanias. They continued working for a settlement in the talks that followed. Rhinon and his associates were later commended for their goodwill towards the democracy, and Rhinon was immediately elected a general following the conclusion of the agreement.

But even more significant was the fact that the leaders in the Piraeus contained several of the most prominent leaders of the faction led by Theramenes prior to the rise of the Thirty. In describing the political situation in Athens after the peace agreement with Sparta in 404, Aristotle distinguished three main groups: those who wanted to preserve the democracy, whom he calls the *demotikoi*; the club fraternity and returned exiles who wanted an oligarchy; and those whom he describes as citizens of the highest reputation whose goal was to re-establish the ancestral constitution. He says this group was led by Theramenes, and among his supporters he singles out four individuals: Archinus, Anytus, Cleitophon and Phormisius.

Cleitophon, an intellectual with links to Socrates and Theophrastus, and a well-known supporter of the concept of the *patrios politeia* in 411, is not known to have been involved in the resistance to the Thirty, but the other three were prominent in it. They were among the many moderate oligarchs who soon became disillusioned with their behaviour and who were forced into exile by the regime's determination to get rid of all potential opponents, and especially those with wealth whose property they coveted. Anytus and Archinus were key figures in the uprising spearheaded by Thrasybulus at Phyle and at the Piraeus, and they also played leading political roles in Athens following the reconciliation settlement. Phormisius is not mentioned among those at Phyle but he was in the Piraeus, and was also to the fore in events after the settlement.[2]

Thrasybulus, the courageous and inspiring leader who was most responsible for the downfall of the Thirty, had a more complex political background.

He played a major role in defeating the oligarchic conspiracy among the leaders of the Samian forces in 411. He helped to cement democracy within Samos itself and to secure a commitment under oath from the Athenian troops to maintain democracy at Athens and to oppose the Four Hundred. It was he who organised the first armed resistance to the Thirty, and who built it and skilfully led it to victory in the Piraeus. But while his commitment to the rule of the *demos* cannot be questioned, the evidence for his career after the Samian army broke with Athens suggests that his vision of democracy had a moderate practical cast that made him sympathetic to aspects of the reforms advocated by proponents of the ancestral constitution.

After securing the loyalty of the Samian troops to democracy, Thrasybulus had then persuaded them to recall Alcibiades, believing that his help was necessary to win the war. Alcibiades promptly arrived in Samos, and the soldiers not only elected him a general along with those already holding the office, including Thrasybulus and Thrasyllus, but gave him overall control of affairs. When envoys from the Four Hundred arrived in Samos soon afterwards, the soldiers reacted angrily to their presentation and wanted to sail at once for the Piraeus. Alcibiades not only managed to restrain them but to get their acquiescence in a message to the regime in Athens that might well have provoked their dissent. He told the envoys that he would not oppose a rule of Five Thousand, but that the Four Hundred must be abolished and the traditional Council of Five Hundred restored.

A regime very much along these lines was, of course, soon afterwards established at Athens, and its leading figure, Theramenes, quickly secured passage through the Assembly of a decree to recall Alcibiades, endorsing what Thrasybulus and the soldiers had earlier done at Samos. There was now a rapprochement between the Samian forces and the government at Athens, and it was largely the work of Thrasybulus, Alcibiades and Theramenes. Later in 411 all three linked up again in a highly successful campaign in the Hellespont which resulted in the spring of 410 in an overwhelming victory over the Spartan fleet at Cyzicus.

But then the public mood in Athens shifted again. There was a resurgence of populism, helped no doubt by the successes of the navy and a consequent rise in the status of the thetes. The Five Thousand was replaced with a return to full democracy, and there was scope once more for politicians in the mould of the demagogues. Cleophon emerged as an influential figure and was, like all demagogues, an implacable foe of Alcibiades. The new mood was reflected in the fact that Alcibiades, Theramenes and Thrasybulus all failed to get re-elected as generals for 410/09 and for the two years following. But despite their lack of official status, they were left in their posts and continued to extend the control of Athens over the Hellespont, which became complete in 408 with the capture of Byzantium and Chalcedon.

These victories were sufficient to swing popular favour back towards Alcibiades, and a new decree, proposed by Critias, was passed recalling him. He entered Athens in triumph around the middle of 407. Past judgements against him were revoked and he was elected general and supreme commander. Thrasybulus too was finally given recognition for his achievements and was also elected general for 407/6. But a few months later came the setback at Notium, and all of this was reversed. Alcibiades was deposed and with him most of his fellow generals, including Thrasybulus. Cleophon led the drive against Alcibiades and his associates, and he even had Critias, who had sponsored the recall of Alcibiades, forced into exile.

This must have been an especially frustrating time for Thrasybulus. It was he who had regained for Athens the military skills of Alcibiades when he brought him back to lead the forces at Samos. The result had been the restoration of Athenian control over the crucially important area of the Hellespont, and the eventual recognition by the *demos* in 407 that Alcibiades was the best military leader it had. Then suddenly, because of a single reverse, the *demos*, displaying again the erratic volatility and willingness to be led by demagoguery that Thucydides had so roundly condemned following the recall of Alcibiades from Sicily in 415, deposed its supreme commander and almost all of his board of generals, and lost to the state the bulk of its military leadership and its greatest military strategist.

Worse was to follow after the victory at Arginusae in the autumn of 406, when the Assembly, led by raw emotion, impulsively voted the death penalty without due process for eight of the generals who achieved the victory, blaming them for a failure to rescue shipwrecked sailors. Six were executed and two escaped into exile. Thrasybulus and Theramenes were at the centre of the controversy. They were at the battle as trierarchs, and it was they who were deputed to pick up the shipwrecked sailors. While the blame fell mainly on the generals in charge, the trierarchs did not emerge unscathed. Not long afterwards Theramenes was rejected at his preliminary scrutiny (*dokimasia*) for the post of general in 405/4 (Lys. 13.10). Thrasybulus disappears entirely from the record after Arginusae until late 404 when, as an exile in Thebes, he began to organise armed resistance to the Thirty. References to him in the speech of Theramenes at the trial that led to his execution suggest Thrasybulus stayed in the city, did not oppose the rise of the Thirty, but, like many honourable and upright citizens (*kaloi kagathoi*), became antagonised by the misdeeds of the regime and was banished as a result. Theramenes twice links him with Anytus as examples of how the regime had alienated the best elements in the city and made them opponents. According to Diodorus (14.32), the Thirty offered Thrasybulus a place in their regime following the execution of Theramenes in early 403, a statement that stretches credibility. If offered, it certainly was not accepted. Thrasybulus pressed on with his mission to overthrow them.[3]

The overall evidence for the career of Thrasybulus shows him as an honourable, patriotic, upper-class Athenian, more soldier than statesman or political ideologue. He was loyal to the tradition of the democratic ideal, but in the years of internal discord and external threat between 411 and 403 he was more closely associated with Alcibiades and Theramenes than with any more committed champions of democracy. His support for Alcibiades may have been based on a recognition of how badly the state needed his skills, but in turbulent times he seems to have been comfortable with the political views of Theramenes, and it was close friends of Theramenes whom he gathered around him in organising resistance to the Thirty. He was certainly seen by the public as linked to Alcibiades and Theramenes, and his political fortunes waxed and waned with theirs. In this he presents a strong contrast to Thrasyllus, his main ally in 411 in winning the support of the Athenian troops and the townsmen in Samos to the cause of democracy. Thrasyllus was subsequently seen as a far more ardent devotee of democracy than Thrasybulus, and more a foe than a friend of Alcibiades. He especially enjoyed the favour of the *demos* when Alcibiades lost it.

All of the leaders in the Piraeus were therefore upper-class Athenians of moderate political views. They had experienced at first hand, not once but twice, the extremes and evils to which the rule of elite minorities was prone. *Oligarchia* was now a discredited concept and no longer an option. As Lysias later wrote, the disasters that had happened left reminders sufficient to prevent even the oligarchs' descendants from wanting a different constitution than the ancestral democracy. Isocrates, in many ways a reluctant democrat, asserted in his speech *On the Peace* that 'the madness of the Thirty has made us all more democratic than those who occupied Phyle'.[4]

But the men in the Piraeus had also experienced the poor judgement and dangerously erratic impulsiveness of popular government when it was badly led and unconstrained by a well-embedded, clearly defined code of law. This was the great concern of the moderate reformers, who were as opposed to the politics of confrontation and demagoguery of a Cleophon as to the amoral and power-hungry supremacism of a Critias. Athens had a new generation of leaders matured by the experiences of brutal civil strife and failed departures from traditional values. They were intent on achieving reconciliation and uniting all classes behind a re-established democracy guided by an agreed, updated, clearly defined written code of law based on fundamental ancestral principles. They joined with moderates in the city, such as Rhinon, to achieve their goals.

Reconciliation was pursued with determination. There were no reprisals. The most extreme elements of the Thirty and their adherents were sequestered in a safe haven. The amnesty for all others was comprehensive, and it proved a powerful means of closing a door to the past and moving to a fresh start.

The implementation of the reconciliation agreement was thorough, and where difficulties arose they were kept from escalating into confrontation. When a returned exile attempted to infringe the amnesty, Archinus persuaded the Council to sentence him to death without a trial as a warning to others. Aristotle says no one else attempted to act in violation of the amnesty. To set an example of generosity in regard to settlement of property disputes arising from confiscations under the Thirty, Thrasybulus and Anytus gave up their claims to large amounts of property that had been taken from them. A debt of over 100 talents owed to Sparta and incurred by the Thirty was paid by decision of the people from the public treasury, even though the agreement specified that each side would be responsible for its own debts. When Thrasybulus understandably wanted to reward the many metics and slaves who had fought to overthrow the oligarchy and introduced a measure to grant them citizenship, Archinus, aware of the strong feelings of many against such extensions of citizenship and determined to avoid divisions, blocked the measure by indicting Thrasybulus for introducing an illegal motion (*graphe paranomon*). But compromise rather than conflict resolved the matter. In 401 those who had served at Phyle were given citizenship, the others the privilege of equal tax status with citizens (*isotelia*).

Phormisius introduced a proposal to limit full citizenship to landowners, but it was rejected. The proposal represented a last effort to give a more oligarchic cast to the constitution by those who believed that the franchise should be confined to those best able to serve the state 'by their persons and property'. But such thinking no longer carried credibility. The internal trauma of recent times was the work of oligarchic interests. It was the *demos* that had emerged with greater credit. No argument any longer remained for the exclusion of any Athenian from sharing in the rights of citizens.

A final major act of reconciliation took place in 401. When the Athenians heard that the oligarchs in Eleusis were hiring mercenaries, they marched in mass against them, executed the leaders and, with the help of friends and relatives of the others, achieved a lasting reconciliation in accordance with the terms of the amnesty.[5]

Socrates

The one great blot on the work of reconciliation was the trial and condemnation to death of Socrates in 399. An extraordinary and pivotal figure in the history of philosophy, Socrates has been immortalised by his pupil Plato, who made him the main interlocutor in his dialogues. Further evidence of his life, character and teachings is provided by another great admirer, Xenophon. Aristotle, Plato's pupil, never knew Socrates, but he recognised his seminal contribution to philosophy, and emphasises in particular his development of inductive reasoning and constant pursuit of universal definitions that would clarify the true meaning of key ideas. Down the centuries Socrates has been seen as a man of monumental intellect and unshakeable moral integrity whose sole purpose was to seek out what was good for human beings and how best to attain it. The manner of his death has therefore tended to be regarded as an abominable act of repression against a genius and a saint. But that is a judgement of hindsight, and his condemnation must be viewed in the context of the particular circumstances surrounding it.

Socrates, born about 470, was the son of a stonemason and, so far as is known, initially followed his father's profession. He did his duty as a citizen and served with distinction as a soldier during the Peloponnesian War. He deliberately did not take any leading role in the Assembly because, according to his own testimony, he knew that if he expressed his true opinions, which would often have meant opposing the view of the mass (*plethos*), he would not have survived. In the one office that he ever held, that of Councillor, he had found himself opposing the wish of the people when he refused, as a member of the presiding *prytaneis*, to support the illegal proposal to try as a body all ten generals who commanded at Arginusae. His stance was met with shouts for his prosecution.[6]

In any event Socrates was being drawn in a direction away from active political involvement. His nimble intellect pulled him into the milieu of the new intellectual movements. Initially he was engaged with the natural sciences, but abandoned them when he concluded that they dealt with things unknowable and irrelevant to what mattered most: human beings and how they should live. In Cicero's words, 'he called philosophy back from the sky and placed it in cities, and brought it into people's homes, and forced it to investigate life and morals and good and evil'.[7]

His focus received new impetus when his ebullient and admiring friend Chaerephon asked the Delphic Oracle if there was anyone wiser than Socrates, and received the answer that there was not. Socrates, who believed he had no wisdom, great or small, was so perplexed by this that he felt obliged to find out what the god meant. So he began to go around Athens and question all manner of people – statesmen, poets, dramatists, artisans – expecting to prove that in all those areas there were people wiser than he. But he found no true wisdom among any of them. They had reputation and certain talents, and this made them think they were wise overall, which was in no way the case. He himself had at least the advantage of not thinking he knew what he did not know.

He concluded that what the god meant was that what humans saw as wise was not wisdom. True wisdom was concerned with something more spiritual in human beings, the *psyche*, the real self, the thinking, reasoning element, and the sole source of wisdom. He further believed that the god's response was giving him a mission to disabuse people of their delusions and lead them to care for this true self and to seek to understand it and what was good and bad for it. So he continued this role of gadfly and midwife, jolting people out of their complacency and leading them on to a clearer perception of the good and its components.

He was also willing to give time to young people, but only to those he thought he could benefit. He emphasised that he was not a teacher in the sense of one who imparts knowledge, because he believed he had none and therefore refused to accept fees. He strongly objected to the claims of the traditional Sophists that they could teach political *arete*, and he strongly criticised their amoral approach to rhetoric. He saw his role with the young as that of a moral and intellectual midwife, drawing out their inner capacity to understand the true self and what was good for it, and helping to lead them to that under-standing by searching for general definitions of the components of the good through the techniques of dialectics and inductive reasoning.[8]

By the 420s he was a famous figure in Athens, well known for his odd, satyr-like, dishevelled appearance and readiness to debate and expound. Despite the fundamental differences that he saw between himself and the Sophists as a whole, he was inevitably classed as one of them in the public mind, an intel-lectual, a teacher, a clever talker and debater. Not surprisingly, he attracted the attention of the writers of comedy, and when Aristophanes decided in 423 to write his play the *Clouds* satirising the Sophists, he made Socrates the central figure, obviously seeing him as the ideal character through which to lampoon every form of inane scientific speculation and specious rhetorical trickery that could be associated with the new learning.[9]

Socrates believed his mission was lifelong and that he could not abandon it without disobeying the god. For him, there was no greater good in life than discussing virtue every day and examining himself and others, because he believed 'the unexamined life was not worth living'. For decades he followed this course without threat or hindrance. This raises the question as to why he found himself in court on capital charges in 399.[10]

He faced two charges, the first accusing him of refusing to recognise the gods of the state and introducing new divinities, the second accusing him of corrupting the youth. The first charge seems to have been largely based on his early involvement with the natural sciences, which were commonly associated with atheism, and on his rather startling claim that from childhood he was guided by some kind of divine or spiritual inner voice (*daimonion*) which deterred him from certain courses of action. If these were the only grounds for prosecution, it is unlikely he would ever have been convicted or even brought to court. They were charges that could have been brought at any time during the previous two decades, and were probably only made in 399 to buttress the second charge, corrupting the young, which formed the heart of the case against him.[11]

This second charge was triggered by the calamities of the late fifth century and the belief that Socrates bore some responsibility for them to the extent that the worst of them were caused by men who had been his disciples. There were some grounds for that belief. It was well known that Socrates had an especially close relationship with many leading lights of the aristocratic young radicals who had grown up in the golden era of power and prosperity and intellectual revolution. Their radical views and ambitions and role in the breakdown of stability and in the eventual civil upheavals of the late fifth century have been discussed earlier. Socrates' eccentric but magnetic personality, his exceptional skill in dialectics and the notoriety that attended his constant challenging of all who laid claim to wisdom had attracted to him many of the leisured rich. He alludes to this in the course of his defence. They often accompanied him on his rounds of the city, revelling in his interrogation of those who engaged with him. Socrates clearly enjoyed their company and enthusiasm. He dined with them, held discussions with them, and undoubtedly acted as mentor and teacher, though in a very different manner than the Sophists. Many of them, such as those listed in Plato's *Apology*, were undoubtedly upright citizens. Xenophon gives a further list of Socratic disciples who were above reproach.

But there were also many who belonged to the more extreme wing of the young radicals, most notably Alcibiades and Critias, the two men who, it could be argued, caused, more than any others, the worst of the disasters that befell Athens in the late fifth century. Charmides, uncle of Plato and first cousin of Critias, was another intimate of Socrates who had a leading role in the regime of the Thirty. He was one of the Ten entrusted with the defence of the Piraeus, a group that, along with the Ten who succeeded the Thirty, and the Eleven who had carried out the judicial murders under the Thirty, were specifically excluded from the amnesty. Charmides was killed, along with Critias, at the battle of Munychia in 403. All three of these Socratic disciples had also been convicted of involvement in the affair of the herms and the Mysteries in 415, together with at least four others who also had links to Socrates.[12]

It is understandable that this particularly close public association with the younger aristocratic elite, so many of whom, and most notoriously Alcibiades and Critias, later turned to revolution, gave rise to the belief that Socrates was a pernicious influence on the young. There can be no doubt that it was this that drove the prosecution and brought the conviction. It was certainly what motivated Anytus, the prime mover behind the trial, who had witnessed the havoc wrought by Critias and his circle, and had himself been exiled and had his property confiscated. He was well known for his hatred of the Sophists and all they represented, and would have seen Socrates as a prime example of the dangerous new forms of intellectual speculation associated with them. He told the jury that the execution of Socrates was necessary to save their sons from destruction as a result of practising what he taught. The whole issue of the relationship of Socrates with Alcibiades and Critias featured prominently in the trial, and there is clear evidence in Aeschines that Socrates was put to death because he was seen as the teacher of Critias.[13]

His case was not helped by the fact that he did little to disguise his aversion to radical democracy and to the notion that, when it came to the critical function of ruling the state, concern for ability and expertise should be set aside and the view of every citizen considered of equal value. He had publicly voiced his particular objection to the choice of magistrates by lot. Xenophon makes clear his low opinion of the collective wisdom of the Assembly; his statement at the trial that, if he had attended the Assembly and expressed his true opinions, he would not have survived has been mentioned earlier.

Socrates also did little to confront specifically the issue of the relationship with Alcibiades and Critias. He never mentions either of them, and falls back on a broad defence against the charge of corrupting the young to the effect that he could not be held responsible for the kind of person anyone who conversed with him or listened to what he said turned out to be, because he never taught, or promised to teach, anyone anything. That would hardly have impressed the jury. Neither would his response when, as was his right, he was asked to suggest a penalty following his conviction. He said he did not want to choose imprisonment or exile. He believed that what he deserved was free meals in the Prytaneum so he could continue his beneficial work, but, since he knew that would not be acceptable, he was willing to pay a fine, and with the help of his friends could pay 30 minae. The alternative was death, and the majority in favour of it was higher than that for his conviction.[14]

History has been able, with the help of Plato and other contemporaries, to appreciate the uniqueness of Socrates, the brilliance of his mind and the sheer nobleness of his character. But the jury of five hundred ordinary citizens in 399 only knew him as an eccentric public presence who disturbingly challenged people's normal assumptions and values, and was generally surrounded by a coterie of the younger aristocratic elite. They had fresh memories of the trauma of two revolutions in which leading figures were members of that elite and known followers of Socrates. It was not difficult to convince them that he was more a threat than a benefit to the democracy. Nothing he said in his defence would have given them reason to believe otherwise.

Socrates was a victim of uniquely turbulent times, of his own brutal honesty, and of the exceptional waywardness of some of those known to have been his disciples. His execution in such circumstances is not a reliable gauge of the commitment to reconciliation or of the level of freedom of speech and thought in fourth-century Athens.[15]

Legal and Constitutional Reform

Reform and updating of the laws was the other urgent issue in the minds of the leaders in the Piraeus, and they confronted it quickly. As soon as they entered the city an interim committee of twenty was elected to manage public affairs until a revised code of law could be enacted. Meantime the laws of Solon and Draco were to remain in force. A Council was chosen by lot and lawgivers were elected. The magistrates were soon restored and normal government resumed.

The lawgivers were expected to work quickly and they did. A level of law reform had been continuing since 411, when the oligarchs appointed two separate commissions to create a new written constitution. The proposals that emerged, while purportedly based on ancestral principles, were chiefly designed to entrench oligarchic rule. They were never implemented, but after the Assembly replaced the Four Hundred with the Five Thousand, there were, according to Thucydides, other frequent meetings of the Assembly that appointed new law commissions and approved other matters related to the constitution. Information about the work of these commissions between 410 and 403 is sparse, but the job of one commission, known as the *anagrapheis*, involved assembling the body of existing law, principally the laws of Solon, and preparing definitive texts for publication. Making emendations was also part of the task.[16]

It is clear that there was a growing realisation that the rule of law, which was a seminal ancestral principle underlying the evolution of Athenian democracy, needed to be strengthened afresh by a comprehensive review and codification of the body of existing law. Obscurities and ambiguities in the codes of Draco and Solon needed to be clarified, and overlaps, inconsistencies and general inadequacies in the mass of laws and decrees passed in the course of almost two centuries since Draco and Solon, and only haphazardly recorded in different forms and different places, needed to be eliminated. The codes of Draco and

Solon were furthermore primarily concerned with private and criminal law, and constitutional law therefore especially needed to be addressed.[17]

The legal reforms undertaken in 403 were more comprehensive than earlier efforts and more far-reaching in their effects. The speech of Andocides, *On the Mysteries*, provides the main evidence for the actions taken. The Assembly voted that all the laws should be scrutinised and those approved inscribed on the wall of the Stoa Basileios in the Agora. To achieve this, a decree, proposed by Teisamenus, prescribed that two new boards of *nomothetai* be established. The first board, which was chosen by the Council, appears to have been given the task of continuing the work of the *anagrapheis* appointed by the Five Thousand, which would have involved completing the compilation and consolidation of existing law into a consistent whole with definitive texts and necessary additions. Their work was to be posted for all to see in the Agora.

The second board represented a totally new departure. It comprised five hundred *nomothetai* elected by the demes who, acting with the Council, were charged with scrutinising all the laws put forward by the first board and ratifying those that they approved. Any citizen had the right to appear before the Council to make their input into the process. The laws that were ratified were to be inscribed, as the Assembly had voted earlier, on the wall of the Stoa Basileios. The final provision in the decree of Teisamenus gave the Council of the Areopagus responsibility to ensure that magistrates adhered to the established laws.

The work of reform further clarified the place of law in the restored democracy and established new procedures for regular review of the body of established law and for any changes to it. The status of law was enhanced by a clear distinction between laws (*nomoi*) and decrees (*psephismata*), a distinction that had become blurred in the fifth century. Laws were now defined as general rules or norms intended to have permanent effect. They had to apply to all citizens and could not be directed against an individual. Decrees were decisions of the Assembly to deal with a particular situation at a particular time. They were limited both with respect to scope and duration. No decree of Council or Assembly could have higher authority than a law. New laws that conflicted with existing decrees invalidated the decrees, and new decrees that conflicted with existing law were nullified, and the proposer was liable to prosecution for introducing an illegal proposal under the procedure known as the *graphe paranomon*. Another provision brought greater certainty to the operation of the law. Magistrates were required to use only the established body of written law. Unwritten or customary law could not be applied for any reason.[18]

The restored democracy did not regard the new code as immutable, and provided several opportunities for change. Every year during the first presidency, the Assembly reviewed the various segments of the code and decided whether any change was required in any area. The board of *thesmothetai*, which comprised the six junior archons and administered the business of the jury courts and presided over public prosecutions (*graphai*), also had the task of regularly reviewing the laws to see if any inconsistencies or invalid laws had crept in. If any were found, they initiated procedures in the Assembly to deal with them. In addition, any citizen at any time could introduce proposals to change the code.

There was a marked conservatism, however, in the forms of change permitted, which is evident also in a set of new procedures created to govern change. New legislation could only involve altering or replacing an existing law rather than breaking new legal ground and adding to the body of legal principles. The new procedures for enacting legislation were far more elaborate and deliberate than before, requiring repeated debate in the Assembly over an extended period, opportunity for other forms of public engagement and a totally new procedure to add a further test of the merits of the proposed change to the law.

Legislative proposals now had to be written down before being presented to the Assembly, and had to be posted in the Agora for public inspection. A meeting of the Assembly decided if the new law was needed or the existing laws were adequate. If it voted for the new law, there was then a pause and the matter was deferred to the second-next meeting of the Assembly for further action. In the interval the proposal remained posted in the Agora, and any member of the public who had reservations could pass them on to the proposer. At the second meeting the Assembly made arrangements for the final stage, which was the convening of a panel of citizens randomly chosen from the jury lists, and probably of varying size like juries, to sit in judgement on the merits of the new law. These panels were known as *nomethetai*, and the procedure they followed took the form of a trial, with five citizens chosen by the Assembly arguing the case for the existing law and the proposer the case for change. The verdict of the panel, as in the case of trials, was final, and if they voted for the proposed change, it became law.

Further protection of established law against ill-conceived change was afforded by a new measure providing for indictment on a charge of having secured passage of a law that was in conflict with existing law or otherwise not in the public interest. The older *graphe paranomon* no longer applied to laws, but continued to be used in the case of decrees.[19]

There was one further development around the time of the reforms that had constitutional significance. Pay was introduced for attendance at meetings of the Assembly. It quickly rose to three obols a day, the same sum that was paid to jurors. By the time of Aristotle it had doubled to a drachma, and by then the number of fixed meetings had also increased to forty a year. The measure was obviously designed to facilitate attendance, especially by the lower classes, who could least afford to sacrifice a day's wages from their regular employment.

It is not certain when pay for public office was restored. It had been suspended by the Four Hundred for the duration of the war, but the suspension was more firmly set in place after the Five Thousand came to power. The most reasonable assumption is that it was restored in 410, when the Five Thousand was deposed and full democracy was re-established. Recent victories in the Hellespont had greatly increased Athenian revenues and weakened the economic argument for restricting pay to the armed forces. This was the era when Cleophon was especially active and introduced his controversial and short-lived dole (*diobelia*) of two obols a day, presumably to help the impoverished. It was a likely environment for a resumption of pay for public office, which would have further improved the position of the poor.

Some historians question whether it was ever restored, but that possibility seems unlikely. Pay for public office was seen as an integral part of full democracy. It was essential to broad political participation and equality of political opportunity. Aristotle lists it as a defining characteristic of democracy, in the same way that its absence was characteristic of oligarchy. He could hardly have said that had it not been a feature of the democracy of his day, which he portrayed as an extreme form. It is also highly improbable that such a distinctively oligarchic feature, which had such important implications for the political role of the *demos*, would have been left in place when all others were being removed. Failure to restore it would in practice have precluded the poorest class from holding public office, which would have been totally inconsistent with the introduction around the time of the reforms of pay for attendance at the Assembly, a move obviously designed to complete a process of democratisation, begun by Pericles, to remove barriers to fuller political engagement by all citizens.[20]

The Effects of the Reforms

The most obvious and important effect of the reforms was that Athens acquired a comprehensive, coherent, updated, definitive code of written law, covering private, criminal and constitutional law, substantive and procedural. The new code was given ratification, not by plenipotentiary powers of lawgivers, but by a new and elaborate procedure designed to maximise the participation of the whole citizen body in the determination and validation of the body of the laws that would define the values and systems of their state. The posting of the laws in the Agora for public inspection; the right of any citizen to appear before the Council to make recommendations; the involvement of every deme in the state along with the Council, which was also representative of every deme, in scrutinising every law and in the final validation – all of these illustrate the special importance attached to the exercise. No meeting of the Assembly could have achieved such wide public engagement or minute scrutiny of the code, or provided as authoritative a mode of validation as the unique arrangements prescribed by the decree of Teisamenus.

The separation of laws and decrees, the higher authority given to laws, and the requirement to apply only statutory law and avoid the use of customary law for any reason were further measures that elevated the place of law within the democracy. But it was perhaps the changes made in procedures for making law (*nomothesia*) that most clearly showed the depth of the renewed commitment to the rule of law. The three new features of the procedures – the requirement that proposals be posted to allow the public to have direct input into the framing of legislation, that they be discussed at two well-spaced meetings of the Assembly and that those approved should be subject to a final verdict by, in effect, a jury of as many as a thousand citizens – gave layers of protection against hasty, poorly judged legislation, and ensured that whatever passed into law had full and well-informed popular sanction.

Overall, the reforms were a powerful reaffirmation of the rule of law as a fundamental principle of Athenian democracy. They represented an unequivocal commitment to constitutionalism and a rejection of absolutism in any form. Athens now indisputably had, in the words of James Harrington, a 'government of laws, not of men'.

This was not, however, a radical new departure for Athenian democracy. Solon, who was revered by many as the father of the ancestral constitution, and whose laws still stood and had been placed at the centre of the new code, had eloquently exposed the evils of absolutism and enshrined in Athenian political culture the doctrine that a state must be subject to a body of just law that commands respect, is applied equally to all and is superior to those who administer it. The place of law and justice in the Periclean vision of democracy has been discussed earlier. Euripides specifically emphasises written law as a guardian of equal justice and a protection against the tyrant. The introduction of the *graphe paranomon* well before the reforms at the end of the century is another indicator of a continuing respect for established law and a reluctance to alter it, let alone override it.[21]

The reforms were nonetheless a landmark in the history of democracy in that Athens now had a comprehensive body of law that had been thoroughly reordered, updated, clarified in definitive written form and revalidated in the most authoritative manner. Even more important, the place of law was elevated to a status that unequivocally established it as the highest authority in the state. This was a decisive turning away from the waywardness that marked popular rule in the later stages of the war and that refused to accept any constraint on the right of the *demos* to do as it pleased. The reforms reimposed the discipline of law on all organs of government, and fulfilled one of the primary objectives of those who had led the people back to power from the Piraeus.

The reforms have also been seen, most notably by Mogens Hansen, as having wider constitutional implications leading to a separation of powers in the fourth century which made legislation and jurisdiction the monopoly of the six thousand citizens each year who had sworn the Heliastic Oath and served as legislators (*nomothetai*) and jurors (*dikastai*), and confined the role of the Assembly to foreign affairs and administrative decrees. The role of the jury courts in the democracy will be considered later, but the notion that the *nomothetai* took over the legislative function from the Assembly seems grossly misleading, and entirely at odds with the intent behind their creation and their impact in practice on the working of the constitution.[22]

The overriding concerns of the reformers in 403 were to achieve reconciliation and unite the state behind an agreed body of law. The task of revising, updating and codifying the existing body of law was immediately launched and quickly completed. The painstaking process of scrutiny, public consultation and ratification of the new code has already been described. The speed and diligence of the whole exercise testified to the depth of the commitment of the general public and its leaders to the rule of law and to defining in written, publicly inscribed form the body of general, permanent rules by which the society agreed to be governed.

The commitment was accompanied by a conservative attitude towards changes to the code, and the Assembly imposed upon itself an exceptionally elaborate process for the making of new law, involving public posting of proposals, two well-spaced meetings of the Assembly to give time for due deliberation and suggestions from individual citizens. To provide further insurance against rash or unwarranted alteration of the laws, the Assembly added a final check in the form of what was in essence a special jury commissioned to give a final judgement on the soundness of the new law.

There is no shred of contemporary evidence to show that this was seen as a curtailment of the Assembly's authority, and in practice it had no impact on the character of Athenian democracy. The *nomothetai* were not a separate, permanent, independent authority sharing power with the Assembly, but a large subset of the Assembly's members who were on the current jury list, and were randomly appointed by the Assembly for one day only to listen again to the arguments for or against a new law, and give a final verdict in the manner of all juries.

The *nomothetai* in no sense took over the legislative function. Legislation still had to be initiated in the Assembly, and it was the Assembly that decided whether to proceed with it and in what form. It entirely controlled the substance of Athenian law. Its apprehensions about legal change caused it to surround the process of lawmaking with an extraordinary series of checks. It did not see that as a derogation of its sovereignty, but as a precaution against error in a matter of the highest importance.

It should also be remembered that the Assembly took yet another step in this period to protect against faulty legislation by means of a law that provided for indictment of any proposer of new legislation who secured passage of a law that was not expedient (*epitedeios*). Under this procedure any new law passed by the Assembly could theoretically be overturned in the courts. The *graphe paranomon* allowed a similar overturning of decrees. These safeguards were not essentially different from the safeguard provided by the *nomothetai*. The Assembly accepted that it made mistakes. It put the blame, however, on its leaders, and was happy to have wrong decisions reversed in court.

The reforms of 403 were not aimed at diluting or moderating the later fifth-century democracy, or at meeting the aspirations of proponents of the so-called *patrios politeia* who sought limitations on the franchise or restoration of oligarchic features in existence before the reforms of Ephialtes and Pericles. The failure of the proposal of Phormisius showed there was no longer any sympathy for oligarchic sensibilities. Belief in the merits of rule by the people was at its height in 403. Oligarchic sentiment no longer had credit. The constitution that emerged was a more mature, better ordered, and strongly law-based democracy, but it remained a pure democracy.

The ancient evidence supports these conclusions. Demosthenes praises the new procedures for making law and describes them as civilised and democratic (*demotikos*). He also praises the conservatism of the *demos* in regard to changing the law, and says the mass of the people (the *hoi polloi*) are the only just and effective guardian of the laws, with a right no one can take from them to decide what is best. He obviously did not see the *nomothetai* as eroding that right.

The Aristotelian *Constitution of Athens*, which presents the restored democracy as the eleventh change of constitution in the history of Athens, certainly did not see it as a more moderate version of the democracy that preceded the Thirty, but as a final step in the progress of that democracy towards the most extreme form. In the *Politics*, which discusses democracy in all its facets and stages, Aristotle emphatically reinforces that view. Though he has no direct discussion of the reforms of 403, he describes in several places the democracy of his day as the ultimate (*teleutaia*) form, democracy in the highest degree (*malista*), the culmination of a series of additions to the power of the people by a succession of populist leaders from Ephialtes and Pericles onwards. In his history of the different forms of democracy he classes it as the fourth variety, and the most extreme, based on a concept of numerical equality that he believed failed the test of justice and reason, left no scope for merit or a balance of power between classes, but prescribed that all political decisions must be made by all. The result was a concentration of power in an Assembly in which an incompetent and morally defective underclass had a numerical superiority that it was sooner or later certain to use to pursue its own interests and pervert the constitution. Such a form of popular rule he compares to an oligarchy that had become dynastic, or a monarchy that had become tyrannical.[23]

Aristotle's analysis is, of course, open to criticism. It ignores the many stabilising factors built into the workings of the constitution of his day, which promoted social harmony, gave scope for merit, and created a balance between the roles of mass and elite. It takes no account of the reforms of 403 and the commitment made in them to the rule of law, a commitment that was strictly adhered to throughout his lifetime. It similarly ignores the fact that it was self-centred ambition and amoral extremism within the upper class that brought the revolutions of 411 and 404 and the brutal excesses and disregard for law of the reign of the Thirty, and that it was the *demos* that brought down the tyrants and showed the real civic virtue, as Thrasybulus emphasised when he led the people back from the Piraeus. These omissions are indicative of Aristotle's unrelenting theory-based aversion to radical democracy, but they give no grounds for rejecting his repeated assertions that the constitution under which he lived was the most complete form of rule by the people in the history of the democracy.

CHAPTER 7

Athenian Democracy in its Fullest Form

There was some continuing evolution of the system of government in the course of the fourth century, and this period has a character of its own and constitutes an important part of the story of Athenian democracy. It has attracted less interest because it lacks the dramatic highs and lows and colourful personalities and cultural breakthroughs of the fifth century. But Athenian political life in the fourth century had a new stability and maturity, and a surer sense of its guiding principles and superior merits. It is also the best-documented era of the democracy and provides the fullest information of how the system functioned. The following sections will review the structures and functioning of the democratic constitution in this final period when it achieved its fullest development and when the democratic ideal received its most complete discussion and clearest articulation.[1]

The Council of Five Hundred

There were no fundamental changes in the role of the Council. It remained a pivotal adjunct of the Assembly. It continued to provide the probouleutic and organisational supports for the Assembly assigned to it in the early stages of the democracy. The wider role that it acquired in the course of the fifth century as the state's full-time umbrella administrative body with responsibility to ensure the efficient implementation of the will of the Assembly also continued. The Aristotelian *Constitution of Athens* provides a detailed breakdown of the functions and powers that these broad responsibilities entailed in the fourth century. While the account shows few major changes to the position held by the Council in the fifth century, some aspects of the Council's work did assume greater importance in the restored democracy, and the lengthy catalogue of functions demonstrates how pervasive was its reach into virtually every area of public administration. The public finances, the preparedness of the armed forces, care of the navy and the dockyards, relations with other states, the religious festivals, public works, fair trading practices – all of these came within its sphere of responsibility. It was the ubiquitous watchdog on behalf of the Assembly, working in collaboration with most of the boards of magistrates to ensure efficiency and integrity in the performance of public officials. It had the judicial power to enforce its wishes and could impose fines on offenders of up to 500 drachmae. If it considered a higher penalty necessary, it could refer the case for final decision to a jury court.[2]

But the Council also had much wider judicial functions in regard to the accountability of magistrates and the prosecution of those accused of any form of malfeasance or behaviour seen as injurious to the state, and it was in this area in particular that its role assumed a greater importance in the fourth century.

The right to hold magistrates accountable was, according to Aristotle, conferred on the people by Solon. Aristotle considered it a basic democratic right, and the reason Solon was often regarded as the creator of Athenian democracy. The Athenians took it very seriously indeed. The ethos of collective decision-making, based on a strong principle of political equality and direct popular control of the course of public affairs, made them wary of delegating power to individuals or creating a strong executive. The Athenians had a lingering fear of tyranny, emphasised by Thucydides and well illustrated by the popular paranoia that erupted after the mutilation of the herms. Memories of 411 and 404 will have kept alive the spectre of unscrupulous leaders abusing the public trust to conspire against the state or advance their own ends at the expense of the public interest. There was a well-rooted conviction that those entrusted with executive power needed watching, should be required to account for their stewardship and should be promptly brought to justice for any offences damaging to the interests of the state. This concern about malfeasance and abuse of power by magistrates was part of a broader concern to build defences against all political threats to the laws and the constitution. There resulted a regime of accountability and a watchfulness to forestall harm to the public interest that reached a peak in the fourth century. The Council had a central role in enforcing this ethos of vigilance.[3]

The evolution of the legal procedures generated by these concerns to control magistrates and protect the state had a long history, and many aspects of that history and the resultant procedures are poorly documented and remain controversial.

The Council of the Areopagus originally had responsibility for supervising the most important areas of political life and protecting the laws and the institutions of the state. It had full powers to call magistrates to account (*euthynein*) and traditionally vetted new magistrates before they entered office, the process that became known as *dokimasia*. Solon reaffirmed the role of the Areopagus, made it the protector of his laws and gave it a specific right to try those who conspired to overthrow the constitution under a procedure that the Aristotelian *Constitution of Athens* called *eisangelia*. No further details of the procedure in that period are provided.

But Solon also, as part of his concern to establish a balance of power between the upper class and the masses, gave the people new judicial powers, most especially through the establishment of the appellate court of the people entitled the Heliaia. The evidence for the composition and powers of the court is sparse, but points to the conclusion that the Heliaia was the full Assembly meeting as a court, and that its right to hear appeals was wide-ranging. It is often argued that there was no appeal against decisions of the Areopagus, but Aristotle clearly states in two different passages in the *Politics* that Solon gave the people the right to hold magistrates accountable. These would be seriously misleading statements if the verdicts of the body with front-line responsibility for the accountability of the magistrates were inappellable.

All the indications are that Solon's judicial reforms were significant and had lasting effects. They are sometimes played down and presented as a sop to the people to make them more amenable to the rule of the elite, but this view ignores Solon's vehement excoriation of the depravity of that elite and its irresponsible use of power. He was clearly determined to remedy the abuses. He diluted the power of the old aristocracy by empowering the nouveaux riches. He sought an active citizenry whose engagement in politics would help combat the factionalism of the nobility. Above all, he sought a system of justice that would end the crooked judgements of a corrupt ruling class. A people's court of appeal with wide powers to review verdicts of magistrates and the Areopagus was very much in line with the goals of his reform programme. In any event, it is certain that by the early fifth century the Heliaia had the right of final decision in cases involving offences against the state. Accounts of six such trials survive. They include trials of such notable figures as Miltiades, Themistocles and Cimon. In all of them it was a popular court that decided the outcome.[4]

But it was not until the reforms of Ephialtes in 462 that jurisdiction in matters of the accountability of magistrates and prosecution of offences against the state was fully transferred from the Areopagus to the Council and *demos*. The Council was given responsibility for the *dokimasia* of incoming Councillors and archons, and always retained this responsibility, though later there was a right of appeal against its judgements to a jury court. The *dokimasia* of all other magistrates, whose members and functions steadily grew, was conducted by the jury courts. The Council also had charge of the examination of the performance of magistrates, the *euthyna*. The procedures governing the *euthyna* in the fifth century are very poorly documented and there is little that can be said with any certainty about them. But there is no indication that the elaborate system recorded for the fourth century was in use by the fifth, and it seems most probable that a tougher, more thorough structure of accountability for magistrates was written into the revision of the laws of 403/2, reflecting a drive for tighter control of public officials by the *demos* after a decade of upheaval.

There were several distinct elements in the system of accountability that operated in the fourth century. Magistrates were now monitored on an ongoing basis by a committee of ten councillors (*logistai*) chosen by the Council each year to audit the accounts of magistrates once in every prytany. Prosecution would obviously follow any evidence of abuses. In addition all public officials, whether holding the title of magistrate (*arche*) or not, were subject to a comprehensive examination of their performance at the end of their term. This was the formal *euthyna* and the process had two separate parts. A national committee of ten auditors, one from each tribe, selected by lot from all citizens of the tribe, had the task of examining the financial accounts. They had ten assistants (*synegoroi*), similarly chosen, who led any prosecutions that might result from the audit. All the audits, whether or not improprieties were found, had to be submitted to a jury court for a final verdict.

The second and more comprehensive part of the process was under the control of the Council and gave an opportunity to any citizen to charge any retiring official with any form of unlawful behaviour during his term. A committee of ten councillors, one from each tribe, selected by lot by the Council, and known as *euthynoi*, had charge of this process. For three days following the conclusion of the audit they sat by the monument of the Eponymous Heroes in the Agora to receive in writing from citizens any charges they wished to make of misconduct in office by any official who had undergone the audit. Each *euthynos* was assisted by two assessors (*paredroi*). Charges were handed to the *euthynos* from the tribe of the accused magistrate. If a charge seemed justified, a fine could be imposed, but if it involved a serious offence against the state it was referred to the *thesmothetai*, the six archons responsible for the administration of the courts who, if satisfied, arranged to bring the case to trial.[5]

The third, and the most significant, judicial responsibility that devolved on the Council following the reforms of Ephialtes concerned the prosecution of major offences against the state that were tried under the procedure known as *eisangelia*. As noted earlier, Solon is credited with introducing this measure into his laws to enable the Areopagus to carry out its responsibility to safeguard the laws and the constitution. Many aspects of the procedure and the forms of crime that fell within its scope remain controversial but, allowing for the fact that there was a certain lack of precision and consistency in the legal system, as evidenced by the frequency of disputes about the interpretation of laws and legal procedures, it is possible to reach some broad conclusions.

The range of public offences that could give rise to an *eisangelia* was wide, and included charges such as impiety, treason, peculation, conspiracy, accepting bribes as a *rhetor* to give bad advice to the people, making false promises to the people, betraying a city, fleet, land or sea force, consorting with the enemy. Later tradition added an open-ended category of public crimes not covered in written law.

An *eisangelia* could arise in several different ways. A Councillor could at any stage initiate a case in the Council, or *eisangeliai* could result from the supervisory functions of the Council. Private citizens could at any time bring an *eisangelia* to the Council charging a magistrate with acting outside the law. Charges brought by private citizens at the *euthyna* of magistrates could also lead to an *eisangelia*.

Cases could also arise from proceedings in the Assembly. At one principal meeting (*kyria ecclesia*) held once in each prytany, the people were asked to vote on whether they considered the magistrates were conducting their office well. If any magistrate got a negative vote he was deposed (*apocheirotonia*) and a trial normally followed in the form of an *eisangelia*. The Assembly had always exercised the right to recall magistrates during their term, and had used it extensively, especially against generals, in the fifth century. But the process for doing so was more thorough and systematic in the fourth century, formally giving the people an opportunity ten times a year to consider whether any such recalls with resultant *eisangeliai* were justified. At these same principal meetings, anyone who wished to bring forward any other form of *eisangelia* could do so.

It is clear that *eisangelia* was developed in the fourth century as a powerful weapon of popular vigilance against subversion and abuse of power. It was used with great regularity throughout the period and, according to Demosthenes, with shameful frequency against generals. The many opportunities that were now placed in the hands of the mass of citizens to sound alarms and initiate prosecutions of major figures marked an extension of direct involvement by the people in surveillance and criminal jurisdiction. It represented a greater democratisation of the constitution, a trend also visible in other aspects of the operation of government in the fourth century. It also illustrates the climate of heightened concern mentioned earlier to forestall any recurrence of the upheavals of the recent past. The restored democracy was leaving little scope for any threats to its stability.

The procedures followed in cases of *eisangelia* have generated the most controversy, sometimes unnecessarily. It is clear that the transfer by Ephialtes of the oversight of magistrates and the guardianship of the constitution from the Areopagus to the Council and *demos* meant the conduct of *eisangeliai*, the main instrument for the pre-emption and suppression of threats to the state, was in the hands of the Council and Assembly. The Council, in line with its broad probouleutic role, was given the right to conduct the first hearing, acting as a court of first instance. It could make a final determination in the case of minor offences, but had to refer more serious offences to the Assembly for a final verdict. The Assembly was performing the task assigned to it by Solon in its role as the Heliaia. When the growing burden of judicial functions in a rapidly expanding state made it necessary to subdivide the Heliaia in the form of the jury courts, most cases were referred to these courts, and the Assembly confined its involvement to cases of exceptional importance. It eventually relinquished all involvement in political prosecutions around the middle of the fourth century.

It is more difficult to be certain about the procedures followed in the cases that arose from proceedings in the Assembly, but there is no compelling evidence that *eisangeliai* that were first aired in the Assembly did not subsequently follow the customary procedure. Given the strict regulation requiring a *probouleuma* of some form before the Assembly could decide an issue, it would be surprising if the Council were not involved. Besides, there are several recorded instances where *eisangeliai* first raised in the Assembly were referred to the Council for preliminary discussion, or advice about how the final trial should proceed, and it is reasonable to assume that this was the standard practice.

The recall of a magistrate and the legal proceedings associated with it constitute a special case. The debate on the performance of magistrates was placed on the agenda by the *prytaneis*, but it was an obligatory item and was not accompanied by any form of *probouleuma*. But the debate involved a decision, and if the recall of a magistrate was voted, that constituted a preliminary judgement that misconduct had taken place. That would have made any further preliminary consideration by the Council redundant. Besides, the Aristotelian *Constitution of Athens* clearly states that a decision to recall led on to a trial in a jury court. It would seem this was the one form of political prosecution in which the Council had no involvement.[6]

Overall there was no weakening of the central position of the Council in the fourth century. There were some administrative changes in its secretarial support, and the chairing of meetings of Council and Assembly was transferred from the presidents to a new board of councillors known as *proedroi*. There were nine *proedroi*, who held their presiding role for just one day, with a chairman chosen by lot from the nine. All were chosen by lot on the morning of the day of the meeting of Council or Assembly, one from each tribe, excluding the tribe that held the presidency. The changes would seem to have had two purposes: to give charge of the chairing of meetings of Council and Assembly to a smaller, more broadly representative and constantly changing group of Councillors; and to prevent any risk of bribery or manipulation by selecting them, as in the case of jurors, on the morning of the day of the meeting.[7]

But the secretarial changes and creation of the *proedri* were purely administrative reforms and did not change the Council's continuing wide-ranging role. It remained the overseer and coordinator of the entire apparatus of government. Aristotle expressly attests to that. Its functions in the supervision and accountability of magistrates and all public officials, and in the guardianship of the constitution and the public safety, arguably increased. Its continuing role as a political training ground for citizens of all classes from every deme in the state remained at least as important as before. It placed its members during their year in office, and especially during the month when their tribe held the presidency, in the forefront of all the major activities of government at the highest level. The annual rotation of its membership, with reselection permitted only once in a lifetime, meant that a very large cross-section of citizens shared this intense apprenticeship. The limited period of service also meant there was no opportunity for influential figures to build a base of power in the Council in the way they might in the Assembly.

The Council was a changing forum where new blood from diverse backgrounds dominated and learned the workings of government. It was the greatest contributor to the informed citizenry of which Pericles boasted, and to what Josiah Ober has termed the dispersal and aggregation of knowledge within the citizen body, the ideal foundation on which to build the stability and success of government by the people. This was all the more significant in the fourth century when, as we shall see below, the people's main forum, the Assembly, ruled with a tighter rein and was less dominated by big personalities.[8]

The Council of the Areopagus

The Areopagus had been deprived of its main political powers by the reforms of Ephialtes in 462, and there is no evidence that it played any significant role in public affairs throughout most of the remainder of the fifth century. Its powers were restored, however, and the jury courts abolished when the Thirty took power in 404. The reforms of 403 reversed that, but the decree of Teisamenus, which created the law reform boards, had a clause that restored to the Areopagus the guardianship of the laws and responsibility for ensuring that magistrates only applied established laws.

This was consistent with the determination of the reformers to fortify the rule of law with as many protections as possible. Though seen by many as an oligarchic symbol, the Areopagus still retained an aura of respectability and authority. It had a long tradition of guardianship of the institutions of the state and had shown itself a bulwark of the constitution, especially in troubled times. In his pamphlet the *Areopagiticus*, written in the late 350s, Isocrates speaks about the high birth and high virtue of members of the early Areopagus, and adds that, despite the fall in moral standards in his day, even the disreputable on entering the Council act in accordance with its traditions rather than their own evil instincts. He urges a restoration of the Council's earlier powers to re-create a society with the moral fibre of its ancestors, and to put an end to the present woes which have brought Athens war and poverty, the hatred of its allies and the contempt of the barbarian. Lycurgus also has high praise for the Areopagus, calling it the most righteous Council and the chief saviour of the state following the defeat by Philip at Chaeronea in 338.[9]

The Assembly of the fourth century was quite willing to turn to the Areopagus for help when it had particular fears about the safety of the state. That was commonly the case in the 340s and 330s when the threat from Philip was reaching its peak, and internal divisions were growing. During this period the role of the Areopagus increased considerably. A new judicial procedure was introduced, known as *apophasis*, under which the Assembly might ask the Areopagus to investigate charges of treason and report its findings to the Assembly. The Areopagus might itself also initiate such actions. In both instances it reported to the Assembly, which then decided whether to send the case to a jury court for a final verdict. There are also instances of the Areopagus intervening in appointments made by the Assembly in relation to embassies and military commands. But the greatest boost to its power came from a decree carried by Demosthenes in the late 340s giving a blanket authority to the Areopagus to punish, in accordance with the ancestral laws, anyone who offended against the law. This may well have been a political stroke by Demosthenes at the height of his power carried out in the belief that he had the support of the Areopagus for his policies, and that he could use the Council to bring down his enemies.

In any event there was a limit to the trust of the *demos* in the Areopagus, and a few years later another decree reinforced the law of Demophantus passed in 410 against subversion of the democracy or participation in public office after its suppression, and specifically prescribed that any members of the Areopagus who cooperated in the overthrow of the democracy in such a way would suffer loss of civic rights and property. It was a pointed warning that the

Areopagus was not above suspicion or beyond the reach of popular retribution. While the Council featured more prominently in the political affairs of the latter part of the fourth century, it only had the power that the Assembly allowed it, and it was never a constraint on the rule of the people.[10]

The Magistrates

According to the Aristotelian *Constitution of Athens*, the number of magistrates administering domestic affairs rose to seven hundred in the course of the fifth century. The number is often regarded as an exaggeration, but without adequate reason. It is unlikely that fewer were required in the fourth century. The surviving evidence from the period provides a list of 450 magistrates in charge of seventy-one different functions, but new inscriptions keep uncovering additional boards of magistrates, and the number of seven hundred may yet be proven accurate.[11]

About a hundred magistrates were elected by the Assembly. Candidates were proposed at the meeting, and voting was by show of hands. The magistrates involved included all senior military commanders and those responsible for the training of the Ephebes, young citizens who had to undergo a comprehensive programme of military training and moral and religious education in their eighteenth and nineteenth years before becoming part of the body of full citizens. Senior financial officers and certain religious officials were also elected.

But as many as 1,100 other magistrates, including the five hundred Councillors, were chosen annually by lot from citizens who volunteered, who were over thirty years of age and who had not suffered any loss of civic rights (*atimia*). If a property requirement was still on the books, it had long been a dead letter. There were special procedures for the selection of Councillors and archons. Councillors continued to be selected by the demes. Each deme was assigned a quota of representatives in proportion to its number of citizens, and those chosen then went forward as part of the fifty members each tribe contributed to the Council.

The selection of archons involved two stages. Each tribe selected ten candidates by lot, one of whom would emerge as the representative of the tribe through a subsequent central process of allotment. The result was a group of ten, three of whom filled the posts of chief archon, archon basileus and polemarch, six of whom formed the board of *thesmothetai*, who administered the courts, and one of whom acted as secretary to the board. The other magistracies were filled from eligible candidates at proceedings in the Theseion presided over by the *thesmothetai*. Election for military commanders took place early in the seventh prytany (February), and presumably the other elections and appointments by lot happened not long afterwards, since time had to be allowed for the *dokimasia* which all incoming magistrates had to undergo before entering office at the start of the new year in July.

Magistrates usually operated as boards, generally numbering ten, with one member from each tribe. All had equal authority, and if a dispute arose it was resolved by a vote. This general principle of collegiality did not, however, preclude individual members of a board being assigned a specific task with individual responsibility for it. The principle of annual rotation and a ban on reappointment applied, except in the case of generals and certain financial officials. But there was no bar to holding a different office, except that the accountability procedures, which extended into the year following tenure of an office, precluded appointment to office in successive years.

In the case of the elective offices, there does not appear to have been any shortage of candidates, and the inscriptional evidence shows no gaps in the membership of the Council. There are some gaps in the records of other offices, but the literary evidence indicates that, at least in many cases, there was plenty of demand and keen competition.

Aristotle provides a list in the *Politics* of the main administrative departments required in any state. It corresponds with what we know of the structures in Athens in the fourth century, and no doubt reflects them. He describes as necessary offices those that administer religious affairs, the marketplace and fair-trading regulations, public works and facilities, rural affairs, the justice system, custody of prisoners and implementation of sentences.

He classifies as equally necessary but of a higher order, because the holders must have greater expertise and trustworthiness, the offices dealing with military affairs and the public finances. These were also the areas of the executive that saw the greatest change in the fourth century, and they require more detailed discussion.[12]

Defence

There were some significant reforms aimed at increasing the professionalism of the army. Athens was a great naval power, with seamen of superior quality. Its citizens were accustomed to the sea and seafaring and, according to the Old Oligarch, skilled in seamanship from an early age. But the army, which was a citizen militia, had no such claims to distinction. The infantry was largely drawn from the hoplite class, Aristotle's *mesoi*, the cavalry from the upper classes. Neither was regarded as a fighting force of the first rank, and neither was well suited to the lengthy campaigns, often at far distances from Athens, that characterised warfare in the late fifth and fourth centuries.

Various efforts were made to address these issues. I mentioned earlier the lengthy and intense regime of training in military, civic and ethical areas for citizens who had just come of age, the Ephebes. It was in place by the middle of the fourth century, and possibly earlier. It provided those who would form the future infantry and cavalry with expert instruction in the use of various forms of weaponry. This was accompanied by physical training and programmes of civic conditioning by older elected supervisors. The second year of this two-year apprenticeship was spent in military operations, patrolling and manning guard posts around the country.[13]

Problems of manpower shortages from losses in the plague and the Peloponnesian and civil wars, and the hardship that high military demands placed on citizens, and especially on poorer farmers, were addressed by greater use of mercenaries, an increasingly common phenomenon throughout Greece in the fourth century. The Athenians had hired Thracian mercenaries to send to Sicily with Demosthenes in 413, and they had long used mercenaries to supplement their own rowers in the fleet. But their use of mercenaries to bolster the effectiveness of the infantry became common practice in the fourth century. Mercenaries offered great advantages in land wars. Unlike a citizen militia, they could serve continuously for long periods, and could be trained and disciplined in ways not possible in the case of a part-time citizen army. Their value was well demonstrated in the Corinthian War of 395–386, when an innovative Athenian general, Iphicrates, used them as light-armed troops (peltasts), and trained them in new tactics and in the use of more effective weaponry. His success became legendary.

After the Corinthian War the use of mercenaries by Athens became still more prevalent. There are signs that there was a reluctance among the hoplite class to serve because of low pay or no pay and, in the case of overseas campaigns, long absences, all of which meant serious financial losses, especially for farmers. Demosthenes felt compelled to argue in the *First Philippic* in 351 for a move away from reliance on mercenary forces, proposing that a quarter of the infantry and cavalry should be citizens, serving for short periods and provided with basic rations, with further remuneration coming from the proceeds of war.

But the role of mercenaries tends to be exaggerated in the orators. Athens certainly continued to have military commitments in the fourth century greater than it could meet from its own manpower, and it needed mercenaries to bridge the gap. They were used especially where a standing army was required during lengthy year-round operations abroad. But citizens continued to fight in large numbers, especially in the shorter campaigns on the Greek mainland. Athens could not have afforded a largely mercenary army. There is abundant evidence that, in the great land battles of the fourth century such as Mantinea and Chaeronea, it was the citizens who bore the brunt.[14]

Changing times also brought changes in the office of general. The precise date of the changes is uncertain, but they were in force by the middle of the century. Five generals were now assigned specific posts: one to command the hoplites, one to guard the borders of Attica, two to protect the approaches to the Piraeus and one to administer the trierarchy, the important liturgy that required wealthy citizens to equip and command a trireme for a year. The remaining five generals were available to be deployed as needed.

These divisions of labour gave a clearer set of responsibilities to the office and the individuals holding it, while maintaining enough flexibility to cope with whatever military needs arose. Demosthenes derided the change, claiming it turned generals into ceremonial showpieces and domestic administrators rather than front-line commanders. Some of the posts were indeed primarily administrative, but they were important to the security of Athens and Attica and the state's capacity to wage war.

Those who were placed in charge of military campaigns were those who had high professional skills suited to deal with a new type of army and a more tactical form of warfare. Most of the great commanders of the fourth century were professional soldiers who devoted themselves to the business of war. They were repeatedly elected, commonly ten to twenty times. One remarkable leader, Phocion, held the office of general forty-six times.[15]

All of the changes mentioned above contributed to a separation of the roles of general and politician. The skills required for the two roles in the fourth century were markedly different. The professional requirements for success as a military commander in the changing military environment left little time or opportunity to acquire the skills or the power-base necessary for sustained political influence. Long absences from Athens were a further barrier to building favour and credibility with the *demos*. But it was the rise of the art of rhetoric that was most of all responsible for the transfer of political leadership from generals to a new breed of politician, the *rhetor*. These well-trained, able orators who lived by their eloquence had a decisive advantage in a mass Assembly where the power of persuasion was always a potent force and, as we shall see later, the right of initiative did not belong to any official leadership but to anyone (*ho boulomenos*) who had the ambition and ability to seize it.

As Aristotle notes in the *Politics*, generals and political leaders now had separate skills and professions. The able speakers had the ear of the people, but were not appointed generals because they lacked military expertise. But those who had the expertise rarely had the power of persuasion. And so the divide developed. The generalship took on a very different character. No Pericles emerged in the fourth century. The era of the great general dominating the course of politics was over.[16]

Finance

There were substantial changes too in the course of the fourth century in the structure and management of the state's finances. Athens faced severe economic challenges following the war and the subsequent civil upheaval. There was an enormous drop in the state income. The tribute from the allies and all other imperial income ceased immediately. All overseas possessions were also lost, and all Athenians in all states of the Aegean were forced back to Athens by Lysander. Pericles had put the figure for the tribute at 600 talents a year in the speech attributed to him by Thucydides before the outbreak of the war. The figure is higher than our other evidence indicates, but possibly correct if Pericles stretched it to include all imperial revenues. According to Xenophon, the total state income amounted to 1,000 talents at the beginning of the war. This meant that 400 talents were being raised from domestic sources, mainly customs dues and harbour taxes, leasing of the silver mines at Laurium and other public properties, taxes on metics, court fees, fines and confiscations. The system of liturgies and a war tax (*eisphora*), levied as required, supplemented these permanent sources of revenue.[17]

But many of these permanent sources ceased or seriously declined as a result of the war. Commerce was particularly badly affected. During the Periclean era the Piraeus had become the great commercial centre of the Aegean, the hub that attracted the ships of all the major trading cities, where Athens not only imported goods for its own needs, but for sale to others. The commercial primacy of the Piraeus was guaranteed by mastery of the sea, which enabled Athens to control the flow of trade and compel traders to use the Piraeus as their market.

But the humiliating defeat and subsequent civil upheaval, and the loss of the fleet and the empire, changed all that. Athens no longer had the wealth or power to sustain its position as the world's emporium and magnet for trade and investment. The Piraeus did remain a major trading centre in the fourth century, and was still producing 36 talents in customs duty in 399, which represented a volume of trade worth about 1,800 talents. But the available evidence suggests that figure was less than half the volume of trade before the loss of empire. The many other commercial benefits enjoyed by Athens as the imperial capital, such as the hosting of foreign embassies and sundry delegations, allies involved in court cases, visitors attracted by its fame and culture, were also greatly diminished. Isocrates later lamented the way foreigners, metics and overseas merchants deserted the city during the Social War of 357–355. The conflicts of the late fifth century would have given reason for a far more extensive exodus.[18]

Other areas of the economy also suffered. The nine-year occupation of Decelea had several economically damaging effects, which are given special emphasis by Thucydides, as discussed earlier. The desertion of more than twenty thousand slaves, many of them skilled, had a particular effect on the mining industry, a major source of public revenue. It went into a long-term decline and did not return to full production until the second half of the century.[19]

It is difficult to quantify the precise extent of the economic crisis of the fourth century or to determine how long it lasted. Figures in the sources are a rarity. But there is sufficient evidence to show that private capital had diminished, that poverty was widespread and that economic issues were very much to the fore. Andocides alludes to calls for cancellation of debts in 403. The last two extant plays of Aristophanes, the *Ecclesiazusae,* produced in 392, and the *Plutus,* produced in 388, are focused on money, and those individuals with too little of it and those with too much, in a state that badly needed rescuing. Aristophanes' solutions are, as usual, burlesque fantasies, but the themes obviously reflect a social reality. Xenophon lists the urgent matters left undone because of the lack of money: relief for the poor; repair of the docks, the walls and the temples; and the restoration of a reserve. Lysias speaks in general terms about the scarcity of money and refers to the state's inability to repay debts to Sparta and Boeotia or to repair crumbling walls and shipyard sheds. He also refers to situations where the Council was led to accept *eisangeliai* and resorted to confiscations to find money to administer the state. Demosthenes has many references to financial difficulties, private and public, that forced respectable citizens to do menial tasks to survive, brought suspension of the courts and meetings of the Council because there was no money to pay jurors or Councillors, and resulted in failure to pay soldiers or provide adequate resources for their commanders. He also gives the only figure that shows how low the public revenues dropped on occasion, when he reminds his audience in the *Fourth Philippic* in 341/40 that it was not long ago that the state's annual income did not exceed 130 talents. The same passage confirms that better times had currently brought public revenues back to 400 talents.

There can be no doubt that the events of the final thirty years of the fifth century left Athens a weaker and poorer state, with a depleted population and depleted private wealth and public revenues. Even the reserve of 6,000 talents kept on the Acropolis for use in emergencies was gone. The hard times prevailed at varying levels throughout most of the first half of the century and were especially severe in times of war, when Athens struggled to meet its obligations and was limited in the initiatives it could take on any front. It was not until the advent of a more peaceful era in the late 350s, and the emergence of an influential statesman, Eubulus, who was committed to a strategy of peace, that the recovery noted by Demosthenes began.[20]

A number of administrative reforms were made to bring greater control and efficiency to the collection and management of state revenues. A new structure of budgeting was introduced in the early decades of the century. It replaced a system of ad hoc allocations to the various organs of government as authorised by the Assembly with a structure of fixed budgets (*merismos*) for each area. The budgets were established by a law rather than a decree, and alterations therefore had to go through the complex procedure involved in changing a law. The arrangement was clearly designed to impose a rigid budgetary discipline, though it had the obvious disadvantage of limiting flexibility to respond to changed circumstances or priorities.[21]

Significant changes were also made to increase state revenues. Throughout most of the fifth century it had not been necessary to impose any form of regular direct taxation. Revenues came from the variety of indirect taxes listed earlier. These were supplemented by the long-established system of liturgies, under which the rich were required to support the great religious festivals, which were a central feature of civic life, and to help fund the mainstay of Athenian military might, the navy. Tribute from the allies was the other great contributor to the treasury. It covered most of the military costs, helped build the architectural splendours of the Periclean era, facilitated the introduction of pay for jurors and public office, enabled the accumulation of a significant reserve, and contributed to the general prosperity resulting from increased trade and employment.

It was only when the ravages of the plague and the costs of the escalating Peloponnesian War overstretched the public finances in 428 that the Athenians resorted to direct taxation and imposed a temporary property tax, the *eisphora*. It had to be imposed again a number of times in the later years of the war, but it remained very much an emergency expedient for use in military crises.[22]

But the scale of the financial difficulties in the fourth century required a more extensive and structured system of revenue generation to maintain the solvency of the state. The *eisphora* and the most significant of the liturgies, the trierarchy, were now required on an almost constant basis. The trierarchy was a particularly onerous liturgy and could cost between 4,000 and 6,000 drachmae. To ease the burden, it became possible in the fourth century for two people to share it. There was also a rather peculiar process known as *antidosis*, which allowed anyone who felt unfairly treated in being chosen for a trierarchy to challenge another citizen whom he believed was richer either to undertake it instead or to exchange properties. If no agreement was reached, the case went to court.[23]

In 357 a whole new system was introduced under a law proposed by Periander, which was obviously intended to increase efficiency, fairness and affordability. It created a register of 1,200 of the wealthiest individuals who would have sole liability for the trierarchy. There were exemptions, however, for orphans, the disabled, heiresses and those whose property lay outside Attica or was in joint ownership. Using a structure similar to one earlier created for the collection of the *eisphora*, those on the register were divided into twenty groups called symmories, and all members contributed equally to the cost of equipping whatever ships were assigned to the group. One of the generals had charge of the symmories and appointed the trierarchs.

But there were still inequities in the system in that it placed equal burdens on the richest and poorest alike within a group, and in 340 Demosthenes introduced a law that required that the wealthiest pay strictly in proportion to their capital worth. This meant that the three hundred who formed the top tier of the wealthy would bear the main cost of the trierarchy. Demosthenes says that as a result of his law one man had to equip two ships instead of paying one-sixteenth of the cost of one.[24]

It is difficult to determine how severe a burden the trierarchy represented for the wealthy. It is fair to say, however, that significant efforts were made to ensure the burden fell mainly on those best able to afford it. The provisions for exemptions and the remedy of the *antidosis* gave protection against hardship and any major unfairness. The reforms of Periander defined responsibility more clearly and spread the costs in a way that may have increased frequency of liability but avoided heavy impositions in one year. The law of Demosthenes ironed out remaining inequities in the system of symmories.

The sources also show that volunteering for the trierarchy continued to be seen as an act of high patriotism, and that it continued to be used extensively as a means to political advancement. Lycurgus says that it is only the trierarchy and other forms of contribution to the state's defences that truly deserve the gratitude of the people. Boasts about voluntary trierarchies beyond the legal requirements abound in the orators. This level of volunteering for the liturgy would indicate that the legal demands did not overstretch the resources of the wealthy. Demosthenes certainly had no sympathy for those who complained or shirked their responsibility, and at one stage he proposed an expansion of the system to ensure the state had adequate fleets.[25]

The *eisphora* became a regular feature of Athenian life from early in the fourth century. A major reform in 378 made it a far more rigorously organised regime. In that year a new census of property was taken, which assessed the taxable capital for the state at 6,000 talents. To expedite collection of the tax whenever a levy was voted, the system of symmories was created in 378/7 which divided those liable for tax into one hundred groups, each group being responsible for delivering the full assessment of that group. Later, to counter evasion and default, three of the richest citizens in each group were appointed and required to pay in advance the full amount due from the symmory. They then recovered what they could from the other members. This prepayment, known as the *proeisphora*, was regarded as a liturgy and would therefore, like all liturgies, last only one year. It presumably rotated among the wealthiest tier of the symmory.[26]

There is widespread disagreement about both the rate of the *eisphora* and the number and categories of citizens who were liable for it. J.K. Davies in his detailed study of wealth in classical Athens concluded that the 1,200 individuals on the trierarchic register constituted the entire leisure class, those commonly known as the *plousioi*. He reckoned they had a capital worth of one talent or more, and were the only group with the capacity to pay taxes.

It seems almost certain, however, that liability for the *eisphora* extended well beyond the 1,200 on the trierarchic register. The proposal of Demosthenes in 354 (14.14) that the number on the trierarchic register should be increased to two thousand shows that at least that number could be reasonably argued to have sufficient wealth to afford participation in the trierarchy. There is also strong evidence from the period of the Thirty that those described as *plousioi* formed a wider group than the 1,200. The Thirty had selected three thousand hardline oligarchic supporters in 404 who were to share in government with them. These clearly did not come from the staunchly democratic hoplite class, but were part of the wealthier elite where oligarchic sentiment was strongest. They were later known as the men of the City. Thrasybulus addressed them after he led the *demos* back from the Piraeus, and he described them as richer (*plousioteroi*) than any of the common people. There may well have been considerable variations in wealth within the Three Thousand, but it is a safe assumption that they were liable for the *eisphora* in proportion to their capital worth.

There are also arguments to support the view that the tax liability extended still further to include the class that Aristotle described as the *mesoi*, the 'middling' working farmers of moderate means. Demosthenes states in a speech from the late 350s that the *plethos*, the common term for the mass of citizens, were worn out from paying taxes. It is hard to believe such a term could have been used to describe an elite group of the state's wealthiest. Elsewhere he talks about frugal tillers of the soil struggling to feed their children, run their homes and pay their taxes. A tax in times of public need, ranging beyond class to all

who had a capacity to contribute something, was consistent with the democratic spirit of communal solidarity, and with the appeals to patriotism and
public service so prevalent in the orators. A broad-based tax linked to capacity
to pay would also blunt perceptions that taxation was a class issue, only
targeting the rich.[27]

The rate at which the *eisphora* was levied is the most vexed question. The
tax was not progressive, but the higher the capital valuation, the greater the tax,
so the richest bore the brunt. The clearest indication of the level of the *eisphora*
comes from statements in Demosthenes. He says that a levy of 1 per cent would
be expected to yield 60 talents, and he confirms that this was the rate levied
in 352. Elsewhere he says levies that were designed to raise about 300 talents
were imposed between 377 and 357. There is no indication of the frequency
of the levy in those years, but a return of 300 talents over twenty years would
mean an annualised rate of only 0.02 per cent. The rate could probably
fluctuate somewhat depending on the severity of the financial need, but it
was clearly kept within moderate levels and was designed solely to deal with
military requirements.[28]

Another method of increasing state revenues in times of need that made its
appearance in the fourth century has been mentioned earlier. It was known as
the *epidosis*, a word meaning a voluntary contribution. Isaeus uses the word to
describe a benefaction to the state in 392 but, according to Demosthenes, it was
not until the expedition to Euboea in 357 that *epidosis* became an official term
for a procedure in the Assembly to raise funds through a special appeal for
voluntary contributions. Any citizen could make a proposal for such an appeal.
If adopted, members were asked to pledge donations immediately. There was
no compulsion to donate. The only pressure was moral and social. As noted
earlier, voluntary public giving was seen as an act of high patriotism in Athens,
and was highly prized and certain to win popular favour. The *epidosis* was a
formal challenge from the *demos* to the rich to show the level of their public-
spirited generosity in a time of need. Those who failed to respond risked public
disapproval and were likely to hear about their failure from their opponents.
The speech of Demosthenes against the wealthy but seemingly stingy politician Meidias shows how effectively a lack of public generosity could be used to
discredit a prominent figure. The *epidosis* was a relatively common phenomenon in the fourth century, and is a good example of how the democratic
system contrived to divert part of the surplus wealth of the elite to public
purposes without compulsion, or any appearance of attacking the right of
private property or of seeking redistribution of wealth.[29]

There was one further significant development in the management of the
public finances in the latter half of the fourth century: the re-creation of the

Theoric Fund, first introduced by Pericles to provide a payment to citizens to cover the cost of attending the theatre during festivals. The reform is attributed to Eubulus, who emerged as a dominant figure in the period from the end of the Social War in 355 until the late 340s. His great concern was to maintain peace and increase economic prosperity and the level of state revenues, and avoid in particular overseas military involvements that were not essential to the security of Athens. The Theoric Fund was re-established soon after the end of the Social War. It made payments to citizens on festival days in line with the intent of Pericles, but it soon acquired a much wider role. All surplus revenues were paid into it. Initially it may have been headed by a single official but by the 330s a board of magistrates had been created to administer it. The office was elective. The monies were used for a wide range of public works and military purposes including roads, the dockyards, naval equipment and the city's fortifications. Aeschines says, with considerable exaggeration no doubt, that the office controlled almost the entire administration of the public finances.[30]

When the influence of Eubulus declined at the end of the 340s and Demosthenes and his associates became more dominant, the Theoric Fund lost some of its importance, and more of the surpluses were diverted to the Military Fund which was the chief priority of Demosthenes. But this seems to have changed again in the early 330s when Lycurgus, a member of the old nobility and a formidable orator, emerged as a powerful advocate of the policies of Eubulus. He appears to have been elected to a new office, which is described by his contemporary Hyperides as the management of the public finances. Whatever his precise official position he was a dominant figure in the 330s, credited with increasing revenues, an extensive building programme, and expansion of the fleet and of the dockyards and harbours.[31]

It is clear that in the latter half of the fourth century new financial offices emerged as the most powerful magistracies and the source of greatest political influence. Politicians such as Eubulus and Lycurgus came closest to achieving the level of influence wielded by leading generals of the fifth century. This is not entirely surprising. After the prolonged economic difficulties of the first half of the century, the most urgent need when more peaceful times and greater prosperity returned was to maximise public revenues and use them to restore the state's infrastructure and boost defences and commercial potential. The powerful new financial offices were clearly designed to do that. The *demos* was never reluctant to delegate significant power in challenging times to individuals who had proven ability and who had won its trust. Alongside its equalitarian ethos of collective control of public affairs, it had always recognised its need for able leaders and the benefits of exploiting talent, especially in times of need. It was a flexibility that served the democracy well.

Overall, however, the democracy did not favour a strong executive. The idea violated too many basic tenets of government by the people. Aristotle lists the principles that defined the place and character of the executive branch in the form of democracy that prevailed in his day. Magistrates should be elected by all from all; all should rule each, and each in turn should rule all; selection should be by lot except where special skills and experience were required; there should be no property qualification for office, or the lowest possible; with the exception of military offices, no one should hold the same office twice except in rare instances; tenure of all offices, or of as many as possible, should be short; magistrates, like all others performing public services, should be paid if at all possible. Theophrastus adds one further principle to Aristotle's list: that magistrates should operate as boards, not individuals.

With respect to functions, Aristotle records that democracy in its final form allowed magistrates no power to make decisions regarding public policy; that was the prerogative of the deliberative Assembly of all citizens. The role of magistrates was confined to preliminary evaluation of issues and the administration of the departments of government in line with the wishes of the people. They were in all matters subordinate to the Assembly, and in all forms of democracy were accountable to the people.[32]

Aristotle's analysis is consistent with the evidence for the practices of his time, and sets out very clearly the depth of the commitment of the Athenian democratic ideal to the realisation of its two closely linked, primal principles of liberty and equality. In the Athenian view, true liberty could only be attained in a state that had true political as well as legal equality for all citizens, and true political equality meant numerical equality, with each citizen counting as one and no one counting as more than one. The corollary of that was that the vote of the majority was supreme, and that whatever the majority decided had to be accepted as final and just.

But government required implementation as well as deliberation, a function that could not be discharged by direct action of the mass of citizens (*to plethos*). It required delegation of power to individuals or groups. But equal liberty required that this too be done on a basis of equality. This gave rise to the principle of rule and be ruled, which meant not only the equal right to seek office but, outside the situation where special skills were required, the equal opportunity to hold it. Hence the short tenure, the general ban on re-election to the same office, the use of the lot for all offices outside the specialist areas, the absence of a property qualification and pay for service. The whole system was geared towards a communitarian culture of intense citizen engagement with public affairs and active participation on a large scale. As noted earlier in regard to the Council, the educative effects of the exposure of the citizenry on such a scale to a broad range of executive offices contributed greatly to the capacity of the *demos* to govern effectively.

The system was also designed to safeguard the rule of the people and protect against individual power-building or the emergence of a ruling elite able to threaten the supremacy of the mass. The short tenure and the ban on re-election to the same office, along with the collegial structure of most magistracies, gave little scope for the use of political office as a path to dominance. But the greatest protection came from the constant vigilance exercised through the frequent rigorous forms of accountability and swift retribution for any conduct deemed injurious to the state. This was especially important in regard to the military and financial offices, where re-election was allowed. Generals received the strictest scrutiny of all, and suffered the most frequent prosecutions. The absence of serious factional strife or class divisions in the fourth century shows how securely the system was functioning.

The Courts (*Dikasteria*)

The main elements of the judicial system were in place by the end of the fifth century but, as in the case of the other areas of government, there was consider-able further development during the fourth century. The greater volume of information about the period in general, and the particularly extensive evidence for the system of justice provided by the sizeable corpus of extant speeches from the great orators of the age, such as Lysias, Demosthenes and Aeschines, give a fuller picture than is attainable from any other era of the pivotal place of the courts within the structures of the democracy, and of their importance in cementing popular control of government.

As noted earlier in this chapter, the jury courts came into being when the court of the people, the Heliaia, which comprised the full Assembly, was sub-divided into a number of courts to cope with the greatly expanded volume of judicial business arising from the reforms of Ephialtes and a rapidly expanding state. The Assembly reserved to itself only the most important political cases, and in the middle of the fourth century it transferred even those to the jury courts.

The range of responsibility of the jury courts continued to grow. In addition to making judgements in matters relating to *dokimasia*, *euthyna* and political crimes, they also dealt with charges of misconduct against those who put them-selves forward as politicians (*hoi politeumenoi*) and professed to have a concern for the state. Demosthenes described the laws relating to the behaviour of such politicians as rightfully tough to deter them from harming the public good. The laws included such offences as accepting bribes to mislead the people, making false promises to the people, and making proposals that contravened existing laws and decrees. The courts had a tight rein on anyone who exercised power by virtue of a magistracy or by their influence as *rhetores* in the Assembly. They also gradually took over the whole range of civil and criminal cases previously dealt with by magistrates, and especially archons. The role of magistrates was now confined to resolving trivial cases involving fines below ten drachmae, and to preliminary evaluations and presiding over the jury courts. The developed court system represented a further major step towards what Aristotle called the final form of democracy operating in his day (*teleuteia demokratia*), in which magistrates decided nothing, merely conducting preliminary investigations.[33]

The jury courts were a constant feature of the civic life of Athens in a society that appears to have had an enormous appetite for litigation. They could sit on any day other than annual festival days, Assembly days and a number of other days considered inauspicious. It appears they did sit with great regularity, as often as 175–225 days a year, according to evidence assembled by Mogens Hansen.[34]

The overall administration of the courts was the responsibility of the six junior archons, the *thesmothetai*, who also presided over political trials. The courts dealing with other types of cases were presided over by other magistrates. Jurors had to be over thirty years of age and in full possession of their citizen rights. They were paid three obols a day for their services, a figure that remained unchanged from the late fifth century despite the fact that pay for attendance at the Assembly increased from three obols in the 390s to six obols in Aristotle's day, rising to nine for plenary sessions. This suggests there was no shortage of volunteers for jury service. Juries varied in size between 201 and 401 in private lawsuits, depending on the seriousness of the issue, and 501–1,001 in public prosecutions, though that could rise beyond 2,000 in political trials of exceptional importance. Jurors apparently did not deliberate among themselves. Voting was by secret ballot and a verdict required only a simple majority. Except where penalties were fixed by law, each party was allowed to propose and justify a penalty, and the jurors chose one of them by another vote. They were not free to devise a penalty of their own.

The number of days of court sittings and the size of the juries, combined with a high volume and rapid turnover of cases, which are estimated to have required up to two thousand jurors every court day, meant a level of participation by the citizen population of huge proportions. The social composition of jurors is hard to determine, but the fact that the scanty evidence is conflicting suggests that there was a social spread.[35]

The national panel of six thousand, from which juries were drawn, was recruited annually by lot from those who put their names forward. The nine archons along with the secretary of the *thesmothetai* oversaw the selection, each recruiting six hundred from within his tribe. There was no ban on reselection. Those chosen had to swear the Heliastic Oath, sections of which are quoted in various forensic speeches. The jurors swore: to vote in accordance with the laws and decrees of the *demos* and Council, and in accordance with their judgement of the just where there was no law; to give an impartial hearing to both sides; never to vote for tyranny or oligarchy, or to follow anyone proposing to subvert the democracy. After swearing the Oath, the juror received a small identification plaque, which in the fourth century was made of bronze and had the juror's name inscribed on it.[36]

The process of selecting and assigning the jurors needed for the courts that were sitting on a particular day underwent major changes in the early decades of the fourth century. It was moved to the morning of the court sittings, and the jurors were selected from those who presented themselves for jury service on the day. The full body of volunteers was first organised by tribes, and one-tenth of the jurors needed for the day were chosen by random selection from each tribe. A second sortition from the resulting list assigned each juror to a particular court, again by a method designed to give fair representation to each tribe on every jury. The archons and the secretary to the *thesmothetai* presided over the entire procedure. Later in the century the presiding magistrates, though informed ahead of time of the days when they would be needed, also began to be assigned by lot to a particular court only on the morning of the day of the sitting.

This elaborately designed system had two purposes. One was to make it impossible for anyone to know ahead of time who would be serving on the jury of a particular court on a particular day, a powerful protection against bribery of jurors or any form of prearranged pact to secure a particular verdict. The second purpose was to ensure that every jury had, as far as was possible, equal representation from all ten tribes, and therefore represented a genuine cross section of the entire citizen population.[37]

The procedures for the initiation and conduct of lawsuits also tell a good deal about the character of the system of justice and its reliance on ordinary citizens to discharge the critical functions. As in the case of the Assembly, the judicial system was designed to give maximum control to the mass of citizens, and to minimise the role of any elite. This was true in respect of both private cases (*dikai*) and public prosecutions, i.e. those affecting the public interest (*graphai*).

Private cases had to be brought and argued by the injured person, except in exceptional circumstances, though it was possible, if the jury agreed, for the plaintiff to share his allocated time with unpaid supporters (*synegoroi*). Defendants similarly had to conduct their own defence, but could also have unpaid supporters in court. Both sides could employ speechwriters (*logographoi*), though the practice was frowned upon. Witnesses were allowed and were important, not so much in establishing the facts as in confirming the assertions of the litigants. From early in the fourth century witnesses had to submit their evidence in writing, which was read out in court, with the witness present merely to confirm it.[38]

But before reaching the courts, almost all private cases were referred to an arbitrator (*diaitetes*), an office established at the beginning of the fourth century. Arbitrators were citizens in their fifty-ninth year who had reached the end of their liability for military service. No one was exempt unless holding office or absent abroad. The arbitrators were organised in ten groups by tribe, each group dealing with cases that arose within its tribe. From start to finish ordinary citizens dominated the process. There was no dependence on any professional elite. The role of magistrates was also peripheral. They conducted preliminary hearings (the *anakrisis*), which seem to have been concerned largely with establishing the legal basis of the action and that everything was in order to let it go forward to court. Magistrates also presided over the court hearing, but their task was to ensure that the proceedings moved to a conclusion in accordance with the rules. They had no power to instruct the jury, no right of summing up, no control over what the jury heard and no role in determining penalties.

The same procedures applied in public prosecutions. As discussed earlier, there were special procedures governing *eisangeliai* and cases related to the *euthyna*, but otherwise the initiative in bringing public prosecutions rested with private citizens. There were no state prosecutors, and the system could not have functioned if citizens were not ready to come forward as accusers, acting in the public interest. Exposing the guilty preserved the democracy. It was seen as a duty as well as a right. Lycurgus said the just citizen will regard those who break his country's laws as his private enemies. As in private lawsuits, both prosecutor and defendant had to conduct their cases in person, aided only by the evidence of witnesses, by whatever *synegoroi* the jury allowed and by whatever services they purchased from the professional speechwriters.[39]

There were some financial incentives to bring prosecutions in certain cases where debts to the state or misuse or misappropriation of state assets were involved. The prosecutor received a proportion of any gains that accrued to the state from such cases. This carried the risk, however, of fostering a culture of snooping and informing, and in the late fifth century gave rise to a breed of prosecutors memorably lampooned in Aristophanes, who were known as sycophants, made a profession of prosecuting and sometimes used the threat of prosecution as a method of blackmail. The system had other risks also in that it gave scope for frivolous or malicious prosecutions to embarrass or damage one's enemies.

The Athenians were aware of the dangers inherent in giving citizens an untrammelled right to act as prosecutors, and they took a number of measures to protect against abuses. Accusers who did not see a case through to the end, or failed to get the votes of one-fifth of the jurors, faced fines of 1,000 drachmae and possible loss of citizen rights. There were also laws dealing with *sycophantia*. No details survive, but Isocrates describes them as tougher than those against any other form of wrongdoing, and charges could be brought under a number of procedures. The Athenians were committed to their system of justice and preserving its integrity.[40]

The courts were a pivotal arm of government and, as noted earlier, some modern historians, especially Mogens Hansen, have argued that they constituted a separate, sovereign element of the constitution that ended the Assembly's previously supreme control over the government of the state. The assertion, if true, would have major implications for the character of Athenian democracy, but the entire body of evidence relating to the origin, structure, procedures and functions of the courts would seem to contradict it.[41]

The courts were established when the scale of the judicial responsibilities transferred from the Areopagus by Ephialtes to the *demos* and Council made it impractical for the Assembly as a body to attempt to discharge them, so the function was delegated to a cross-section of the *demos* randomly selected in equal numbers from all the tribes and changing annually. It is likely that the system began to be developed soon after the reforms of Ephialtes. It was certainly in full operation in the Periclean era, when Pericles introduced pay for jurors to help ensure the large numbers of citizens required for jury duty would be available.

It is implausible in itself that Pericles, the man seen by both Plato and Aristotle as the prime architect of radical democracy, would have helped embed the system, if it meant a dilution of the powers of the Assembly or an end to its position as the state's supreme governing authority. Pericles defined democracy as the system that gave *kratos*, not to the few, but to the greater number, which meant rule by majority decisions of the full mass of citizens. The Assembly was the only forum that provided for a gathering of the mass, the *to plethos*, or what the inscriptional evidence refers to as the *demos plethuon*, the *demos* in its full form. The Assembly was certainly supreme in the time of Pericles, and it was the Assembly that provided the power-base for his ascendancy. A century later the same Assembly was the base that gave Demosthenes his period of dominance. That was the time when Aristotle was writing in the *Politics* that, in a democracy, the principle of numerical equality meant of necessity that the mass, the *to plethos*, must be supreme, and that what the greater number decide must be taken as final and just. There is no ancient evidence that contradicts that statement of Aristotle.[42]

But, as emphasised previously, the Assembly did need supporting institutions to assist it in the task of governing. The Council and the body of magistrates provided such support from the beginning, and the reforms of Ephialtes led on to the creation of the courts. All of these auxiliary bodies were organised and conducted their affairs along strict democratic lines, observing the principles of equality and of rule and be ruled. They remained the domain of the mass of citizens, showing democracy in action, and enabling broad participation by a wide range of citizens, not only in the deliberative and legislative functions, but in the executive and judicial functions. This was participatory democracy on a grand scale.

All of these institutions contributed to the more effective functioning of the democracy, but none of them had independent power to make policy or take the big decisions that determined the course of political affairs. Their role was supportive, to implement or uphold the will of a supreme Assembly.

The courts had an especially pivotal role, as the orators and Aristotle made clear. But they, above all, were a domain of the mass of citizens, free of any special role for a professional or aristocratic elite. The jurors numbered six thousand, the number required for a quorum at a plenary meeting of the Assembly, hardly a coincidence. It had special significance for Athenians, clearly seen as the number that could be accepted as genuinely representative of the body of citizens.

There are many references in the orators that show jurors were closely associated with the *demos* and were regarded as acting on behalf of the *demos*. Dinarchus tells a jury that they have been assembled on behalf of the *demos* and are sworn to obey the laws and decrees of the *demos*. There are other references that present jurors as the same people who attend the Assembly, or identify them with decisions of the Assembly.

The courts were not designed to check or balance the power of the Assembly. Their function was expressly the opposite. It was spelled out in the Heliastic Oath, which stated as its first injunctions that jurors must vote in accordance with the laws and decrees of the *demos* and Council, and refuse to support tyranny or oligarchy or anyone who attempted to subvert the democracy. Demosthenes had it read out at the trial of Timarchus to drive home his point that the state is governed by laws and decrees, and that, if the courts should lose their power to uphold the law, the democracy would crumble. Elsewhere he says laws are but written texts without courts to enforce them. The courts were therefore seen as a necessary support for the democracy, ensuring the will of the people was enforced and the constitution protected.[43]

The views of Aristotle are in line with those of the orators. He considered the creation of the courts, far from diluting the democracy, as the decisive event that made possible the emergence of extreme democracy, extending the control of the mass into a crucial area of government. He emphasises that a full democracy required that the judicial function be controlled by the mass of citizens. The right to share in the administration of justice, along with the right to share in the deliberative function of the Assembly, defined citizenship in a democracy. But he explicitly says that the judicial right, while it belonged to all citizens, could be exercised either by all collectively or by those selected from all. In either case, in Aristotle's view, the courts were in the hands of the masses, and were an organ of popular rule that cemented and protected the power of the masses. The Aristotelian *Constitution of Athens* is even more explicit in identifying the courts with the *demos*, when it summarises the final state of the constitution in the fourth century: 'the *demos* has made itself supreme in all matters, and decides everything by the decrees of the Assembly and the decisions of the courts, where it holds sway'.[44]

It is difficult to argue that the constitution of the fourth century was other than democracy in its fullest form. The power of the *demos* was pervasive. The evidence that the Assembly remained the supreme governing authority, through a strict rule of law, seems conclusive. There was no disposition for checks, other than the law, on the power of the *demos*, after the dire experiences with the champions of oligarchy. The courts, from their inception, were seen as institutions of the people, protecting the rule of the people and giving effect to the will of the people as expressed through the Assembly.

The Assembly

The continuing dominant position of the Assembly in the fourth century has been adequately discussed in the previous section. The changes in procedures for enacting new laws had relatively little effect in practice on the way the state was governed. The definition of laws in the reforms confined them to general permanent rules akin to the provisions of modern written constitutions. The Athenians were content that virtually all the particular, time-limited decisions involved in administering the state, many of which would require statutory sanction in modern systems, should be made simply by decree. Foreign affairs were entirely managed by decree. No aspect, even matters as significant as peace settlements or alliances, was deemed to require passage of a law. This, combined with a strong aversion in principle to altering established law and the complex procedures required to achieve it, seems to have made new legislation a rare occurrence in fourth-century Athens. There is no record of any law being passed between 403 and 375. There is inscriptional evidence for only seven laws altogether, compared with 488 decrees. There were certain financial matters connected with customs and foreign trade, mining and the fixing of the *merismos* that were regulated by law, but even where laws were needed, their introduction and content were entirely in the hands of the Assembly. The latter very much remained in control of the course of public affairs.[45]

That control continued to be strengthened throughout the century by a succession of developments designed to increase the level of involvement of the Assembly and make it as representative as possible of the mass of citizens by expanding participation. The introduction of pay at the start of the century, a time of particular financial stringency, was a determined effort to boost attendance, especially by the lower classes. About the same time there was another major expenditure on the Assembly when its main meeting place on the Pnyx was totally reconstructed, creating a fully enclosed and enlarged theatre-shaped space with seating. The building of such an elaborate facility in straitened times was a strong statement of the importance attached to the Assembly, but it also facilitated the Assembly's work and ensured there was adequate accommodation for larger numbers.[46]

But the most significant development was an increase in the number of fixed meetings. In the fifth century it is likely there were only ten such meetings annually, one in each prytany, with others summoned on an ad hoc basis as required. The number was increased to four in each prytany in the course of the fourth century. The date of the increase is uncertain, and it may have been gradual, but it meant a more heavily engaged Assembly, exercising more direct managerial control. Dates of meetings were fixed in advance and agendas were published five days ahead of the meeting, facilitating the planning and preparation of attendees.

The first meeting in each prytany was a plenary session (*kyria ecclesia*), which required a quorum of six thousand. It was obviously seen as the meeting that dealt with the most important business. Top of the agenda was a vote on the performance of magistrates and, as mentioned earlier, a negative vote generally meant recall and subsequent prosecution. Plenary sessions also gave citizens an opportunity to bring forward any form of *eisangelia* that they wished to pursue. The Assembly was ruling with a tight rein. The vigilance was unrelenting.[47]

There is no explicit evidence for the numbers attending, but there are several indications that they were high, and that the quorum of six thousand required for plenary sessions was a usual turnout. There were several forms of business transacted outside the plenary meetings that required the same quorum, a strong indication that assembling such numbers was not problematic. Aristophanes certainly gives the impression that the problem was not too few attending, but the size of the throngs scrambling for admission. In the two surviving plays from the fourth century mentioned earlier, he satirises the pushing and shoving of the lower classes to get into the Assembly so they could draw their pay. He is writing burlesque political comedy, of course, but beneath the hyperbole and farce there had to be, as always, a base of truth. The unemployed or self-employed, such as the shoemakers who get special mention from Aristophanes, would have found three obols, which later became six, an attractive reward for what was probably, in most instances, a half-day meeting. Small farmers, who had the flexibility to manage their time and could add to their earnings without loss of income from their primary occupation, would also have found the pay attractive.

But the passion for political engagement among the general mass of Athenian citizens should not be underestimated. The level of participation required to man Council, juries, magistracies, Assembly and the armed services shows a society where public service pervaded the lives of citizens. The restoration after 403 of true participatory democracy with political equality for all was hard-earned, but it had brought with it a new consensus. The overthrow of the brutal reign of the Thirty had purged the state of oligarchic intrigue and discredited oligarchic dogma. The merits of rule by the people were no longer a source of debate or controversy outside the schools of philosophy. But rule by the people came with an obligation on the people to participate in that rule. Citizenship meant a share in the constitution, but it was a sharing that was inseparable from civic engagement. The themes of service and participation to preserve a strong democracy are constantly sounded by the orators in addressing popular audiences in the Assembly and courts. They were obviously core elements of the prevailing democratic ethos.[48]

The social balance among those attending the Assembly is another issue that has obvious importance for the character of the fourth-century democracy. The evidence is spotty and conflicting, but the Assembly certainly was not a body dominated by the upper classes. All the indications are that, while the balance would have varied somewhat depending on the issues that were to the fore at any particular time, the social mix was broadly representative of the social divisions in the state as a whole. That meant there would always be a preponderance of those who had to work for a living, those of hoplite and thetic status, who were lumped together by the ancient writers as constituting the poor.

All the points made earlier in regard to participation levels support this conclusion. If the numbers attending were normally of the order of six thousand, that represented about a quarter of the citizen population of the fourth century, the great majority of whom had to come from the hoplite and thetic classes, since the so-called leisure class in its entirety almost certainly numbered no more than three thousand.

There are other reasons to believe the Assembly was a genuinely popular arena. Its decisions are always portrayed in the sources as decisions of the mass. Where they went wrong, writers like Thucydides are quick to blame the *demos* in its sense of the multitude (*to plethos* or *homilos*). There is no hint in the orators that decrees represented anything other than the will of the people. Aristotle always presents the Assembly as the chief forum of the mass of poorer citizens, the nerve centre of radical democracy. That was the main basis of his fear that a pure democracy would degenerate into a tyranny of the poor. The Assembly was synonymous with the rule of the people, which is why it was a prime target of the revolutionaries of 411 and 404. But it was the *demos* that emerged victorious from the upheavals of the late fifth century and, following the restoration of democracy in 403, the grip of the people's Assembly on the course of political affairs was at its tightest. It met more often, its oversight of all public officials was constant, pay for attendance facilitated higher participation, popular juries enforced its decrees.[49]

What did not change, however, was the reliance of the Assembly on good leadership. I have mentioned in an earlier chapter the curiously unstructured nature of decision-making in the Assembly and the unofficial character of the Assembly's leadership. Its procedures scrupulously followed the democratic principle of *isegoria*, the equal right of all citizens to have their say. There was therefore no hierarchy of speakers, no one who was authorised to lead. Even magistrates had no special role. The Council prepared the agenda and, apart from certain fixed items, everything that came before the Assembly had a preliminary recommendation from the Council (*probouleuma*), which was presented by a member of Council. But often the *probouleumata* merely put forward an issue for debate without a specific recommendation, and even when there was a specific proposal, the Assembly could reject or amend it, or substitute a totally different motion. Everything therefore hinged on the debate, and the debate began with the chairman inviting anyone who wished to speak (*ho boulomenos*) to do so. Those who emerged as political leaders were therefore those who had the ambition and confidence to stand forth as advisors and shapers of policy, and who had the skills and distinction to carry authority and credibility. It was a daunting task for the ordinary citizen to seek to impress an audience notorious for its intolerance of incompetent speakers or poorly reasoned argument. It was also hazardous in that proposers of motions were open to prosecution for making illegal proposals or misleading people.[50]

In practice, therefore, those who were the main architects of public policy and were accepted as experts and leaders were those who regularly took to the platform and who had the special talents, distinction and expertise needed to persuade their audience. Through most of the fifth century they were predominantly aristocrats whose birth, wealth, connections and training gave them unrivalled political advantages. In an era of great wars and the growth of empire those who excelled as military leaders carried particular authority and tended to dominate politically as well as militarily. The system had the great benefit not only of exploiting the greater leisure and superior training of the elite but of maintaining, with the free consent of the people, a leading place within the new democratic order for the traditional ruling class, rivalling each other for the public trust. It forged a strong consensus between the classes behind the democratic ideal.

The strains of plague and prolonged, damaging warfare, and the ineffectiveness of aristocratic leadership, caused a breakdown of that consensus in the final decades of the fifth century, and gave scope for the demagogues and for the radicalism and reckless militarism of a new generation of oligarchic dissenters. But the reforms of 403 forged a new consensus, which saw a return to a stable rule of the people, still led by an elite of birth or wealth, who had their rivalries and divided opinions, but showed no signs of lingering oligarchic yearnings.

But, as noted earlier, the character of that leadership changed considerably in the course of the fourth century, as military leadership became more professional and full time, and the flowering of the art of rhetoric opened a new pathway to political influence for gifted orators, especially those whose birth, wealth, achievements and personality added to their status and credibility. The new politicians were commonly known as *rhetores*. They were self-appointed leaders and had no special legal status, but through their ambition to lead and mastery of the art of persuasion they acquired recognition as expert, far-sighted, right-minded citizens capable of providing prudent leadership.

But the lack of any official mandate did not free the *rhetores* from accountability for the manner in which they exercised their leadership. They were liable to prosecution under the laws forbidding the introduction of decrees or legislation that violated existing law. Such prosecutions were commonplace, often brought by *rhetores* against their political rivals. There is a famous example of the experience of one prominent *rhetor*, Aristophon, who was reportedly prosecuted seventy-five times under the *graphe paranomon*.

Rhetores could also be indicted by *eisangelia* for failing to keep their promises to the people or for accepting bribes to give bad advice to the people. Demosthenes complains that, after the defeat of Athens and Thebes by Philip at Chaeroneia, he lived under constant threat of prosecution on a variety of grounds. Accountability hung over the head of everyone who achieved a position of leadership whether through official or unofficial means.[51]

All the known political orators came from the leisure class, though by no means all belonged to the old nobility of the clans, the *gennetai*. Lycurgus certainly did, but few others can be definitely identified as *gennetai*. There were prominent figures among them, such as Aeschines and Demades, who most likely emerged from lower-class backgrounds. The overall number of *rhetores* appears to have been relatively small. Hansen, who has compiled lists of known *rhetores* between 403 and 322, estimates that the total number was under a hundred and that the number active at any one time was never more than twenty.

But the *rhetores* were not the only citizens who participated in debates in the Assembly. It is clear from Isocrates that ordinary citizens from the ranks of the *phauloi*, the common throng, did speak, and sometimes to good effect. Members of the Council had to propose *probouleumata* that recommended a particular course of action. Hansen's listings led him to conclude that 700–1,400 citizens were involved in proposing decrees over the period of the fourth-century democracy. Certainty about the numbers is not attainable, but it is clear that participation in debates of the Assembly extended well beyond the elite corps of *rhetores*.[52]

The divide between generals and *rhetores* is a striking feature of fourth-century politics, but it was never total. It developed gradually and was essentially a phenomenon of the second half of the century. The first half-century of the restored democracy saw Athens again embroiled in a succession of wars. During that period the most prominent leaders all held generalships at one time or another, many repeatedly.

Thrasybulus, Agyrrhius and Conon provide examples from the 390s and early 380s. Callistratus was another leader who combined important political and military roles. He was a central figure in shaping Athenian policy in the 370s and 360s, a general in 378 and chief architect of the Second Athenian League, which was established in that year. He was a general again in 372 and led the negotiations with Sparta that resulted in the Peace of Callias in 371. He continued to support a pro-Spartan policy and was the key figure behind the decision of Athens to align itself with Sparta against Thebes in the 360s. It is also clear that other outstanding generals of the first half of the century, such as Iphicrates, Chabrias and Timotheus, were well connected politically. But the list of influential leaders who never held a generalship is also long, and includes such figures as Eubulus, Demosthenes, Aeschines, Hyperides, Demades, Dinarchus, Lycurgus, Androtion and Aristophon.

But the most notable example of a soldier statesman in the fourth century was Phocion, who became the subject of one of Plutarch's *Lives*. Plutarch portrays him as a man of the highest virtue, a good man and a great statesman in the mould of Pericles, Aristides and Solon. He combined a considerable military talent with an austere but effective style of oratory marked by brevity. He never tried to humour the people and often opposed their wishes, but they trusted him and elected him general forty-five times during the final half century of the democracy. He never achieved the status of a Pericles, but he remained a key political and military leader to the end of the democracy.[53]

These examples show that the Athenians continued to use talent where they found it, and gave leadership in both the political and military spheres to those they believed had the necessary skills in both. But as these skills became rarer and Athens entered a period of relative peace following the end of the Social War in 355, political leadership became increasingly monopolised by a select group of talented *rhetores*, none of whom, with the exception of Phocion, ever held a generalship.

The nature of the power-base of the leading *rhetores* and the dynamics of power in the Assembly of the fourth century have been the subject of much discussion. The role of parties, factions and other forms of coalition has been a recurring question. Recent scholarship has tended to move away from presenting the politics of the fourth century in these terms, but the debate seems far from over. The ancient sources, however, provide little indication that political leaders were backed by stable factions among the elite or organised followings among the wider body of citizens, or that such action groups were a significant force in the decision-making of the Assembly.

There is plenty of evidence of intense rivalries and bitter enmities among political leaders, and prominent politicians undoubtedly had networks of friends and personal connections whom they naturally sought to rally to their support. Like-minded politicians who had shared views about big issues such as war and peace and taxation would also not surprisingly support each other in Assembly debates. But these types of informal cooperation based on personal connections and common political views are a far cry from ideas of stable factions pooling their influence and assembling their followings to exert pressure on the Assembly to adopt their agendas. That brand of factional politics ran directly counter to the democratic vision of a mass Assembly where every citizen was free to express his personal opinion and vote in accordance with his personal judgement, and where decisions represented the cumulative wisdom of the many and were genuine expressions of the will of the people. Factional machinations or power blocs of any kind seeking to manipulate decisions of the Assembly were a perversion of that ideal. The democracy required that political leaders should have one source of power: the support of the people. That was what had carried Cleisthenes to power in 508. As Herodotus put it, he made the people his *hetaireia*.

The demotic uprising of 508 was a repudiation of factional politics and the *stasis* that went with it, and the democratic order that followed was determined it would not return. The radical expedient of ostracism was devised to remove anyone from the state whose influence had reached a point where it posed a threat to the supreme right of the mass freely to decide the course of political affairs. Suspicion of the intentions of upper-class networks of *philoi* and of elite social clubs in particular (*hetaireiai*) grew in the course of the fifth century and was fed by demagogues like Cleon. The terms *hetaireia* and *hetairoi* became increasingly associated with the idea of a conspiracy to overthrow the democracy. Following the role of the political social clubs in 411 and 404, all such associations were outlawed, a reflection of an ingrained popular aversion to cliques of the elite.

I mentioned in an earlier chapter other features of the democracy and of Athenian society that guarded against the emergence of powerful individuals or groups: the inclusiveness of the political system that promoted participation and gave a meaningful role to the lower classes; the absence of any system of clientage or any institution of government dominated by the elite that gave scope for power-building; the structure of the armed forces, whose core was the hoplites and thetes, the most loyal democrats of all. The character and procedures of the Assembly also militated against manipulation of decision-making by organised groups. The unpredictability of the attendance; the random seating; the strong role of a Council comprised of broadly representative, annually rotating members; a presiding board of nine *proedroi*, one member drawn from each tribe, excluding the tribe holding the prytany, chosen by lot for one day and on the day of the meeting to exclude any form of manipulation – all of these features made controlling or tampering with decisions of the Assembly difficult in the extreme.

But it is the almost total lack of reference in the ancient sources to factions or action groups in fourth-century politics that most strongly argues against their existence. There are some references to broad divisions between the mass of the democratic poor and the respectable men of means, and differences in interests and outlook between these two main social classes inevitably caused occasional frictions, but any ongoing factional strife along class lines is simply not in evidence in the fourth century.

There are a few references in Demosthenes that might suggest action groups featured in debates in the Assembly. On one occasion (18.143) he accuses Aeschines of having a group of supporters around him to interrupt the speech of Demosthenes. The Assembly was notorious for heckling speakers, and accusing an opponent of organising it was an obvious line of attack and can hardly be taken as hard evidence of ongoing class or factional divides. In two other speeches (2.29; 13.20) Demosthenes alleges that symmories were acting as organised pressure groups, shouting their support for a *rhetor* who was presumably advocating a measure they wanted adopted. But Demosthenes is roundly denouncing such behaviour as a new phenomenon and urging that it must cease. If it had been commonplace, Demosthenes would almost certainly have had a lot more to say about it, as would the critics of democracy, especially the philosophers. But no contemporary source suggests that factions were a regular feature of fourth-century politics. Aristotle saw the *demos* as a mono-lith, and his concern was that its control was far too absolute. He associated factions with oligarchies, which he regarded as especially prone to factious rivalries within their own ranks. He believed democracies were far more stable and free of divisions among their adherents, at odds only with any oligarchic opposition.

There was certainly nothing that could be characterised as an oligarchic party or opposition in fourth-century Athens. Those who secured positions of leadership were champions of democracy and defenders of the will of the Council and Assembly. There was no one in political life who dared voice oligar-chic sentiment. The *demos* was, as Aristotle insists, fully in control, and was far too jealous of its prerogatives, and far too vigilant and intent on safeguarding the rule of the people, to tolerate factional power plays or the machinations of groups seeking to impose their will on the people's supreme governing body.[54]

CHAPTER 8

Achievements and Shortcomings

Athens faced several formidable internal challenges in the aftermath of the bitter defeat in the Peloponnesian War, the brutal reign of the Thirty and the ravages of the subsequent civil war. It had to build reconciliation and a new consensus. It needed to achieve law reform and safeguard the sanctity of the rule of law in the aftermath of the breakdown of constitutional government. It had to deal with the problems of a shattered economy. Its position as an autonomous state was precarious. Its defence and armaments were destroyed and, while it had domestic autonomy, it was subservient to Sparta in foreign policy. In addition it had to cope with the two inveterate fault lines, likely to be aggravated in difficult times, that had always posed challenges for democracy and its ideals of equality among citizens: wide inequality in the distribution of wealth between mass and elite; and a class structure with an aristocracy long accustomed to rule and imbued with the idea that political power should follow good breeding and the special talents and all-round excellence (*arete*) that characterised the noble and good (*kaloi kagathoi*).

Summary of Achievements

On the domestic front, though it struggled with the financial challenge, Athens succeeded in achieving over the eighty-two years of the life of the fourth-century democracy a remarkable level of political and social stability that realised the democratic ideal in its fullest form. The determination and statesmanship with which reconciliation was pursued, and which won the admiration of Aristotle, have already been discussed. The amnesty was respected, and the reforms allayed the concerns of moderate dissenters by addressing the main flaws and excesses that had tarnished the working of democracy in the later fifth century. A thorough review and codification of existing law were achieved, the status of law was enhanced, and new procedures for the making of law guarded against ill-considered alterations or additions to the body of law.

The economic difficulties were eased by more stringent budgeting and tighter administrative controls, and by a programme of taxation that undoubtedly placed heavier burdens on the wealthy and generated grumbling, but stopped well short of provoking a social crisis. There was no attack on acknowledged rights of private property. The severity of the financial crisis could well have triggered a movement for a greater equalisation of wealth, and such ideas were circulating in the intellectual milieu, but they never took hold in the political arena. There is no reason to believe that the Athenian democratic ideal ever favoured a communitarian ethos that denied rights of private property, or leaned towards the extreme Platonic view that all property must be seen as ultimately belonging to the state and must be used for the benefit of society as a whole. Solon, who was so widely accepted as the father of the principle of the rule of law and basic democratic rights, had laid down very different precepts in regard to private property and the distribution of wealth. His views have been discussed in an earlier chapter and can be briefly summarised here. He believed that justice required protection of the poor against oppression or exploitation by the rich, but did not believe that justice required that all should share equally in a country's wealth. That would entail injustice to those who had justly acquired their property and went beyond what was needed to achieve a just balance between the social classes. While he decried the pursuit of excess wealth and saw large-scale inequality in wealth as a barrier to social harmony, he defended the right to property justly secured and accepted that disparity in wealth was part of the natural order that could not be upset without social turmoil. His purpose was to find a just balance between the rights of rich and poor that allowed neither to perpetrate injustice against the other.[1]

Aristotle also provides an extensive discussion of wealth and property rights in the *Politics* that gives a valuable insight into Greek views of economic justice. He saw wealth as a good, and a measure of prosperity as essential to the harmony and safety of a state, as well as personal well-being and fulfilment. But it was a means to an end and had a natural limit determined by its capacity to contribute to the public good and personal happiness. Its unlimited acquisition was a perversion of its purpose, and had the negative social effect of creating a gulf between rich and poor that was destructive of civil harmony and communal solidarity.

But despite the risks to society from extremes of wealth and poverty, Aristotle found overriding reasons why the right to property must be respected and state regulation of the distribution of wealth must be limited. Some of these views have been referred to earlier. His reasons were a mixture of the moral and the expedient. He argues that people have certain natural needs and instincts as human beings that must be respected and that are too fundamental to be swept away in the interest of a presumed public good. He sees the desire for family relationships and friendship in this light, and also possessions that people can think of as their own. This feeling that something is one's own (*idion*) he regards as making a difference beyond words in the pleasure derived from it. He links the feeling to a sense of self, a form of self-love that is not selfish, but is a moderate, natural (*physikon*) and more or less universal level of egotism.

He further argues that it is private property that makes possible acts of kindness to others and is the source of liberality (*eleutheriotes*) in general, which he considers another pleasurable and noble quality of human nature and a bond of society. All these things are lost where the state is excessively communitarian. He clearly believed, in a manner reminiscent of Pericles in the Funeral Oration, that there must be a private domain for the individual within the public association that is the state. He completely rejected Plato's communistic vision of society, which submerged individual identity and subordinated even the most basic private needs to an excessive preoccupation with the public good.

Aristotle also advances more pragmatic reasons for safeguarding property rights. Harmony is best achieved when everyone has his own possessions and controls their use. So is efficiency, since people apply themselves more diligently to what is their own. Reward then follows effort and ability, which is just, and interference with that breeds resentment among the most able. In addition, threats to private possessions create a climate of fear among the wealthy. He considers this especially true in democratic systems, where the rich feel most insecure and the temptation to infringe their property rights is greatest.

Aristotle did, however, favour limited state intervention to relieve extreme poverty, which he saw as a cause of civic dissension and crime. He was opposed to simple hand-outs which he compared to filling a leaky jar. Instead, grants to the poor should be designed to lift them out of poverty, and he therefore advocated that surplus revenues should be collected and distributed to the poor, and where possible in amounts adequate to buy a small farm or at least get started in trade or agriculture.

But at a broader level he believed that the best means to greater economic levelling and harmony between rich and poor lay in creating through education a culture that would curb the irrational drive for wealth beyond need, and instil a spirit of good citizenship and civic responsibility that accepted that, while ownership of property should be private, its use should be common. This meant the rich should give voluntarily but generously to advance the public interest, and especially to meet critical social needs. This included having surpluses in revenue go to help the impoverished, providing the extra funds needed to protect against particular threats to the security of the state, and even meeting the costs of pay for attending the Assembly and manning the courts when times were hard. The rich should also avoid luxury and excess in their own lifestyle. He linked liberality and temperance (*sophrosyne*) as the twin virtues that should govern the use of wealth and provide protection against class tensions. Aristotle's views, more Solonian than Platonic, reflected in many ways the outlook and practice of Athenian society in the fifth and fourth centuries.[2]

There was a marked preference in both centuries for methods of generating state revenues that did not involve compulsory levies on property or any form of private wealth. The whole system of liturgies was largely built on an ethos of voluntary giving and benefaction (*euergesia*) by the wealthy, and there were benefits for both the givers and the public. Generous use of wealth for the public good was undoubtedly an effective means to political power. It gave claims to leadership and inspired trust. It earned goodwill and gratitude (*charis*). Political leaders omitted no opportunity to advertise the extent of their public giving.

Private philanthropy also built favour with the public and was a common phenomenon. Cimon provides an early example. He became famous for his broad generosity. He removed fences from his fields so that anyone who wished could have access to the crops. He gave free dinners to his demesmen on a daily basis, and the young men around him regularly gave gifts of money and clothing to the needy. Gorgias says that he made money to spend it, and he spent it to win *time*. The pursuit of honour through high prominence and achievement in public life remained the driving ambition of the *kaloi kagathoi*. In democratic Athens that meant first acquiring popular trust and favour, and public-minded liberality was an important means to that end.[3]

But the financial plight in which Athens found itself in the fourth century made greater impositions on the wealthy unavoidable and their enforcement progressively more stringent. But the organisation of a more structured, regular system of compulsory revenue generation was approached in a careful, conservative spirit. The purpose was strictly limited to raising funds for military operations. As it evolved care was taken to provide for the possibility of exemptions and for remedies against unfairness. The main burden was placed on those best able to afford it. The rate at which the *eisphora* was levied appears to have been moderate by any standard, and the fact that over the twenty-year period between 377 and 357, a time of almost continuous warfare, only 300 talents were raised shows how modest the level of taxation was. It was so modest, in fact, that the funding it produced often fell far below what the state required for its military campaigns. There are instances of the efforts of generals being thwarted by a shortage of funds, and other instances where they were forced to find the resources to support and pay their troops from the spoils of war or booty from raids. Sometimes the funds ran out and servicemen were left unpaid altogether. In a campaign in the late 370s to keep Corcyra out of Spartan hands, Iphicrates was so short of money that he had to hire out his crews as farm labourers.

But there was a clear reluctance on the part of the upper classes to pay higher taxes. Complaints about existing levels and instances of evasion and arrears are well documented. Significantly, the Assembly, with its large majority of the poor, did not insist, and the introduction of the *epidosis* is a very clear example of an overall aversion to compulsory levies on wealth, and a preference for voluntary giving based on a sense of patriotic duty.

The restored democracy's approach to addressing its many financial challenges and securing adequate public revenues was therefore cautious and limited. There was no social agenda. The need to repair the economy and alleviate the worst consequences of the multiple blows it had suffered was largely ignored. No measures were taken to relieve the poverty and hardship that must have followed the fall in employment, the disruption of agriculture, the devastation of the countryside, the closure of the mines, and the disruption of trade and commerce.

The tax reforms were not concerned with issues of social justice or economic stimulus. None of the money went to help the poor. There was no attempt to establish even a rudimentary welfare system. The Theoric Fund, which probably did not come into being until the middle of the century, gave hand-outs to the public during the great festivals, and Eubulus also used the Fund to invest in major capital infrastructural developments, which would have provided an economic stimulus and increased employment. But the *eisphora* did not contribute to this Fund, which was financed by surpluses that derived from income provided by state assets and indirect taxes. In the final decades of the democracy these surpluses increasingly went into the Military Fund in times of war. Much more could have been done to revitalise the economy and improve the lot of the working classes if some of the *eisphora* had been used to increase domestic productivity rather than support expansionist wars that offered dubious benefit to the state. Aristotle saw the wisdom of helping the impoverished become productive, self-supporting citizens. The Athenian leadership and public did not.

The sole purpose of the *eisphora* remained the funding of the wars that were especially frequent in the first half of the century. Involvement in these wars, which will be reviewed in more detail later, was dictated by a prudent concern to ensure the security of Athens by maintaining it as a major power and by keeping its main rivals, Sparta and Thebes, as weak as possible. But there was also a hawkish, imperialist edge to Athenian policy inspired by a lingering yearning for the primacy and glories of the fifth century, and it sometimes led to a militarism bordering on naked imperialism. That yearning appears to have been shared by leaders and public alike, though the uncertainty of the rewards and the prospect of long campaigns abroad lessened enthusiasm for service, and mercenaries continued to be used extensively both on ships and on land.

In summary, the financial policies of the fourth century are open to some serious criticism. Too little revenue was raised from direct taxation, and it was spent exclusively on wars that did more to impoverish than benefit the state. Domestic needs were neglected. But what the reformed trierarchy and *eisphora* did achieve was to enable Athens to regain full autonomy and its place as a leading power, and for a time to recover mastery of the seas with the security and commercial benefits that went with that. Of perhaps greater significance, the increased tax burdens were implemented without alienation of the wealthy or any serious damage to social harmony or the political consensus.[4]

Social and political stability were also reinforced by the continued readiness of the restored democracy to give opportunities to the upper class to play a leading role in the political life of the state. A lot has been said about this already, but it is such a crucial phenomenon in understanding the harmony of the orders that prevailed in the fourth century, in a strictly class-based society operating a political system based on a principle of absolute political equality that gave power to the multitude, that it is worth reviewing its main features. The democratic ideal, as it evolved in the fifth and fourth centuries, never accepted that anyone was born to rule or endowed by birth or wealth with the right to political privilege or primacy. But it did accept that democracy required leaders with special talent and expertise to guide the state in the most critical areas of the deliberative and executive functions of government. As a result the decision-making of the *demos* was led by authoritative figures who commanded its trust, and power was freely delegated to those who proved their *arete* and capacity to benefit the state.

The criteria by which the *demos* measured ability and trustworthiness always favoured those of high birth and high wealth. The *demos* of Athens, like the *populus* of Rome, had an aristocratic bent which inspired a respect for those with a famous lineage that conferred a certain standing, authority and credentials for leadership. The Athenians never strove for a classless society. They were content to live with differences in wealth and social status. Solon had institutionalised the social and financial divide, and saw it as the order of nature.

Wealth fortified the benefits of high birth. It also opened the way to political prominence for those of humbler ancestry who had talent and ambition. It gave the leisure necessary for the demands of a political career. It gave numerous opportunities to win public favour through public and private benefaction. Above all it made possible the high level of education that became increasingly necessary for political success in the fourth century. The aristocratic ideal had traditionally given pride of place to a form of physical and moral education designed to generate martial prowess, courage and endurance and a striving for *time*. But the arrival of the Sophists shifted the focus to the development of the mind as well as the body. Figures such as Protagoras and Gorgias helped establish the power of speech honed by a proficient intellect as the great new pathway to political influence. The fourth century brought the full flowering of the art of persuasion. The Athenian public relished rhetorical virtuosity, and eloquence could make the difference and carry the day in all of the three main fora of decision-making under the democracy: the Council, Assembly and courts.

There were worries about the dangers of rhetoric and its power to deceive. Sycophants provided a ready example of the dangers. The term Sophist also developed derogatory connotations and became associated with a specious and manipulative cleverness. But on the whole the Athenians were in love with eloquence, and oratorical skills offered the surest route to political leadership. Of course, military success continued to garner public favour, but generals who lacked eloquence had difficulty in winning their way in debate.

But oratorical and military skills were both beyond the reach of the ordinary citizen, and in consequence the leaders of the fourth century continued to be drawn from the upper classes. There were a few whose families were new to politics, but none was poor. The constitution as it functioned in practice therefore had an oligarchic cast, but one that arose by act and consent of the people, a factor that undoubtedly provides the main explanation for the remarkable level of cohesion and stability that prevailed in the fourth century.

But there was never a risk that the upper class could achieve control or form a ruling elite. More than at any time in its history, the democracy of the fourth century represented a true example of rule by the people. Two pillars of the democracy ensured this would remain the case: the high level of accountability for all in positions of leadership; and a high level of active participation in public affairs by an engaged and informed citizenry. The oligarchic cast of the leadership was balanced by this culture of vigilance and direct engagement of the mass in every major area of government.

The rigour and regularity of accountability have been fully discussed earlier. They left no room for incompetence or malfeasance or any hint of disloyalty to the democracy. Every citizen was a watchdog for the interests of the people, with the right to initiate prosecution. The catalogue of leaders, military and political, who were indicted, and the high number convicted show how vigorously the system of accountability was enforced. The vigilance and gradual separation of military and political roles left little scope for any leader to build a dangerous level of power. No one came close to reaching the degree of ascendancy achieved by Pericles, and it is noteworthy that the Assembly never found it necessary to resort to ostracism to remove a leader perceived to be a risk.[5]

Direct participation by the mass of citizens in the government of the state was always a prominent feature of Athenian democracy. Its central place and importance are well described by Pericles in the Funeral Oration. But it was in the fourth century that it reached its peak and led Aristotle to describe the constitution of his day as the most complete form of democracy (*teleutaia demokratia*), in which the *demos* took more power to itself and controlled everything.

The civic spirit that inspired and sustained broad direct participation by the mass in government ultimately derived from the communitarian ethos that characterised the *polis* in general. That ethos was based on the belief that human beings gathered in states to achieve a more secure and fulfilling life through the fellowship and mutual support that a well-ordered association with others could provide. The association existed to advance the good of all, the common good, and required for its success the dedicated commitment of all its members to that end, subordinating private advantage to the public good.

Aristotle provides the fullest and most memorable expression of this collectivist view of the state. In the *Politics* he famously describes man as a political animal. By his nature he is neither solitary nor self-sufficient, but designed for life in society and equipped with a variety of social aptitudes, most notably a moral sense of what is good and bad, right and wrong. It is a partnership in these qualities that makes a household and a state.

Man is therefore born for citizenship. On his own he is incapable of achieving fulfilment of his true being. He who is stateless (*apolis*), whether because he is incapable of human fellowship or does not need it, is either subhuman or superhuman, a beast or a god.

But Aristotle repeatedly emphasises that citizenship brought obligations as well as benefits. Individually and collectively all citizens had a responsibility to work for the common welfare, and to give it precedence over any personal interest. The well-being of the state was the function (*ergon*) of citizenship, as it was the function of governments, transcending other considerations.

The Spartans, as we have seen, were to take these communitarian ideas to extremes. Athenian democracy translated them into a very different political order, with a different view of the rights and duties of citizenship. It stood for the principle that all citizens are free and equal members of their state, but its view of equality extended far beyond Spartan concepts of *isoi* and *homoioi*. Equality at Athens meant not only being equal in freedom and before the law, but entitled to share in an equal direct way in the ruling of the state. For that entitlement to be meaningful there had to be a willingness and a high level of equality of opportunity to exercise it, so that political power genuinely rested with the full body of citizens, the *demos*. Without broad participation the concept of rule by the people was a sham.[6]

Participatory Democracy at its Height

Participation intensified in the fourth century at several levels. The Assembly, which was always the main forum for the exercise of the people's power, saw the greatest expansion of its role. The changes have been described earlier. They all contributed to more frequent engagement by larger gatherings of citizens who were now paid to attend. The plenary sessions in particular, which centred on the performance of magistrates and amounted to a review each prytany of the state of the nation, gave the *demos* the opportunity to exercise greater vigilance and more direct managerial control.

The other main organs of government – the Council, executive magistracies and courts – were all structured in a way that provided the maximum opportunity for ordinary citizens from all parts of the state to participate at a variety of levels in the business of government. Councillors, jurors and all holders of magistracies had to be over thirty, so this segment of the population was especially intensively involved in public life.

The Council's composition, with its membership drawn from all the demes on a basis of proportional representation and rotating annually, with re-election allowed only once in a lifetime, meant a broad spectrum of the entire body of citizens participated in this high office. The fact that it met every day apart from holidays also meant that involvement was full time and for a full year.

There were about seven hundred other magistrates required each year for the various administrative departments, the great bulk of them chosen by lot from those who put their names forward. Re-election to the same magistracies was not permitted, except for the main electoral offices, but the same person could hold a variety of different offices. The literary evidence indicates there was no shortage of candidates.

But it was the jury courts that brought the greatest number of Athenian citizens into the thick of political affairs. Their function was centrally political. As we have seen, private cases, mostly settled by arbitration, were a small part of their responsibility. Many forms of crime, including murder, were also dealt with elsewhere. It was the high volume of political responsibilities assigned to the courts that formed the great bulk of their work. These included: the *dokimasia* of magistrates other than Councillors; oversight of the letting of public contracts and the sale of confiscated property; prosecutions arising from *euthynai* and *eisangeliai*; the frequent challenging of the legality of decrees and changes in law proposed to the Assembly. It was jurors also who formed the panels of *nomothetai* when required.

The high number of court days in the year (around two hundred) and the high number of jurors on those days (1,500–2,000) meant that a large and varying segment of the citizens over thirty years of age was regularly involved in jury service and exposed to the array of political trials, and the political issues underlying them, that dominated the agenda of the courts. The mode of selection of the annual panel, which recruited six hundred volunteers by lot from each of the ten tribes, and the fact that each jury was also selected by lot in a way that, to the extent possible, gave equal representation to each tribe, meant participation was not only large but spread across the entire citizen body.

The courts, manned by this large and broad cross-section of ordinary citizens, were a central pillar of the democracy. They were the people's watchdog, sworn to protect the democracy and enforce the laws and the decrees of the *demos* and Council. Both the orators and Aristotle emphasised their critical importance in protecting the rule of law and the rule of the people. Aristotle viewed the courts and the Assembly as the two main organs of government in a democracy, and the right to participate in both as the defining characteristic of democratic citizenship.

The intense participatory character of all the main governmental structures of the democracy kept the mass of citizens at the heart of the political process. But it is noteworthy that the system was totally dependent on volunteering. Apart from military service, citizens were not compelled by law to participate in public life. The fact that they continued to do so in such numbers was undoubtedly in part due to the introduction of pay for attending the Assembly and serving as jurors or office-holders, but it was also due to a culture of participation that underpinned the very notion of Athenian democracy. Pericles emphasised in the Funeral Oration that the word democracy itself entailed management by the many and created a system that poured scorn on those who shunned public affairs, the *apragmones*, and drew strength from collective debate and the greater understanding and resolution that considered decision-making bestowed. There was no dichotomy here between state and civil society. The citizens were the state, equal partners in a *koinonia* to advance the common interest, collectively deciding and enforcing its laws and policies, and ensuring that those it chose to lead them met their responsibilities.[7]

The broad participation by the mass of citizens in every facet of government obviously helped entrench the rule of the people, but it also had other effects that strengthened the quality and stability of the political system. The experience gained by so many in the four main divisions of government meant that a broad, first-hand knowledge of public affairs was dispersed throughout the citizen population, ensuring a public that was politically aware and capable of informed decision-making.

The dispersal of knowledge was further aided by a traditional concern of the democracy to put as much political information as possible into the public domain. Excavations in the Agora in the twentieth century reveal a dramatic increase in the number of inscriptions following the reforms of Ephialtes. They deal with all forms of public decisions and accounts, decrees of the Assembly, lists of tribute from the allies, relations with foreign states, details of military affairs and of Athenian dead. At the end of the fifth century a state archive was created in the Agora when the Old Bouleuterion was converted into a state archive, the Metroon, housing important public documents, which were available to citizens on request. The legal reforms at the end of the fifth century, which required that the body of revised, ratified law must be inscribed on the wall of the Stoa Basileios in the Agora, and that all proposals for new legislation must be posted in the Agora to allow public perusal and input before the final vote in the Assembly, contributed further to a well-informed citizenry.

The importance of a knowledgeable public in a democracy has been a common theme of political analysts and proponents of democracy. In the Funeral Oration, Pericles showed his awareness of the importance of knowledge in the workings of democracy when he praised the grasp of public affairs that existed among the people. James Madison, the fourth president of the United States, famously wrote that 'a popular government without popular information is but a prologue to a farce or a tragedy, or perhaps both. A people who mean to be their own governors must arm themselves with the power knowledge brings.' Similar sentiments have been reiterated many times since. Athens provides a first and notable example of a popular government well armed with popular information, a factor that contemporaries saw as a strength, and that must be included among the contributors to the success and stability in internal government that characterised the democracy, especially in the fourth century.[8]

Broad participation also gave the people a sense of ownership of their political destiny which instilled loyalty to the constitution and belief in the superiority of its laws and systems and of the way of life that it made possible. Pericles gave prominence to all these features of the democracy in the Funeral Oration and stressed the pride in the system and the commitment to defend it that resulted. The superiority of the democratic order and the duty of all citizens to protect it became commonplaces in Athenian oratory.

In his discussion of how to preserve constitutions in the *Politics*, Aristotle put the primary emphasis on the commitment of citizens to their form of government, and argued that this commitment could only be achieved if citizens were trained by habit and education in the ethos of the constitution and acquired the will to live by its values. There could be no more effective method of habituating people to the democratic way and fostering democratic values than the Athenian emphasis on active participation by the mass at all levels of government.

There were flaws in Athenian society under the democracy and in the domestic statesmanship of the fourth century, as we shall see below, but by the standards of the time the restored democracy created a successful society and achieved the greatest level of harmony and consensus of any period in the history of the democracy. There were dissenting voices among the intelligentsia, notably Plato, Aristotle and, to a lesser degree, Isocrates, and probably among the *apragmones* who stayed out of politics, but there was no open dissent among the politically active.

None of Aristotle's fears for radical democracy materialised. There were no major constitutional crises, no disregard of the rule of law, no assault on the property of the rich, no serious factional conflicts, no oligarchic conspiracies or coups, no extreme populism from demagogues, and no repetition of the indiscipline that marked the behaviour of the *demos* in the late fifth century.

The society also preserved an environment that allowed the cultural supremacy of Athens to continue. Pericles had described his fellow citizens as lovers of beauty and wisdom, and the entire state as the school of Greece, exemplar of human capacity at its most accomplished, versatile and graceful. Isocrates could still boast, in speeches dating from the 380s and 350s, about the cultural and intellectual dominance of Athens. He talks about its great festivals which excel not only in their spectacles, but in their testing of the intellect (*gnome*) and of rhetorical and artistic skills. He glories especially in the fact that it was Athens that gave philosophy to the world, and that it honoured oratory and acquired such a reputation for all the skills related to eloquence that it became the world's hub for all aspiring orators.

Oratory and philosophy were undoubtedly the crowning cultural achievements of fourth-century Athens. The philosophical and rhetorical schools headed by Plato and Isocrates drew students from all over the world. Other cultural achievements did not match the heights of the fifth century, though history remained an important literary genre, and the festivals continued to encourage the writing of new plays. But little of the history or drama survived for long. The enduring cultural impact came chiefly from philosophy and rhetoric, but the legacy of Plato, Aristotle and the orators proved such a formative force in European thought and education that the fourth century, like the fifth, deserves to rank as a pivotal era in the history of western civilisation.[9]

Shortcomings

The political achievements of Athenian democracy undoubtedly represent a legacy of enduring importance, and their continuing relevance to modern democratic thought and the challenges facing modern democracies will be further reviewed in the Epilogue.

But Athenian democracy also had its flaws, and was far from being a model society by the standards of modern liberal democracies. Its great achievement was to extend to all male citizens, irrespective of their economic or social status, equal political and legal rights, and to create a constitution that enabled them to exercise these rights directly, freely and equally. But the vision had limitations. It claimed to give power to the many but, as noted earlier, the many did not include three significant elements of the population: women, slaves and resident aliens known as metics (*metoikoi*). The place of these three groups in Athenian society is an integral part of the story of democracy, and must be taken into account in any evaluation of the extent and value of the Athenian achievement.

Women

The new political thinking brought nothing new in relation to the rights of women, and took no steps to advance gender equality. Athenian women, though they had the status of citizens, did not possess those political rights that Aristotle described as the essence of citizenship – the right to share (*metechein*) in the administration of justice and in the holding of public office. In fact, they had no political rights of any description. They also had limited legal rights. Throughout their lives they were subject to a guardian, their father or their husband, or, if they had neither, their male next-of-kin. They could not bring legal action except in the case of divorce. They could not own property. A woman whose father had no sons could inherit, but an heiress did not fully own the inheritance (*kleros*). She was known as an *epikleros*, and her responsibility was to see that the inheritance was kept intact and passed on to the nearest legitimate male heir.[10]

There were many other aspects of Athenian life and customs that kept women in a position of subordination and seclusion. Gender roles were sharply defined and greatly limited women's freedoms and opportunities. Men were seen as the natural leaders, protectors and providers. In the public arena they had major political, judicial and military functions. In the household (*oikos*) they were the masters (*kyrioi*), the ultimate controllers. Women were regarded as the weaker sex, more suited to obeying and preserving than to leading, and they had a wholly separate set of roles. They had no involvement in the public arena outside certain religious festivals. Their domain was the household, their tasks connected with motherhood and the running of the home. Xenophon's *Oeconomicus*, which deals with estate and home management, provides an interesting glimpse of Greek perceptions of gender roles and the domestic responsibilities of a wife. The main character, Ischomachus, tells Socrates the instructions he gave his new young wife who was not yet fifteen.

> Your duty will be to remain indoors and send out those servants whose work is outside, and superintend those who are to work indoors, and to receive the incomings and distribute so much of them as must be spent, and watch over so much as is to be kept in store, and take care that the sum laid by for a year is not spent in a month. And when wool is brought to you, you must see that cloaks are made for those who want them. You must see too that the dry corn is in good condition for making food. One of the duties that will fall to you, however, will perhaps seem rather thankless: you will have to see that any servant who is ill is cared for. (Loeb trans.)[11]

These perceptions of difference in character and roles led on to differences in the rearing and education of boys and girls, and in the qualities valued in men and women. There was no publicly established system of education in Athens, and no required level of educational attainment, but there was a system of private schools that would seem to have been well established by the end of the sixth century. Boys, at least those from the more well-to-do families, began to attend school from about age seven. Very little is known about the primary level, but the teacher was called a *grammatistes*, and the emphasis was clearly on literacy and probably arithmetic. These were skills essential for participation in public life. Training in music and physical education was also associated with this stage. With the advent of the Sophists there were opportunities at higher levels for advanced forms of education that prepared the ambitious for political leadership.

There is no evidence that girls attended school. The skills they required for their roles were easily acquired in the home. The main concern with daughters was to get them suitably married, and this tended to happen at an early age, sometimes as young as fourteen. This lack of educational opportunity further circumscribed the lives of women and was a powerful impediment to any progress towards gender equality.[12]

Differences in the qualities valued in men and women in this male-dominated society further contributed to the subordinate, isolated position of women. Physical power and courage, martial valour, patriotic devotion to duty and the common good, pursuit of honour, nobility of character (*kalokagathia*) – these were the hallmarks of male *arete*. Feminine *arete* put the stress on chaste self-restraint (*sophrosyne*), fidelity, obedience, silence, modest avoidance of the limelight. When Pericles addresses the widows of the fallen in the Funeral Oration, he alludes to feminine *arete* and gives his advice in one sentence: 'Your great glory is not to fall short of what your nature has given you, and great glory is also hers of whom there is least talk among men in praise or in blame.' Aristotle has a lot to say in the *Politics* about the difference in the *arete* of men and women, and, to illustrate a feminine virtue not appropriate in a man, he quotes a line from the *Ajax* of Sophocles: 'Silence does credit to a woman.'[13]

In the field of sexuality the difference in the standards of behaviour expected from men and women was especially pronounced. Virginity was a requirement for women before marriage. An unmarried woman caught having an affair could be sold into slavery under a law of Solon. A married woman who had sexual relations with any man other than her husband was guilty of adultery, for which the penalties were divorce and public humiliation such as exclusion from participation in public festivals.

In the case of men, it was considered acceptable for them, whether married or not, to have homosexual relationships or liaisons with courtesans, prostitutes or slaves. A man was considered guilty of adultery only if he had sexual relations with a married female citizen. In that case he could be killed by the husband if caught in the act. A speech of Lysias records one such incident, where the husband exercised his right and killed the adulterer. The alternative was a monetary settlement.[14]

The qualities most valued in women also contributed to the notion that women should appear as little as possible in public, and in particular should not associate with men who were not related to them. Better-off women had slaves to run their errands, and had less reason to go out, and did not normally appear in public spaces except in the case of funerals or religious festivals, especially the Panathenaea and Thesmophoria. They may also have attended the theatre, though the evidence is not conclusive.

Male concern with ensuring the fidelity of their wives and the legitimacy of their heirs added to the seclusion. The most extreme example of this was the exclusion of wives from the husband's entertainment of friends in the home. There was a separate space in the house, the men's quarters (*andrōn*), where guests dined. The only women present were slaves and prostitutes who supplied the entertainment. The speeches of Lysias and Demosthenes provide other examples of the vigilance of husbands, and highlight the impropriety of any contact between strangers and girls or wives. It must be emphasised in all of this, of course, that the lives of poorer women were very different from those of the better-off. Poorer women had to run their own errands, and often had to go out to work, hiring out their services as washerwomen, woolworkers, childminders and midwives, or selling their wares. In rural areas they must also have worked alongside their husbands on smallholdings. Their lives were physically harder, but freer and more varied.[15]

There were also positive aspects to Athenian social structures and attitudes towards women. There were many features of Athenian law that were protective of them. Every female citizen had to be provided with a dowry, which was intended to be a lifelong support for her. Income from the dowry could be used, but the dowry itself had to be preserved intact. In the case of divorce the husband had to return the dowry, which provided some continuing source of support for the woman and gave her the prospect of remarriage.

A marriage could be ended by mutual consent, or the husband could end it by sending the wife back to her father or guardian. The wife could also end the marriage, but in her case she had to lodge a formal statement with the archon that she was leaving her husband. Andocides and Plutarch record a dramatic example. Hipparete, wife of Alcibiades, outraged by his flagrant liaisons with courtesans of all types, went herself, as required, to lodge her declaration before the archon that she was leaving her husband. She was intercepted, however, by Alcibiades, and physically carried back from the Agora to their home. Hipparete apparently chose not to pursue the matter further, but the regulation regarding dowries and divorce did give women a certain level of lifelong financial security, and freed them from the threat of being trapped in unhappy or abusive marriages.[16]

There was a number of other laws designed to protect the vulnerable, many of them women. The archon had responsibility to oversee the enforcement of these social protections, and to conduct the preliminary hearings involving violations. Parents had to be cared for by their children until death and given a proper burial. There were laws protecting orphans and heiresses against anyone who wronged them, and laws forcing guardians to fulfil their obligations. The archon took care of widows whose husbands had died while they were pregnant, and looked after the affairs of orphans and heiresses until they were fourteen years old.[17]

This was not a society with any marked misogynistic leanings, nor did it lack concern for the well-being of its female citizens. But it was a society culturally locked into centuries of acceptance of a divide between the character and civil functions of the sexes that should not be crossed.

Could the democracy have brought a more enlightened view and confronted the issue of gender equality? To what extent does its failure to do so vitiate what it did achieve, and bring into question the validity of calling the rule of the *demos* a genuine democracy? Any significant change to the political or social position of women in the fifth or fourth centuries B.C. would have involved a form of revolution for which there was no paradigm in the Greek world, which would not occur in western civilisation for another 2,400 years and which, when it did, proved contentious, made halting advances and is still, in the minds of many, a work in progress.

Major political or social revolutions generally have long gestation periods and deep roots in broad civic disillusionment and a profound sense of grievance. These were the factors that brought the age of revolution in Greece in the seventh and sixth centuries, helped entrench fundamentally important principles of government such as the rule of law, and at Athens broke the hold of the elite of birth and wealth on political power. But there was no impetus for extending the revolution to the sphere of gender equality, no groundswell of social unrest demanding it, no champions capable of altering mindsets hardened by centuries of tradition. Athens did not and could not resolve all of the complex challenges involved in the ongoing search for a more just, equal and stable society, but it did bring to light and sought to implement a set of core political principles that form the essence of the democratic ideal. Its democracy was far from perfect by modern standards, but it had created the kernel.

Slavery

The democracy's acceptance of the institution of slavery must also be viewed in its historical context. To the modern liberal mind, slavery is a social abomination. But it was a worldwide phenomenon in ancient times, and remained prevalent until the late nineteenth century. The spread of Christianity made astonishingly little difference. The church did not condemn it or seek its abolition. We find one pope ordering the enslavement of Florentines in the late fourteenth century, and another accepting a gift of one hundred Moorish slaves in the fifteenth century. Slavery was also commonplace in the Muslim world. The discovery of America greatly extended the level of slavery in the Western Hemisphere and led to the infamous trade in black African slaves in the sixteenth and seventeenth centuries. The influence of the Enlightenment in the eighteenth century helped turn opinion against slavery, but it was not until the mid-to-late nineteenth century that slavery was abolished in European countries and their colonies, and in the United States and Latin America.

Athens, like all Greek *poleis*, had a significant population of slaves. There are no reliable figures for the actual number at any period, but there are plausible grounds for assuming a figure in the region of 100,000 for the mid- and late fifth century, with the number reducing considerably with the drop in the free population and in mining following the Peloponnesian War.

The main sources of slaves were those conquered in war or otherwise made captive. Children of slaves were also slaves. Greeks had qualms about enslaving fellow Greeks, and the bulk of Athenian slaves were imported and were so-called barbarians, whom the Greeks viewed as inferior beings. They came mostly from Thrace, the area around the Black Sea and the interior of Asia Minor. There was a slave market in the Agora, and Xenophon says a tax on imported slaves was an important source of revenue for the state.[18]

Slaves were used for a variety of functions. There were public slaves (*demosiai*), some of whom acted as assistants to magistrates and the Council. Others worked as labourers on public projects and in the dockyards, and there was a select group of three hundred, known as the Scythian Archers, who policed the Assembly and courts and enforced the orders of magistrates. Slaves were not used in the armed forces in combat roles, but they did serve as rowers in the fleet and as batmen for hoplites.[19]

But the great bulk of slaves were in private ownership. A large component were household slaves, many of them women. They provided a range of domestic services for better-off families. Slaves were used in agriculture but the scale of use is uncertain. Small farmers most likely could not afford slaves and almost certainly did not need full-time help, given the seasonal nature of labour requirements in agriculture. But larger landholders did require a workforce, and such evidence as survives suggests that it consisted largely of slaves. Casual free labourers may have supplemented the slaves at peak periods.

Significant numbers of slaves were employed in industry. The state-owned mines at Laurium were leased out in sections to contractors, who used almost exclusively slave labour. The work was so dangerous and gruelling that it was shunned by free labour. There were also numbers of sizeable workshops (*ergasteria*) where slave labour predominated. Sometimes the labour was hired from wealthy citizens whose business was investing in slaves and hiring them out to big farmers, state contractors or manufacturers. Nicias is the best-known example, said by Xenophon to have owned one thousand slaves whom he hired out to mining contractors at an obol a day per slave.

Slaves do not appear to have been used to the same extent in major state building projects. Fragments of accounts from construction of the Erechtheum show that out of 86 workmen listed, 24 were citizens, 42 were metics and 20 were slaves. The highly skilled nature of the work may account for the relatively low number of slaves.[20]

Other uses of slaves involved arrangements whereby an owner set up a group of slaves in a business or workshop of their own and took a proportion of their earnings in return. Slaves in this situation enjoyed a high degree of independence and had an incentive for high productivity, which would enable them to build up profits with which they could buy their freedom. Slaves with the right talents were also given responsibilities as foremen or managers.

There were obviously big differences in the quality of life of slaves depending on their skills and occupations.[21] But slavery was in all cases a grim and degrading condition. Euripides wrote in the *Ion* (854): 'the name alone brings shame upon the slave.' The slave was seen as a chattel, what Aristotle called 'an animate piece of property' (*Pol.*1253b32), was wholly subject to the will of the owner, and had only minimal legal rights or recognition as a member of the society.

There is evidence, however, that the democracy showed slaves a great deal more humanity than did other Greek regimes. Slaves had some legal rights. The owner could not legally kill a slave. He could impose many forms of severe punishment, but only a court could impose a death sentence. There was also a law on *hybris*, quoted by Demosthenes, which made it an indictable offence for anyone to assault or treat unlawfully any child, woman or man, free or slave. Demosthenes makes great play of the fact that Athenian law protected slaves in this humane way.

The indulgent attitude of the democracy towards both slaves and metics is highlighted by the Old Oligarch. He complains about their unbridled behaviour (*akolasia*), the fact that one is not allowed to strike them, that they will not get out of your way, that they are indistinguishable in dress and appearance from the citizens. He believes the democracy favours all of this, blurring distinctions between slave and free, allowing slaves to live sumptuously and earn money and gain their freedom, and have no fear and speak their mind. He contrasts this with the very different situation in Sparta. He thinks the reason for all this indulgence is the services slaves and metics give the navy, the great bulwark of the democracy.

Plato and Aristotle also consider greater freedom and privileges for slaves as characteristic of radical democracy. Plato cites as the most extreme aspect of freedom in a radical democracy the fact that men and women who have been purchased are no less free that those who purchased them. Aristotle similarly considers lack of control (*anarchia*) over slaves a feature of democracy, though he thinks that, up to a point, such an attitude towards slaves could be a benefit.[22]

But while the lives and opportunities of slaves in Athens may have been marginally better than in other Greek states, the fact remains that the democracy did not fundamentally change the institution of slavery. Throughout the Greek world slavery was a fact taken for granted, and slave labour formed part of virtually every facet of the labour force. It was an integral part of the Greek social fabric. The morality of slavery was certainly debated, at least among the intelligentsia, and there were those who argued that no one is a slave by nature, and that slavery was a consequence of a convention that those conquered in war could be enslaved by the victors, and had no moral justification. Aristotle goes to considerable lengths to refute this, arguing that slaves are a natural and necessary part of society, and that throughout all nature there are superiors and inferiors. Man rules the animals, the soul the body, the mind the appetites. Similarly human beings with superior gifts rightly rule those who lack full human capabilities. Aristotle was forced to admit, of course that in real life it was often raw force rather than superior intelligence or moral excellence that determined who was slave and who was free, and in general his defence of slavery lacks the intellectual incisiveness and rigour that normally mark his theoretical writings. In any event, there is no sign that slavery raised any moral concerns among the mass of Athenians. Their greater concern was to have the benefit of slave labour. Xenophon says: 'those who are able buy slaves so they can have fellow workers.'[23]

Two questions have arisen regarding the degree to which the democracy was dependent on the benefits of slave labour. The first concerns the extent to which slave labour generated the revenues needed to meet the cost of democratic government, the second concerns the extent to which slave labour created the leisure for citizens to participate in public life at the high levels required for the stable functioning of the democracy. The first question is less important for most of the fifth century when the state's revenue came primarily from the tribute paid by the allies, and from other fruits of empire. The treasury was in surplus and able to build reserves, but there is no basis for attributing any of this to the benefits of slavery.

The Peloponnesian War and its outcome brought a very different situation. The financial consequences of defeat have been described in some detail in the preceding chapter. Athens struggled to raise sufficient revenues in the fourth century, and failed repeatedly to fund adequately its military operations. But it had many successes and did manage to maintain stable government and bring the democracy to its fullest form. It is still difficult, however, to identify ways in which slave labour propped up significantly any aspect of the fourth-century democracy.

A sizeable proportion of the slave population was employed in the households of the better-off. These were, by and large, not wealth-producing, though on country estates they may sometimes have worked on the land as well as in the home. But on balance they were a cost, not a benefit, enhancing the quality of life and status of their owners, but not contributing to the public finances.

Slaves employed in agriculture, mining, the building industry, manufacturing and services such as banking undoubtedly contributed to the creation of wealth. But very little of this wealth found its way into the public coffers. The main gains went to the big farmers, to private entrepreneurs, such as the father of Demosthenes, who established their own workshops or small factories, to traders who might use slave crews for their ships and to state contractors. All of these might use slaves they owned, though larger concerns, and especially state contractors, would generally hire slave labour from another group who made big profits from slavery, entrepreneurs whose business consisted in buying and leasing slaves.[24]

The only way by which the state could get a share in the benefits of slave labour was through taxation. But, as we have seen, Athenian culture, with its emphasis on the right to private property and aversion to any redistribution of wealth, was also averse to direct taxation or any compulsory levies on the wealthy except in emergencies. Athens never sought to impose a direct tax on income, and the tax on capital assets, the *eisphora*, which it eventually introduced was for military uses only, brought complaints, evasion and concealment of assets, was set at a low rate and raised very little money. Slaves were a capital asset, and would have been included in the capital valuation but, given the rate and the overall yield, the gain to the treasury would not have been significant.

There was one other way in which the state might have capitalised on slave labour. It owned the most valuable capital asset in Attica, the silver mines at Laurium. But the only revenue derived from the mines was the sum paid by contractors for mining concessions. For at least the first sixty years of the fourth century that was a paltry sum, no more than three talents a year, because of a failure to repair the damage done to the mines by the Spartan occupation of Decelea. Xenophon strongly urged in the *Poroi* that the mines should be developed to their full potential, but he is especially insistent that the state must not simply lease the mines, but acquire and lease the slave labour needed to work them. He believed this could eventually yield 100 talents a year for the treasury. But the *demos* never sought to exploit the financial benefits of slave labour in such a way.

Xenophon's essay makes clear beyond question that the profitability of slavery lay in owning slaves for hire, or productively using them in one's own enterprises. The Athenian state did not do either of these, nor did it devise an effective system for taxing the profits of those who did. The conclusion of Jones that a negligible proportion of Athenian revenue came from slave labour seems entirely correct.[25]

The degree to which slavery facilitated the participation of citizens in public life is a more vexed question, because there is no reliable data about the numbers of Athenians who owned slaves. We know that in the American South about a quarter of whites owned slaves, and the proportion is likely to have been not much greater in Athens because of the high number of the population living at subsistence level.

It is certain that the wealthy minority, whom Aristotle describes as the *euporoi, plousioi* or *gnorimoi*, the well-off and notable, had multiple slaves for reasons of status as well as utility. But they were a minority leisure class, who could live off their wealth and had no need to work for a living. Political life was their natural métier. Slavery had nothing to do with their political participation. The rest of the citizen population Aristotle describes as the *aporoi, penetes* or *demos*, the badly off, the mass of ordinary citizens. They formed the large majority and included many categories: farmers, craftsmen, traders, merchant seamen, ferrymen, fishermen, unskilled labourers. These were the people who had to work for a living. They were also the heart of the democracy, the dominant force in the all-important Assembly, which provided the great popular forum where the *demos* exercised its *kratos*.[26]

But was the exercise of 'people power' possible only because slave labour enabled the mass of citizens to leave their work and participate in such a fulsome fashion in political life? There is no certain proof either way, but the balance of the evidence suggests that the participatory character and stable functioning of Athenian democracy were not dependent in any significant way on slavery.[27]

First, it is worth noting that no ancient source, not even Aristotle, who devoted so much space to discussion of radical democracy, and to its evolution and, to his mind, its domination by the poor, ever suggests that slavery had any bearing on the character and functioning of the democracy. Second, there are good reasons to believe that the great majority of the so-called poor did not own slaves. The most valuable information about the social structure and standard of living of the citizen population comes from the very rare statistics that appear in the sources. One relates to the settlement forced on Athens after its defeat in the Lamian War in 322. The Macedonian general Antipater required it to change its constitution and restrict political rights to those with a property valuation above 20 minae (2,000 drachmae). As a result, 22,000 citizens were disenfranchised, leaving only nine thousand with full political rights.[28]

These numbers show that more than two-thirds of the citizen population in the fourth century were truly poor. Demosthenes records a man telling a court how difficult it was to live on an inheritance of 45 minae. It is further evident that the great bulk of the 22,000 were peasant farmers. Thucydides tells us that the majority of Athenians still lived in the countryside at the time of the Peloponnesian War. A second statistic provided by the historian Dionysius of Halicarnassus, who lived in Rome in the first century B.C., would seem to confirm that this was still the case in the fourth century. In his introduction to a speech of Lysias opposing the proposal of Phormisius in 403 to limit citizenship to landowners, he says that the proposal would have disenfranchised five thousand citizens. This figure would indicate that three-quarters or more of the 22,000 with capital evaluations below 20 minae were landowners, and presumably made their living chiefly from the land. But their farms must have been extremely small. Lysias provides the only evidence of land prices in Attica in the fourth century, and it shows that an acre of land was valued at about 360 drachmae. This would mean that a farm valued at 20 minae could not be much larger than five acres, if some allowance is made for a house and equipment. Farms of a lower valuation would obviously be smaller still. Farmers with such modest holdings would not have the need or the resources for slave labour. The land, even if intensively farmed, could easily have been worked by the farmer and his family, and such evidence as we possess suggests this is what happened. A slave on a farm of five acres would have been a costly, if not unaffordable, extravagance.[29]

Those who had no wealth in land, whom Aristotle contemptuously described as inferior types (*phauloteroi*), artisans (*banausoi*), traders (*agoraioi*) and labourers for hire (*thetikoi*), comprised the urban proletariat. Aristotle stressed that they had easy access to the Assembly, and the level of their political dominance was one of his greatest objections to radical democracy. Some of them may have been reasonably well-off and owned slaves. Artisans who had large workshops certainly used some slave labour. But any causal connection between that and the fact that they availed themselves of their right to participate in the state's main political institutions, which were located so close to them, seems far-fetched.

Many of those among the citizen population with capital valuations above 20 minae would still have been relatively poor. The smaller farmers among them are likely to have used an element of slave labour, but they certainly could not afford to dispense with their own labour. Aristotle stresses that farmers with moderate amounts of property have no leisure. Their time is spent on their farmwork. I have discussed the political participation of this group, who comprised the core of the hoplite class, in an earlier chapter. It may have been expedited to some degree by slave labour, but it was not dependent on it.[30]

There are several explanations for the high participation levels in Athenian democracy that are far more compelling than slavery. They have been identified in earlier discussion of political participation. Pay was an important factor. Aristotle says pay gave leisure to the poor, enabling them to exercise their citizenship. The city was a focal point for citizens for many reasons – commercial, cultural, recreational and religious, as well as political. People were used to travelling there and combining different purposes.[31] But participation certainly entailed effort and, for many, probably some cost. It took strong motivation and intense loyalty to the ideal of the rule of the people to sustain it. That came from a deep-rooted culture of civic engagement fostered first of all at the level of the deme, and further strengthened by the system of tribes and their activities and the opportunity for so many to go on and serve in the Council. It also came from the fact that the rule of the *demos* was hard-earned and was almost lost in the convulsions of the late fifth century. That intensified the determination to protect it and make it work, as the particularly high levels of vigilance and accountability in the fourth century demonstrate. The citizens were willing to expend effort to preserve what they treasured. Their democracy was not a parasite feeding off slavery. Its effectiveness and stability rested on other pillars.

Metics (*Metoikoi*)

Metoikoi was the name given to freeborn foreigners who took up long-term residence in Athens. Their place and treatment in Athenian society tell a happier story than the situation of women and slaves. They were almost exclusively Greeks, as the record of gravestones shows, obviously attracted to Athens by the fact that it was a great commercial and cultural hub that welcomed foreigners who had skills, and gave them the freedom to use their talents and flourish financially. The only initial requirements were that they have an Athenian citizen as a sponsor (*prostates*) and that they register within a month of taking up residence. They were registered in the deme in which they resided. Slaves who were manumitted, a relatively rare occurrence in Athens, were also given the status of metics.

Despite the generally welcoming attitude of Athenians, metics did suffer a variety of disabilities. Not surprisingly, they had no political rights. They also could not own land or houses. Athenians adhered strictly to the principle, apparently common to all Greek cities, that only citizens could own the real estate of their country. Likewise metics could not contract a valid marriage with an Athenian citizen, and any children of such a union were denied citizenship. They also had to pay a poll tax (*metoikion*), which was 12 drachmae a year for a man, six for a woman. They were not eligible for any state hand-outs or supports, but were liable for liturgies, with the exception of the trierarchy, and for the *eisphora*. They were also liable for military service as sailors or hoplites.[32]

On the positive side they had the full protection of the law and had direct access to the courts, though in some Greek states metics had to act through a patron. They had full freedom to engage in trade and industry, and seem to have been especially prominent in commerce and banking. A census towards the end of the fourth century records ten thousand metics in Attica, but that figure represents only males eligible for military call-up, and the full number, including women, was probably two, and possibly three, times larger.

It seems clear that metics on the whole flourished in Athens, and that their contribution to the economy and society generally was well appreciated. Xenophon puts forward several proposals in the *Poroi* to encourage more metics to settle in Athens and thereby boost the economy. He says that they should be released from the obligation to serve as hoplites and should be allowed to serve in the cavalry, and that the most worthy among them should be allowed to buy vacant lots in the city and build houses on them. On the one hand the proposals show how disadvantaged metics were in comparison with citizens, but on the other hand they show, especially the proposal to confer the right to own real estate, how important metics were seen to be to expanding the non-agricultural areas of the economy. Xenophon's proposals, however, went unheeded.[33]

We know of several metics who achieved high prominence in Athenian society. The orator Lysias provides a particularly good example. His father, Cephalus, a Syracusan who had migrated to Athens on the invitation of Pericles and had settled in the Piraeus, where the family established a thriving business manufacturing shields, was a member of the Socratic circle. Plato chose their house as the setting for the dialogue the *Republic*, with Cephalus and his three sons, Lysias, Polemarchus and Euthydemus all present. Lysias also features prominently in the *Phaedrus*. The family fell foul of the Thirty Tyrants: Polemarchus was killed and Lysias had to flee from Athens, though he gave sterling support to Thrasybulus and the democrats in Phyle and the Piraeus, which won him an award of citizenship on the proposal of Thrasybulus. But some error in procedure nullified the decree and he remained a metic.

In the fourth century Lysias turned his attention to speechwriting, where he had extraordinary talents and was highly successful. Dionysius of Halicarnassus knew of 230 speeches. In 388 he had the honour of delivering an oration at the Olympic Games, in which he urged unity against what he saw as the two great threats to Greece, Dionysius of Syracuse and the king of Persia, and castigated the behaviour of Sparta. He may not have been a citizen, but he achieved high success and high standing in the society in which he lived.[34]

The banker Pasion was another well-known metic, though strikingly different from Lysias. He began life as a slave, working in the bank of his owner, where he achieved such profits that he was given his freedom. He acquired control of the bank and became the richest man in Athens, his total worth estimated at 60 talents. He eventually managed to secure citizenship. It is a wondrous tale, which shows that metics in Athens did have opportunity, and could achieve recognition for their success.[35]

There are relatively few examples of metics who achieved the heights of Lysias and Pasion, but as a body they were welcomed and accepted, and they proved loyal adherents of the democracy, as their fulsome support for the men in the Piraeus illustrates. The Athenian failure to give them a pathway to citizenship reflects a culture that believed citizenship derived from what later became known as *ius sanguinis*, a blood right, which for the Athenians meant descent from parents both of whom were citizens. The idea of eventual citizenship for resident aliens through naturalisation, an almost universal feature of modern democracies, was not favoured, though it did happen, and Cleisthenes reportedly gave citizenship to large numbers of metics and slaves after the revolution of 508/7. But in general Athens wanted a different kind of relationship with resident aliens that did not involve citizenship, but was based on mutual benefit. It was a relationship that appears to have functioned to the satisfaction of both sides.[36]

Foreign Policy

Flaws in foreign policy had cost Athens dearly in the fifth century. Some of the same flaws appeared in the policies of the fourth, with even more serious consequences. The activist spirit of the *demos* had not been blunted by defeat, and a hankering to repeat old glories persisted. The risk that ambition might overreach itself was increased by the fact that the right of the Assembly to decide foreign policy had few checks in law, a constitutional weakness that had not been remedied in the reforms of 403. When it came to international relations, including issues of war and peace, the power of the *demos* was unchecked. It could rule by decree.[37]

The Road Back from Defeat

Under the terms of the settlement of 404 Athens was left without walls or any significant armaments and reduced to the status of a subordinate ally of Sparta. It was a deeply humiliating and vulnerable position for the former leading imperial power, but Athens was careful to abide by the terms of the settlement over the following nine years. By 395, however, opportunities to recover its full autonomy and reclaim its place as a leading Greek power began to appear, and the restored democracy was not slow to grasp them.

Sparta's use of victory had disappointed and alienated much of the Greek world. Key allies such as Corinth and Thebes had pressed for far more severe treatment of Athens to eliminate it as a military and commercial rival, but were disregarded. Sparta had posed as the liberator of the Greek states of the Aegean from the oppressive imperialism of Athens, but it decided to take control of the Aegean itself by imposing oligarchic regimes, backed by Spartan garrisons and overseen by Spartan governors or harmosts, on most of the former dependencies of Athens.

Sparta's uncharacteristic eagerness for involvement outside the Peloponnesus was in evidence again in 401 when it decided to intervene in Persia in support of Cyrus, who was in rebellion against his older brother, King Artaxerxes. But Cyrus was defeated and killed at Cunaxa in 401, and that ended the rebellion. Sparta, however, led by a new king, Argesilaus, who was an advocate of extending Spartan influence, continued its challenge to Persian might by dispatching an army led by Argesilaus himself to Asia Minor in 396 to assist the Ionian cities, which were threatened with annexation by Persia. Artaxerxes responded by expanding the Persian navy and appointing Conon, the Athenian commander at Aegospotami, who had subsequently wisely taken refuge in Cyprus, to command it.

These developments had been watched with great interest at Athens, and hopes were raised that Conon could help Persia break the power of Sparta. At the same time Persian envoys were busily working to incite Sparta's Peloponnesian allies, along with Athens and Thebes, to go to war with Sparta, and promising Persian gold in support. Matters came to a head in 395, when a dispute between the minor states of Locris and Phocis led Thebes to intervene on the side of its ally Locris. The Phocians in turn sought and secured the support of Sparta. Thebes asked Athens for help, and the Assembly unanimously took a momentous decision towards the end of 395 to ally itself with Thebes and the Boeotian League. Athens was back at war with Sparta. Corinth and Argos soon joined the Theban/Athenian coalition. The allies gathered in Corinth in the summer of 394, and the so-called Corinthian War began.

Sparta had some initial successes, but all was changed when Conon inflicted a catastrophic defeat on the Spartan fleet at Cnidus in August 394. Accompanied by the Persian satrap Pharnabazus, the Persian fleet then headed for Laconia under Conon, who ravaged the coast and was given permission to bring the fleet to the Piraeus, with funds to rebuild the Long Walls and the fortifications of the harbour and of Athens. He was welcomed as a hero. By 391 Athens had its pride and its defences restored, and its shattered economy boosted by the injection of Persian capital.[38]

But Athens did not rest content with this extraordinary reversal of fortune. The Corinthian War on land soon developed into something of a stalemate, but there was an eagerness in the Assembly to begin to recover mastery of the Aegean. In the course of 393, with support from Conon and his Persian fleet and funds, the strategically important islands of Lemnos, Scyros and Imbros were brought back under Athenian control. But the Spartans, now anxious for peace with Persia and alarmed by the activities of Conon, sent a delegation to the Persian satrap Tiribazus in 392, offering terms of peace that would give Persia control of the Ionian Greeks, and accusing Conon of misusing the king's resources. The Athenians sent a counter-delegation led by Conon, but Tiribazus was on the side of the Spartans and had Conon imprisoned. He was soon released or escaped, but died in Cyprus in 392.

This setback caused Athens to send an embassy to Sparta later in 392. It was led by Andocides and Epicrates, who were given full powers to negotiate a settlement. They came back with proposals that the Greek states in Asia would be under the control of Persia, and all other Greek states would be autonomous, with the exception of Lemnos, Scyros and Imbros, which would belong to Athens. The envoys brought the proposals before the Assembly, and Andocides urged their acceptance with a series of powerful arguments exalting the proven benefits of peace to Athens, emphasising the frequency with which the Assembly had opted in the past for war rather than peace, and always to its detriment, and describing the gains that Athens had made since 404 and that left no justification for continuing the war. The Assembly, however, not only rejected the deal, but voted to prosecute the envoys for treason. They had to flee into exile.[39]

The decision is telling evidence of the mood of the *demos*, intent once more on adding to the catalogue of decisions favouring war, not peace, and determined that Athens, not Sparta, would rule the Aegean. The Persian fleet and Persian gold were gone, but there was an immediate resolve to build a substantial new fleet. An *eisphora* was levied, and forty ships were commissioned. This was the doing of the mass rather than the elite. In the *Ecclesiazusae* of Aristophanes, produced at this very time, the leading character says that when it comes to launching ships the poor vote in favour, the rich and the farmers vote against. The play, behind the irreverent burlesque façade of stage comedy, has a serious political message. It presents a society ruled by an erratic *demos* eager for war, that increasingly selects worthless types (*poneroi*) as leaders. Aristophanes uses Agyrrhius as a prime example, a populist who, by his introduction of pay for attending the Assembly, has brought people flocking to draw their wages who do not trust those who want to help them, and fawn on those who do not.

The author of the *Hellenica Oxyrhynchia* presents what was probably the substratum of truth underlying the colourful dialogue of Aristophanes. He identifies a divide between the many populist politicians (*hoi polloi kai demotikoi*) and the propertied gentry (*epieikeis* who had *ousia*), the *demotikoi* gaining the favour of the people because of their support for the recovery of the empire. The imperial urge had returned to Athens.[40]

The immediate goal was to keep Sparta from gaining a foothold in major Aegean states such as Rhodes or Cyprus, but securing control of the Hellespont and the trade routes to the Black Sea, the major source of the Athenian grain supply, was also an urgent priority. Thrasybulus was placed in command of the new fleet. He went first to the Hellespont and gained control of the Propontis and Bosporus, but failed to dislodge the Spartans from their stronghold at Abydos at the mouth of the Hellespont. He soon headed for Rhodes, but a foraging expedition en route caused his death in 389.

But the Athenians persisted with the Aegean strategy and sent a number of leading generals to the northern Aegean in 389/8. But a new Spartan commander, Antalcidas, outmanoeuvred them in 387 and reinforced the Spartan hold on the Hellespont. The Athenians failed to dislodge him. Athens now had little choice but to consider peace. The Persian king was also anxious to settle the issue of the Ionian Greeks and stabilise Greek affairs generally. Towards the end of 387 envoys from the Greek states were invited to Sardis to hear the king's terms. His proposals were identical to those Andocides and his fellow envoys had brought back from Sparta in 391, with a concluding statement that the king would make war on anyone who did not accept the peace. The Athenians accepted, as did Thebes eventually, and by early 386 all the participants in the Corinthian War had sworn to observe the terms prescribed by the king.[41]

The so-called King's Peace caused great disappointment in Athens, where high ambitions had been dashed by the setback in the Hellespont. As usual, the *demos* vented its anger on its generals. Four commanders were prosecuted, and almost certainly condemned. But the *demos* had only itself to blame. It had angrily scorned the advice of Andocides and had once again opted for war to its cost, and in the end had to settle for peace on terms available much earlier.[42]

The Peace did little to ease the rivalry and conflict that was endemic in Greece. Sparta emerged in the strongest position, and over the rest of the 380s worked to press its advantage and create a secure supremacy. It tightened its hold on the Peloponnesus, and in 382 responded to a call to intervene in a dispute between Olynthus and some of the large Chalcidian cities. By 379 it had forced Olynthus to surrender and had dissolved the Chalcidian League and made its members dependent allies. More significantly, it had gained virtual control of Thebes. In 382, when its army was moving north on its way to Olynthus and was encamped near Thebes, a pro-Spartan Theban polemarch, Leontiades, enabled the Spartan commander Phoebidas to enter the city and seize the Acropolis and install Leontiades in power. The Spartan authorities approved what had happened and maintained a garrison in the Theban Acropolis. Spartan dominance had now reached alarming heights. The King's Peace had neither protected the autonomy of Greek states nor limited the imperial ambitions of Sparta.

Athens carefully avoided military involvements during the latter half of the 380s, concentrating on building its military resources. The fleet was increased from about seventy ships in 387 to a hundred in 378. It also began seeking alliances with key Aegean states, and concluded a defensive pact with Chios in 384. But it did nothing to provoke Sparta.

The situation suddenly changed in the winter of 379/8. A coup led by Theban exiles, with some help from Athenian border forces, overthrew the government in Thebes, and the Spartan garrison had to withdraw. Sparta immediately sent an army into Boeotia, but it turned back without attacking Thebes, leaving behind a force under a commander named Sphodrias. Early in 378 he made a night raid deep into Attica with the intention, according to Xenophon, of seizing the Piraeus, but when dawn broke before he got there, he retreated. There was outrage in Athens, magnified when the Spartans put Sphodrias on trial but acquitted him. The Athenians now went on to a war footing, put gates on the Piraeus, built more ships and gave their fullest support to the Boeotians. They also intensified their efforts to forge new alliances.[43]

The Second Athenian League

In the winter of 378/7 an ambitious, far-reaching initiative was launched that resulted in the formation of what is commonly called the Second Athenian League or Alliance. A decree proposed by Aristoteles, a prominent *rhetor*, which has been largely preserved, sets out important features of the initiative. It shows that an invitation was issued to all autonomous Greek states to join in a defensive alliance under the leadership of Athens so that they could enjoy their freedom, independence and possessions secure from encroachment by Sparta. Extensive assurances were also given against any intrusions by Athens. It could not impose garrisons or levy tribute on member states, and its citizens could not own or acquire land in any of these states. The flaws that had converted the Delian League from an alliance (*summachia*) to an empire (*arche*) were being carefully avoided.

Other evidence provides information about the structures and procedures of the League. A resident Council (*synedrion*) was set up in Athens comprising representatives of all member states. Each member state had one vote and decisions were taken on a majority basis. Athens was not a member, but the Athenian Assembly and the *synedrion* had equal power, and decisions had to have the consent of both. All members had to contribute ships or money for the operations approved by the allies, but the meagre evidence does not allow much certainty about how this aspect of the alliance worked. There is no sign, however, that the contributions, initially at least, were a source of friction or division, though Isocrates alleged the Athenians later forcefully exacted contributions from the allies.

The range of states that joined the alliance is impressive. They included powerful Aegean states such as Chios, Mytilene, Rhodes, Byzantium, the cities of the Chalcidian League, Corcyra to the west, most of the cities of Euboea and, most remarkable of all, Thebes. The growth was gradual, but eventually the number of members may have gone as high as seventy.[44]

The League was a far-sighted initiative that created a broad alliance of Greek states that offered genuine mutual benefits, respected the traditions and independence of each member, and gave protection against domination by the leading power. It did not require a high level of political integration of the allies, but did provide a high level of added security through collective action jointly agreed and implemented using the experienced leadership that Athens could provide. It was a model of a federation that had the potential to counteract the volatility of Greek politics and break the ruinous cycle of war between Greeks. It could also provide a stronger bulwark against external threats.

Callistratus is often regarded as the main architect of the League, though the evidence is meagre. He was elected general in 378 at the time of its formation, and again in 372, and was prominent in every major political development of the 370s. He was a powerful orator, greatly admired by Demosthenes, and a diligent statesman, according to Theopompus. But he also directly involved himself in military operations and had close relations with one of the most successful military leaders of the decade, Chabrias. Whatever his role in creating the League, he was a central figure in Athenian politics in the 370s.[45]

The League was highly successful in its primary goal of containing Sparta's expansionist ambitions. Efforts to subdue Boeotia in successive invasions in the early 370s were repulsed. Athens led a successful naval war against the Spartan fleet. A major victory by Chabrias at Naxos in 376 led to mastery of the Aegean by that League. That same year Timotheus, son of Conon, was sent around the Peloponnesus, and he gained the support of Corcyra and the cities of Cephallenia.

But a lack of funds was limiting the capacity of the League to achieve its objectives. Thebes aggravated the situation by failing to make its contribution.

Athens wanted an end to the war, and in the summer of 371 a conference was held in Sparta to discuss peace. Callistratus and Callias were the chief Athenian envoys. Terms were agreed similar to those of the King's Peace, affirming again the autonomy of all Greek states. Thebes again demanded that Boeotia be recognised as a single political entity, but this was again refused. The Theban envoys, led by a new Theban boeotarch, Epaminondas, then refused to swear acceptance of the agreement, and the name of Thebes was deleted from the treaty.

Sparta reacted immediately and sent an army to attack Thebes. The decisive encounter took place in the middle of 371 at Leuctra, where Epaminondas showed his military skills and inflicted a crushing defeat on the Spartans. The power of Sparta north of the Isthmus was at an end.[46]

Leuctra also had implications for Athens and the future of the Second League. Thebes was now going it alone, and its rising military power was potentially a greater threat to Athens than the greatly weakened Sparta. The first reaction of the Athenians was to summon a conference at Athens in late 371 of all states that wished to be part of the King's Peace. The participants swore to abide by the terms of the Peace and decrees of the Athenians and their allies, and to help any state that had sworn the oath, if attacked. The hope obviously was that this would deter any Theban aggression.

Events then moved quickly. The cities of Arcadia saw the weakness of Sparta as an opportunity to establish their full independence, and formed a union under a single broadly democratic government. The Spartans sent an army under Agesilaus to quell the initiative. The Arcadians appealed for help to Athens and Thebes. Athens refused, but Thebes responded positively and Epaminondas led his first invasion of the Peloponnesus in late 370. By the time he reached Arcadia, Agesilaus had withdrawn. Epaminondas proceeded into Laconia and came within sight of Sparta. He did not attack the city, however, but contented himself with burning the dockyards at Gytheion and then headed for Messenia where the Messenian serfs rallied to his support. He established Messenia as an autonomous state and began the building of a new capital, Messene, on the slopes of Mount Ithome.

His expedition had far-reaching effects. It enabled Arcadia to cement its union and go on to build a well-fortified federal capital, Megalopolis. It deprived Sparta of a bulwark of its power, Messenia, and left it with two hostile powers on its borders. Sparta's place as a major Greek power was permanently diminished. Epaminondas began his return to Thebes in early 369.

News of these events caused further soul-searching in Athens. The Council summoned the Assembly, which heard from Spartan envoys and allies. There was divided opinion, but, according to Xenophon, the Assembly was swayed by the fear of a powerful, hostile Thebes on its border if it failed to help Sparta, and by the hope that help in these dire straits might bind the Spartans to Athens as firm, long-time allies. With Callistratus as its chief proponent, a decision was taken to send an army under Iphicrates to the Peloponnesus.[47]

It was a fateful decision. Leuctra and its aftermath proved as big a turning point for Athens as for Sparta. Athens was now committed to war with Thebes, a recent ally and primary source of the power of the Second League, and had forged an alliance with Sparta, its recent enemy whose ambitions the League had been established to keep in check. But the subsequent behaviour of Athens indicates that it was motivated by more than fear of Thebes or naïve hopes of lasting friendship with Sparta. Its real hope was that it could use the new alliance to lever support for its enduring ambition to regain control of Amphipolis and the Chersonese, which would entrench its domination of the northern Aegean and provide the springboard for a renewed mastery of the sea.

The relationship between Athens and Amphipolis was close and of long-standing. After two failed attempts, a successful colony had been established in Amphipolis in 437/6 by Hagnon, son of Nicias, though the majority of the settlers had come from neighbouring allies in Chalcidice and Thrace because of a shortage of Athenian citizens. It was strategically significant, located at an important crossing of the Strymon commanding trade routes to the north and surrounded by large timber and mineral resources. When Athens lost Amphipolis to Brasidas in 424, it was a bitter blow, and Thucydides the historian, who was blamed for not saving the city, paid the price with a twenty-year exile. Athens did its utmost to recover Amphipolis as part of the Peace of Nicias. It failed, and the loss always rankled.

The Chersonese commanded the trade routes into the Black Sea. Pericles had settled a cleruchy there c. 350 with a thousand colonists. Plutarch describes the settlement as one of the best-remembered and cherished achievements of Pericles, pacifying a fertile wheat-producing region and securing the area of the Hellespont.[48]

At a further meeting at Athens late in 469 with Sparta and its allies to decide the terms of the new alliance and the chain of command, the Athenians were quick to capitalise on their offer of help to Sparta by pressing for support for their traditional claims to Amphipolis and the Chersonese. According to Demosthenes, their claims were not only recognised by all Greeks but by the Persian king as well. This was a major quid pro quo for the *volte-face* that aligned Athens with Sparta and against Thebes, and it marked the beginning of a new determined drive for old imperial glories.[49]

But the price proved to be very high. The new Athenian direction embroiled it in a further fifteen years of almost continuous warfare that impoverished the state and left it with annual public revenues of as little as 130 talents in the late

350s. Worst of all, it brought the final dissolution of the main elements of the Second League.

Military action in the Peloponnesus over the next several years was desultory and changed little. The Theban interest was centred more on northern Greece, where instability in Thessaly and Macedonia gave scope for expansion of Theban influence. Athens was also preoccupied with its plans in the northern region. In 368 Iphicrates was dispatched with a fleet to the northern Aegean. Amphipolis was, of course, the main target, but Amphipolis was prepared to resist any effort by Athens to impose control, and Iphicrates seems to have concentrated his efforts on Macedonia where he intervened in a struggle for the throne at the invitation of Queen Eurydice, mother of two future kings, Perdiccas and Philip II. Iphicrates drove out the pretender Pausanias, but not long afterwards Thebes succeeded in forcing Macedonia into alliance with it.

In 366 Athens sent a further expedition to the eastern Aegean under the command of Timotheus. He gained control of Samos, where a cleruchy was established, a favourite tool of empire in the Periclean era. Timotheus replaced Iphicrates in the north in 365. He worked in cooperation with the Persian satrap Ariobarzanes, and with his help gained possession of two important centres in the Chersonese, Sestos and Krithote. Two attempts to take Amphipolis failed, but Timotheus had legendary success along the northwestern coast, capturing more than twenty cities, including Methone, Pydna, Potidaea and Torone. Another cleruchy was established in Potidaea. Athens could again claim to be an imperial power.[50]

In the late 360s the focus of attention again switched to the Peloponnesus, when division within the Arcadian League, and between the League and Elis, gave Sparta hope of regaining some of its lost power and caused Epaminondas to lead his fourth expedition into the Peloponnesus in 362. After initial skirmishes that saw Theban forces fighting in the streets of Sparta, the decisive encounter took place at Mantinea between the combined forces of both sides. Armies from Athens, Sparta, Elis, Achaea and the Arcadian cities opposed to Thebes were ranged against the Thebans, Argives, Messenians and Arcadians loyal to Thebes. The Theban side put their opponents to flight, but Epaminondas was killed, and the Thebans failed to seal their victory. In Xenophon's view Mantinea changed nothing, and left Greece in greater confusion and disorder than before.[51]

Athens soon faced further setbacks. The Second League was approaching the final stages of disintegration. The end of the 360s brought trouble in the straits and the Chersonese. With help from Chalcedon and Cyzicus, Byzantium, previously a leading member of the Second League, began to impede the Athenian grain fleet in 362. Athens had to send warships to protect it, a practice it had to continue for several years. In 360 the Thracian king, Cotys, seized Sestos, and Athenian control of the Chersonese was threatened. Sestos was not recovered until 357 when Chares, who had emerged in the second half of the 360s as a decisive, talented military leader, was placed in command.[52]

The degree of dissatisfaction at Athens in this period with the course of its foreign policy is reflected in a large number of high-level prosecutions. Several of the generals who had served in the Chersonese and the Hellespont in the late 360s and early 350s were indicted and condemned. But two of the city's most senior statesmen were also put on trial. Callistratus, who had so ably served Athens over many years, was condemned to death in 361 and had to flee into exile. The charge is not recorded but most likely related to a foreign-policy issue. Aristophon, a well-known leader since the end of the fifth century, was accused in connection with the handling of a dispute with the island of Ceos in 362. He was acquitted by two votes. The mood in Athens was at its most unforgiving.[53]

Athens did achieve a significant success in 357 when Euboea, which had sided with Thebes after Leuctra, was recovered as an ally. But soon afterwards the most important remaining members of the Second League, Byzantium, Chios, Rhodes and Cos, formally seceded. Their action spelled the end of any meaningful role for the League in Greek affairs, but the disintegration of the alliance had begun much earlier. Thebes was obviously no longer a member after 369. Euboea sided with Thebes. Athenian moves against Amphipolis alienated the Chalcidians and Olynthus. Corcyra had seceded by 360. Ceos had sought to secede around 366 and Athens had had to negotiate a new settlement with the island.

The states that seceded in 357 had long been moving in that direction. When Epaminondas led a fleet of a hundred ships into the Aegean in 364 he was welcomed by Byzantium, Chios and Rhodes to their cities, though they stopped short of offering him support. Soon afterwards Byzantium was again harassing Athenian grain ships. The decision to make the break in 357 may have been spurred by offers of help from the ambitious satrap of Caria, Mausolus, who was intent on extending his influence over the Aegean islands, but disillusionment with Athens had been building for some time.[54]

The reasons are easy to understand. Athens had declared war in 369 on the League's most powerful member and taken the side of the state that the League was established to resist. At least one important member, Mantinea, had difficulty with that decision, and there is no indication that the *synedrion* approved it or was asked to do so. But subsequent Athenian actions in the Aegean were a far more blatant departure from the purposes of the League. Athens had embarked on a unilateral agenda to gain control of Greek states that were posing no threat to any member of the League, and that had a right to independence under the terms of the King's Peace, which the League had sworn to uphold at the conference in 369. Nothing could be more at variance with the defensive mission of the League, or could have more fatally undermined its functioning as intended. Athens had squandered an opportunity to lead a powerful coalition of the willing that could have been a stabilising influence in Greece and an effective protection against external enemies.

But Athens was not now prepared to allow the seceding states to leave the alliance, confirming its posture as an imperial master, not a leader of free allies. Chares was sent with sixty ships to attack Chios, and the so-called Social War began. Chios received help from Byzantium, Rhodes, Cos and Mausolus, and defeated Chares in early 356. Reinforcements were sent under Iphicrates, his son Menestheus and Timotheus, but Chares suffered another defeat at Embata in the strait between Chios and the mainland in the autumn of 356. His colleagues, who disagreed with his decision to fight in bad weather, had not properly supported him and were later prosecuted. Iphicrates and his son were acquitted, but Timotheus was fined 100 talents and went into exile in Chalcis, where he died soon afterwards. The defeats, combined with pressure from the Persian king, persuaded Athens to make peace in 355/4. The secessionists got their independence. The League was left with a rump of minor powers.[55]

Athens also suffered further setbacks in the early 350s. Macedonia got a new king in 359, Philip II, son of Eurydice, the queen whom Iphicrates had assisted almost a decade earlier. Philip was a leader of extraordinary energy and ability and ruthless ambition. He quickly managed to unify Macedonia and reorganise the army, creating the famed Macedonian phalanx, and he was intent on extending Macedonian control along its borders. In 357 he moved eastwards and captured Amphipolis, and in the following years took Pydna, Potidaea and Methone. The achievements of Timotheus and Athenian imperial ambitions had been brought to nought. Athens declared war after the capture of Amphipolis, but took no action.[56]

Athens was at a low ebb by the mid-350s. The democracy remained stable, but the state's finances and foreign policy were in tatters. Its plight gave rise to two discourses by two prominent Athenians of very different personality and background, Xenophon and Isocrates. They are thoughtful essays by two significant contemporary witnesses, and provide a valuable insight into the character of the political debate in Athens in the 350s.

Xenophon's brief essay, entitled *Revenues (Poroi)*, provides a comprehensive catalogue of the wealth of natural resources available to Athens, which he believes should enable it to produce abundant revenues for the needs of the state provided there is peace. He lists its moderate climate, productive seas, extensive silver and stone deposits, and its central location which made it a stopping point for all travellers by land or sea. He dwells on its unrivalled advantages as a commercial centre with its location and safe harbours. Nowhere can those with things to buy or sell do better than in Athens. He offers a variety of proposals for capital projects to exploit these advantages. But all is contingent on securing a lasting peace. He goes so far as to propose appointing Guardians of Peace (*eirenophylakes*). Peace would make Athens a hub for shipowners and merchants, for those with corn, wine, oil or cattle. It would attract investors, craftsmen, Sophists, poets, anyone interested in things worth seeing or hearing (5.2–4).

But Xenophon is aware that there are those who want hegemony and still think it can more likely be achieved by war than peace. He reminds them that it was not coercion but services to Greece that gave Athens leadership of the Delian League, and it was excessive harshness that caused it to lose it (5.6). In an obvious reference to the Second League he says the islanders again gave the leading place to Athens because of its just behaviour, though he leaves unspoken the implied message that again that hegemony was lost by bad behaviour. But now, because of the turmoil in Greece, he believes Athens could win back the Greeks by reconciling the warring states. He proposes sending embassies up and down Greece to bring peace. If Athens showed it was striving for peace in every land and on every sea, it would have the prayers of everyone (5.10). He accepts, however, that Athens would have to go to war if wronged, but if Athens had wronged nobody, the enemy would have trouble finding allies, and vengeance could come quickly.

He ends by summarising the benefits of his proposals: greater friendship with Greeks, a safer life, a higher reputation, no war taxes, an ample supply of the necessities of life for the *demos*. Instead of war draining the treasury, there would be a large surplus for festivals and for repair of temples, walls and docks (5. 11–12).

Isocrates provides a more elaborate rhetorical, passionate discourse, entitled *On the Peace (Peri Eirenes)* and cast in the form of a speech to the Assembly meeting to consider peace at the end of the Social War. It is a valuable, revealing, contemporary analysis of the dark side of imperialism, and a scathing indictment of Athenian imperialist policies and mistreatment of allies in the recent past.

Isocrates begins by recognising the activist impulse of Athenians to recover past glories, their readiness to man triremes and their propensity for involvement in wars, but says he is urging them to make peace, not only with the Rhodians, Chians, Byzantines and Coans, but with all mankind in accordance with the terms of the King's Peace. He extols peace, listing benefits similar to those mentioned by Xenophon – greater safety, domestic harmony, prosperity with no war taxes or trierarchies, freedom to till the soil and sail the seas, increased revenues and a city full of merchants, metics and visitors, all of whom have now deserted Athens. Peace would also win back for Athens the esteem of fellow Greeks, the most important benefit of all (12, 16, 18–21).

Three main themes dominate the bulk of the speech: the evil and folly of imperialism (*arche*); the continuing addiction of Athenians to this form of coercive rule; and the need for new directions based on a commitment to peace and justice. He condemns the form of rule called *arche* as despotic. It compels rather than leads, thinks injustice more expedient than justice, covets the possessions of others, believes the strong should rule the weak, and breeds war and interventionism (*polypragmosune*). He equates it with tyrannical one-man rule within states. The evils that despots do are the evils that imperial states perpetrate, and for the same reason. Absolute power corrupts, and replaces justice with injustice, and discipline and moderation with licence and arrogance (29–32, 91, 114–15).

He cites Athens and Sparta as the two great examples of imperialism corrupting and destroying. It brought the ruin of Athens, which proceeded to abuse the hegemony freely given to it by its allies in the Delian League, and to engage in such extreme behaviour as the insane adventurism of the Sicilian expedition. It ended in the near-destruction of the state. Imperialism similarly brought the ruin of Sparta, which wronged almost every state in Greece before its insolence brought it to disaster at Leuctra (84–85, 91–92, 95–100, 105, 116).

His condemnation of imperialism provides the backdrop for trenchant criticism of recent Athenian imperialist behaviour and failure to learn the lessons of history. He accuses his audience of still persisting in the belief that mastery of the sea is the greatest of goods and that, if they sail with many triremes and force other states to pay contributions and deny those who refuse the right to sail the sea, they have achieved something of value. Their ancestors fought and overcame the barbarians to preserve the safety of Greeks, while they have hired barbarians to fight Greeks on their behalf, and have extorted money from their allies to pay them. Instead of liberating the cities of Greece they seek to enslave them. They still covet an empire that is neither just, attainable nor beneficial. He asks how Athens could now acquire an empire in its impoverished state, since it could not retain one when it had 10,000 talents at its disposal. Even if it could, it would be a road to disaster, as in previous times (29, 42–43, 66, 70).

He ends with a clear set of messages. Athens must stop longing for mastery of the sea, refrain from fruitless wars and loathe all forms of despotic rule. It must treat its allies as it would its friends and give them real independence, leading them not as a master but as a comrade. It must work to secure the esteem of all Greeks and stand forth as the champion of freedom; a saviour, not a destroyer. It must prepare for war and build its power, but as a deterrent, not a threat. Its power must be linked to justice, an instrument for deliverance, not enslavement. This is the path to honour and hegemony (64, 133–44).

Around this time Isocrates wrote another discourse, the *Areopagiticus*, to which I have alluded earlier. Its principal theme was the need to revert to the ancestral constitution, restore the powers of the Areopagus and re-create the golden era of Athens as a disciplined, morally responsible leader in Greece. Isocrates contrasts with that the current sad state of Athens, and reiterates the core argument of *On the Peace* that the decadence and flawed public policy of his day are only bringing the state internal woes and external hatred and dishonour.[57]

Xenophon and Isocrates, both writing in the late 350s, are in broad agreement on many points. Both argue for peace and avoidance of wars of aggression, policies that would build the wealth and power of Athens. Both believe that hegemony would follow if Athenians refrained from injustice and used their resources and power, not for coercion, but to champion lasting peace and freedom for Greeks. Both, though in varying degrees, are critical of recent Athenian foreign policy, which they clearly show had an imperialist agenda to impose Athenian rule over the Aegean, and which involved Athens in abuse of allies and oppression of other Greeks, and ended in failure.

The essays of Xenophon and Isocrates put the spotlight on one of the great failures of the Greek states as a whole during what was in many ways a golden age of Greek civilisation in the fifth and fourth centuries, namely the failure to find a way of halting the endless cycle of internecine warfare and create national agreements and structures that would work for unity and peace and the common welfare of all Greeks. There were alliances in abundance, but they were generally leagues of neighbouring or kindred states designed to protect their members against other Greek coalitions, and were almost invariably led by a dominant *hegemon* whose chief concern was its own power.

The Greeks fully recognised the many bonds between them – shared ethnicity, cultural heritage and religious traditions. They were also very aware of the ruinous effects of war, the benefits of peace and the vulnerability of a fragmented Greece to external threats. Panhellenism was a well-worn theme, but it remained a pious, romantic notion, sounded at great Panhellenic occasions such as the Olympic Games. The *Panegyricus* of Isocrates, generally acknowledged to be his masterpiece, provides the outstanding example of Panhellenic rhetoric, calling for an end to the chronic, calamitous warfare between Greeks against the great common threat, Persia. Gorgias and Lysias were other orators who made similar pleas on Olympic occasions.

But Panhellenism was a forlorn hope, pushing against the weight of history. There were stronger forces dividing Greeks than uniting them. The tribal divide between Dorians and Ionians ran deep, a serious barrier to trust and cooperation between the most powerful states, the Dorian Spartans and the Ionian Athenians.[58] In many ways the culture of the *polis* was a culture of separateness, of independence (*autonomia*), and self-sufficiency (*autarkeia*), of exclusive attitudes towards citizenship, of belonging to and sharing in a close-knit, self-governing political community, all of which contributed to a strong sense of political identity and place. Greece in the classical era was divided into about 750 such separate political entities, widely varying in size and citizen population. None of this precluded cooperation and peaceful coexistence, but it did present barriers to any close political integration, and gave scope within any form of alliance for the powerful and the imperial-minded to exert dominance.

Athens was given opportunities both in the fifth and fourth centuries to overcome such obstacles and create and lead sustainable, broad-based coalitions committed, under agreed overarching structures, to protect against common threats and to promote peace. It is hard to argue with the judgement of Xenophon and Isocrates that on both occasions Athens, intent on empire-building and mastery of the sea, abused its position of leadership and betrayed its mission. With regard to the Delian League, Pericles bears much of the blame. He wanted only one superpower in Greece, and one that ruled rather than led its allies, a policy that eventually embroiled Athens in a major war and, according to Thucydides, aroused such anger against Athens that, at the start of the Peloponnesian War, the majority of Greeks favoured Sparta, hoping to be freed from the yoke of Athens or fearing they would fall under it. After the death of Pericles harder edges of Athenian imperialism made their appearance, and the conduct of the war was dominated by a hardline militarism, new imperial ventures and a reluctance to make peace without victory. It all ended in a humiliating surrender.[59]

The Second League, with a membership as high as seventy states and a charter that guarded against excessive intrusions or controls by Athens, should have had better prospects of achieving a sustainable alliance that could provide a showcase of the benefits, military and economic, of a broad-based union committed to protecting peace. But after Leuctra, partly no doubt out of fear of a hated rival, Thebes, but also sensing opportunity, Athens embarked on a solo agenda of aggrandisement that made the League irrelevant and turned Athens once more into an aggressor against the freedom of Greeks.[60]

The role of the political leadership in determining Athenian foreign policy in the first half of the fourth century is hard to establish. After the deaths of Conon and Thrasybulus the period produced no outstanding leaders and certainly none of the stature of a Themistocles or a Pericles. Callistratus was to the fore in establishing the Second League, and seems to have taken a leading part in the decision to align with Sparta in 369. But the extent of his influence remains in doubt, and he ended up in exile in 361. The other leaders most prominent in the sources, Iphicrates, Chabrias, Timotheus and Chares, were professional soldiers more than politicians. They were elected for their military skills, and survived only as long as they were successful. Phocion stands out as both a political and a military leader who commanded the trust and respect of the *demos*, but he lacked the authority and charisma to sway the Assembly, and his consistent advocacy of prudence and peace fell on deaf ears.

The hawkish, imperialist mentality behind much of Athenian foreign policy in the first half of the fourth century was emanating from the *demos* itself. The will to power, so evident in the rhetoric and conduct of the Peloponnesian War, had not diminished. No lessons had been learned. Isocrates does not blame the leadership for the plight of Athens in the 350s; he blames the people themselves and their hunger for empire. The democracy, which achieved so much domestically, did nothing to alter the culture of war with its ruinous consequences.

Athens paid a heavy price for its failed leadership of the Second League, and in the aftermath of the Social War there was a genuine desire for peace and new directions. The great military giants of preceding decades, Chabrias, Iphicrates and Timotheus, were all off the scene. New political leaders were coming to the fore who were more disposed towards peace. Chief among them was Eubulus, about whom little is known until the 350s, when he quickly came to prominence and achieved a position of high influence as director of the restored Theoric Fund. His role in steering Athens towards a more conservative defensive foreign policy and his success in increasing state revenues have been mentioned earlier. Aeschines records that he had the trust of the people. He capitalised on that to acquire a large measure of control over the public revenues and to build the Theoric Fund into a major department of state for social and infrastructural development. Laws were passed requiring that all moneys left over from the administration of the various departments should go into the Fund. Athens began to get the kind of capital investment recommended by Xenophon.[61]

The Growing Threat from Macedonia

Athens steered clear of military involvements during the latter half of the 350s. It ignored a plea for help from the Megalopolitans in 353, when Sparta made a move to recover control of Messenia and Arcadia. It similarly refused support around the same time for a democratic revolt in Rhodes against an oligarchic regime imposed by Mausolus after the Social War, and stayed on the fringes of a major conflict involving Phocis and Thebes centred around control of the sanctuary at Delphi, despite the fact that Phocis was an ally.

But the continuing expansionist activities of Philip of Macedonia threatened the mood of peace. In 352 he moved into Thessaly and seemed intent on taking control of Thermopylae, the gateway to central Greece. Athens felt compelled to send an expedition to defend it, but Philip withdrew and turned his attention to Thrace and the Chersonese, the one remaining Athenian foothold in the straits and vital to the security of the city's food supply. The Assembly voted to send a fleet of sixty ships and to levy an *eisphora* of 60 talents. But illness prevented Philip pursuing the campaign. Athens was prepared to go to war when its vital interests were at stake, but had no appetite for going on the offensive.[62]

Not everyone agreed with this policy of restraint. The late 350s saw the rise to prominence of Demosthenes, who quickly became a forceful advocate of war against Philip and a formidable counterweight to the policies of Eubulus. Son of a wealthy factory owner, he was a versatile orator of extraordinary ability with strong ideas and a ruthless streak. He had honed his skills in the courts before entering the political arena. His vision of the destiny of Athens harked back to the days of Athenian glory in the fifth century, and he had a Periclean view of the Athenian character as that of a people who led and acted with resolve, tolerated no injury, and were driven by patriotic fervour to fight and make sacrifices for their state and its ideals. His early political speeches were in support of the Megalopolitans and Rhodians, and of a better-organised and extended system of symmories. All had fallen on deaf ears. His first attempt in 350 to rouse the Assembly against Philip, in a speech known as the *First Philippic*, also failed to make an impact. It enumerated the failures of Athens to check the rise of Philip and proposed the immediate marshalling of large-scale land and sea forces, and especially the citizen army, to attack where opportune and defend where necessary. It was powerful, well-reasoned oratory, but Athens was not yet ready to heed the rhetoric of war.[63]

Philip's next actions, however, brought a shift in the public mood. In 349 he moved against the Chalcidian League and Olynthus. He now seemed set on gaining control of the entire Thracian coast, including the Chersonese. Demosthenes pressed for a decisive response in his three Olynthiac Orations. He again berated the Assembly for allowing Philip to pick off Athenian possessions one by one, and argued that Philip must now be stopped while he was beatable and far away and before the war was transferred from Olynthus to Athens. To find funds he proposed repeal of the laws dealing with the Theoric Fund, which he claimed was diverting revenues from military needs to trivial purposes. The Athenians finally accepted the need for action, but their response was piecemeal, much of the help arrived too late and Olynthus fell in 348.[64]

The fall of Olynthus further increased Athenian fear of Philip's power and intentions. Eubulus persuaded the Assembly to send an embassy to the Peloponnesians to seek to recruit allies to oppose Philip. One of the envoys was Aeschines, who had spoken in favour of the proposal of Eubulus. It was his first recorded speech before the Assembly. He had previously served with distinction as a hoplite under Phocion, who befriended him, and later as public secretary to the Council and Assembly. He had also spent time as a tragic actor, had a powerful voice, and his three surviving speeches show a rhetorical nimbleness that made him a match for Demosthenes. The embassy to the Peloponnesus had little success, and when Philip soon afterwards indicated that he wanted peace and an alliance with Athens, there was general agreement in the Assembly that peace was the best option.[65]

An embassy of ten was dispatched to negotiate. It included Demosthenes, Aeschines and Philocrates, proposer of the embassy. It met with Philip at Pella in late 347. It was agreed that both sides should retain what they had, which meant Athens gave up its claims to Amphipolis, but was guaranteed control of the Chersonese. Philip sent a letter back with the embassy indicating that he wanted an alliance as well as peace, and was sending envoys to discuss this. The envoys pressed the case for an alliance and stipulated that the peace should apply only to Athens and the members of the allied *synedrion*. A motion to accept the terms, put forward by an ally of Eubulus, Philocrates, was accepted and was ratified by the *synedrion*. A second embassy with the same personnel was dispatched to get Philip to swear to the peace and negotiate any further benefits they could. Philip and his allies swore the oath about the middle of 346.

Demosthenes was unhappy with the outcome of the second embassy. He had disagreed with Aeschines about how the further negotiations with Philip should be handled, and he felt they had got nothing but vague promises, especially in regard to Phocis. But the Assembly voted to extend the treaty and alliance to Philip's descendants, and to join in action against the Phocians if they did not surrender the temple at Delphi. A third embassy was sent to update Philip. Demosthenes refused to serve on it.

Philip next moved to end the Sacred War and quickly gained control of Thermopylae and Phocis, and called a meeting of the Amphictionic Council to decide the fate of the Phocians. The third embassy was directed to change its itinerary and attend the Council, where Aeschines argued for leniency. But the punishment was harsh. The cities of Phocis were destroyed and the inhabitants forced to live in small villages.[66]

There was outrage in Athens. The Assembly had been led to believe that Philip would save the Phocians from any such fate. But even Demosthenes agreed that this was not the time to break the peace.[67] It was to last until 340, but was never stable. Philip, a great opportunist and master of brinkmanship, was a slippery ally who did not inspire trust. Athenian suspicion of his intentions continued to harden, stoked by relentless efforts by Demosthenes to present him as an enemy who was bent on the destruction of Athens.

The influence of Demosthenes grew steadily throughout the 340s, as he used his powerful oratorical skills to turn the *demos* towards war. In 344, in a speech in the Assembly, the *Second Philippic*, he denounced Philip and the peace and called for a change in policy. The following year the leading proponents of peace, Philocrates and Aeschines, were charged with treason. An ally of Demosthenes, Hyperides, conducted the prosecution of Philocrates and won a conviction and sentence of death. Philocrates fled before the verdict. Demosthenes himself conducted the prosecution of his long-time adversary Aeschines, reviving charges of treasonable behaviour on the second embassy that he had first made in an abortive prosecution in 346.

It was a memorable encounter between the two foremost orators of the day. Both speeches survive. Aeschines won, but by a narrow margin. His effectiveness as a counterforce to Demosthenes went into decline. Little is heard of him in the years after the trial, and his main allies, Eubulus, Phocion and another respected general and political leader, Nausicles, also seem to have lost their earlier prominence. Demosthenes was now approaching the peak of his ascendancy.[68]

Continuing interventions by Philip in Greek affairs in 343/2 heightened tensions further and gave Demosthenes additional credibility. He was in the forefront of efforts during those years to win allies for Athens, and succeeded in gaining alliances with the Achaeans, Argives and Messenians, and with Megalopolis and its associated Arcadian cities. He was also instrumental in winning Euboea to the side of Athens through an agreement with Callias, leader of Chalchis, that a new federation of Euboean cities led by Chalchis should be formed and become allied with Athens. In 341 he was awarded a golden crown by the Assembly for his efforts.[69]

Philip was well aware of the increasing hostility towards him in Athens, and in 343 he sent an embassy offering to consider modifications of the peace, but hardline responses from the Assembly prevented any progress. Athens was soon in dispute with Philip on another front, in the Chersonese, where it had sent its general Diopeithes to shore up its defences with additional cleruchs. He got into a dispute with the city of Cardia in the northwest, which denied it was part of the Chersonese. The Cardians refused to accept cleruchs and appealed to Philip. He sent troops to support them. Diopeithes responded by raiding allies of Philip on the Thracian coast. When Philip protested to Athens, Demosthenes delivered his speech *On the Chersonese* in the Assembly in early 341, defending Diopeithes, urging reinforcements for him, warning about a threat to Byzantium from Philip, asserting that Philip was in fact at war with Athens and had broken the peace. A few months later he delivered a still more vehement call to war in the *Third Philippic*, upbraiding the Athenians for their inaction in the face of mounting evidence that Philip had no intention of observing the peace, and warning that he must be resisted now before he became unstoppable. He proposed immediate preparation for war, the procurement of ships, money and troops, and the dispatch of envoys to seek help from the Peloponnesus, the islands and the Persian King.[70]

The worsening confrontation between Philip and Athens came to a head in 340, when Philip attacked two of his former allies, Perinthos and Byzantium in the Propontis. Control of those cities by Philip would create a serious threat to the food supply of Athens, the reality of which was made starkly clear later in 340 when Philip seized the Athenian grain fleet. The response from the Assembly was swift and emphatic. On the motion of Demosthenes it voted for war and the stele on which the peace proposed by Philocrates was inscribed was taken down and smashed. Phocion was sent with a fleet to assist the Byzantines. Demosthenes introduced his reform of the trierarchy aimed at providing more adequate funding for the fleet by increasing the burdens on the wealthiest.

Philip failed to take Byzantium or Perinthos and left the area in 339 to settle a dispute with the Scythians. But by the end of 339 he was ready to confront the situation in Greece. Athens prepared for the war ahead. A reform long sought by Demosthenes, to use the resources of the Theoric Fund for military purposes when needed, was passed. An alliance with Thebes was advocated by Demosthenes and successfully negotiated by an embassy, which he led. Philip apparently made final overtures to Athens, but once again Demosthenes prevailed over the advocates of peace, who included Phocion and probably Aeschines. In August 338 the fateful encounter took place at Chaeronea in Boeotia. The main allied forces comprised the Athenians, Boeotians, Euboeans, Achaeans, Megarians, Corinthians and Corcyraeans. The numbers on either side were probably close to even, but the result was a decisive victory for Philip.[71]

Athens feared the worst and made frantic preparations to defend the city. But Philip wanted peace. His mind was now fixed on a grander design: the conquest of Asia Minor. He concluded agreements with the various major states and then sought to bind them together in a common peace. Athens was given a highly favourable settlement, negotiated by an embassy that contained Aeschines, Phocion and a rising political newcomer, Demades. It retained its independence; the citizens taken captive at Chaeronea were restored without ransom; Oropus, taken over by Thebes in 366, was returned to Athens. The Second League had to be formally disbanded, but it had long ceased to be a meaningful body.

Thebes got harsher treatment. Some of its leaders were executed, others banished. Exiles were restored and given prominent positions. A Macedonian garrison was installed in the Kadmeia. Sparta also suffered when it refused to surrender border regions claimed by neighbouring states that were allies of Philip. Laconia was devastated and its hostile neighbours strengthened.[72]

Philip next attempted to create a new stability throughout Greece. In the winter of 338/7 he convened representatives of the Greek states at Corinth and proposed the formation of a league of the states as partners in peace. Under the terms agreed all states were guaranteed autonomy, but under the hegemony of Macedonia. All pledged to maintain internal stability and refrain from interference in other states. A *synedrion* was created comprised of representatives of all states, the number of delegates presumably proportionate to the military contribution of each state to the forces of the alliance. The function of the *synedrion* was to deal with disputes or violations of the agreement and decide matters of war and peace. One of its first acts was to declare war on Persia and appoint Philip as leader of the Greek forces. As a further assurance of political stability and Macedonian supremacy, Philip maintained garrisons in at least three strategic locations, Corinth, Thebes and Ambracia.[73]

The events leading to Chaeronea again raise questions about the democracy's handling of foreign policy. The *demos* faced a difficult and threatening situation in the late 340s. The large surviving corpus of speeches from Demosthenes, along with the evidence of Aeschines, provides a rare close-up view of the intensity of the discussion in Assembly and courts, and the complexity of the decisions that the *demos* (which met, according to Aeschines, in many extraordinary sessions in the years before Chaeronea) was called upon to make. Opinion was sharply divided. There were able advocates of peace such as Eubulus, Aeschines and Phocion, and the Assembly was certainly made aware of the benefits of a peaceful solution. But, in a familiar pattern, it was the rhetoric of war that again won the day. Demosthenes provided it with rare power and passion. His speeches *On the Chersonese*, delivered in early 341, and the *Third Philippic*, a couple of months later, were particularly forceful calls to arms against an enemy that he declared was inexorably hostile to Athens and to its system of democracy, and was intent not only on subduing but annihilating it. It was therefore a struggle for its very existence. He recalled the glories of the past and appealed to the integrity and nobility of spirit that achieved them. Athens must again lead the way and save Greece. The *demos*, still eager for power and primacy, followed his lead.

But Demosthenes was misguided in several respects, as events would show. Philip was not intent on the destruction of Athens or its democracy. As stated above, his grand design, undoubtedly formed by the late 340s, was to conquer

Asia Minor and break the power of Persia. To achieve that he needed to eliminate threats to Macedonia from hostile neighbours in Thessaly, Epirus, Illyria and Thrace. He also needed the goodwill of Greece, and above all he wanted an alliance with Athens, which would give him what he especially lacked, naval power.

He never closed the door on negotiations with Athens. He made several attempts in the late 340s to address Athenian unhappiness with the terms of the peace, especially in 343 when he sent a delegation, led by Pytho of Byzantium, to Athens to invite proposals for modification of the peace. The Athenian response, engineered by Hegesippus, a hardline populist who shared the antagonism of Demosthenes towards Philip, made demands that Philip was never going to accept. But he came back with a pledge to defend the freedom of Greeks, and proposed, among other things, to submit disputes between himself and Athens to arbitration. But Hegesippus attacked the proposals and they came to nothing. Other overtures from Philip fared similarly.[74]

But the greatest misjudgement of Demosthenes was his apparent belief that Athens had the capacity to resist Philip successfully. After its failure to hold the Second League together, Athens had neither the financial resources nor the manpower to match the military might of Macedonia. It struggled continuously in the fourth century to find the funds to support its military ventures, even when the Second League was functioning at its best. Demosthenes repeatedly upbraided the Athenians for their unwillingness to pay more taxes to fund military needs. He tried to remedy the situation with his reform of the symmories and the trierarchy, but the yields remained inadequate. He finally managed to get monies normally destined for the Theoric Fund diverted to the military fund, but that only happened shortly before Chaeronea. Athens, without the benefits of empire or the support of a strong alliance, simply lacked the capacity to be a dominant power in Greece.

Athens was particularly badly placed to fight a land war against such a formidable foe as Philip. The real source of Athenian military power had always been its fleet. Its infantry, according to the Old Oligarch, was not highly regarded even by Athenians. Pericles certainly showed little faith in it when he decided at the start of the Peloponnesian War that he could not afford to confront the Spartans in a land battle. He saw the fleet as the means to victory. The condition of the Athenian army when Athens declared war on Philip in 340 was weaker still. It managed to field ten thousand hoplites at Chaeronea, but it was a force with little combat experience, and none against the Macedonian phalanx. Athens had relied on mercenaries in earlier action against Macedonia. The last time an Athenian citizen army had seen major action was at Mantinea, twenty-four years earlier. Athens had worked to secure allies, and with considerable success, but it had no help from Sparta, or most of the rest of the Peloponnesus, and the outcome of the battle was always going to depend on the forces of the two significant powers, Athens and Thebes. The Athenian infantry fared badly, and the Theban forces were unable to save the day.[75]

The favoured treatment given Athens after Chaeronea belied all the dire predictions of Demosthenes about the intentions of Philip. Its unfailing ambition and propensity for war, combined with faulty leadership, had led Athens to make another poor decision in foreign policy, but Philip had no desire to see it humbled, and it went on to flourish under the strong leadership of Lycurgus for another fourteen years, enjoying increased prosperity and one of its lengthiest periods of peace. Lycurgus acquired an ascendancy soon after Chaeronea that lasted for more than a dozen years and gave him a level of influence that came closest to rivalling that of Pericles. His skilful management of the finances raised annual revenues as high as 1,200 talents. His achievements are listed in the decree of Stratocles passed in his honour in 307/6, including his capital investments, his disbursements from the Theoric Fund, his strengthening of the city's defences, his creation of a fleet of four hundred triremes and his increased emphasis on the worship of Athena. It is also attested that Ephebic service became more rigorous and inclusive during his tenure. Lycurgus, an ally of Demosthenes, and friend of Hyperides, was no pacifist. He left Athens more prosperous and militarily stronger than it had been for much of the fourth century.[76]

Alexander

Philip did not long survive the creation of the so-called League of Corinth. In the summer of 336 he was assassinated at the wedding of his daughter by Pausanias, a member of his bodyguard. Pausanias was killed, but the instigators of the plot were never revealed. Philip's leading generals, Antipater and Parmenio, quickly installed Philip's son Alexander as the new king.

The death of Philip brought rejoicing at Athens and offerings of thanksgiving, but any hope that the grip of Macedonia might be loosened was soon dispelled. Alexander quickly came south and had the *synedrion* confirm him as *hegemon* with authority to lead a war against Persia. He then left to deal with trouble in Thrace and Illyria. A rumour that he had been killed caused the Thebans to revolt, but Alexander immediately marched from Illyria and took Thebes by storm. The city was levelled, the surviving inhabitants were sold into slavery and the land was divided among Boeotian states that had sided with Alexander. The Athenians had carefully refrained from sending help to Thebes and showed themselves eager for good relations with Alexander. Chaeronea had thoroughly dampened the warlike spirit that Demosthenes had so fervently promoted in the late 340s.

In 334 Alexander led an army into Asia and began the war with Persia. His legendary conquests over the following twelve years transformed the history of the eastern Mediterranean and Asia, and relations between east and west. But in June 323, after his return to Babylon from India, he fell ill and died. He was thirty-two.[77]

The death of Alexander created new hope in Athens that Macedonia could be successfully challenged. The death threatened the stability of Macedonia and of the whole of Alexander's empire. There was no heir to take his place. The rivalry between his generals and satraps was intense. Antipater had charge of Macedonia and Greece, but before his death Alexander had appointed one of his leading commanders, Craterus, to replace him. Conflict between them was likely. The Athenians now saw a credible opportunity to break free of Macedonian domination. They were encouraged by the fact that a force of eight thousand mercenaries, who had been discharged by Alexander or had defected, had gathered in southern Laconia, was available for hire and had chosen an Athenian, Leosthenes, as their leader.

The decision for war was made in the autumn of 323. Leosthenes was appointed general and given 50 talents to pay his troops. Envoys were sent to the Greek states to invite them to join Athens in a fight for liberty. There was strong popular support for war. The benefits of the previous fifteen years of peace and prosperity could not overcome the urge to be fully free, and free especially from any control by a state that was not seen as truly Greek. Lycurgus had died about a year earlier, and the most prominent leader in 323 was Hyperides, another able orator, a pupil of Isocrates and friend of Leosthenes, who was leading the mercenaries in southern Laconia, and a long-time asso-ciate and ally of Demosthenes in promoting the war against Philip. He was the leading advocate of war against Antipater. The only known voice in opposition was Phocion, who tried to calm the popular ardour and make the people consider the realities of what was being undertaken.[78]

Demosthenes had no voice in these decisions. He had been convicted a year earlier of accepting bribes from Alexander's treasurer in Babylon, Harpalus, who had embezzled a large sum of money. Harpalus had fled and sought refuge in Athens after Alexander returned to Babylon from India. Demosthenes was fined 50 talents and, unable to pay, had fled into exile. Demades was accused of the same crime and had gone into exile without awaiting trial. Both were now recalled, and Demosthenes was able to lend his support to the plans for war. Leosthenes advanced into Aetolia, where he received strong support. The Thessalians also joined him. The Athenians sent five thousand citizen infantry, five hundred cavalry and two thousand merce-naries. Leosthenes had several successes in the early stages and hemmed in Antipater in Lamia in Malis where he kept him under siege over the winter of 323/2. When Antipater offered to negotiate, the response was a demand for an unconditional surrender.[79]

But the Athenians fared badly in the naval war. They suffered successive defeats and failed to prevent Leonnatus, satrap in Hellespontine Phrygia, and Craterus from crossing into Europe to reinforce Antipater. The Greek allies suffered other setbacks early in 322. Leosthenes was killed in a skirmish. The Aetolians went home, the reason unknown. The siege of Lamia had to be aban-doned. The Greek forces were now reduced to about 25,000 infantry and 3,500 cavalry. Antipater's reinforced army had 40,000 infantry and 5,000 cavalry. The armies faced each other at Crannon in central Thessaly in August 322 and the Greeks were defeated. Losses on both sides were light, but the battle ended the war. It was now clear to all that Macedonian power in Greece had not been undermined by the death of Alexander. The Greek effort on the other hand had been undermined by a lack of unity and strength of purpose and effective lead-ership, and above all by the surprising ineffectiveness of the Athenian navy. Phocion had warned that, while Leosthenes and his forces might have some success in the short term, Athens did not have the money, ships or hoplites for a long war. It had superiority neither on land nor at sea, and in 322 it had little choice but to negotiate the best terms it could.[80]

Athens paid a heavy price for its decision to go to war. Phocion and Demades were the chief negotiators. Antipater imposed four conditions: Athens had to pay a war indemnity; it had to accept a Macedonian garrison in Munychia in the Piraeus; it had to surrender the leading anti-Macedonian activists, most notably Hyperides and Demosthenes; and, finally, it had to change its constitu-tion and restrict political rights to those who had a property qualification above 20 minae. The Assembly accepted the terms. Hyperides and Demosthenes had already fled, but Antipater had them pursued. Hyperides was captured and killed. Demosthenes took poison rather than surrender.

The constitutional requirement had the most radical consequences by far. According to Plutarch, it disenfranchised over twelve thousand citizens. Diodorus gives a figure of 22,000, which seems more credible. A figure of nine thousand is generally agreed for those who had the necessary property qualifi-cation. Whatever the precise numbers, the result was that henceforth Athens was ruled by a minority. *Kratos* no longer rested with the *demos*. The principle of political equality and majority rule no longer prevailed. The democracy, developed to its fullest form in the fourth century, came to an end in September 322, when the Assembly accepted the terms prescribed by Antipater.[81]

But the demise of the democracy cannot be ascribed merely to the dictates of a conqueror. The democracy was largely responsible for its own destruction, and it was flaws in its foreign policy that proved to be its Achilles heel. As I have stressed before, the vigour and heady ambition of Athenian foreign policy had their roots in the demotic revolution of 508/7, which created the democracy, and which not only empowered the mass of citizens but energised them and generated an exuberant self-confidence that encouraged risk-taking and the will to achieve. These were the qualities to which Alcibiades appealed when he urged the Assembly to undertake the Sicilian expedition. It was a culture that had been strongly reinforced by the successes in the Persian Wars and the ascendancy achieved with the leadership of the Delian League and the evolution of a powerful empire. It is stirringly glorified in the Funeral Oration of Pericles.

But this culture took on a more extremist edge after the start of the Peloponnesian War, fed by a series of leaders who lacked the calculated ambition of a Pericles and were more recklessly bent on dominion for Athens. Whether one calls them demagogues, radicals or just imperialists, from the death of Pericles onwards, Athens seldom lacked a Cleon, or an Alcibiades, or a Cleophon, or an Agyrrhius, or a Demosthenes, or a Hyperides to stoke the native chauvinism of the populace and urge them towards war. The result was a democracy that was always more disposed to war than peace, and more likely to choose dominion rather than the role of *primus inter pares*. Isocrates cogently drove home in his discourse *On the Peace* the grip this imperialist impulse and propensity for war had on the Athenian psyche, and the harm that it brought. Both he and Xenophon agreed that this was at the root of the repeated failure of Athens to maintain an enduring primacy in Greece.[82]

But the lessons were not learned. A greatly weakened Athens, bereft of allies and adequate military resources, was again induced in 340 to choose war over peace by the persuasive eloquence of Demosthenes, speaking the language of patriotism, and appealing to pride and past glories, and the destiny of Athens to lead and save Greece. It survived that mistake through the benevolence of Philip but, despite experiencing the benefits of a lengthy era of peace, it risked all once more in 323, and lost again. This time Antipater was determined that the democracy would have no more opportunities to pursue its restless urge for glory and dominion, and he imposed a new order, no longer the rule of the *demos*, but of the wealthier minority.

But the failures in foreign policy should not obscure the remarkable domestic achievements of the democracy of the fourth century. This was the period when the basic tenets of the democratic ideal were most fully implemented. Athens had to recover in 403 from a lawless, brutal tyranny, which had come on top of the crushing defeat in the Peloponnesian War. It did so with remarkable resilience, embarked on a determined programme of reconciliation and reinstated the democracy, making it more firmly a government of laws, based on a body of law that was updated, codified, written down, comprehensively agreed and protected against hasty or ill-considered change. The result was an enduring level of political consensus and stability, grounded in strong principles of freedom and equality. The *demos* firmly controlled the Assembly and the courts, and participation in public life reached its highest level, creating an experienced and informed citizenry. Power was freely delegated to those who proved their ability, which meant in practice that the people were led by the elite, a further aid to political consensus and social cohesion. But the mass remained vigilant, and accountability for those who led was strict and unforgiving. Inequality in the distribution of wealth was not challenged, but the wealthy bore the brunt of military expenditure, and a strong culture of public benefaction prevailed and met to some degree Aristotle's prescription that private wealth should be used for public good. Social unrest was not in evidence. Measured against the standards of the time, it was a successful society.

The democracy came to an end in 322, but the ideal, and the bold new vision of the purpose and nature of the state and of citizenship and of government that underpinned it, could not be eradicated, and was to change the character of western political thought and eventually the course of its constitutional history. That legacy, which has enduring relevance for modern concepts of democracy, will be discussed more fully in the Epilogue.[83]

Epilogue

The period of the world's first democracy represents a remarkable, eventful era in European history, an era of great energy, of cultural and intellectual peaks, and of groundbreaking advances in political and social thinking. It is an era that will always have enormous intrinsic interest. But its legacy to the modern world also has a broader importance, which this Epilogue will seek to explore.

The scale of the cultural achievement has been discussed in an earlier chapter. The lasting significance of that achievement is not in dispute. It has shaped the literary, artistic and intellectual life of Europe and the western world in crucial ways. Its study will always have value for its own sake, and for an understanding of the roots of European civilisation.

The extent of the political legacy is a more vexed issue. Two main questions arise. The first concerns the extent to which the Athenian democratic ideal inspired the re-emergence of democratic sentiment in the seventeenth and eighteenth centuries and shaped the democratic forms that subsequently evolved. The second concerns the lessons that the Athenian experience may still have to offer a world that seems in love with the concept of democracy, but where there is no real consensus about what democracy entails, and where many professedly democratic states are struggling to preserve even the most basic democratic principles.

The first question is the more difficult to answer, but it is also perhaps the less important. The revolutionary movements that emerged in America and Europe in the later eighteenth century were not unlike those that swept through the Greek world almost 2,500 years earlier. They were rebellions against oppressive systems of absolute monarchy and aristocratic elites that the revolutionaries believed had failed. Like Cleisthenes and his followers in 508 B.C., they were in search of a new order, and they could look for some guidance to the models of Athens and republican Rome, which were well known to those leading the movements for change.

In America there was certainly interest in democratic and republican ideas, but there were particular fears that if power were vested in the mass of ordinary citizens, it would lead to chaotic government and a tyranny of the majority that would govern in its own interest, which was precisely the fear of Plato and Aristotle about radical democracy. Two of the most prominent framers of the American Constitution, Alexander Hamilton and James Madison, accepted that for practical reasons, as well as reasons of order and the protection of minorities, the new government could not be the pure democracy of the city-state, but instead what Hamilton described as a representative democracy. Madison agreed, but felt it should more properly be called a republic than a democracy, with 'a government which derives its powers directly or indirectly from the great body of the people, and is administered by persons holding their offices during pleasure, or for a limited period, or during good behaviour'.[1]

The protracted, turbulent, multifaceted French Revolution produced a far more varied and radical range of views than the American. It was more fiercely hostile to aristocratic privilege, more concerned with political equality, with some in search of economic equality as well. But there was no one agitating for direct democracy along Athenian lines. Even the most democratically minded saw difficulties with it. Emmanuel Sieyes, a passionate foe of privilege, and proponent of the place and importance of the common throng, the Third Estate, accepted that the mass could never be an effective governing agent in a large state. A select group, chosen by the people, must represent it and be its voice. Robespierre, who was far more radically egalitarian and a fervent devotee of democracy, similarly accepted that democracy should not be defined as 'a state in which the people, continuously assembled, regulates by itself all public affairs'. He saw it instead as 'a state in which the sovereign people, guided by laws which are its own work, does by itself all it can do well, and by delegates all that it could not'.[2]

Thomas Paine, the influential contemporary essayist and supporter of the American and French revolutions, did not consider the representative system a dilution of democracy, but an extension of its range to large states. For him, the new American government was Athens writ large. He calls it 'representation engrafted on democracy' and adds: 'what Athens was in miniature, America will be in magnitude. The one is the wonder of the ancient world, the other is becoming the admiration, the model of the present.'[3]

Power to the people that would be directly exercised by them was therefore not seen as a practical option for large modern states, but the concept of power to the people remained at the core of democratic sentiment in the eighteenth century, and the Greek word that expressed it, *demokratia*, soon became the universal title for the democratic forms that evolved on both sides of the Atlantic. It did so because the word carried connotations that became increasingly irresistible. It was a word that implied rejection of political or legal privilege, or of claims by any individual or group that political power was their birthright. It affirmed instead the principle that it was the body of citizens alone who had the ultimate right to decide their own destiny, their own values and the rules by which they should live with one another. Delegating that right to representatives was seen as necessary in large states, but was not seen as negating the ultimate sovereignty of the people, provided those given power were representatives holding office for a defined period, chosen by the people, accountable to the people, acting in the interests of the people and attentive to the will of the people. So democracy still meant power to the people, and the word, and all it implied, was the first significant legacy of Athens to modern democracy.

There were, of course, many other influences shaping the character of the new political systems that emerged in the late eighteenth century, most notably republicanism, which originated in Rome with the expulsion of the kings in 510 B.C. Over the next two centuries the Romans created a form of government which they called *respublica*, the property of the people, and which they described as a mixed constitution, a balanced blend of the three basic forms, monarchy, aristocracy and democracy, a mix designed to spread power in a way that would prevent tyranny by the mass or the elite, and achieve stability.

But Roman republicanism had a strong aristocratic bias. Cicero, its great admirer and exponent, saw it as the ideal form of government, which guaranteed the people strict equality before the law, and constituted them as the state's highest authority, the electoral and law-making body. But it was designed to put the real governing power in the hands of those of greatest excellence (*virtus*) and standing (*dignitas*). Cicero saw this as the ideal mix of power, which guaranteed freedom (*libertas*) for the people, and a controlling authority (*auctoritas*) for the most worthy, producing able government by the talented few with the free consent of the people.[4]

The republican tradition, with its aristocratic bias and concern to preclude domination by the few or the many, had a considerable impact on the character of the emerging forms of modern democracy, and its effort to prevent the dominance of any social element by splitting power along social lines evolved into the concept of separation of powers based on the main functions of government, the executive, the legislative and the judicial. The concept envisaged constituting these three areas as independent branches of government, creating a system of checks and balances, and precluding the risks of tyranny inherent in centring all power in one institution. The separation of powers was built into the American Constitution, and variations of it form part of all modern liberal democracies, especially the aspect of judicial independence.[5]

The achievement of Athens, however, not surprisingly retained a prominent place in the thinking of the theorists and political leaders throughout the revolutionary era of the late eighteenth and early nineteenth centuries. It was not always praised or seen as a model, but it was part of the debate, and had its admirers, ranging from Thomas Paine to George Grote. Its two cardinal principles, freedom and equality, which Aristotle considered the essence of its democratic ideal, also became fundamental principles of modern democracy. I have reviewed in an earlier chapter the Athenian concept of freedom as expounded by Pericles which, alongside its communitarian spirit and ethos of civic engagement, showed a level of appreciation of the importance of personal freedom that foreshadowed the thrust of the liberal thinking that began to emerge in the later eighteenth century with the writings of theorists such as Paine, John Locke and John Stuart Mill.[6]

None of the emerging democracies reproduced the radical egalitarian character of Athenian democracy, or believed it was possible or desirable. The belief persisted, however, that the people were the proper ultimate judges of how their society should function and be governed, and that, accordingly, the collective will of the people should be sovereign. With respect to the law, strict equality under a rule of law became an essential characteristic of all the new democracies, a principle that went back to the lawgivers of Greece and was the major legacy of Solon to Athens.[7]

No precise assessment of the impact of Athenian ideas on the re-emergence of democracy is possible. It is clear, however, that the Athenian system was well studied and was part of the debate, and the congruency of thought evident in core values of both Athenian and early modern democratic systems suggests a strong causal connection between the old and the new. A telling remark by John Adams, in 1782 in a letter to the Marquis de Lafayette, who played a prominent part in both the American and French Revolutions, is further evidence that the tide of influence from the classical world, so strongly evident in other aspects of western civilisation, was also flowing in the political arena. Adams wrote: 'I am a republican on principle. Almost everything that is estimable in civil life has originated under such governments. Two republican powers, Athens and Rome, have done more honour to our species than all the rest of it. A new country can be planted only by such a government.'

Of greater importance is the second question, regarding the lessons that the Athenian experience can offer to a world still in transition following the collapse of communism, which brought a dramatic swing away from all forms of absolute or oligarchic rule, and a renewed appetite for power to the people. For some, the end of the history of ideas and of ideological division had come. But many established democracies are wandering farther away from their democratic heritage, and many inchoate democracies are struggling to engraft democratic values on traditions sharply at variance with them. History is not over, and the ideological battle is not won. The example of Athens is more relevant than at any time since the eighteenth century.[8]

Before attempting to identify the learning that can be extracted from the Athenian experience, it is important to review the main elements of the Athenian achievement and the salient characteristics that brought their democracy stability, loyalty to a political ideal, resilience and durability. The evolution of Athenian democracy crystallised and extended the 'isonomic' trends that swept across the Greek world in the seventh century. Solon laid the first foundations of the future democracy and embedded in the Athenian psyche two interconnected concepts that lie at the heart of the democratic ideal: freedom and the rule of law. His first reform was the *seisachtheia*, which vindicated the right of all citizens to freedom in the negative sense of not being subject to the arbitrary control of another. But his primary mission and greatest achievement was the creation of a written body of law, grounded in justice and applying equally to all, which would protect the rights and freedoms of citizens and define the procedures and rules that would govern their lives. Significantly it extended freedom into the positive sphere, giving all citizens the right to a significant, though not a controlling, say in the government of their state.

About three-quarters of a century later Cleisthenes, backed by a populace weary of tyrannical oppression and oligarchic factionalism, took the reforms of Solon a step further, and put power in the hands of the body of citizens itself. Every citizen would henceforth have the positive right to participate on an equal basis in determining the course of public affairs, and the collective will of the people would be sovereign. The fundamental elements of the democratic ideal had been born.

But equal political rights meant little without the opportunity to exercise them. Cleisthenes showed his awareness of this, and his reforms included an elaborate new system of local and national government designed to facilitate participation and promote a culture of civic engagement. The structure of demes, phratries, tribes and Council, along with annual rotation of offices, has been described in earlier chapters. It brought levels of participation and social interaction, and a form of political apprenticeship that created a citizenry that was politically aware and politically educated, and that had a sense of loyalty to a constitution of which it could feel it had ownership. In the Funeral Oration, Pericles emphasised the motivating power of self-rule and the manner in which it inspired loyalty and moved people to act with greater courage and decisiveness in pursuing actions that they themselves had deliberated and decided. High participation and the benefits that came with it were to prove an enduring source of the stability and capability of the democracy.

Ephialtes carried the direct political involvement of the populace a major step further by transferring judicial power and the scrutiny of magistrates from the oligarchic Council of the Areopagus to the Council and Assembly of the people, which led to the creation of the jury courts.

The Periclean era brought further democratisation, and further boosted participation. All offices were opened to the hoplite class, a trend that would eventually, in practice, open all offices to all citizens. Pay was introduced for jury service and gradually for all magistrates, for those serving in the army and navy, and for members of the Council. Perhaps most significant of all in its implications for fuller equality of political rights and opportunity and wider participation was the introduction of selection by lot of jurors, members of the Council and all holding executive offices other than those requiring specialist skills.

The further reforms following the trauma of the Peloponnesian War and the revolutions of 411 and 404 did not change the fundamental elements of the constitution, but greatly strengthened the operation of many of them. The introduction of pay for attending the Assembly gave another boost to participation, but the most significant changes came in the area of the law. The details of the changes have been discussed in an earlier chapter. They produced a new definitive, permanent, written body of law that was fully agreed by the entire body of citizens. The thoroughness of the process of review, scrutiny and consultation before the code was submitted to the Assembly for final ratification showed the commitment of the democracy to a strict rule of law, as binding on the bodies of government as on the individual citizen. So did the multiple safeguards that were put in place to guard against hasty or ill-considered alterations. The Athenians had found a shared sense of the values and rules by which they wished to live and be governed, and they were determined to preserve them. The sanctity of law remained a hallmark of Athenian democracy, its guardianship the sacred duty of every citizen.[9]

Another notable feature of the democracy that contributed to unity and stability was its diligence in protecting against two of the most insidious threats to good government: corruption and factionalism. The rigour of its system of accountability for all entrusted with public office left little scope for malfeasance or corrupt behaviour. The Council had a special role in overseeing the conduct of magistrates, but every citizen was a watchdog for the interests of the state, empowered to indict anyone suspected of corrupt or treasonable behaviour.

The meticulous care taken to eliminate the possibility of tampering with juries, or of influencing those presiding over Council or Assembly, is a good measure of the almost obsessive determination to eradicate corruption.

It was the evils of factionalism that sparked the demotic revolution of 508 and led Cleisthenes to conceive of a radically different political order. The *demos* subsequently showed no tolerance for any recurrence of factional politics or for the rise of any power grouping likely to encroach upon the free rule of the people. It went so far as to devise the expedient of ostracism to remove any individual whose influence seemed to pose a threat. When the danger from the political clubs (*hetaireiai*) became evident in 411 and 404, lessons were learned and all such associations were banned. There was no space allowed in democratic Athens for the factions, parties or special interest groups so feared by Madison as a danger in democratic and republican systems.[10]

The democracy was also successful in effecting radical political change without precipitating major unrest or class conflict. The *demos* never threatened the property of the wealthy, belying the predictions of critics of pure democracy such as Aristotle and Madison. There was no ideological clash surrounding the distribution of wealth in Athenian politics, no Gracchus Babeuf beating the drum of economic equality. On the contrary, it adopted a highly conservative attitude towards taxation or impositions of any kind on the better-off, and relied instead on a culture of voluntary public beneficence (*euergesia*), aided by the fact that the use of wealth for the public good was both expected and politically rewarded. Aside from the short-lived oligarchic revolutions of 411 and 404, there was harmony of the orders in Athens, and a prominent place for the elite with the willing assent of the mass.[11]

Modern Democracy and the Athenian Model

A comprehensive review of the state of modern democracy is well beyond the range of this study. The following are some general reflections that highlight areas where modern democracy is stumbling and in danger of losing its bearings, and where the Athenian experience may have most to offer. It must first be emphasised that modern liberal democracies have advanced human progress in ways that extend well beyond the Athenian achievement. The abolition of slavery, the emancipation of women, the emphasis on civil rights and the equal worth and dignity of every individual, and the increased international cooperation and agreements to define and protect these shared human attributes represent significant progress in the ongoing search for forms of political association capable of protecting and improving the lives of all their members.

But, as I have outlined in the introduction to this book, great challenges still face modern democracies. The high hopes following the collapse of communism have faded. Events since 1989 have shown how serious the obstacles to embedding and sustaining democratic ideals are. They are especially formidable in cultures where democratic values have little or no history. Supplanting long-standing authoritarian traditions and power structures, political and religious, with a supreme rule of law that respects the rights and liberties inherent in the democratic ideal, and is equally binding on ruler and ruled alike, is a daunting task. Enforcing such a rule of law in a manner safe from corruption is more daunting still. The most recent Freedom House Survey, which has been mentioned earlier, and which shows more declines than gains in the efforts to build societies that enjoy genuine freedom, illustrates the scale of the challenge. The impediments to democracy taking root in cultures to which its basic tenets are alien may well prove insuperable. At best it will be a long and rocky road. But Athens travelled that road. The problems it faced were not, of course, the same as those facing the modern complex, multicultural states in which democracy is currently struggling to gain a foothold. But it did have to go from the unequal, divided world of Solon, ruled by an entrenched, oppressive, faction-ridden elite, to a society governed by an agreed code of law, which recognised the equal intrinsic worth and dignity of every citizen, and the right of every citizen to an equal voice in deciding the public good. Athens remains a striking and valuable example of how a socially divided, unstable oligarchic society can radically transform itself and live by new values of freedom and equality and popular government under a strictly enforced rule of law.

But the Athenian achievement also has lessons for modern developed democracies, which have increasingly eroded the role of the people and are now pale shadows of the Athenian concept of government by the people. The label democracy has largely become what Ronald Syme called Roman republicanism, 'a screen and a sham'.[12]

Many of the elements that gave Athens its vitality and stability are missing, and many others are honoured more in the breech than in the observance. There are of necessity wide differences between the direct democracy of the city-state and large modern representative democracies, but as Paine correctly emphasised, representation and size do not involve discarding the essential principles of the democratic ideal. In particular, they do not negate the most elementary democratic principle, that the voice of the people is the highest law, and that it should be heard and heeded to the greatest degree possible. Many see that as impractical, and even undesirable, and the trend of modern political thought and practice is to confine the role of the people to the electoral function, what John Dunn calls 'one day's rule in four years'. Joseph Schumpeter gave a strong impetus to that view in his book *Capitalism, Socialism and Democracy*, first published in 1942. He considered democracy the 'rule of the politicians', not the rule of the people.[13]

But even the electoral role has been diluted and tarnished by the failure of modern democracies to create fair electoral processes. The bulk of candidates are preselected by political parties and have the benefit of the influence and financial resources of these parties. Independent candidates have no such benefits. More serious is the common situation where candidates are backed by powerful special interests, the egoists and ideologues who use their resources to fund candidates willing, if elected, to do their bidding. This amounts to corruption, the purchasing of political power. The rise of the mass media, which can give large-scale exposure to those who have the resources to use it, has increased the threat to free and fair elections from the power of money. So has globalisation, which has speeded the growth of multinational conglomerates with the capacity to influence the outcome of elections and the resultant direction of government. A recent notable example of the disturbing level of influence that well-resourced special interests can exert on government is provided by the ability of the gun lobby in the United States, spearheaded by the National Riflemen's Association, to block gun-control legislation which opinion polls clearly show has the support of the majority of the American people.

The electoral function can only achieve its purpose if those elected represent the informed choice of the people. The people can only make that choice if the candidates and their views are presented to them on a more or less equal basis. That requires that all candidates have a more or less equal opportunity to promote themselves and explain their views and goals. Regulation of campaign spending and of the level of contributions to individual candidates by one person or body is the only method of achieving that requirement. Some states have taken steps to do this, but the efforts have struggled to win acceptance and have proved hard to enforce. A severe blow has been dealt to prospects for effective regulation by a recent ruling of the US Supreme Court, which held that it is not an acceptable governmental objective 'to level electoral opportunities or equalise the financial resources of the candidates'. The Court considered that a limitation on campaign spending would constitute an infringement of freedom of speech. This is a far cry from the Athenian determination to root out corruption and forestall the possibility of any power group being able to control or manipulate the decision-making of government. It opens the door to the rule of money, the antithesis of all that democracy represents.

The rule of the people over public affairs is further diminished by the lack of any adequate system of accountability for politicians. When the Athenian *demos* delegated power to office-holders, that power came with a rigorous regime of accountability for its use. In modern democracies, where the power to rule is delegated in its entirety, there is no such regime. The electorate can replace those who no longer command its favour at the next election, but the prospect of losing one's seat is a feeble safeguard against bad government or abuse of power. Even if democracy must be reduced to 'the rule of the politicians', it should be a rule that is answerable to the people who conferred the power to rule, and it should be subject to swift retribution for any abuse of the people's trust.

Representative democracy in its modern guise seems to be gliding inexorably towards oligarchy. The dismemberment of the people's power has cleared the field for party insiders and the special interests, what Dunn calls 'the order of egoism', for whom political influence means personal gain. The spirit of civic engagement is giving way to political apathy and cynicism about politics and politicians. In many states, large numbers are too disengaged from political affairs even to exercise their right to vote. The pride in citizenship, the public-spirited communitarian ethos, the sense of having a real say in directing the public good – characteristics that gave Athens its social cohesion and vigour, and unprecedented levels of political engagement – are all becoming casualties of modern popular disempowerment.[14]

The concept of democracy, however, still retains its allure, but it is difficult to see how it can sustain its claim to be the system that ensures the government of a state is carried out in line with the wishes of the majority of the people unless the people have a more meaningful role in debating and shaping the significant decisions that will deeply affect their lives. Modern democracy may, of necessity, have to be representative, but that does not mean that it cannot be more broadly deliberative. It can mean more than skeletal electoral democracy.

But how does one answer the view that governing is best left to those whom the public judge to be best qualified to govern, or the view that has persisted since Plato and that underlies the elitist republican tradition that Cicero so eloquently expounded and helped perpetuate, that governing should be the domain of the most expert and worthy? First of all, there is no guarantee, and little likelihood, that those who present themselves for election, whether chosen by their parties or running as independent candidates, represent the best talent or the wisest heads in the society. Secondly, political judgement and wisdom are elusive qualities. They undoubtedly require a base of knowledge and experience but are mostly gifts of nature. Good judgement, being able to see the right course – what Thucydides called *gnōme*, and considered the special attribute of Pericles – though it certainly needs a level of political knowledge, is not a necessary consequence of advanced education or any form of specialised learning. Great intellectuals do not necessarily make great politicians. It is not possible to say that political wisdom is the preserve of any social class or group of specialists. It is a quality that, to an extent, is within the grasp of everyone.[15]

That was certainly the premise on which Athenian democracy was founded and flourished. It was self-rule, born out of disillusionment with all other forms of rule, trusting in the native instincts and capacities of the people themselves to decide collectively, and on a basis of equality, their common destiny and how best to secure the common interest. Thucydides has left us in the Funeral Oration of Pericles an inspiring vision of what that new form of government entailed, with the people deliberating, deciding, implementing, no longer oppressed, but freely consenting, motivated, engaged. Government was a communal enterprise, participation its lifeblood.

Even Aristotle, a great thinker but no great admirer of democracy, conceded that political wisdom was not the exclusive preserve of an elite, and that a plausible argument could be made for popular rule. He made it in his so-called summation theory, mentioned earlier, which held that, while each individual within the mass (hoi polloi) may not have superior excellence, everyone has a share in goodness and practical wisdom (phronesis), and can contribute something, and the sum of those contributions makes the collective judgement of the many more likely to be right than that of the more expert few.[16]

The Athenians put their faith in the judgement of the many, and saw democracy as society's best hope for free, equitable, consensual and effective government precisely because the key decisions most deeply affecting the character and life of their society were debated and decided, not by any few, but directly by the people themselves. That level of direct democracy, as already stressed, is clearly impractical in large modern states, but if the essence of the democratic ideal is to be preserved, representative democracy must find a way of coexisting with a form of deliberative democracy that allows the voice of the people to be heard in an organised manner in the deliberation of issues of high national importance. Without a genuine deliberative role for the public, democracy is a hollow shell, robbed of its core.

The benefits of a wider deliberative role for the people are many. It is the only way by which the collective creativity and practical good sense and the often hidden wisdom that lie within the broad body of citizens can be harvested and used to enlighten the decisions of government. The other benefits have been referred to many times in the course of this study. They relate to the social benefits of high civic engagement – a communal spirit, social solidarity, political stability, and the high morale and motivation that derive from a sense of empowerment. A more participatory democracy is also a more vigilant democracy, a protection against corruption, and against the domination of cliques or factions or special interests, and the degeneration of the democracy into the oligarchy which Syme saw lurking behind the façade of every form of government, and which Robert Michels saw as the inevitable fate of all democracies because of the political apathy of the masses, their need for leaders and their tendency to venerate leaders who won their admiration. But it need not be so. The story of Athenian democracy belies both of these theses.[17]

The great challenge, of course, is to find ways by which the voice of the people can have a meaningful say within a representative democracy in the shaping of binding decisions that will determine the character of their society. There is one essential prerequisite for such participation: a public that understands its constitution and form of government and its rights and responsibilities as citizens, and that has ready access to a continuing flow of information about public affairs. This is a theme that has often been sounded since Aristotle, who was insistent that citizens must be educated so they understand the particular character (*ēthos*) of the constitution (*politeia*) under which they live and their communal duty to preserve it. I have cited earlier the strong language in which both Madison and Adams drove home the need for knowledge of public affairs to be disseminated throughout the general population. In the political arena they rightly saw ignorance as especially dangerous and disempowering. Athenians acquired most of the necessary learning by doing, but they did acquire it. Josiah Ober's recent valuable study *Democracy and Knowledge* has shown how thoroughly political knowledge was aggregated and dispersed throughout the Athenian citizen body.[18]

In modern society more of that knowledge will have to come through the educational system. Preparing young people for responsible citizenship should be a goal of education at every level. The ethos of civic engagement should be fostered by all the organs of state and by early involvement in local community activities. Athenian democracy drew strength from the vibrant community life of the demes.

When it comes to the availability of knowledge of current political issues and challenges, modern society has an advantage over the Athenians. The rise of the mass media, and especially digital media, has led to a knowledge revolution, and a vastly easier and wider access to information. Equally important has been the emergence of broad agreement, at least in the mature democracies, about a range of rights covering the area of free speech. These include freedom of thought and expression, the right of individuals to be informed and to seek, receive and impart information, and the right of the mass media to investigate and publish information and opinion on all matters in which the public have a legitimate interest, and about which they have a right to know. In free societies these rights are now firmly embedded in constitutions, laws and court judgements, and have been affirmed in international proclamations such as the UN

Universal Declaration of Human Rights and the European Convention on Human Rights.

A vigorous free press is potentially an important arm of a healthy democracy. Its protected position carries two important public responsibilities. It has a duty to provide the public with a continuous flow of accurate information about what is happening in its society and in the world around it. It has the further duty to hold government to account, to subject the performance of government to rigorous scrutiny and to investigate any evidence of irregularity or corruption. This function, properly discharged, can mitigate the effects of the otherwise weak level of accountability for politicians in modern democracy. Modern jurisprudence has seen it as an especially important function, and has described the press as the eyes and ears of the public.

But in many respects the mass media are failing the public. Large elements of the print media are shifting their focus from informing to entertaining, filling their pages with the sensational and the prurient. A more serious development is the concentration of significant news organisations in fewer hands, leading to powerful media conglomerates that have dangerous levels of political leverage. Media moguls tend to have their own agendas and can become another interest group capable of distorting the free working of the democratic process. Regulation and strict codes of practice are clearly necessary, but finding appropriate forms of regulation and defining the boundaries of press freedom without undermining the capacity of the press to fulfil its societal functions is a challenging task. The outcome must be acceptable to the media and to government, and must command the confidence of the public. Above all, the regulatory body itself must be independent of both media and government to ensure its objectivity and credibility. Free news media operating under broadly acceptable, independent regulation remain an important watchdog of the public interest and are essential to maintaining a well-informed citizenry.[19]

But even the best-informed citizenry can have little impact on the course of public affairs unless opportunities are provided for the voice of the people to be heard on major issues and reflected in the decisions of government. Identifying what these opportunities might be is a very large question indeed, and again well beyond the scope of this study. I can only touch briefly on the subject here.

The challenge of providing a meaningful deliberative role for the public in modern democracies may not be as great as first appears. It is worth noting that the ancient Greeks had variations in the way popular rule was exercised. Aristotle emphasises that there are several ways by which the people can exercise their deliberative function without meeting en masse. He cites the example of Miletus, where the body of citizens made decisions by meeting in sections by turns, so that all citizens participated equally, but in relays, so all were involved equally, but all were not involved in all decisions. It must also be remembered that the meetings of the Athenian Assembly were attended by only about six thousand citizens, often fewer. It was, to some extent at least, a changing six thousand, but nonetheless decisions were taken by about 20 per cent of the adult citizen population, and no one questioned that these decisions truly represented the will of the *demos*. Turnouts in modern elections and referenda can be as low as 30 per cent, but the results are accepted as the judgement of the people.[20]

Democracy has never involved, and never will involve, all of the people all of the time in the deliberation of the big public issues. It is not possible nor is it necessary for achieving a genuine deliberative role for the people. There has been a recent resurgence of interest in democratising democracy and redirecting it back to its original communal deliberative character, and it has rightly focused on how small-group deliberation, backed up by modern communications technology, can achieve these goals.

Robert Dahl in his major study *Democracy and its Critics*, published in 1989, suggested the idea of the 'minipopulus', a group of about a thousand citizens, randomly chosen from the entire population, commissioned to deliberate on a major public issue, 'meeting' by teleconferencing, and supported by a committee of scholars, specialists and researchers. Its conclusions would be fed into the deliberative processes of government, supplementing rather than replacing them. Numerous such groups could be used to deal with different issues.

Since then there has been a flurry of publications on deliberative democracy and how it could, and why it should, be strengthened. More important, the theories are being tested by states and independent bodies. Canada has used what it called a Citizens' Assembly to consider electoral reform, a group not involving elites but ordinary citizens, randomly chosen. A similar model of a bottom-up process of participation by citizens to elicit the views of a cross section of the public has been used in the Netherlands. In Ireland a group of academics recently devised and organised a Citizens' Assembly of randomly chosen people who were charged with making decisions about a range of issues that preliminary regional meetings and opinion polls had determined were of greatest concern to the public. They were briefed about the issues and the arguments surrounding them. They could further inform themselves by interviewing expert witnesses. Assurances were sought from government that proposals from the Assembly would be taken on board.[21]

These are examples of how the public can be re-engaged with the deliberative process, and how the sum of the varied components of wisdom that Aristotle believed resides in the body politic can be gathered and used to advance the common good. There may well be covert resistance by governments and the 'order of egoism' to such efforts to extend power beyond their circles, but there now seems to be a momentum for change that provides the hope that the downward slide of democracy towards the fate predicted by Michels can be arrested, and that it can more meaningfully lay claim to its name.

In a broader sense the whole remarkable eruption of democratic sentiment that has swept the world since 1989 is testimony that the revolutionary Athenian ideal of the state as a community of free and equal citizens governing themselves and working together under their own laws to secure the good life for all continues to inspire. It is a noble aspiration, far from fully attained in Athens or any modern state, but its pursuit remains the best hope for a more stable, peaceful, equitable and productive world.

Notes

Introduction

1. Kagan, *Pericles*, 2.
2. Schumpeter, *Capitalism, Socialism and Democracy*, 269. Huntington, *The Third Wave*, 9–10.
3. Syme, *Roman Revolution*, 15.

Chapter 1

1. Great advances have been made in recent times in knowledge and understanding of the *polis* by the work of the Copenhagen Polis Project directed by Mogens Hansen. Cf. Hansen and Nielsen (eds), *An Inventory of Archaic and Classical Poleis*. Hansen, *Polis: An Introduction to the Greek City State*.
2. Arist. *Pol.* 1270a38. Hansen and Nielsen (eds), *Inventory*, Part I, 70–73, 138–43. Part II, *passim*.
3. Cf. Raaflaub, *The Ancient Greek City-State*, ed. Hansen, 41–59; *Demokratia*, ed. Ober and Hedrick, 150ff. Scully, 'The *Polis* in Homer'. Finley, *World of Odysseus*.
4. In the *Odyssey*, Homer gives a detailed picture of the *polis* of the Phaeacians, the life contrasted with that of the Cyclops. Cf. *Od.* 6.4–10, 259–72; 7.84–130; 9.105–15, 189. For *dike* in Homer cf. *Il.* 16.388; 18, 505ff. *Od.* 19.109ff. For Assemblies of the *demos* cf. *Il.* 2.50ff., 206ff., 9.9–172. *Od.* 2.6–256.
5. Hes. *WD* 22–36, 298–324.
6. Hes. *WD* 203–80. *Theog.* 79–98. Cf. North, *Sophrosyne*, 9ff. Jaeger, *Paideia*, trans. Highet, I, ch. 4. Solmsen, *Hesiod and Aeschylus*.
7. Hes. *WD* 200–85. *Theog.* 900ff. Cf. Jaeger, *Paideia* I, ch. 4. Morris, *Demokratia*, 28ff. Raaflaub, *Ancient Greek City-State*, ed. Hansen, 41–105.
8. Hes. *WD* 239–40, 250–51, 258, 263, 280, 322–24. *WD* 105–202 recounts the five ages. He offers another explanation of evil at *WD* 45–104, the myth of the original sin of Prometheus, who stole fire from heaven and caused Zeus to create Pandora and her box filled with all the forms of evil that beset mankind. On his use of myth cf. Jaeger, *Paideia* I, 65ff. Raaflaub, *Cambridge History of Greek and Roman Political Thought*, 34–37.
9. For colonisation cf. Boardman, *The Greeks Overseas*. Finley, *Bronze and Archaic Ages*. For hoplites and the origins of democracy cf. Hansen, *Demokratia*, 289–312. Snodgrass, 'The Hoplite Reform and History'. Forrest, *Emergence of Greek Democracy*, 88ff.
10. The latter half of the seventh century produced the potent, acerbic iambic poetry of Archilochus, the deeply personal Aeolian lyrics of Sappho and Alcaeus from Lesbos, and the stirring military elegiacs of the Spartan Tyrtaeus; at the start of the sixth century came the reflective, political elegies of Solon. Cf. Jaeger, *Paideia* I, ch. 7. Bowra, *Greek Lyric Poetry*. Raaflaub, *Cambridge History of Greek and Roman Political Thought*, 37–48.
11. Cf. Boardman, *Greek Art*. Robertson, *History of Greek Art*.

12. For the main surviving ancient texts cf. Kirk, Raven and Schofield, *Presocratic Philosophers*. Useful general accounts provided by Jaeger, *Paideia* I, ch. 9. Burnet, *Early Greek Philosophy*. Luce, *Introduction to Greek Philosophy*. Fornara, *Archaic Times to the End of the Peloponnesian War* provides a useful compendium in translation of surviving fragmentary sources from the Archaic period and the fifth century.

13. Theognis was an elegiac poet from Megara who lived in the late sixth century. About 1,400 lines of his poetry survive, though some of it was clearly written by other poets. He laments the decline in the wealth and power of the traditional aristocracy (*agathoi*), who alone had true nobility of spirit, true *arete*, and are now being displaced by the lowly (*kakoi*), who have no breeding and no capacity for true *arete*. Cf. excellent analysis of Jaeger, *Paideia* I, ch. 10.

14. Aristotle cites many examples of revolution in Greece in the late seventh and sixth centuries in his analysis in *Pol.* 1302aff. of the causes of revolution. Cf. Wallace, *Origins of Democracy in Ancient Greece*, 73–74. Andrewes, *Greek Tyrants* remains a valuable general account of the phenomenon of the tyrants. Cf. Pleket, 'The Archaic *tyrannis*'.

15. For the early history of Sparta, Lycurgus and the Great Rhetra cf. Cartledge, *Sparta and Laconia*. Ehrenberg, *Solon to Socrates*, ch. 2. Forrest, *History of Sparta*. Murray, *Early Greece*. The main primary sources are Tyrtaeus, frgs 4, 5, 8 (West). Hdt. 1.65.2. Thuc. 1.18.1, 101, 2–3; 4.80.2–3. Arist. *Pol.* 1269a37ff, 1306b29–1307a4, 1313a26ff. Plato *Laws* 776c–777. Plut. *Lyc.* 6. Polyb. 6.3; 10.46–50.

16. Arist. *Pol.* 1294b20–39. Xen. *Lak. Pol.* 8.3, 9, 13, 15. Isocr. *Panath.* 153ff., 176–84. Plato *Laws* 692a–693a, 712d–e. Plut. *Lyc.* 6–7, 26. The final line of the Rhetra in Plutarch's version, as emended in line with Tyrtaeus' account, would suggest that the people had the final power to decide, but the text is far from certain, and Plut. *Lyc.* 6.4 says that, if the *demos* made unjust (*skolia*) decisions, the *gerousia* and kings could set them aside. Arist. *Pol.* 1273a5ff. indicates that when kings and *gerousia* were unanimous they were not required to consult the *demos*. Cf. Wallace, *Democracy 2500?*, 12–14.

17. Xen. *Lak. Pol.* 2.5, 9, 11–12. Plut. *Lyc.* 10, 12, 14, 16, 19, 21, 24. Arist. *Pol.* 1333b12–1334a10.

18. For references to Tyrtaeus as the inspirational poet who glorified military valour cf. Plato *Laws* 629a–630. Plut. *Cleom.* 2.3. *Lyc.*, *Leoc.* 106. Arist. *Pol.* 1306b40. Diod. 8.27.1–2. Horace, *Ars Poetica*, 101–3. Cf. Tyrtaeus frgs 10, 11, 12 (West). Jaeger, *Paideia* I, 85–98.

19. Plut. *Lyc.* 25.3. Tyrtaeus frg. 4 (West).

20. Aristotle (*Pol.* 1295b25) says that 'it is preferable that a state should consist as much as possible of those who are equal (*isoi*) and of similar status (*homoioi*)'. Cf. Cartledge, *Demokratia*, 175–85. Aristotle strongly criticises the fact that Ephors were not held accountable: *Pol.* 1271a5ff.

21. Cf. Arist. *Pol.* 1294b18–30 on common meals and education; 1270a15–b7, 1271a30ff., 1307a35–37 on differences in wealth. Xen. *Lak. Pol.* 5. Plut. *Lyc.* 10, 12.

22. Arist. *Pol.* 1270b18–26. Cf. 1294b35–40, 1309b17ff. *Eth. Nic.* 9.6.

23. For Tyrtaeus' poem, *eunomia*, cf. frg. 4 (West) Arist. *Pol.* 1306b40. Strabo 8.4.10. Hdt. 1.65.2; 7.104. Thuc. 1.18.1, 84.3. Xen. *Lak. Pol.* 8.

24. Cf. above notes 16 and 17, and Arist. *Pol.* 1269b–1271b16.

25. Rawson, *The Spartan Tradition in European Thought*, has an excellent account.

26. For other Greek lawgivers cf. Arist. *Pol.* 1274a23ff.

27. Polyb. 6.10–14. Cic. *Rep.* 1.69. Cf. McClelland, *History of Western Political Thought*, 324–37. Hahm, *Cambridge History of Greek and Roman Political Thought*, 464–76.

28. Arist. *Ath. Pol.* 1–4, 41.2. Cf. Rhodes, *Com. Ath. Pol.*, 65ff. Thuc. 1.126. Fornara, *Archaic Times*, no. 15.

29. The main primary sources are Arist. *Ath. Pol.* 5–12, 14.2, 41.2. Arist. *Pol.* 1266b17ff., 1273b35–1274a22, 1281b33ff. Isocr. 7.16; 15.232. Plut. *Solon*. The fragments from Solon's writings have been collected by M.L. West, *Iambi et Elegi Graeci*. Cf. Jaeger, *Paideia* I, ch. 8. Rhodes, *Com. Ath. Pol.*, 118–79. Murray, *Early Greece*. De Ste Croix, *Athenian Democratic Origins*, chs 1–4. Lewis, *Solon the Thinker*.

30. Dem. 19.255. Arist. *Ath. Pol.* 5.2–3. Solon, frg. 13 (West). Plut. *Solon* 14.2, 25.6.

31. For Solon's attachment to the idea of the Mean cf. Arist. *Ath. Pol.* 12.1–2. Dem. 19.251–55. Aesch. 1.6–7. Arist. *Eth. Nic.* 1179aff. Plut. *Solon* 14. North, *Sophrosyne*, 12, 14–16.

32. Arist. *Ath. Pol.* 6–10. Cf. Rhodes, *Com. Ath. Pol.*, 125–69. For his views about the distribution of wealth cf. Arist. *Ath. Pol.* 12.1–3.

33. For Solon's judicial reforms cf. Plut. *Solon* 18. Arist. *Ath. Pol.* 9.1. Ostwald, *Popular Sovereignty,* 5–15. Rhodes, *Com. Ath. Pol.*, 160–61. Hansen, 'The Athenian Heliaia from Solon to Aristotle', 9–47. Wallace, *Democracy 2500?,* 11–29. Murray, *Early Greece,* 190ff.

34. Arist. *Ath. Pol.* 7.3–4; 8.5. Plut. *Solon* 18.1–2. Cf. Wallace, *Areopagus.*

35. Arist. *Ath. Pol.* 8.4. Plut. *Solon* 19.1–2. Cf. Rhodes, *Com. Ath. Pol.*, 153–54. Mossé, *Athenian Democracy,* ed. Rhodes, 242–59. Raaflaub, Ober and Wallace (eds), *Origins of Democracy,* 36–48. Wallace, *Democracy 2500?,* 19–20.

36. Arist. *Pol.* 1273b36–42, 1274a11–22, 1281b30–34. Cf. 1294a30–1294b41. Cic. *Rep.* 1.68–69. Wallace, *Democracy 2500?,* 11–29, presents a different view of Solon's achievements, arguing that his reforms took power out of the hands of the *eupatridae* and put it by law in the hands of the people, and that he should therefore be seen as the creator of Athenian democracy. He expresses largely similar views in *Origins of Democracy,* ch. 3. But Solon's own words and the evidence of Aristotle cited above do not support such an interpretation.

37. The main ancient sources are Arist. *Ath. Pol.* 14–19. Arist. *Pol.* 1305a10ff., 1315b21. Hdt. 1.59–64. Thuc. 6.53–54. Cf. Fornara, *Archaic Times,* no. 31. Rhodes, *Com. Ath. Pol.*, 189–240.

38. The cultural impact of the reign of Peisistratus is well discussed by Jaeger, *Paideia* I, ch. 11. Cf. Forrest, *Emergence of Greek Democracy,* ch. 7. Andrewes, *Greek Tyrants,* 100–15. Ober, *Mass and Elite,* 65ff.

39. Arist. *Ath. Pol.* 17–19. Hdt. 5.55–66; 6.123. Thuc. 1.20; 6.53–59.

40. It should be emphasised that democractic movements also developed in many other Greek states, but the evidence for them is very limited. A comprehensive discussion is provided by Robinson, *The First Democracies.*

Chapter 2

1. Arist. *Ath. Pol.* 17–20. Hdt. 5.66, 69–78; 6.123. Thuc. 1.20.2; 6.53–49. Cf. Ostwald, *Popular Sovereignty,* 16–18. Ehrenberg, *Solon to Socrates,* 85–88. Ober, *The Athenian Revolution,* ch. 4. Arist. *Ath. Pol.* 20.3 says Cleomenes attempted to dissolve the *boule,* but it resisted. The Council in question is sometimes considered to be the Areopagus, not the Solonian Council, but Arist. *Ath. Pol.* never elsewhere uses the term *boule* in relation to the Areopagus. Cf. Rhodes, *Com. Ath. Pol.*, 246.

2. On the social structure of the sixth century cf. Forrest, *Emergence of Greek Democracy,* esp. 50ff., 191ff. Lambert, *Phratries of Attica.* Traill, *The Political Organisation of Attica.*

3. Arist. *Ath. Pol.* 20–21. Arist. *Pol.* 1310a13–19, 1319b20–28, 1337a10–20. There has been a great deal of important recent work on the political reorganisation of Attica by Cleisthenes, and its significance. In addition to the works cited in note 2 above, cf. Lewis, *Athenian Democracy,* ed. Rhodes, 287–309. Whitehead, *The Demes of Attica.* Jones, *Rural Athens under the Democracy.* Ober, *Athenian Legacies,* ch. 4; *Democracy and Knowledge,* esp. 134–55. Osborne, *Athens and Athenian Democracy,* ch. 3.

4. Arist. *Ath. Pol.* 21. Arist. *Pol.* 1319b20–28. Rhodes has produced the definitive work on the Council. Cf. *Com. Ath. Pol.*, 258ff., and *Athenian Boule,* esp. ch. 5.

5. Ober has valuable analysis of the significance of the reforms of Cleisthenes in *Athenian Legacies,* ch. 2; *Democracy and Knowledge,* ch. 4. Cf. articles by Ober, Raaflaub, Cartledge and Farrar in *Origins of Democracy,* ed. Raaflaub, Ober and Wallace.

6. Arist. *Ath. Pol.* 20.1. Hdt. 3.80.6; 5.78; 7.142ff. Cf. Raaflaub, *Demokratia,* 140ff.

7. For ostracism cf. Arist. *Ath. Pol.* 22.2, 43.5. Arist. *Pol.* 1284a18ff., 1284b15ff., 1302b18ff. Thuc. 8.73. Ps. Andoc. 4.35. Cf. Kagan, 'The Origin and Purposes of Ostracism'. De Ste Croix, *Athenian Democratic Origins,* 180–214. Forsdyke, *Exile, Ostracism, and Democracy.*

8. Hdt. 6.131. Arist. *Pol.* 1273b36ff., 1281b33ff. Arist. *Ath. Pol.* 22.1, 29.3. Plut. *Cimon* 15.2. Isocr. *Areop.* 16–17; *Antid.* 306.

9. Grote, *History of Greece*, 3.372–79. The 2,500th anniversary of the events of 508/7 produced an important volume of papers entitled *Democracy 2500?*, ed. Morris and Raaflaub, on the character and significance of the democratic ideal. For the view that the reforms of Cleisthenes did not establish full democracy as Athenians in the fifth century understood it, cf. Ostwald, *Popular Sovereignty*, 27–28. Raaflaub, *Democracy 2500?*, chs 3 and 5. The contrary view is argued by Ober, *Democracy 2500?*, ch. 4. Cf. Ober, *The Athenian Revolution*, ch. 4.

10. Definition of *demokratia* in Thuc. 2.37. Cf. Harris, 'Pericles' Praise of Athenian Democracy: Thucydides 2.37.1'. Herodotus uses the term in 6.43. There are no earlier uses, but that proves little, since so few texts survive from the late sixth and early fifth centuries. It would be surprising if the word did not emerge quickly in conjunction with, or in the wake of, the revolutionary changes introduced by Cleisthenes. The most significant later power acquired by the *demos* was control of the lawcourts which Aristotle (*Pol.* 1274a3ff.; cf. *Ath. Pol.* 9.1) considered important but, as Aristotle also emphasises, Solon had already given the people considerable judicial power and the right to hold magistrates accountable.

11. Hdt. 5.74–78.

12. For Athens as the mother of Ionians cf. Arist. *Ath. Pol.* 5. Thuc. 1.12.4. Herodotus is the main source for the Ionian revolt: 5.30–126; 6.1–30.

13. Hdt. 6.94–116. Plut. *Arist.* 5. Nepos *Milt.* 2–8.

14. Hdt. 7, 53–138, 161. For the role of Themistocles cf. Hdt. 143–44. Thuc. 1.14, 18, 74, 90–93. Plut. *Them.* 3–5.

15. On Thermopylae and Artemisium cf. Hdt. 7.175–238; 8.10–18. Plut. *Them.* 8.2. On Salamis cf. Hdt. 8.51–53, 72–115. Thuc. 1.74. Arist. *Ath. Pol.* 23.1. Plut. *Them.* 10–15; *Cim.* 5; *Arist.* 8–9. On Plataea cf. Hdt. 8.140; 9.71 ff. Plut. *Arist.* 10–19. Diod. 11.31–32. On Mycale cf. Hdt. 9.90, 96–106, 120–21. Cf. Meiggs, *Athenian Empire*, 33ff.

16. Thuc. 1.23, 88–97. The digression is commonly referred to as the Pentecontaetia, the fifty-year period. Thucydides mentions Hellanicus as the only one who touched on this period, but only briefly and inaccurately.

17. Hdt. 9.106, 114–21. Thuc. 1.75, 89.2, 96–97; 3.10.2. Arist. *Ath. Pol.* 23.5. Diod. 11.47. Cf. Meiggs, *Athenian Empire*, 39ff., 50ff. Plut. *Arist.* 24–25. The structures of the League are controversial. I have followed the well-reasoned conclusions of Meiggs, *Athenian Empire*, 460–68. Cf. also Kagan, *The Outbreak of the Peloponnesian War*, esp. ch. 2, and Eddy, 'The Cold War between Athens and Persia', who argues that the Persian threat did not wholly disappear until the end of the Peloponnesian War.

18. Thuc. 1.97–101; 3, 10.3–4. Plut. *Cim.* 6–9, 13. Diod. 11.60. Cf. Meiggs, *Athenian Empire*, 68–91, 376. Meiggs dates the revolt of Naxos to 467, Thasos to 465. It should be emphasised that the character of Athenian imperialism is highly controversial. More will be said about this in chapter 3. Cf. recent discussions in Low (ed.), *The Athenian Empire*, and Ma, Papazardakas and Parker (eds), *Interpreting the Athenian Empire*.

19. Thuc. 1.89–92. Plut. *Them.* 19.

20. Plut. *Cim.* 3.10; *Arist.* 2.4–5; *Nic.* 3–4.1. Arist. *Ath. Pol.* 28.2. Cf. Davies, *Athenian Propertied Families* and *Wealth and the Power of Wealth.* Connor, *New Politicians.* Ober, *Mass and Elite*, chs 3–7. Calhoun, *Athenian Clubs.* On the treatment of incompetent speakers cf. Plato *Prot.* 319b–c; *Rep.* 492b. Xen. *Mem.* 3.6.1. Aesch. 1.80–84; 2.51; 3.224. Lys. 12.73. Hansen, *Athenian Assembly*, 70ff. Ober, *Mass and Elite*, 138.

21. Hdt. 6.104.2, 109.10. Arist. *Ath. Pol.* 22.2; 44.4; 62.3. For the development of the office of general cf. de Ste Croix, *Athenian Democratic Origins*, 215ff.

22. Hdt. 6.136; 8.79.1. Nepos *Milt.* 8–9. Plut. *Arist.* 7.2; *Them.* 20.4, 22.3. Arist. *Ath. Pol.* 22.8.

23. Cf. note 28 below.

24. The Salamis decree (IG I³1, ML) provides the first recorded use of *edoxe toi demoi*. For other key decisions made by the *demos* cf. Hdt. 5.97; 7.142–43; 8.144; 9.6. Plut. *Them.* 10.20; *Arist.* 10.5–8.

25. For the number of thetes cf. Jones, *Ath. Dem.*, 79ff. Cf. Arist. *Pol.* 1279b38–1280a5. For the political implications of the increased military role for thetes cf. Ps. Xen. 1.2. Plato

Laws 706c–707a. Arist. *Pol.* 1321a14ff.; *Ath. Pol.* 27.1. Raaflaub, *Democracy 2500?*, 45ff., 95ff.

26. Arist. *Ath. Pol.* 22.2–5. Cf. Rhodes, *Com. Ath. Pol.*, 263–66, 272–74.
27. For the role of the Areopagus in the wake of the Persian Wars cf. Arist. *Pol.* 1304a20ff.; *Ath. Pol.* 23.1–2; 25.1. Rhodes, *Com. Ath. Pol.*, 287ff.
28. The reforms of Ephialtes are still a subject of wide debate. The scanty primary sources are Arist. *Ath. Pol.* 25; *Pol.* 1274a7ff. Plut. *Cim.* 15–16; *Per.* 9.2–5. Thuc. 1.102. Aristides may have helped pave the way for the reforms. Cf. Plut. *Arist.* 22. Cf. Ostwald, *Popular Sovereignty*, 47–83. Raaflaub, *Democracy 2500?*, 48ff. Wallace, *Areopagus*, ch. 3. Rhodes, *Boule*, ch. 4. For the size of juries cf. Hansen, *Ath. Dem.*, 187. Andoc. 1.17.
29. Arist. *Pol.* 1273b, 40ff. Arist. *Ath. Pol.* 25.4; 28.2. Plut. *Cim.* 15.2; 17.2. The *patrios politeia* of Solon and Cleisthenes was at the centre of political debate in 411, and the *Areopagiticus* of Isocrates shows it was still a cherished ideal of some in the fourth century.

Chapter 3

1. Thuc. 1.139.3–145. Plut. *Per.* 2–6; 11. Plato *Laches* 180d. Plutarch stresses his ascendancy for forty years at 16.2–3. Cicero cites the same number (*De Or.* 3.138), though it was only after the death of Ephialtes in 361 that he began to achieve real prominence. His first recorded generalship was in 454/3 (Thuc. 1.111.2).
2. Thuc. 1.127.1–3, 139.4; 2.13–65. Plato *Phaedrus* 269e–270a. Plut. *Per. passim.* Cicero, *De Or.* 1.216; 2.93; 3.59, 138. *Brutus* 28, 44. *Orator* 15.29.119. For the hostile view cf. Plato *Gorg.* 515e. Arist. *Pol.* 1274a7ff.; *Ath. Pol.* 27.1–4. Connor, *New Politicians*, Finley, 'Athenian Demagogues', 3–23, Ostwald, *Popular Sovereignty*, 181ff., Kagan, *Pericles of Athens* have useful discussions of the Periclean era.
3. Plutarch records several links between Pericles and Ephialtes. Both were bitter opponents of Cimon. Cf. Plut. *Per.* 7.6, 9–10; *Cim.* 14.4, 15.2. Arist. *Pol.* 1274a7ff.; *Ath. Pol.* 27.1ff.
4. Admission of *zeugitae* to archonship recorded in Arist. *Ath. Pol.* 26.2. There is no specific evidence that the thetes were ever legally admitted to the archonship, but it seems clear from Ps. Xen 1.2 and Arist. *Ath. Pol* 7.4 that the ban was not enforced. Cf. Rhodes, *Com. Ath. Pol.*, 145–46. On pay for jurors and public office cf. Arist. *Ath. Pol.* 24.3, 27.3; *Pol.* 1274a7ff. Pay was not extended to attendance at the Assembly until shortly after 400. Arist. *Ath. Pol.* 41.3.
5. Arist. *Ath. Pol.* 26.4; *Pol.* 1278a26–34. Plut. *Per.* 37.3. Cf. Rhodes, *Com. Ath. Pol.*, 331–35. Shapiro, *Dem. Emp. Arts*, 127–51. Modern commentators tend to shy away from using words such as nation, nationalism, rights, even patriotism, in regard to Greek political theory on the grounds that they are anachronistic, but these concepts were well understood in ancient Greece. Aristotle has an important discussion of the elements and character of a true *polis* in *Pol.* 1274b–1276b.
6. Arist. *Ath. Pol.* 8.1 says Solon introduced selection of archons from preselected candidates, but this is contradicted by Arist. *Pol.* 1274a.2ff. Cf. Rhodes, *Com. Ath. Pol.*, 146ff. It does appear, however, that Solon did use selection by lot for treasurers of Athens (*Ath. Pol.* 47.1), and that Cleisthenes used sortition for the selection of priests for new cults in the demes. Cf. Ostwald, *Popular Sovereignty*, 139. For selection of the Council by lot cf. Thuc. 8.69. Arist. *Ath. Pol.* 22.5, 32.1. Rhodes, *Boule*, 6–7.
7. Arist. *Pol.* 1274a, 1276a, 1273a, 1294b, 1317b. Hdt. 3.80.6. Plato records the view of Protagoras in *Prot.* 320–23. Aristotle presents the argument (sometimes called the summation theory) for the greater wisdom of the collective view of the many in *Pol.* 1281a1ff. In Thuc. 6.38–39 Athenagoras in the Syracusan Assembly argues the justice and wisdom of inclusiveness and equality in decision-making. Cf. Raaflaub, *Demokratia*, 140ff.
8. For the consequences of pay for public office cf. Arist. *Pol.* 1274a7ff., 1292a10ff., 1293a5ff., 1300a2ff., 1305a30ff., 1317b7ff. Plato *Gorg.* 515e. Withdrawal of pay for public service was one of the first proposals of the oligarchs in 411. Arist. *Ath. Pol.* 29.5. Thuc. 8.65.

9. The author of the pamphlet, commonly referred to as the Old Oligarch, is unknown. It has been wrongly ascribed to Xenophon in the tradition. It is generally agreed that it was written in the early stages of the Peloponnesian War. The usual form of citation is Ps. Xen.

10. Ps. Xen. 1.3. Arist. *Ath. Pol.* 28.2. Plut. *Per.* 11.1-2, 12.2,14. This was the period when the terms *demokratia*, *oligarchia* and *aristokratia* made their appearance, evidence of continuing debate about the merits of the rule of the few and the many. Cf. Hdt. 6.43. Thuc. 2.37. Andrewes, 'The Opposition to Pericles', and articles by Raaflaub and Eder in *Democracy 2500?*, 33-37, 112-13.

11. The Oration is recorded in Thuc. 2.34-46. The bibliography on Thucydides and his historical method is voluminous. I cite here works I found most useful: Finley, Introduction to Rex Warner's translation of the *History of the Peloponnesian War*. De Ste Croix, *Historia* (1954-55), 1-41; *Origins of the Peloponnesian War* (1972), esp. the Introduction. Connor, *Thucydides* (1985). N. Loraux, *The Invention of Athens*, trans. A. Sheridan. Hornblower, *Thucydides*. Low, *Interstate Relations in Classical Greece*, esp. ch. 6; *The Athenian Empire* (2008), esp. the Introduction. Two detailed commentaries – Gomme, Andrewes and Dover, *Historical Commentary on Thucydides*, and Hornblower, *Commentary on Thucydides* – are immensely valuable.

12. Dem. 20.105-8; 18.123; 24.192-93. Aesch. 1.195. Wallace, *Demokratia*, 105-19; *Athenian Identity and Civic Ideology*, 127-55.

13. Plato *Rep.* 557. Isocr. 7.20. Arist. *Pol.* 1310a30-36, 1263b1-5.

14. Dem. 21.47. Arist. *Ath. Pol.* 56.2. Hansen and Wallace have useful accounts in *Demokratia*, 91-119, of individual rights and protections in Athenian law. Cf. Ober, *Athenian Legacies*, 92-127. Fustel de Coulanges, *The Ancient City*, cites many instances of intrusion by the state into private life, but many of his examples are questionable and certainly do not warrant his conclusion that there was no real liberty in Athens. Cf. also Fisher, *Hybris*.

15. Dem. 18.123. Aesch. 1.195. Cf. Wallace, *Demokratia*, 112-13.

16. For more detailed discussion of liturgies, taxation, volunteering cf. above, pp. 181-82, 223-26, 247-48, 264, 302. Cf. Liddel, *Obligation and Liberty*, chs 4-5.

17. For religion and the democracy cf. Ostwald, *Popular Sovereignty*, 137-71, 191-98, and Appendices B and C.

18. Grote, *History of Greece*, 5, 71-74. Constant, *Political Writings*, 310-27. Berlin, *Four Essays on Liberty*, 122-34. Gomme, *More Essays in Greek History and Literature*, 139-55. Finley, *Democracy Ancient and Modern*, 116; *Economy and Society*, 92-93. Ostwald, *Demokratia*, 49-61. Hansen, *Demokratia*, 91-104. Wallace, *Demokratia*, 105-19. Wood, *Demokratia*, 131-37. Liddel, *Obligation and Liberty*, 11-16, has a useful summary of modern views on liberty in Athens.

19. Thuc. 1.22.4; 3.81-82. Arist. *Pol.* 1253a1-40, 1263b1-5.

20. Cic. *Rep.* 3.33; *Leg.* 1.18-19, 28-29, 33; *Off.* 3.23, 27-28. Cicero confirms in *Off.* 3.20 that he is following the teaching of the Stoics. Cf. *Rep.* 1.34; 2.27; 4.3 for acknowledgement of his debt to Polybius and Panaetius.

21. For fuller discussion of the place of women and slaves in Athens cf. above, pp. 256-67.

22. Thuc. 1.71.1, 76-77; 3.40.2-3, 48.1; 5.89; 6.83. Recent disclosures about the activities of the US National Security Agency are a good example of the readiness of modern liberal democracies to give precedence to national interests and security over law, national and international.

23. Eur. *Supp.* 433-38. Aesch. 3.233-35 stresses the power of the juror and the courts in protecting democracy. The private citizen is king in a democracy by his power to control politicians by his vote as a juror. Cf. Dem. 24.78. For the Heliastic Oath cf. Dem. 24.149-51. Hansen, *Ath. Dem.*, 182-83.

24. Cf. Thuc. 2.37.3. Andoc. 1.82-85. Cf. above, pp. 201-6. Ostwald, *Popular Sovereignty*, 369-72. Boegehold, *Demokratia*, 203-14. For the *graphe paranomon* cf. Thuc. 3.43.4-5. Andoc. 1.17, 22. Hansen, *Ath. Dem.*, 205-12. Aristotle has a review of the arguments for and against changing the laws in *Pol.* 1268b-1269a27. There is one recorded instance (Xen. *Hell.* 1.7.12) of shouts in the Assembly that it would be a terrible thing (*deinon*) if the *demos* were not allowed to do whatever it wished, but that was an aberration in fraught circumstances which will be discussed later. Cf. above, pp. 177, 186. We know of no repetition.

25. Thuc. 1.69, 102–15, the main source for the events of those years. Cf. Meiggs, *Athenian Empire*, ch. 6.

26. Thuc. 1.104, 109–15. Hdt. 7.151. Isocr. 8.86. Plut. *Cim.* 17.3–18; *Per.* 23. Meiggs, *Athenian Empire*, chs 7–8, provides a superb narrative of this period, with a detailed analysis of the controversial Peace of Callias – and a full listing of sources on pp. 487–88. By 450 Pericles was reaching the height of his ascendancy, with no rival left of comparable stature. Cf. Plut. *Per.* 11–12, 14, 17.

27. Thuc. 1.105, 107–8, 143; 2.13.2–7, 62.6. Plato *Gorg.* 455e. Ps. Xen. 1.

28. Thuc. 1.97; 2.13.2. Plut. *Per.* 12.1; *Arist.* 25.2. The body of epigraphic evidence has been assembled in two collections: Meiggs and Lewis, *Greek Historical Inscriptions* (ML), and Merritt, Wade-Grey and McGregor, *Athenian Tribute Lists*. Cf. Rhodes, *Boule*, 89ff. for decree of Clinias. For the tribute and epigraphic evidence cf. Meiggs, *Athenian Empire*, chs 13 and 14 and Appendix 13. For more recent discussions cf. Rhodes, 'After the Three-Bar Sigma Controversy: The History of Athenian Imperialism Reassessed'. Papazarkadas, 'Epigraphy and the Athenian Empire: Reshuffling the Chronological Cards'. The extent of the use of the tribute to fund the Periclean building programme has begun to be disputed. Cf. articles in Low (ed.), *The Athenian Empire*, by Giovannini, Kallet-Marx and Osborne.

29. Thuc. 2.13.3. Plut. *Per.* 12–14.

30. For adoption of Athenian coinage cf. *Athenian Tribute Lists* 2.61. For the allies and the courts cf. Thuc. 1.77.1. ML52. Ps. Xen. 1.16–18. Isocr. 4.113. Meiggs, *Athenian Empire*, 220ff. Cf. de Ste Croix, 'Notes on Jurisdiction in the Athenian Empire'. For new thinking about the date and significance of the decree concerning coinage, weights and measures cf. Lewis, *Coinage and Administration of the Athenian and Persian Empires*, 53–63. Kroll, *Interpreting the Athenian Empire*, 195–210.

31. Thuc. 1.40.5, 115–17. Plut. *Per.* 24.1. Ps. Xen. 3.11. Arist. *Pol.* 1307b22. For cleruchies cf. Plut. *Per.* 11.4–5. Jones, *Ath. Dem.*, 168ff. Meiggs, *Athenian Empire*, 261ff., also ch. 11. Garrisons do not seem to have been much used before the Peloponnesian War. Cf. Gomme, *HCT* 1.381.

32. *Arche* is the standard word in Thucydides for Athenian rule. Isocrates makes clear the word denoted a despotic form of rule. Cf. 8.94, 102, 114–15, 134, 142. Pericles uses *tyrannis* of Athenian rule (Thuc. 2.63), as does Cleon (Thuc. 3.37).

33. Thuc. 2.48; 4.104.4, 105.1; 5.26. John Finley, *Thucydides*, 8–16 has a good summary of the evidence. Three *vitae* survive from the Byzantine period, but they are considered too unreliable to be of much value.

34. Thuc. 8.1. For his view of Pericles cf. 2.59.1–2, 60.1, 65.1–4, 8–11.

35. Cleon: 3.36.6, 50.1; 4.21.3, 28–30, 39.3, 122.6; 5.2–10, 16. Alcibiades: 5.43, 45, 46.5, 55.3, 84.1; 6.8.2, 15–18, 28–29, 61, 88–92. In 6.89.6 he has Alcibiades call democracy folly (*anoia*). Cf. also 7.18.1; 8.12, 14–17, 26, 45–56, 81–83, 85–86, 88, 97, 108. Diodotus: 2.41–49. Thucydides' final comment about Cleon is especially harsh. In 5.16 he names Cleon and Brasidas as the two men most opposed to peace: 'Brasidas because of the success and honour he got from war, Cleon because he thought that, if there were peace, he would be more clearly revealed as a scoundrel, and his slanders would have less credence.'

36. Thuc. 8.97.2–3. Cf. Arist. *Ath. Pol.* 33.2–3. The Constitution of the Five Thousand and Thucydides' view of it have generated a lot of discussion. Cf. Andrewes, *HCT* 5.331ff. Ostwald, *Popular Sovereignty*, 395ff. De Ste Croix, 'The Constitution of the Five Thousand'. Sealey, *Essays*, 11–32. Rhodes, 'The Five Thousand in the Athenian Revolutions of 411'. Harris, 'The Constitution of the Five Thousand'. For Aristotle's view of a constitution that had a fusion of oligarchic and democratic features. Cf. esp. *Pol.* 1292a–1301a. For the views of Isocrates cf. 7.15–28; 12.114–18.

37. There is a fuller discussion of the events of 411 in the historical narrative of the period below, pp. 172–75. It is interesting to note that Isocrates, in his advocacy of the merits of the ancestral constitution in the *Areopagiticus* (70), with its mix of oligarchic and democratic features, insists that he is no oligarch, but a democrat who wants a just and well-ordered constitution.

38. Thuc. 1.89–118. Thucydides says that he wrote this digression from his story (*ekbole logou*), which is commonly referred to as the Pentecontaetia, to fill in the events of the roughly fifty-year period between the departure of Xerxes from Greece and the outbreak of the Peloponnesian War, because no one else had reliably dealt with it, and it was the time when Athens confirmed its hold over its empire and acquired great strength, creating a fear among the Spartans that Athenian power would keep growing. Thucydides considered this the real cause of the Peloponnesian War (1.88, 118).

39. Thuc. 1.99; 2.41.4–5. Egyptian adventure: 1.104, 109–10. Athenian envoys at Sparta: 1.72–78. Debate and Syracuse: 6.81–87.

40. For the purpose of his history cf. above, pp. 87–88. His insistence on a rule of law and high moral standards within states is well illustrated in his comment on the effect of the plague in Athens (2.53) and the civil war in Corcyra (3.70–84). For an excellent recent discussion of Greek interstate relations, including discussion of the views of Thucydides, cf. Low, *Interstate Relations*. It might be argued that, despite the efforts to create a body of international law through the United Nations and the establishment of the International Criminal Court, little has fundamentally changed in relations between states since the time of Thucydides.

41. Thuc. 1.77.5; 2.8.4–5, 63.2; 3.13.6–7, 37.2; 6.76.2–4; 8.2.1.

42. De Ste Croix, 'The Character of the Athenian Empire'; *The Class Struggle in the Ancient World*. Cf. Bradeen, 'The Popularity of the Athenian Empire'. De Romilly challenges the view of de Ste Croix in 'Thucydides and the Cities of the Athenian Empire'. Cf. also De Romilly, *Thucydides and Athenian Imperialism*. Meiggs, *Athenian Empire*, ch. 23. Ostwald, *Scripta Classica Israelica* (1993), 51–66; *Autonomia: Its Genesis and History*. Hornblower, *Thucydides*, esp. ch. 7.

43. Thuc. 2.8.4–5, 72.1; 4.79–88, 102–16, 120–23. The remarks of Phrynichus are in 8.48.5–6. Isocrates (8.94, 102, 114–15, 134, 142) stresses the alienation of the allies as a result of Athenian oppression. Cf. Xenophon's brief essay *Peri Poron*.

44. Thuc. 1.20–21. For the constancy of human nature and the lessons of history cf. 1.22.4, 76.2–3; 3.82.2; 4.61.5; 5.105.1–2, Finley, Introduction to *Thucydides, History of the Peloponnesian War*, trans. Warner, 19, 24–25.

45. Thuc. 1.73–78; 6.81–87. Some historians believe the threat from Persia never disappeared. It was not imminent, however, in this period. Cf. Eddy, 'The Cold War between Athens and Persia'.

46. On *time* and *arete* cf. Homer *Il.* 6.208; 11.784. Plato *Symp.* 208–9. Arist. *Eth. Nic.* 1.5. Tyrtaeus frgs 10, 13 (West). Hdt. 1.30. Jaeger, *Paideia* I, ch. 1.

47. Hdt. 5.78; 8.3. Thuc. 1.69.1, 73–75; 6.82. Thuc. 1.70 provides the Corinthian view of the Athenian character.

48. For the themes in the speech of greatness and power and the qualities that produced them cf. Thuc. 2.36, 39–40; 41.2–4, 43.1.

49. Cf. Thuc. 2.13.2, 63.

50. Thuc. 2.63.2–3.

51. For a good summary of the effects of empire on the democracy cf. Raaflaub, *Democracy 2500?*, 46ff. For the level of revenues cf. Thuc. 2.13.3. Xen. *Anab.* 7.1.27. Cf. *Ath. Trib. Lists*, 3.344ff. Jones, *Ath. Dem.*, 6–8. For the expansion of the navy cf. Hdt. 8.44. Thuc. 1.141; 2.13, 8. Plut. *Per.* 11. For numbers of hoplites cf. Thuc. 2.13.6–8. For numbers at Marathon and Plataea cf. Hdt. 9.28. Nepos *Milt.* 5.

52. Thuc. 2.56.2; 3.17.3; 6.8.1; 6.31.3. Aristoph. *Plut.* 505ff. Plut. *Per.* 7. Arist. *Ath. Pol.* 24.3 says empire brought affluence for the masses. For fourth-century numbers employed in the docks cf. Garland, *Piraeus*, 97ff. For use of industrial slaves cf. Raaflaub, *Dem. Emp. Art*, 27ff. Davies, *Wealth and Power of Wealth*, 41ff. Jones, *Ath. Emp.*, 14–15. Useful discussions of expenditures and revenues by Finley, 'The Fifth-Century Athenian Empire: A Balance Sheet'. Kallet, *Dem. Emp. Arts*, 46ff. Pritchard, 'Costing Festivals and War: The Spending Priorities of the Athenian Democracy'.

53. On pay for public office and its costs cf. Podes, 'The Introduction of Jury Pay by Pericles: Some Mainly Chronological Considerations'. Kallet, *Dem. Emp. Arts*, 46. Jones, *Ath. Dem.*,

6. For the reserve and its use for buildings cf. Thuc. 2.13.3. Plut. *Per.* 12–14. Cf. above, note 28.

54. On cleruchies and colonies cf. *Ath. Trib. Lists,* 3, 282–97. Jones, *Ath. Dem.,* 168ff. Meiggs, *Athenian Empire,* 260ff.

55. For the grain supply cf. Moreno, *Feeding the Democracy.*

56. Thuc. 2.38.2. Ps. Xen. 1.17–18; 2.7, 11–12. Isocr. 4.42. For metics cf. Ps. Xen. 1.12. Aristoph. *Ach.* 507–8. Hansen, *Ath. Dem.,* 116–20. Jones, *Ath. Dem.,* 10–11. Finley, *Ancient Economy,* 163ff.

57. Cf. Jones, *Ath. Dem.,* 161ff. Hansen, *AJAH* 7 (1982), 172–89. Ober, *Mass and Elite,* 127ff. On the balance sheet of empire, cf. Meiggs, *Ath. Emp.,* ch. 14. Finley, 'The Fifth-Century Athenian Empire: A Balance Sheet'.

58. Arist. *Pol.* 1322b12–37; *Ath. Pol.* 24.3. Cf. Rhodes, *Com. Ath. Pol.,* 302ff. Hansen, *Ath. Dem.,* ch. 9; 'Seven Hundred *Archai* in Classical Athens'. Meiggs, *Athenian. Empire,* 215.

59. Rhodes, *The Athenian Boule,* has written the most comprehensive study of the Athenian Council, and the account here is largely based on it.

60. For participation cf. Hansen, *Ath. Dem.,* 313ff. Raaflaub, *Dem. Emp. Arts,* 20ff. Sealey, *Demosthenes,* 30ff.

61. For *graphe paranomon* cf. Andoc. 1.17. Ostwald, *Popular Sovereignty,* 125ff.

62. Ps. Xen. 1.1, 4–8.

63. Ps. Xen. 1.2; 3.1, 9. Cf. Frisch, *Constitution of Athens.*

64. Plato's *Seventh Epistle,* almost universally accepted as genuine, gives interesting insight into his life and political experience. Cf. *Rep.* 496c. Grube, *Plato's Thought,* 259ff.

65. For the task and education of the statesman cf. *Prot.* 319ff.; *Gorg.* 513ff.; *Rep.* 342eff., 376d–414, 519b–522; *Laws* 689–90. For the social divisions and their roles cf. *Rep.* 413c, 415a–427. For the characteristics of the ideal state cf. *Rep.* 427e, 428b–434e. Unity is emphasised in *Rep.* 422e; *Alc.* 126c; *Clit.* 409d–e; *Laws* 701d. In the *Politicus,* Plato is even more emphatic that the state must be directed by *episteme.* A rigid rule of laws carefully assembled and sanctioned would be a second-best option, but a poor one. Cf. *Pol.* 300–1. It should be noted that there are many scholars who do not believe that the dialogues *Alcibiades* and *Clitopho* are genuine works of Plato.

66. Law sanctioned by oldest and best: 659d; serving the common interest: 697d, 715b; magistrates servants of the law: 715d; laws must persuade: 718b, 723a–d. Cf. 693b–c, 701d.

67. Mixed constitution: *Laws* 693d, 701e. Sparta an example: 692, also Persia, 694a–b. Bks 5ff. provide details of the complex mix of oligarchy and democracy.

68. *Laws* 698b–699e; *Gorg.* 515c–517c, 518c–519b; *Rep.* 557–559; *Laws* 688e–699. There is a voluminous bibliography on Plato. I found the following helpful: Williams, *Plato: The Invention of Philosophy.* Annas, *Introduction to Plato's Republic.* Vlastos, *Interpretations of Plato.* Grube, *Plato's Thought.*

69. Flaws of oligarchy: *Pol.* 1290b2–30, 1305a35–1306b21. Definition of democracy: *Pol.* 1278b13, 1279b18, 1280a13. Polity closest to democracy: 1293b34. *Eth. Nic.* 1160a31ff. Freedom: *Pol.* 1279a21–22, 1310a30–35. Democracy more stable than oligarchy: 1302a9. Rule and be ruled: 1283b42–1284a1. Importance of majority support for constitution: 1270b21ff., 1296b15ff., 1309b16ff. Summation theory: 1281a42–1281b16. Cf. 1286a22ff. Dahl, *Democracy and its Critics,* 97ff., has an interesting modern variation' on the summation theory which he calls 'The Strong Principle of Equality'.

70. Arist. *Pol.* 1296b20ff. Merits of the *hoi mesoi:* 1295a37ff., 1295b25–1296a21. Cf. 1292b25ff., 1318b6ff. Aristotle's view of this middle population as the stable anchor of a state appears in Aeschylus and in the *Suppliants* of Euripides, 238–45, where he says the *moira en meso* is the saviour of cities.

71. The navy and democracy: *Pol.* 1303b11–12, 1304a22–25, 1321a14–17. Cf. 1327b1ff. Ephialtes and Pericles: *Pol.* 1274a7–11.

72. *Teleutaia demokratia: Pol.* 1298a28–33, 1319b1–27. The inferior proletariat: *Pol.* 1319a21–32, cf. 1277a35–1277b8, 1278a8–15, 1328b38–41. Aristotle also refers to the *teleutaia demokratia* as a fifth form of democracy (*Pol.* 1292a4–19), in which the multitude (*plethos*), not the law, is supreme (*kyrios*), and the people become a collective monarchy and grow into tyranny.

73. Freedom and equality: *Pol.* 1255b20–21, 1280a12–14, 1295b25–26, 1302a26–30, 1310a26–36, 1317a40–41, 1317b10, 1318a3–7, 1319b30. The true purpose of the state: 1279a24–33, 1280b–1281a1–8.
74. *Pol.* 1317b12–17, cf. 1310a26–36. Cf. Plato *Rep.* 557b. Isocr. 7.37.
75. Artisans (*banausoi*) and labourers (thetes) as citizens and office-holders: *Pol.* 1277b34–1278a40, 1281b24–1282a23, 1300a10–1300b5, 1309a30, 1318b6–1319a5, 1328b10–41. Pay for public office and Assembly: 1300a1–4, 1308a32–1309b10, 1321a32–35. For the dangers of exclusion and need for some sharing (*methexis*) for all citizens in the deliberative and executive functions cf. 1278a26, 1281b30–31. But their share must not empower them to change the constitution: 1298b31–33.
76. *Pol.* 1298a28–34. Cf. 1299b39–1300a4.
77. *Pol.* 1276b1–15, 1276b30–31, 1278b9–15, 1279a17–22, 1289a1–25, 1295b1. Cf. Isocr. 7.14; 12.138. Dem. 24.210. Stability through education and balance of power between classes: 1295b1–1296a21, 1310a15–19. Aristotle's ideal state, the polity, a blend (*mixis*) of oligarchy and democracy, sought to create the right balance with the *mesoi* as the anchor. Cf. *Pol.* 1293b32–1294b43.
78. Cf. above, pp. 75–76, and pp. 201–6.
79. No figures for number of thetes; Jones, *Ath. Dem.*, 9, provides estimates. Cf. Ostwald, *Popular Sovereignty*, 230. Ships on patrol: Plut. *Per.* 11.4. Evidence and analysis for colonies and cleruchies provided by Jones, *Ath. Dem.*, 161–80.
80. Arist. *Pol.* 1278a25; *Ath. Pol.* 7.4. Cf. Rhodes, *Com. Ath. Pol.*, 142. Cf. Davies, *Wealth and the Power of Wealth*, ch. 4. Connor, *New Politicians*, 85–136. Jones, *Ath. Dem.*, 8–9. It was difficult for thetes to achieve influence in the Assembly, where eloquence and credibility were the tools of leadership, and those without them were heckled or shouted down. Cf. Plut. *Dem.* 6.3. Arist. *Rhet.* 1355a2–3. Aesch. 1.80–84; 3.224. Hansen, *Ath. Dem.*, 146.
81. Thuc. 2.13–16. Hdt. 5.77–78. The evidence for the social composition of the Assembly is meagre and inconclusive. Plato *Prot.* 319c–d and Xen. *Mem.* 3.7.6 give lists of the types of people attending the Assembly, but all they indicate is that the citizen population was broadly represented. Cf. Ober, *Mass and Elite*, 137ff.; *Democracy and Knowledge*, ch. 4. Carter, *The Quiet Athenian*, esp. ch. 4.
82. Special powers of generals in war: Thuc. 4.66, 76, 118.14. Cf. Jones, *Ath. Dem.*, 124–25.
83. Ps. Xen. 1.3.
84. The centrality of the concept of equality in Athenian democracy is well documented. Hdt. 3.80.6; 5.78. Eur. *Supp.* 350–53, 429–41. Thuc. 2.37.1; 6.38.5–39.1. Dem. 21.69. But when it came to the most important office the prejudice in favour of the elite remained strong. An interesting symbol of that is the use of the word *dunatoi* in contrast to *demos* in Ps. Xen. 1.3 and Thuc. 2.65.2 to denote the upper class. The word had connotations of both power and ability, implying these were attributes that characterised the elite and entitled them to leadership.
85. Ps. Xen. 1.13. Cf. articles by Wolin, Wood, Raaflaub, Cartledge and Roberts in *Demokratia*, ed. Ober and Hedrick.

Chapter 4

1. For a comprehensive overview of modern theories of the causes of the cultural upswing cf. *Dem. Emp. Arts.* Webster, *Athenian Culture and Society* connects many elements of the cultural revolution to the democracy.
2. For the building programme of Peisistratus and patronage of the arts cf. Boersma, *Athenian Building Policy*, 11–27. Jaeger, *Paideia* I, 228–33. For the origins of tragedy and comedy cf. Arist. *Poetics* 4ff. Lesky, *Greek Tragedy*, trans. Frankfort, ch. 2.
3. Plut. *Cim.* 5. Cf. Hölscher, *Dem. Emp. Arts*, 164–67.
4. Plut. *Per.* 13.5–9. Cf. articles by Shapiro and Hölscher in *Dem. Emp. Arts*, chs 6 and 7. Kallet-Marx, 'Did Tribute Fund the Parthenon?' Robertson, *History of Greek Art*, and Boardman's many writings on Greek art, especially *Greek Sculpture: The Archaic Period* and *The Parthenon and its Sculptures*, provide good general studies of Greek art and architecture.

5. Hdt. 2.35; 3.60. Thuc. 1.10.1. Isocr. 7.66. Dem. 22.76–77. Plut. *Per.* 12–14. Cf. Kallet, *Dem. Emp. Arts*, 46–51.

6. The Panhellenic Congress: Plut. *Per.* 17. Athena and the Panathenaea: Hdt. 8.55. Jameson, *Dem. 2500?*, 177–79. Lisa Maurizio, 'The Panathenaic Procession: Athens' Participatory Democracy on Display?' in *Democracy, Empire, and the Arts in Fifth-Century Athens*, Deborah Boedeker and K.A. Raaflaub (eds), Cambridge: Harvard University Press, 1987, ch. 14. Meiggs, *Ath. Emp.*, 166, 273–93.

7. Erechtheus: Homer *Il.* 2.547; *Od.* 7.81. Athena Nike: Hölscher, *Dem. Emp. Arts*, 173–76.

8. Cf. Meiggs, *Ath. Emp.*, 289. Boersma, *Athenian Building Policy*, 65–82. Jameson, *Democracy 2500?*, 185.

9. Thuc. 2.15. Euripides, *Supp.* 334–58, 403–8, 426–55. Plut. *Theseus passim*; *Cim.* 8.3. Cf. Boedeker, *Dem. Emp. Arts*, 186–89. Francis, *Image and Idea*. Hölscher, *Dem. Emp. Arts*, 160–61.

10. Hdt. 5.78. Thuc. 1.70.3; 2.36.4, 42.1, 43.1.

11. Thuc. 2.38–39. Ps. Xen. 1.13, 2.9, 3.2, 8. Cf. Kallet, *Dem. Emp. Arts*, 46–58. Jameson, *Democracy 2500?*, 176–77.

12. Plato *Symp.* 175e. *Theorika*: Plut. *Per.* 9.1. A good general account of the festivals is provided by Pickard-Cambridge, *Dramatic Festivals*.

13. Dem. 18.120. Lys. 21.1–5. Arist. *Ath. Pol.* 56. Cf. Rhodes, *Com. Ath. Pol.*, 622ff. Saïd, *Dem. Emp. Arts*, 275–76. Expenditure on festival liturgies: Thuc. 6.16.3. Plut. *Nic.*, 3.2–6. Connor, *New Politicians*, 21ff. Davies, *Athenian Propertied Families*, XXI–XXII. Kallet, *Dem. Emp. Arts*, 54–58.

14. Arist. *Poetics* 4–22. Drama and politics: Goldhill, *Reading Greek Tragedy* (1986). Goldhill and Osborne (eds), *Performance Culture and Athenian Democracy*. Saïd, *Dem. Emp. Arts*, 276–84. Plato describes tragedy in *Gorg.* 502c as *demegoria* (popular oratory). Cf. *Minos* 321a.

15. Cf. above, pp. 69–70. Ps. Xen. 2.18. Aristoph. *Ach.* 377–82. Cf. Henderson, *Dem. Emp. Arts*, 255–73.

16. Thuc. 2.38–41, 60.6. Arist. *Pol.* 1341a27–32.

17. Very little of the writings of the Sophists has survived. The dialogues of Plato are the main source of information, and Plato was a fierce critic. There has been a great debate about the fairness of Plato's evidence, but broad agreement in modern times that the questions they raised about education, religion, morality and politics have enduring importance. Valuable modern studies include Guthrie, *The Sophists*. Jaeger, *Paideia* I, 286–331. Kerferd, *The Sophistic Movement*.

18. Plato *Prot.* 328b, 349a; *Meno* 91c–92b. Xen. *Mem.* 1.6.13. Isocr. 15.155–58. Subjects taught: Plato *Prot.* 318d–e, 339a; *Hipp. Min.* 368 b–e. Views of Gorgias: *Meno* 71e, 73a–d, 95c; *Gorg.* 452d, 454b–457c, 460–61c.

19. Plato *Prot.* 318e–319a, 320d–324d, 327c–328c; *Theaet.* 167c–d, 170a–d. Cf. Farrar, *Origins of Democratic Thinking*, ch. 3.

20. Thuc. 3.38.7. Plato *Hipp. Min.* 364a; *Meno* 70b. Isocr. 12.1–4, 45. Gorgias stirred enormous interest on visits to Athens and Olympia. Diod. 12.53.3. Philostr. *VS* 1.9. There was also a level of reaction against the Sophists. There are reports of a prosecution of Protagoras and of his books being burned. Diog. Laert. 9.52, 54, 55. Cf. Ostwald, *Popular Sovereignty*, 532–53. Wallace, *Dem. Emp. Arts*, 203–22. Plato *Meno* 91e says that for forty years Protagoras practised his art without anyone in Greece noticing that he corrupted the youth.

21. For the legacy of the Sophists to education cf. Jaeger, *Paideia* I, 316ff.

22. Cf. Yunis, *Dem. Emp. Arts*, 234ff. J. Finley, *Thucydides*, 44, 101. For a more general discussion of the aims and methods of Thucydides cf. Farrar, *Origins of Democratic Thinking*, ch. 5.

Chapter 5

1. Thuc. 1.23.6. Two particularly useful and relatively recent studies of the origins of the war are Kagan, *Outbreak of the Peloponnesian War*, and de Ste Croix, *Origins of the Peloponnesian War*. But Thucydides remains our best witness. Whether his view that the war was inevitable is right is another question, and more debatable.

2. The Ionian and Dorian divide: Hdt. 5.91. Thuc. 1.102, 124; 6.82. Plut. *Cim.* 16.8. Spartan inaction: Thuc. 1.69, 71, 118.
3. The thinking and strategy of Pericles and the Athenians in this period are spelled out in Thuc. 6.82–83, cf. 1.143.
4. The Corcyraean incident is described in Thuc. 1.31–55. It is clear from the account that war between Athens and Sparta was already seen as imminent. Cf. 1.33.3, 36.1.
5. Potidaea: Thuc. 1.56–65. Megara: Thuc. 1.67.4; 139.1–2; 2.39. De Ste Croix, *Origins of the Peloponnesian War*, 224ff., has a detailed discussion of the Megarian decree.
6. Thuc. 1.66–88, 118–125, 127.3, 139–46; 2.13. Thucydides considered the belief of Pericles that the war could be won was well based: 2.65.5–6. The events leading to the war are discussed in detail in the excellent studies of Kagan, *Outbreak of the Peloponnesian War* and de Ste Croix, *Origins of the Peloponnesian War*. The early stages of the war are well covered by Kagan, *The Archidamian War* (1974).
7. For the accuracy of the claims of Thucydides that the majority of Greece favoured Sparta in the war cf. above, pp. 85–86.
8. Thuc. 2.14–17 has a graphic account of what the Periclean strategy of moving the rural population to Athens entailed. Ravages of the plague: Thuc. 2.47–54; 3.87.
9. Thuc. 2.56–65. Plut. *Per.* 35–38, which includes details of the many private misfortunes of Pericles at the end of his life.
10. Thuc. 2.60.6, 65.8–11. Cf. 1.138.3. Jones, *Ath. Dem.*, 99–133, has a good overview of how the democracy worked.
11. Thuc. 2.65.10. Arist. *Ath. Pol.* 28.1–4. Isocr. 8.126–33.
12. Finley, 'Athenian Demagogues'. Cf. also Connor, *New Politicians*, esp. chs 3–4. Connor's account is, in many ways, a more balanced treatment of the demagogues than Finley's. On the need for expertise on the part of leaders cf. Xen. *Mem.* 3.6. Arist. *Rhet.* 1359a30ff. Connor, *New Politicians*, 122–27. Andrewes, 'The Mytilene Debate: Thucydides 3.36–49'. Hornblower, *Com. on Thuc.*, II, 344ff. Rhodes, 'Political Activity in Classical Athens', 132. It must also be remembered, of course, that the *demos* itself, because of the character of the democratic constitution, which required high levels of participation by the full body of citizens in so many areas of government, was exceptionally well informed about the functioning of the whole system.
13. Arist. *Ath. Pol.* 28.2–3. In 22.3 it says Peisistratus started as a *demagogos* and then became a tyrant.
14. The aristocratic establishment was, of course, far from being a harmonious, monolithic bloc. As we have seen, there were sharp rivalries, divisions about the appropriate limits to democratisation, frequent ostracisms, and the reforms of Ephialtes led to his assassination. But these were divisions within the upper class. Cleon was introducing division between mass and elite, questioning the leadership of the high-born and promoting a more assertive role for the Assembly.
15. Thuc. 3.36.6–40.8, 50.1; 4.21.3, 22.2, 27–28, 122.6; 5.1–3, 10, 16. Aristoph. *Knights passim*. Arist. *Ath. Pol.* 28.3. Schol. Aristoph. *Knights* 44. Connor, *New Politicians*, 91–101. Ostwald, *Popular Sovereignty*, 201–8. Rhodes, *Com. Ath. Pol.*, 351ff. Davies, *Athenian Propertied Families*, 8674.
16. Prominence in the Assembly: Thuc. 3.36.6, 50.1; 4.21.3, 122.6. Demagogues and the courts: Aristoph. *Knights* 305–6, 441–44, 1255. Cf. Ostwald, *Popular Sovereignty*, 208ff. Thucydides, in his final comment on Cleon in 5.16, singles out his penchant for defaming people.
17. Thuc. 3.36–50. Cf. Andrewes, 'The Mytilene Debate: Thucydides 3.36–49'.
18. Pylos and Sphacteria: Thuc. 4.3–23, 26–41. Delium: Thuc. 4.76–77, 89–100. Amphipolis, Mende, Scione: Thuc 4.78–88, 102–23, 129–32; 5.2–11. Cf. Isocr. 12.63. Peace of Nicias: Thuc. 5.13–25. Thucydides has a fascinating section (5.26) on himself, his history and his twenty-year exile after the fall of Amphipolis.
19. Thuc. 4.21.3; 8.65.2. Aristoph. *Knights* 191–93, 217–18, 1128. Cf. *Frogs* 423–25. Arist. *Pol.* 1294a4–38, 1304b20–1305a8, 1313b40. Isocr. 8, 122–34.
20. For examples of Athenian cruelty in the war cf. Thuc. 4.57; 5.3, 32, 116.
21. For the sufferings of Athenians in the war cf. Thuc. 2.47–55, 59 on effects of the plague and overcrowding from the influx of rural inhabitants. For the moral impact cf. 2.53. For

the ravages of the invasions cf. 2.55–57. A fragment of a speech of Andocides (frg. 4 Blass) gives a flavour of the resentment against those crowding into the city from the country.
22. Thuc. 3.81–84.
23. Several plays of Aristophanes, notably the *Knights, Wasps* and *Acharnians*, highlight a generation gap and the frivolities of the young. Cf. Forrest, 'An Athenian Generation Gap'. Ostwald, *Popular Sovereignty,* 229ff. Connor, *New Politicians,* 146–47.
24. Eur. *Supp.* 232–37. Callicles in Plato's *Gorgias* (esp. 483–84c) exemplifies the political outlook of the highbrows of the new generation. Cf. Thuc. 6.89.3–6.
25. Thuc. 2.37.5. Soph. *Antigone* 454ff. Cf. Aeschyl. *Supp.* 241–42, *Eum.* 576. Arist. *Rhet.* 1368b7, 1373b4. Dem. 18.275. These views of the source of true law, extending from Hesiod to Demosthenes, represent the origin of the theory of natural law developed by the Stoics and given eloquent expression in Cicero's *De Republica*. Cf. Guthrie, *Sophists,* ch. 4. Ostwald, *Popular Sovereignty,* 250–73.
26. Plato *Theaet.* 166d, 167c. Xen. *Mem.* 1.2.40–46.
27. Plato *Rep.* 338c–354c; *Gorg.* 482c–484c. Antiphon frg. 44ADK.
28. Aristoph. *Clouds* 1075–78. The power of *physis* is forcibly affirmed in Eur. *Electra* (esp. 939ff.) and in Thuc. 3.82.2, 84.2. For suspicion of the Sophists cf. Plato *Prot.* 316c–d. Plut. *Per.* 4.1–2; *Them.* 4.2. Aristophanes brought together in the *Clouds* all the prejudices that surrounded the Sophists. Cleon's speech in the Mytilenian debate played on popular prejudice against intellectuals.
29. Thuc. 2.53.1, 65.10–11; 3.82, 84.2. Cf. de Ste Croix, *Ath. Dem. Origins,* 11ff.
30. Thuc. 1.73–78.
31. Thuc. 3.37–48. Cf. Ostwald, *Popular Sovereignty,* 307–8.
32. Thuc. 5.43, 52; 6.15, 89; 8.86. Plut. *Alc.* 1–12, 16. Argos initiative: Thuc. 5.45–47, 52, 61.1, 76, 84.1. Plut. *Alc.* 14–15.
33. Plut. *Alc.* 14.2–9; *Nic.* 10.3–8. Hyperbolus: Plut. *Alc.* 13.3–5; *Nic.* 11. Thuc. 8.73.3. Cf. Arist. *Pol.* 1284b23. Cf. Rhodes, 'The Ostracism of Hyperbolus', which argues for dating the ostracism to early 415.
34. Thuc. 5.84–114, 116. Plut. *Alc.* 16.5. Isocr. 16.1.49. Ps. Andoc. 4.22–23. Cf. de Romilly, *Thuc. and Ath. Imp.,* trans. P. Thody, 273–74. Amit, 'The Melian Dialogue and History'. Ostwald, *Popular Sovereignty,* 305–12. Hornblower, *Commentary on Thucydides,* vol. 3, 216–56, which has a thorough discussion of the incident with an extensive bibliography. Thuc. 5.116.3 indicates that treachery from inside played a part in the Athenian capture of the city. Athens clearly had sympathisers among the Melians. Cf. 5.84.3–85.1.
35. Thuc. 6.1–32. Plut. *Alc.* 17–20; *Nic.* 12. Cf. Meiggs, *Ath. Emp.,* 344–50, 375–403. J. Finley, *Thucydides,* ch. 6. Kagan, *The Peace of Nicias and the Sicilian Expedition.*
36. The polarisation has been well described by Ostwald, *Popular Sovereignty,* ch. 5, with extensive references. He also examines the evidence of the dramatists.
37. Thuc. 6.27–29, 53–61. Plut. *Alc.* 18.3–20.1. Andoc. 1 (sections 1–33 deal with the profanation of the Mysteries, sections 34–70 with the mutilation of the herms; cf. esp. sections 48–66; cf. also 2.2, 7, 10). Ostwald, *Popular Sovereignty,* App. C, has assembled all the evidence for those involved in the conspiracy and their backgrounds and associations. Cf. also an important article by Osborne, *Athens and Athenian Democracy,* 341–67.
38. Andoc. 1.61; 2.7, 10. Thuc. 6.28.2, 60.1.
39. Thuc. 7.1–16, 31–87.
40. Thuc. 7.28.3, 8.1–2, 4. Decelea: 7.19.1–2, 27–29; 8.69.1–2. Cf. Kagan, *The Fall of the Athenian Empire,* whose interpretation of the evidence differs occasionally from mine.
41. Thuc. 8.6–44. For a good account of the Ionian War cf. Meiggs, *Ath. Emp.,* ch. 20. For an interesting analysis of the role of Alcibiades in the events leading to the coup of 411 cf. Rhodes, 'Thucydides and Alcibiades'.
42. Thuc. 8.47–48, 54.4. Friendship and politics: Plut. *Arist.* 2.4–5; *Moralia* 806f–807d. Xen. *Mem.* 24.6–7. Cf. Calhoun, *Athenian Clubs.* Connor, *New Politicians,* chs 2–3.
43. Thuc. 3.82.5–6. Hdt. 5.66, 71. Plut. *Per.* 11.1, 14.2; *Nic.* 11.4; *Alc.* 13.4. Ps. Andoc. 4.4.
44. Thuc. 8.65–68. Arist. *Ath. Pol.* 29.5 has a somewhat different version. Cf. Rhodes, *Com. Ath. Pol.,* 380ff. *Ath. Pol.* 29.5 and Lys. 20.16 indicate the body of the Five Thousand was intended to assume the functions of the Assembly and provide the magistrates. Thuc.

8.66 describes the degree to which the *demos* was cowed and fearful of saying or doing anything. The absence of the fleet at Samos would have meant the absence of large numbers of thetes, and an Assembly more amenable to persuasion by Peisander.

45. Antiphon: Thuc. 8.68, 90.1–2. Aristoph. *Wasps* 1301–3. Very little can be known with certainty about his life or writings. Cf. Guthrie, *Sophists*, 285–94. Phrynichus: Thuc. 8.27, 50–51, 68.2. Plut. *Alc.* 25.5–10. Theramenes: Thuc. 8.68.4, 89.2, 92.9. Arist. *Ath. Pol.* 28.5, 32.2. For all three cf. Ostwald, *Popular Sovereignty,* 359–367. Kerferd (ed.), *The Sophists and their Legacy.* Gagarin, *Antiphon the Athenian.*

46. Thuc. 8.65.3, 97.1. Isocr. 7.16–60 provides a detailed fourth-century decription of how admirers of the *patrios politeia* of Solon and Cleisthenes viewed the system. Informative modern discussions can be found in Fuks, *Ancestral Constitution* and Finley, *Ancestral Constitution.* Hansen, *Ath. Dem.,* 296ff.

47. Thuc. 8.70–76, 81–82.

48. Cf. above, pp. 83–85. Thuc. 8.89–97. Arist. *Ath. Pol.* 29–33. Diod. 13.38.2, 42.2.

49. The main sources for the final period of the war are: Xen. *Hell.* bks 1–2, Diod. bks 13–14, and references in the fourth-century orators. For law of Demophantus cf. Andoc. 1.96–98.

50. Xen. *Hell.* 1.5, 6.24–7.35. Plut. *Alc.* 35.2–36.3. Diod. 13.73–74, 97–100. Thuc. 6.15.4 has an interesting comment on the suspicions Athenians developed about Alcibiades, and their ruinous consequences. For Cleophon cf. Arist. *Ath. Pol.* 34.1. Finley, 'Athenian Demagogues', 11, has pointed out that, in the last decade of the Peloponnesian War, the entire rural population had to move to the city. This brought to Athens a large displaced and disgruntled population with the time and opportunity to attend the Assembly. This may account in part for the unusually volatile behaviour of the Assembly in this period.

51. Xen. *Hell.* 2.1.17–2.23. Diod. 13.107; 14.3.2. Lys. 13.14. Andoc. 3.11–12, 39. Plut. *Lys.* 15.1. Arist. *Ath. Pol.* 34.3.

52. Arist. *Ath. Pol.* 34.3–35.1. Xen. *Hell.* 2.3.1–2, 11–14. Lys. 12.43–44, 48. Diod. 14.4. Cf. Ostwald, *Popular Sovereignty,* 475–87. Whitehead, 'Sparta and the Thirty Tyrants'.

53. For Critias cf. Plato *Prot.* 316a; *Char.* 153c; *Critias passim.* Xen. *Mem.* 1.2.12–16, 24–39; *Hell.* 2.3.15–19. Aesch. 1.173. For his involvement in the affair of the herms cf. Andoc. 1.47. Lys. 12.43–44 records his appointment as one of the Ephors. Cf. Guthrie, *Sophists,* 298–304.

54. Arist. *Ath. Pol.* 35–38. Xen. *Hell.* 2.3.15–4.38. Diod. 14.32–33.

55. The role of Persia in the defeat of Athens must not be underestimated. The funding of Lysander's fleet was clearly of enormous importance. Cf. Kagan, *The Fall of the Athenian Empire.*

Chapter 6

1. Terms and views of the settlement: Arist. *Ath. Pol.* 38–40. Xen. *Hell.* 2.4.38–42. Andoc. 1.81, 89–91, 140. Dem. 20.11–12. Lys. 25.27–28. Isocr. 18.34, 42–46. Cf. Ostwald, *Popular Sovereignty,* 497–500.

2. Arist. *Ath. Pol.* 34.3; 38.3–4. Archinus: Dem. 24.135. Aesch. 2.176; 3.187. Arist. *Ath. Pol.* 40.1–2. Anytus: Plato *Meno* 90a–b, 91c–92c; *Apol.* 18b, 23e. Isocr. 18.23. Cleitophon: Arist. *Ath. Pol.* 29.3. Aristoph. *Frogs* 967. Plato *Clit.* 406, 410. Phormisius: Aristoph. *Frogs* 965. Dion. Hal. *Lysias* 32. Ostwald, *Popular Sovereignty,* 472ff., has profiles of all four.

3. For the earlier career of Thrasybulus and sources cf. above, pp. 174–75, 179, 188. For his role under the Thirty and at Phyle and the Piraeus cf. Xen. *Hell.* 2.3.42–44, 2.4.2–42; 3.5.16. Diod. 14.32.

4. Lys. 34.1. Isocr. 8.108.

5. Arist. *Ath. Pol.* 40.1–4. Cf. Rhodes, *Com. Ath. Pol.,* 477–78. Isocr. 7.67. Proposal of Phormisius: Dion. Hal. *Lys.* 32. Lys. 34. Eleusis: Xen. *Hell.* 2.4.43. Arist. *Ath. Pol.* 40.4.

6. The main evidence for the trial and the life of Socrates is the *Apology,* written by Plato, who was present at the trial. It recounts the defence of his life and actions by Socrates. Xenophon, who was on the fringes of the Socratic circle, provides further evidence in

four works, the *Oeconomicus, Apologia, Symposium* and *Memorabilia.* Plato *Apol.* 28d–e refers to Socrates' military service, 31c–d to his absence from the Assembly, 32b to the debate after Arginusae. Socrates also risked his life when ordered by the Thirty to arrest a man they wanted to kill. He went home instead of obeying. Plato *Apol.* 32c.

7. Cic. *Tusc.* 5.4.10; *Acad.* 1.15; *Brut.* 30–31.

8. Plato, *Apol.* 21–23c, 29d–30b, 33b. Xen. *Mem.* 1.2–4. Socrates compares his life to that of a midwife, an art his mother practised, in Plato *Theaet.* 149a–151d. He denies charging fees in Plato *Apol.* 18d.

9. Socrates alludes to the *Clouds* in Plato *Apol.* 19c. Cf. 18b–d. Aesch. 1.173 describes him as a Sophist. Xenophon gives the reasons why Socrates had no interest in the natural sciences in *Mem.* 1.1.11–15. References to his physical appearance abound in Xenophon and Plato. Cf. Xen. *Symp.* 2.18. Plato, *Symp.* 2115b–e. Cf. Guthrie, *Socrates,* 66ff.

10. Plato *Apol.* 29d–30b, 38a.

11. Xen. *Mem.* 1.1.1. Plato *Apol.* 24b–c. References to the *daimonion* occur frequently in Plato and Xenophon. Cf. Plato *Apol.* 31c–d, 40a–c; *Rep.* 496c; *Euthypho* 3b; *Theaet.* 151. Xen. *Symp.* 8.5; *Mem.* 4.8.5; *Apol.* 4.

12. Plato *Apol.* 23c, 33d–34a. Xen. *Mem.* 1.2.48. For disciples of Socrates implicated in the affairs of the herms cf. Ostwald, *Popular Sovereignty,* 539–49.

13. Anytus: Plato *Meno.* 91c–92d; *Apol.* 29c. Aesch. 1.173.

14. Xen. *Mem.* 1.2.9. Cf. *Mem.* 3.9.10. For his opinion of the Assembly cf. Xen. *Mem.* 3.7.6. On the proposed penalty cf. Plato *Apol.* 36b–38b. Xen. *Apol.* 23. Diogenes Laertius (2.38) says that the *demos* repented of its decision, and that Anytus was forced to leave Athens.

15. The trial of Socrates remains a subject of intense debate. For recent contributions on opposing sides cf. Stone, *Trial of Socrates,* and Cartledge, *Ancient Greek Political Thought in Practice,* 76–90.

16. Thuc. 8.97, 1–2. Interim government arrangements recounted by Andoc. 1.81–82. Cf. Xen. *Hell.* 2.4.43. For the work of the *anagrapheis* cf. Lys. 30.2, 25, 28–29. Lysias was prosecuting Nicomachus on the grounds that he refused to submit to an audit. He had been an *anagrapheus* from 410–04, and was reappointed in 403. It is clear that assembling the code was a major task.

17. There was a recognition that the whole body of law needed revision. Cf. Arist. *Ath. Pol.* 35.2. Lys. 10.16–20. Andoc. 1.82. Hansen, *Ath. Dem.,* 162ff.

18. Andoc. 82–89. Cf. MacDowell, 'Law-Making at Athens in the Fourth Century B.C.' Harrison, 'Law-Making at Athens at the End of the Fifth Century B.C.' Ostwald, *Popular Sovereignty,* 513–24. Questions have been raised about the reliability of Andocides as a source for the legislation. Cf. Carawan, *The Athenian Amnesty.*

19. Dem. 20.89–99; 24.17–27, 30, 33, 42–43. Aesch. 3.38–40. Cf. MacDowell, 'Law-Making at Athens in the Fourth Century B.C.', 63–65. For the new measure outlawing proposals contrary to existing laws or proposals disadvantageous to the state cf. Dem. 24.33. Arist. *Ath. Pol.* 59.2. Rhodes, *Com. Ath. Pol.,* 545, 660.

20. On abolition of pay by the Four Hundred and Five Thousand cf. Arist. *Ath. Pol.* 29.5, 33.1. Thuc. 8.97. Xen. *Hell.* 1.1.19–23 describes benefits of victories in the Hellespont. For Cleophon and the dole cf. Arist. *Ath. Pol.* 28.3. Arist. *Ath. Pol.* 41.3 records introduction of Assembly pay, and 62.2 records pay for members of the Council and jurors. Hansen questions whether pay for ordinary offices was ever restored (*Ath. Dem.,* 241), but Aristotle's references to pay for public office as a basic characteristic of democracy and the reason the poor are eager to hold office continuously hardly leave room for doubt. Cf. *Pol.* 1279a13–14, 1309a4–7, 1317b35–37.

21. Cf. above, pp. 28–30, 67–68. Eur. *Supp.* 430–35.

22. Hansen, 'Did the Athenian *Ecclesia* Legislate after 403/2?'. 'Initiative and Decision: The Separation of Powers in Fourth-Century Athens'. Cf. *Ath. Dem.,* 151–55, 300–4. For different views cf. Gomme, *More Essays in Greek History and Literature,* 177–93. MacDowell, 'Law-Making at Athens in the Fourth Century B.C.' Rhodes, 'Nomothesia in Fourth-Century Athens'.

23. Dem. 24.24, 37. Arist. *Ath. Pol.* 41.2; *Pol.* 1274a6–12, 1293a1–12, 1298a32–35, 1298b15–18.

Chapter 7

1. There has been a persistent tendency to view the fifth century as the era of the democracy's greatest achievement and the fourth century as an era of decline. This view has rightly been challenged, notably by Walter Eder, cf. *Democracy 2500?*, 115–21, and *Die athenische Demokratie im 4. Jahrhundert v. Chr.*, 11–28. Cf. also Rhodes, 'Athenian Democracy after 403 B.C.'

2. Arist. *Ath. Pol.* 43.2–49. Cf. Rhodes, *Com. Ath. Pol.*, 510–72; *Boule*, 212.

3. Arist. *Pol.* 1274a15–18, 1281b33–35. Thuc. 6.53–60.

4. Arist. *Ath. Pol.* 8.4. For the Heliaia cf. Arist. *Ath. Pol.* 9.1. Rhodes, *Com. Ath. Pol.*, 160–61. Ostwald, *Popular Sovereignty*, 9–12, 30–37.

5. Reforms of Ephialtes: Arist. *Ath. Pol.* 25.2. Plut. *Cim.* 15.2. Cf. Rhodes, *Boule*, 201–15. Ostwald, *Popular Sovereignty*, 50–62.

6. Solon and *eisangelia*: Arist. *Ath. Pol.* 8.4. For *eisangelia* in fifth and fourth centuries cf. esp. Arist. *Ath. Pol.* 43.4, 45.2. Hyper. 4.7–8. Isocr. 15.314; 16.6. Harpocration s.v. *eisangelia*. Further evidence comes from records of individual cases. The subject has been well studied. Cf. Ostwald, *Popular Sovereignty*, 51–55 and Appendix A, 525–27. Hansen, *Eisangelia*. Rhodes, 'Eisangelia in Athens'; *Boule*, 162–71. Harrison, *Law of Athens*, 2.50–59. For the frequent use, and possible abuse, of *eisangelia* cf. Dem. 4.47. Hansen, *Ath. Dem.*, 216–18 counts 130 prosecutions between 492 and 322, thirty-four of them against generals.

7. Arist. *Ath. Pol.* 44.2–3. Cf. Rhodes, *Boule*, 25–28.

8. Arist. *Pol.* 1322b12–18. Gomme, *More Essays in Greek History and Literature*, 185–86, estimates that 'a quarter to a third of citizens over thirty at any one time had had such political experience as membership of the Council gave'. Cf. Rhodes, *Boule*, 214–15. Ober, *Mass and Elite*, 140; *Democracy and Knowledge*, 142–55.

9. Arist. *Ath. Pol.* 35.2. Andoc. 1.84. Isocr. 7.37–42. Lyc. 1.52.

10. For *apophasis* cf. Dem. 18.133–34. Din. 1.3.51, 54–58, 2.20. Wallace, *Areopagus*, 198ff. Harrison, *Law of Athens*, 2.105. Hansen, *Eisangelia*, 39–40. Rhodes, 'Athenian Democracy after 403 B.C.', 319–20. Decree of Demosthenes: Din. 1.62.3. Law of Demophantus: Andoc. 1.95–98.

11. Arist. *Ath. Pol.* 24.3. Cf. Hansen, 'Seven Hundred *Archai* in Classical Athens'.

12. The main source for magistrates, their selection and duties, is Arist. *Ath. Pol.* 44.4, 51–62. Cf. Arist. *Pol.* 1321b4–1323a10. Aesch. 3.13. Arist. *Ath. Pol.* 7.4. and 47.1 show that the property qualification for office had become a dead letter. Overall evidence suggests office attracted the lower classes. Cf. Ps. Xen. 1.3. Dem. 24.112; 57.25. Arist. *Pol.* 1279a13–14. Jones, *Ath. Dem.*, 104. On the magistrates in general cf. Hansen *Ath. Dem.*, 225–45.

13. Ps. Xen. 1.19–20, 2.1. Xen. *Hipparchicus passim*; *Mem.* 3.21ff. Cf. Jones, *Ath. Dem.*, 99–100. For Ephebes cf. Arist. *Ath. Pol.* 42.2, 53.4. Pélékides, *Histoire de l'éphébie attique*.

14. Mercenaries in fifth century: Thuc. 1.121.3, 143.1; 7.27.29. Mercenaries in fourth century: Dem. 4.19–29. Pritchett, *Greek State at War II*, esp. chs 3 and 4. Jones, *Ath. Dem.*, 30–32. Arist. *Pol.* 1297a10–12 says the poor are willing enough to fight when properly fed.

15. Arist. *Ath. Pol.* 61. Plut. *Phoc.* 7.8. Dem. 4.26.

16. Arist. *Pol.* 1305a10–15. Aesch. 3.146, 229. Isocr. 8.54–55. Cf. Hansen, *Ath. Dem.*, 269–70. Perlman, 'The Politician in the Athenian Democracy of the Fourth Century B.C.' Jones, *Ath. Dem.*, 128. Rhodes, 'Athenian Democracy after 403 B.C.', 314–15.

17. Xen. *Hell.* 2.2.2; *Anab.* 7.1.27. Plut. *Lys.* 2–3. Thuc. 2.13.2–5. Cf. Meiggs, *Ath. Emp.*, 255–72. Strauss, *Athens after Pelop. War*, 42ff. Pritchard, Costing Greek Festivals and War.

18. Ps. Xen. 1.16–18, 2.7. Thuc. 2.38. Isocr. 8.20–21. Cf. Andoc. 1.133–34. Xen. *Poroi* 4. Meiggs, *Ath. Emp.*, 255–57. Strauss, *Athens after Pelop. War*, 50–51.

19. Decelea: Thuc. 7.27. Cf. Lys. 7.6–7. Xen. *Poroi* 4.

20. Andoc. 1.88. Xen. *Poroi* 4.19. Lys. 19.11; 27.1–3; 30.22. Dem. 8.26, 10.37–38, 19.89, 24.96–97. Cf. Jones, *Ath. Dem.*, 9–10, 30–33. For the recovery cf. Sealey, *Demosthenes*, 116ff.

21. *Merismos* IG II² 29, 18–22. Cf. Rhodes, 'Athenian Democracy after 403 B.C.', 310. Also Rhodes and Osborne (eds), *Greek Historical Inscriptions 404–323 B.C.*, 19.

22. Thuc. 3.19.1 records the first *eisphora*, which raised 200 talents. Cf. Meiggs, *Ath. Emp.*, 318 and note 4.
23. For the costs of the trierarchy cf. Lys. 21.1-2; 32.24, 26-27. Dem. 21, 154-55. Antidosis: Arist. *Ath. Pol.* 56.3, 61.1. Dem. 21.80; 42.1, 19. Lys. 4.1; 24.9. Isocr. 15.5, 144-45. Cf. 8.128. Gabrielson, 'The Naukrarii and the Athenian Navy'.
24. Periander's Law: Dem. 14.16-17; 18.102-4; 21.154-55; 47.21-22, 44. Cf. Gabrielson, *Financing the Athenian Fleet*, 212ff. Rhodes, *Com. Ath. Pol.*, 680. Davies (*Wealth and the Power of Wealth*, 9-14, 28-35) reckons this top tier had a capital worth of 3-4 talents. But there were those who had far more, up to 15 talents. Dem. 27.7-9; 28.11; 29.59. Cf. Jones, *Ath. Dem.*, 57.
25. Jones (*Ath. Dem.*, 56-57) has collected instances of a generous level of volunteering. Cf. Isocr. 15.145. Lys. 21.2-6; 19.29. Dem. 21, 154. Lyc. *Leoc.* 139. In his speech on symmories (14.14-17) Demosthenes proposed expanding the register of 1,200 to two thousand. Cf. Liddel, *Civic Obligation*, 270-74.
26. Evidence of resort to the *eisphora* in 390s and 380s in Isocr. 17.41. Lys. 28.3-4. Aristoph. *Eccl.* 197-98, 779-83. Cf. Strauss, *Athens after Pelop. War*, 140, 152. For system of collection cf. Philoch. frg. 41. Dem. 18.103-4; 21.153, 157; 22.44; 42.25. Jones, *Ath. Dem.*, 23-32. De Ste Croix, 'Demosthenes' *timema* and the Athenian *eisphora* in the Fourth Century B.C.' Rhodes, 'Athenian Democracy after 403 B.C.', 311. Thomsen, *Eisphora*.
27. Davies, *Wealth and the Power of Wealth*, 9-37. Dem. 22.65; 24.111, 172. For the ethos of all contributing cf. Dem. 1.20; 2.31. Jones, *Ath. Dem.*, 28-29.
28. Dem. 3.4; 14.19, 27; 22.44; 27.37. Cf. Polyb. 2.62.7. Meiggs, *Athenian Empire*, 257. Jones, *Ath. Dem.*, 29.
29. Plut. *Phoc.* 1.2. Dem. 18, 312; 21.161-62. Isaeus 5.37-38. Din. 1.80.
30. For Pericles and the *theorikon* cf. Plut. *Per.* 9.1-3. For the Theoric Fund of the fourth century cf. Arist. *Ath. Pol.* 43.1; 47.2. Aesch. 3.24-25. Dem. 1.19-20; 3.11; 10.35-45; 13.2. Rhodes. *Com. Ath. Pol.*, 514-15; *Boule*, 105-8. Sealey, *Demosthenes*, App.6. Jones, *Ath. Dem.*, 33-35.
31. It is unclear what office Lycurgus held. The position described by Hyperides (frg. 118) is nowhere mentioned as an office in Arist. *Ath. Pol.* Cf. Rhodes, *Boule*, 107-8. Jones, *Ath. Dem.*, 129-30. Sealey, *Demosthenes*, 209.
32. Arist. *Pol.* 1317a40-1319b32. Theophrastus, *Characters*, 26.1-2.
33. For expansion of role of *dikasteria* cf. Arist. *Ath. Pol.* 3.5; 41.2. Rhodes, *Com. Ath. Pol.*, 318. Holding politicians to account: Dem. 18.250; 24.192-93. Cf. Lys. 25.27. Hyper. 4.27. Aristophon claimed he had been indicted seventy-five times (Aesch. 3.194). Cf. Ober, *Mass and Elite*, 327-28. Hansen, *Ath. Dem.*, 208.
34. Ps. Xen. 3.2 refers to the litigious character of the Athenians. For the number of court days cf. Hansen, 'How Often Did the Athenian *Dikasteria* Meet?'
35. Arist. *Ath. Pol.* 62.2 records jurors' pay; 63.3 their qualifications; 53.3 and 68.1 the size of juries. Cf. Dem. 24.9. Andoc. 1.17. Rhodes, *Com. Ath. Pol.*, 728-29. Hansen, *Ath. Dem.*, 186-89. Arist. *Pol.* 1268b10-17 states jurors did not deliberate among themselves.
36. Arist. *Ath. Pol.* 24.3 records a panel of six thousand. Heliastic Oath: Dem. 24.149. Arist. *Pol.* 1287a25-30 approves the idea that, where the law is unclear, jurors should decide in accordance with what seems right.
37. Arist. *Ath. Pol.* 63-69. The complicated procedure is well described by Rhodes, 'Athenian Democracy after 403 B.C.', 318-19. Cf. *Com. Ath. Pol.*, 697-735. Harrison, *Law of Athens*, 2.44ff. Todd, *Shape of Athenian Law*, 83ff. Dow, 'Aristotle, the Kleroteria and the Courts'.
38. *Synegoroi* and *logographoi*: Dem. 32.32; 58.19; 59.14. Aesch. 1.94. Isocr. 15.36-38. Cf. Todd, *Shape of Athenian Law*, 95-96. Hansen, *Ath. Dem.*, 194. Rhodes, 'Athenian Democracy after 403 B.C.', 315.
39. Arbitrators: Arist. *Ath. Pol.* 53.2. Dem. 47.12. Harrison, *Law of Athens*, 2.65ff. Rhodes, 'Athenian Democracy after 403 B.C.', 316. *Anakrisis*: Dem. 58.8. Role of magistrates: Todd, *Shape of Athenian Law*, 79. Citizens as prosecutors: Lyc. 1.3-6. Dem. 59.104.
40. Sycophants: Dem. 53.1-2; 58.12-13. Isocr. 15.313-15. Lys. 13.67-68; 18.9; 25.3. Cf. Aristoph. *Birds* 1410-69; *Eccl.* 460, 561; *Plut.* 850-958. Hansen, *Ath. Dem.*, 194-95. Osborne, *Essays in Athenian Law*, 83-102, reprinted with new endnote in Osborne,

Athens and Athenian Democracy, 205–28. Osborne disagrees with the standard negative view of sycophants, and argues that they were a necessary part of the democratic legal system.

41. Cf. above, ch. 6, note 22.
42. *Demos plethuon*: IG I³, 105. Cf. Ostwald, *Popular Sovereignty*, 32–34. For power of the Assembly in a democracy cf. Arist. *Pol.* 1275a20–25, 1317a40–1317b30.
43. Din. 1.84; 3.1, 19. Dem. 21.193–94, 214–16; 22.10. 24.149, 154–56; 25.20–22. Aesch. 2.84; 3.8. Cf. Ober, *Mass and Elite*, 144–47.
44. Arist. *Pol.* 1275a20–35, 1317b25–28; Arist. *Ath. Pol.* 41.2.
45. Rhodes, 'Athenian Democracy after 403 B.C.', 306. Hansen, *Ath. Dem.*, 176; 'Did the Athenian *Ecclesia* Legislate after 403/2?' Two recently discovered laws show how carefully new laws were drafted, with great attention to detail – a law on silver coinage (375/4) and a grain tax law (374/3). Cf. Rhodes and Osborne (eds), *Greek Historical Inscriptions 404–323 B.C.*
46. Aristotle considered pay for attending the Assembly and courts a particular trait of radical democracy, ensuring the poor would attend and dominate. *Pol.* 1297a35–37, 1298b13–20. For the Pnyx cf. Thompson, 'The Pnyx in Models'. Forsén and Stanton (eds), *The Pynx in the History of Athens*.
47. Arist. *Ath. Pol.* 43.3–6, 61.2. Cf. Rhodes, *Com. Ath. Pol.*, 520–31. Hansen, *Ath. Dem.*, 133–49.
48. Oligarchs in 411 claimed the numbers attending the Assembly were below five thousand (Thuc. 8.72), but it suited their purpose to minimise the attendance. Cf. Aristoph. *Eccl.* 303–10. *Plut.* 329–30. Cf. Hansen, *Ath. Dem.*, 130–32. Ober, *Mass and Elite*, 132–38.
49. Cf. Thuc. 2.65.4, 8–10; 8.1.1, 4. Arist. *Pol.* 1279b29–30, 1280a1–6, 1317b7–10.
50. *Ho boulomonos*: Dem. 13.11; 18.170; 24.23. Aesch. 2.65. Andoc. 1.23.
51. Cf. above, note 33. Ober, *Mass and Elite*, 106–18. Roberts, *Accountability in Athenian Government*.
52. Hansen, 'The Number of Rhetores in the Athenian Ekklesia, 355–322'. Cf. Davies, *Athenian Propertied Families*. Ober, *Mass and Elite*, 112–18. Sealey, *Demosthenes*, 30–31.
53. Cf. above, note 16. Plut. *Phoc. passim*. Hansen, *Ath. Dem.*, 268–76, has a good discussion.
54. Hyper. 4.7–8 attests the ban on *hetaireiai*. Arist. *Pol.* 1302a talks about the relative freedom of democracies from factional strife. Aesch. 3.233 says 'the private citizen is a king in a democracy by virtue of the law and his vote'. Hell. Oxy. 1.3 alludes to broad social divides but says nothing suggesting factions or parties. For recent scholarship on parties cf. Ober, *Mass and Elite*, 121–25. Hansen, *Ath. Dem.*, 277–87. Strauss, *Athens after Pelop. War*, 4, 18, 26–30, 90. Sealey, *Demosthenes*, 33–35. Jones, *Ath. Dem.*, 130–31.

Chapter 8

1. For Plato's view on property cf. *Rep.* 416–17; *Laws* 739–40. For Solon cf. above, pp. 28–29, 31.
2. Arist. *Pol.* 1263a–1265a. Cf. *Pol.* 1266a35–1267b12, 1320a17–1320b17. Cf. above, p. 73.
3. Plut. *Cim.* 10ff. Lys. 27.10. Lyc. 1.139–40. Cf. detailed discussion of Athenian euergetism and financial obligation by Liddel, *Civic Obligation*, 94–108, 262–79. Ober, *Mass and Elite*, 226–33. The most serious threat to the wealthy in hard times may have come from trumped-up charges brought to mulct the rich. There is some evidence of such cases. Cf. Lys. 19.11; 27.1; 30.22. Hyper. 4.33–36 congratulates juries on resisting such efforts.
4. For taxation and the response to it cf. above, pp. 223–27, 264, 302, with notes. For Theoric Fund cf. Rhodes, *Com. Ath. Pol.*, 514ff. Jones, *Ath. Pol.*, 33–36. Sealey, *Demosthenes*, 256ff. Demosthenes wanted all surpluses to go to the Military Fund. Dem. 3.11. There was also a system of payment of two obols a day to those unable to work because of disability. Arist. *Ath. Pol.* 49.4. Lys. 24.4–18. Aesch. 1.103. Some resented paying taxes while the poor got hand-outs. Dem. 10.35–39; 21.101.
5. On the benefits of high birth and the Athenian readiness to empower those who proved their talent and trustworthiness cf. above, pp. 54–56, 110–13, 142–43, 238–39. Also Ober,

Mass and Elite, 115ff. For the rigours of the system of accountability cf. above, pp. 209–14, 229. Hansen, *Ath. Dem.*, 215ff. Roberts, *Accountability*.

6. Arist. *Pol.* 1253a1–40. Citizenship and participation: 1275b18–22; 1276b1–2, 20; 1278a35–38; 1283b42–43. The task of all cities is the well-being of the community: 1276b29–30, 1278b18–30. Cf. 1279a18–22. Manville, *Demokratia*, 377–99.

7. The Assembly and courts were the two great fora for citizen participation. Cf. Arist. *Pol.* 1275b15–22; *Ath. Pol.* 41.3.

8. Thuc. 2.40.2–3. For the increase in the number of inscriptions cf. Meiggs, *Athenian Empire*, 18ff. For the importance of a well-informed *demos* cf. Thuc. 2.40.2–3. Arist. *Pol.* 1310a14–17, 1337a12–13. Madison's statement is recorded in the *Writings of James Madison*, I, ch. 18, Document 35. John Adams expresses similar sentiments in a 'Dissertation on the Canon and Fuedal Law', *Boston Gazette*, 30 Sept. 1765, when he says: 'Liberty cannot be preserved without a general knowledge among the people. . . . The preservation of the means of knowledge among the lowest ranks is of more importance to the public than all the property of all the rich men in the country. . . . Let every order and degree among the people . . . all become attentive to the grounds and principles of government. . . . Let us . . . contemplate the great examples of Greece and Rome. . . . In a word, let every sluice of knowledge be opened and set a-flowing.' Ober (*Democracy and Knowledge*) has a detailed treatment of the dispersal and aggregation of knowledge under the democracy. The amount of written information being put into the public domain in the fourth century raises the question of the level of literacy among ordinary Athenians. The evidence is scant, but it would seem that a basic literacy must be assumed given the efforts made to provide written information for the body politic. The question has attracted a lot of attention in recent decades cf. Harris, *Ancient Literacy*. Thomas, *Literacy and Orality in Ancient Greece*. Johnson and Parker (eds), *Ancient Literacies*. Missiou, *Literacy and Democracy in Fifth-Century Athens*.

9. Thuc. 2.40.1; 41.1. Isocr. *Panegyr.* 44–50; *Antid.* 295–96.

10. For guardians cf. Harrison, *Law of Athens*, 1.30–32. For *epikleroi* cf. Dem. 51.54. Diog. Laert. 5.11–16. Pomeroy, *Goddesses*, 60–62. Todd, *Shape of Athenian Law*, 228–31. Aristotle (*Pol.* 1269b14–1270a27) strongly disapproves of the law in Sparta that allowed women to own property and have large dowries and inheritances.

11. Xen. *Oec.* 35–37. Earlier in the dialogue Ischomachus had explained that the gods made men as protectors, more capable of endurance and more courageous than women, whose task is indoors and the nourishment of children (17–18, 30). Aristotle has a great deal to say about women, stressing their natural inferiority to men and the different gender roles. Cf. *Pol.* 1254b13–15, 1259a37–1260b30, 1277b22–26. There is another text, entitled *Oeconomicus*, wrongly attributed to Aristotle, which echoes many of the views of Xenophon and Aristotle. Cf. esp. bk 1, 1–4.

12. There is almost nothing in the sources about educating women other than in their domestic duties. Aristotle insists, however, that women and children must be educated with respect to the constitution. Plato favoured educating women equally with men, but in this he appears to be a lone voice. Cf. *Laws* 804d–805b. The evidence of vase-painting indicates that at least some Athenian women were literate. Cf. Too (ed.), *Education in Greek and Roman Antiquity*.

13. Thuc. 2.45.2. Arist. *Pol.* 1260a21–33. Xen. *Oec.* 14, 23ff. Soph. *Ajax* 293. Cf. 586. For the roots of Greek male *arete* cf. Jaeger, *Paideia* I, for female *arete* North, *Sophrosyne, passim*.

14. Plut. *Solon*, 20. Lys. 1, esp. 26–28. Cf. Pomeroy, *Goddesses*, 86–88. Cohen, *Law, Sexuality and Society*. Dover, *Greek Homosexuality*.

15. Xen. *Oec.* 30, 35. Lys. 1.6–14; 3.6–8. Dem. 47.34ff. Cf. Pomeroy, *Goddesses*, 79–83. Cohen, *Law, Sexuality and Society*, ch. 6. For poorer women going out to work cf. Arist. *Pol.* 1300a7–8, 1323a5–6. There is much about everyday life in Athens that cannot be known because of the dearth of information in the sources. There are good accounts in Webster, *Everyday Life in Classical Athens*, and *The World of Athens* from the Joint Association of Classical Teachers, revised by Robin Osborne.

16. Dowries: Aesch. 3.258. Plut. *Arist.* 27.4. Dem. 59.113. Pomeroy, *Goddesses*, 63–65. To obtain a divorce a wife had to lay in person a *gramma apoleipsis* before the archon. Plut.

Alc. 8.2–4. Andoc. 4.13–15. Aristotle, though wedded to the traditional Greek view of the capacities and role of women, stressed that husbands must treat their wives not like an absolute ruler (*basilikōs*), but like a constitutional statesman (*politikōs*), i.e. bound by rules. *Pol.* 1259a37–1259b10.

17. Arist. *Ath. Pol.* 56.6–7. Cf. Rhodes, *Com. Ath. Pol.*, 629–36. Women also had a significant role in religious life as priestesses in a variety of cults, and in festivals such as the Panathenaea and the Thesmophoria. Cf. Strauss, *Democracy 2500?*, 148–49. Just, *Women in Athenian Law and Life,* 23ff. The dominant place of women as central characters in Greek tragedy, generally sympathetically portrayed, is also significant evidence that women had a place of honour in Greek tradition. Pomeroy, *Goddesses,* 58–60, urges caution in evaluating this evidence. Osborne, in his collection of studies of aspects of Athenian democracy, *Athens and Athenian Democracy,* ch. 12, has an interesting thesis that the citizenship law of Pericles enhanced the status of citizen women, a change reflected in how women are represented in the iconography.

18. There are no reliable figures for the numbers of slaves in the fourth century. The census of Demetrius of Phalerum towards the end of the fourth century reportedly recorded 400,000, a figure universally agreed to be impossible. Hyperides is recorded as saying there were 150,000, a more believable figure, but it still seems too high. For the source of and trade in slaves cf. Dem. 21.48. Xen. *Poroi* 4.25. Hansen, *Ath. Pol.*, 122–23. Garlan, *Slavery in Ancient Greece,* 44ff. Finley, *Economy and Society,* 103–4.

19. For public slaves cf. Arist. *Ath. Pol.* 54.1. Scythian archers: Andoc. 3.5. Aesch. 2.173. Plato *Prot.* 319c. Aristoph. *Ach.* 54. Slaves were used as rowers only in emergencies. Cf. Meiggs, *Athenian Empire,* 439.

20. Cf. Jones, *Ath. Dem.*, 12–17. Finley, *Economy and Society,* 99–104. Nicias as slave owner: Xen. *Poroi* 4.14. But slaves by no means displaced free labour. Aristotle (*Pol.* 1291b25) lists the casual labourers (*to chernetikon*) as a separate category of the *demos*. Cf. Finley, *Economy and Society,* 97. Jones, *Ath. Dem.*, 11–12. Erechtheum workmen: cf. Randall, 'The Erechtheum Workmen'.

21. Xen. *Mem.* 2.5.2 says Nicias paid a talent for a slave overseer. There is the example of Pasion, a slave who rose in the banking business and secured his freedom – and eventually citizenship. Cf. above, p. 269.

22. Dem. 21.47–50. Ps. Xen. 1.10–12. Plato *Rep.* 563b. Arist. *Pol.* 1319b28–32. Cf. Ober, *Athenian Legacies,* 110–18. It cannot be assumed, however, that slaves were content with their lot. The fact that twenty thousand sought to make their escape during the occupation of Decelea shows how much they were prepared to risk to get away from their situation in Attica.

23. Arist. *Pol.* 1254a7–1255b15. Xen. *Mem.* 2.3.3.

24. The father of Demosthenes had two factories employing thirty-two knife-makers and twenty bed-makers. Dem. 27.9–11. Lys. (12.17–19) tells how the Thirty killed his brother Polemarchus and took seven hundred shields from their factory, and 120 slaves.

25. Jones, *Ath. Dem.*, 19. For taxation system cf. above, p. 223 and n.4, p. 328. Demosthenes (10.37–38) says that state revenues fell as low as 130 talents for a period in the fourth century when Athens was at war and indirect taxes were affected, showing how little revenue it was raising from direct taxation. The revenues only returned to a normal level of 400 talents around 340 when peace had been restored and harbour dues and other indirect taxes again increased. For the income from mining cf. Crosby, 'The Leases of the Laureion Mines'.

26. Arist. *Pol.* 1291b14–30, 1319a21–33. For those attending the Assembly cf. Xen. *Mem.* 3.7.5–7. Plato *Rep.* 565a; *Prot.* 319d. Cf. above, pp. 107–10, 237–39.

27. There is divided opinion about the importance of slavery to the stability of Athenian democracy. Cf. Jameson, 'Agriculture and Slavery in Classical Athens'. De Ste Croix, *The Class Struggle,* 141–42, 505–6. Raaflaub, *Dem. Emp. Arts,* 26–28. Wood, *Peasant-Citizen and Slave,* chs 2–3. Jones, *Ath. Dem.*, 10–20. Finley, *Ancient Slavery,* 90. Ober, *Mass and Elite,* 24–27. Hansen, *Ath. Dem.*, 317–18. Osborne, *Athens and Athenian Democracy,* ch. 5, provides an important new study of the economics and politics of slavery.

28. Diod. 18.18. Plut. *Phoc.* 25–28. Plutarch's number of twelve thousand for the disenfranchised has been rightly rejected as too low. Cf. Hansen, *Demography and Democracy*, esp. 12–40.

29. Dem. 42.22. Dion. Hal., *De Lysia*, 29–30. Lys. 19.29, 42 gives an example of land costs. Cf. Jones, *Ath. Dem.*, 142, n. 36, 143–4, n. 86. Slaves came at a cost. In *IG II–III²*, 1672 from 329 B.C. three obols a day is allowed for the food of a public slave, which comes to about 180 drachmae a year. Cf. Dem. 27.36. Lys. 32.28. The purchase price of an adult male slave could vary between 100 and 300 drachmae, depending presumably on skills and physical condition. The main evidence in inscription 79aML. Aristotle gives the strong impression that the poor did not own slaves. Cf. *Pol.* 1323a5–7. At *Pol.* 1252b12–13 he says the ox serves the poor in place of the slave. Cf. also 1300a7, which implies poor women had to go outdoors through lack of help to run their errands. Aristoph. *Plut.* 223–24 talks of poor farmers toiling in the fields themselves. Cf. the interesting study of Wood, *Peasant-Citizen and Slave.*

30. Arist. *Pol.* 1319a25. *Pol.* 1292b25–29 says that farmers of moderate means have to work for a living and have no leisure. Cf. 1318b10–14. Dem. 24.172.

31. Arist. *Pol.* 1293a5–10, 1300a1–4, 1317b32–35. Cf. Aristoph. *Eccl.* 184–87, 205. Isocr. 8.130; 15.152. Cf. Hansen, *Ath. Dem.*, 126–27. Cf. above, pp. 107–10, 237–38.

32. Whitehead, *Ideology of the Athenian Metic* provides a valuable, comprehensive study. Cf. Hansen, *Ath. Dem.*, 116–20. Strauss, *Democracy 2500?*, 149–50, has a brief but useful analysis. Cf. also Jones, *Ath. Dem.*, 10–11. Finley, *Economy and Society*, 72, 81. Kamen, *Status in Classical Athens,* 32–61.

33. Arist. *Pol.* 1275a11–15. Lysias clearly represented himself, and spoke on behalf of others. Cf. Lys. 5.1–2; 12. Xen. *Poroi* 2.1–6, 3.5 sets out his proposals to attract more metics. Ps. Xen. 1.10–12 shows there was also some resentment of metics.

34. Lys. 12, against Eratosthenes, has an extensive account of his family and himself. Cf. Plato *Rep.* 1, 1–5; *Phaedrus*, 227–28. The Olympic Oration is preserved in part by Dionysius of Halicarnassus who considered it a good example of the epideictic skills of Lysias. *De Lysia* 29–30. Diod. 14.105 adds further details. Dinarchus and Isaeus were other metics who achieved high prominence as orators. Aristotle too, of course, was a metic. For the efforts to give citizenship to all who had supported the democrats in the Piraeus, and the effort of Thrasybulus to give citizenship to Lysias cf. Arist. *Ath. Pol.* 40.2 and Rhodes, *Com. Ath. Pol.*, 474–76.

35. Pasion features in six extant speeches: Isocr. 16. Dem. 36, 45, 46, 49, 52. Cf. also Trevett, *Apollodorus, the Son of Pasion.*

36. The Athenian attitude towards naturalisation is fully discussed in M.J. Osborne, *Naturalization,* esp. ch. 4. The *ius sanguinis* remains a primary basis for citizenship in modern societies. It is also worth noting that the rights of immigrants and conditions for naturalisation are far from being internationally agreed in the modern world. In matters of citizenship states tend to guard their sovereignty jealously.

37. Cf. Hansen. *Ath. Dem.*, 156–57; *Athenian Assembly*, 183–84.

38. The main sources for the events of the late 400s and 390s are Xen. *Hell.* bks 3–4. Cf. *Anab.*, a fascinating tale in which Xenophon recounts in seven books how the Greek contigent in Cyrus' army fought its way back to the Aegean after the battle of Cunaxa, with Xenophon himself in a leading role. The papyrus known as the *Hellenica Oxyrhynchia* is a valuable source, especially for the mid-390s. Cf. Bruce, *An Historical Commentary on the Hellenica Oxyrhynchia.* Cf. also Diod. bk 14. Paus. bk 3. Strauss, *Athens after Pelop. War.* Cartledge, *Agesilaos.* Hamilton, *Sparta's Bitter Victories; Agesilaus and the Failure of Spartan Hegemony.*

39. Xen. *Hell.* 4.8.6–16. Philoch. FGrH328F14a, F149b. Andoc. 3. Dionysius of Halicarnassus doubted the authenticity of this speech, but recent modern opinion is largely agreed that it is genuine. Andocides, however, is known for his ability to tailor facts to suit his case. Cf. Strauss, *Athens after Pelop. War,* ch. 5.

40. Aristoph. *Eccles.* 105–205. Hell. Oxy. 1.2–3. Cf. Strauss, *Athens after Pelop. War*, 90, 101–4. Sealey, *Demosthenes*, 11–12.

41. Lys. 28.3-4. Xen. *Hell.* 4.8.25-5.1.36. Diod. 14.110. Dem. 19.180 says there were no places more important to Athens than Thermopylae on land and the Hellespont at sea. The Athenians also sent a squadron of ten ships to help Evagoras of Cyprus, who was in conflict with Persia, a move Xenophon (4.8.24) found inexplicable since it was certain to alienate Persia, and may have influenced the timing and terms of the King's Peace. All the ships were captured by a Spartan fleet. There are signs of waywardness in the rule of the *demos* at this point. Cf. Ryder, *Koine Eirene.*

42. Dem. 24.134-35. Lys. 26.23. Cf. Sealey, *Demosthenes*, 16. Strauss, *Athens after Pelop. War*, 159-61.

43. Xen. *Hell.* 5.2-4, 34. Diod. 14.92; 15.19-29. Plut. *Pelop.* 6; *Ages.* 24. For the size of Athenian fleet cf. Polyb. 2.72.6. Diod. 15.29.7 gives two hundred, not a believable figure. Cf. Sinclair, 'The King's Peace and the Employment of Military and Naval Forces 387-78'.

44. For the decree of Aristoteles cf. Tod *GHI* II, 123. Diod. 15.28-30. No reference to the League in Xenophon's *Hell.*, but he does refer to it in *Poroi* 5.6. Diod. 15.30.2 gives the number as seventy. Aesch. 2.70 mentions seventy-five. Cf. R.M. Kallet-Marx, 'Athens, Thebes, and the Foundation of the Second Athenian League'. Sealey, *Demosthenes*, ch. 3. Cargill, *The Second Athenian League.*

45. Dem. 18.219. Aesch. 2.124. Plut. Dem. 5.1-3. Theopompus, FGrH115F97-98.

46. Xen. *Hell.* 5.4.59-6.4.16. Xen. *Hell.* 6.2.1 mentions the failure of Thebes to pay its contributions. Diod. 15.30-50. For Timotheus cf. Isocr. 15.106-13.

47. Xen. *Hell.* 6.5.1-52. Dem. 16.4-5; 59.27.

48. Amphipolis and the Chersonese: Plut. *Per.* 19.1. Thuc. 4. 102-8. Cf. Meiggs, *Athenian. Empire*, 160.

49. Xen. *Hell.* 7.1-15. Dem. 9.16; 19. 137, 253. Ps. Dem. 7.29. Aesch. 2.32. Cf. Sealey, *Demosthenes*, 74-78.

50. Xen. *Hell.* 7.1.15-4.40 has a full narrative of events in the Peloponnesus. For the campaigns of Iphicrates and Timotheus cf. Diod. 15.78-90. Dem. 2.14; 15.9; 23.150-51. Din. 1.14. Isocr. 15.107-13. Aesch. 2.26-29, 70. Sealey, *Demosthenes*, ch. 6.

51. Xen. *Hell.* 7.5.1-27. The *Hellenica*, the only contemporary history of the period, ends with Mantinea. Cf. Diod. 15.82-89. Paus. 8.11.

52. Dem. 15.3; 23.158-62, 170-73. Diod. 16.34.

53. For the prosecutions cf. Hyper. *Euxen.* 1-2. Aesch. 2.124. Lyc. *Leoc.* 93. Sealey, *Demosthenes*, 254.

54. Dem. 22.14; 23.173; 50.4-17. Diod. 15.78-79 records the naval expedition of Epaminondas. Cf. Cawkwell, 'Epaminondas and Thebes', 270-71. For Mausolus cf. Dem. 15.3, 27.

55. Diod. 16.7.3-4, 21.1-16 provides a narrative of the war. Cf. Dem. 20.82. Cf. Cawkwell's useful article 'Notes on the Social War'. Sealey, *Demosthenes*, ch. 5.

56. Diod. 16.8.2-3. Dem. 1.8-9; 2.6. Aesch. 2.21, 70-72. Isocr. 5.2.

57. Cf. Isocr. *Areop.* 6-7, 12, 78, 81-82.

58. Cf. Thuc. 6.80.3, 82.2-3. Part of the Olympic Oration of Lysias (*Lys.* 33) survives. Isocrates returned to the theme of Philhellenism in 346 in *Oration V*, which is cast as an open letter to Philip. By then he had lost hope that Athens could lead a coalition of independent states at peace with each other against the Persian foe, and he looked to Philip to fulfil that role. Cf. *Epistles* 2 and 3. Philip's settlement after Chaeronea bears some resemblance to the vision of Isocrates.

59. Thuc. 2.8.4-5. Cf. above, pp. 136-40, 146-63.

60. It is interesting to compare the achievement of Europe over the past sixty years after it emerged from the trauma of two brutal world wars, which were the culmination of many previous cycles of conflict. Two broad alliances have brought peace, increased prosperity and a high level of security. The European Union, which now has twenty-eight members, has achieved a remarkable degree of cohesion, and continues to move towards greater political and economic integration. The North Atlantic Treaty Organisation (NATO), which is more analogous to the Athenian Second League, is a broader alliance than the EU, a defensive military alliance, which now has forty-eight members including the United States and Canada. The US is by far the most powerful

member, but there is no acknowledged *hegemon*, and the structures are designed to ensure collective decision-making. For the past sixty years NATO has provided an effective defensive shield against external threats to any of its members.

61. Aesch. 3.25. Cf. Rhodes, 'Athenian Democracy after 403 B.C.'; *Boule*, 235–40. Cawkwell, 'Eubulus'. Cf. above, pp. 271–72, 276–84.

62. Dem. 15 and 16 set out the issues in regard to the Megalopolitans and Rhodians. For Philip in Thessaly and Thrace cf. Diod. 16.30–34.

63. Aesch. 3.171–72. Plut. *Dem.* 3–13. Cf. Sealey, *Demosthenes*, 96–101, also App. 4. Worthington (ed.), *Demosthenes*. Worthington, *Demosthenes of Athens and the Fall of Classical Greece.*

64. Dem. 1–3. For the Theoric Fund cf. Dem. 3.11, 19. For Olynthus cf. Diod. 16.53. Dem. 19.263–67.

65. Evidence for the life of Aeschines comes mainly from Dem. 19 and the speeches of Aeschines himself. Cf. Harris, *Aeschines*, 7–40. For moves towards peace cf. Aesch. 2.12–19.

66. Diod. 16.59–60. Dem. 19 and Aesch. 2 provide detailed, though obviously tendentious, accounts of the embassies. Cf. Harris, *Aeschines*, chs 3–4.

67. Dem. 5.13–25; 19.128.

68. Conviction of Philocrates: Aesch. 3.79. Dem. 19.116. Din. 1.28. Hyper. *Euxen.* 29. For the trial of Aeschines and its aftermath cf. Harris, *Aeschines*, 116–23. The supporters of Aeschines are listed in Aesch. 2.184.

69. Dem. 9.72; 18.87. Aesch. 3.95–98. Schol. Aesch. 3.83. Plut. *Dem.* 17. Cf. Sealey, *Demosthenes*, 176–77.

70. Dem. 8; 9.71–73; 10.31–34, 68.

71. Diod. 16.74–76. Plut. *Phoc.* 14.3–7. Philoch. *FGrHist* 328F55, 56a. Aesch. 3.141–45, 222. Dem. 18.102–7, 211–15. Plut. *Dem.* 18.1–3. For the final overtures from Philip cf. Plut. *Dem.* 18.3–4; *Phoc.* 16. Aesch. 3.148–52. For Chaeronea cf. Diod. 16.85–88. Plut. *Dem.* 19.2–20.2. Hammond, *History of Greece*, 567–70.

72. Dem. 18.282, 287. [Demades] 'On the Twelve Years', 9–11. Nepos *Phoc.* 1. Polyb. 5.10.1–7. Diod. 16.87–88. Plut. *Phoc.* 16.3–5. Paus. 1.25, 34.

73. Diod. 16.89. Paus. 1.94. Isocr. *Epistle* 3. Polyb. 3.6.12–16. Cf. Perlman (ed.), *Philip and Athens.*

74. The evidence for the delegation led by Pytho comes mainly from [Dem.] 7, generally agreed to be the speech delivered by Hegesippus. Cf. Aesch. 3.83. Dem. 18.136. Harris, *Aeschines*, 111–14.

75. In Dem. 18.234–38 Demosthenes speaks of the weak state of Athenian military resources when he entered political life after the Social War. He boasts of how greatly he strengthened them, but Chaeronea showed how far the realities of Athenian power fell below its aspirations.

76. Decree of Stratocles: *IG* II, 457. Cf. Hyper. frg. 23. The speech of Lycurgus against Leocrates shows his power and sharp edge as an orator, and his fervent patriotism. Plut. *Dem.* 23.3 and *Phoc.* 17.2 list Lycurgus as one of the leaders Alexander wanted surrendered to him in 355. Cf. Davies, *Athenian Propertied Families*, 348–53. Will, *Athen und Alexander.*

77. Diod. 16.89–95. Plut. *Alex.* 10.4. *Dem.* 21–22. Aesch. 3.160. Theban revolt: Diod. 17.8. Plut. *Alex.* 11.3–6; *Dem.* 23. Alexander in Asia: Arrian, *Anabasis* provides the best narrative of events. Cf. Plut. *Alex.* 15–76. Diod. 17.50–18.4.

78. Diod. 18.8–11. Dem. 19.31 contemptuously describes Philip as a pestilent Macedonian who is not only not a Greek, but has no kinship with Greeks. The main source for Hyperides is a biography in Ps. Plut. *Lives of the Ten Orators*. In speech 5.20–21 his friendship with Demosthenes is mentioned. Athenaeus 8.342 says he studied under Plato and Isocrates. Phocion's opposition to the war is recorded in Plut. *Phoc.* 22.3–23.3.

79. Diod. 18.11–18. Demosthenes was not blamed for Chaeronea, and had a full part in Athenian life until the Harpalus affair. He was chosen to deliver the Funeral Oration for those who died at Chaeronea, served as commissioner on the Theoric Fund, and as commissioner for the repair of the fortifications. Dem. 18.113–19.285. Aesch. 3.17, 24,

27–32. Harpalus affair: Plut. *Dem.* 25–26. Hyper. 5. Din. 1. Diod. 17.108. Cf. Badian, 'Harpalus'.

80. Diod. 18.11–17. Plut. *Phoc.* 23–26.

81. Diod. 18.18. Plut. *Phoc.* 26–28; *Dem.* 28–30.

82. Cf. Pritchard, 'The Symbiosis between Democracy and War', in Pritchard (ed.), *War, Democracy and Culture in Classical Athens,* 1–62.

83. It should be noted that the democractic ideal did not die in 322, and there were recurring, though abortive, efforts to restore it in Athens well into the third century. Cf. Bayliss, *After Demosthenes.* Cf. also Harris, *Democracy and the Rule of Law in Classical Athens.*

Epilogue

1. Hamilton, Jay and Madison, *The Federalist* 39. Hamilton, Madison and John Jay were the authors of the influential *Federalist Papers,* seventy-seven essays, the bulk of them written by Hamilton and Madison, and published anonymously in New York papers during the debate on the Constitution at the Convention in Philadelphia in 1787. They were collected, eight more essays were added and the total of eighty-five was published in 1787–88 under the title *The Federalist. Federalist* 10, written by Madison, was especially influential and expresses views central to his thinking. Cf. Dahl, *How Democratic Is the American Constitution?,* 159–62. Dunn, *Setting the People Free,* 74–80.

2. François (Gracchus) Babeuf and Philippe Buonarroti were the great advocates of economic equality and enemies of the special interests, whom they saw as concerned only with their personal interests and indifferent to the public good. Emmanuel Sieyes, relentless foe of the nobility, published an especially influential pamphlet in 1789 entitled *Qu'est-ce le tiers état?* Robespierre's views are collected in *Discours et rapports à la convention.* Dunn, *Setting the People Free,* 92–118, has a lucid account of the main figures of the French Revolution.

3. Paine, *The Rights of Man,* 176–77.

4. The mixed constitution of Rome is described in Polyb. 6.3–19, and in Cic. *Rep.* 2.41–43, 56–61; *Leg.* 3.24, 28; *Sest.* 137. Cf. Wood, *Cicero's Social and Political Thought,* ch. 9. Mitchell, *Cicero: The Senior Statesman,* 51–56.

5. Montesquieu (1689–1775) is especially associated with the theory of the separation of powers, but the revolution of 1688 in Britain, which brought the Bill of Rights and clear division of power between monarch and parliament, together with Locke's *Second Treatise of Government,* which provided a theoretical justification for the outcome of the revolution, were perhaps more important factors in embedding the theory.

6. Cf. above, pp. 67–69. Liddel, *Civic Obligation* has a good overview in the introductory chapter of the debate about differences between ancient and modern concepts of liberty.

7. Aristotle sets out the first theoretical justification for the principle of popular sovereignty in *Pol.* 1281a40–1281b15. Cf. Dahl's theory of the *Strong Principle of Equality in Democracy and its Critics,* 97–98. Morris, *Demokratia,* 19–48. Roman Republicanism and Cicero's *De Legibus* helped further to embed the principle of the rule of law in western political thought. For countercurrents of anti-democratic thought cf. Roberts, *Athens on Trial.*

8. Cf. Fukuyama, *The End of History and the Last Man.* There is a growing belief that the experience of Athens holds lessons for modern democracy. Cf. *Demokratia,* ed. Ober and Hedrick, 1–6. *A Company of Citizens,* ed. Ober and Manville. Rhodes, *Ancient Democracy and Modern Ideology,* ch. 5. Cartledge, *Ancient Greek Political Thought in Practice,* ch. 11.

9. The sovereignty of law and its central place in society is a recurring theme in the philosophers, dramatists and orators. Notable instances are Thuc. 2.37.3. Eur. *Supp.* 429–38. Plato *Crito* 50b. Arist. *Pol.* 1282b1–14. Dem. 24.5, 75–76. Lys. 2.18–19. Aesch. 1.4. Lyc. *Leoc.* 3–6. Hyper. 4.5.

10. Cf. above, pp. 45–46, 241–43.

11. Cf. Liddel, *Civic Obligation*, esp. 96–98, 281–82. Ober, *Mass and Elite*, 199–247.
12. Syme, *Roman Revolution*, 15.
13. Schumpeter, *Capitalism, Socialism and Democracy*. Cf. esp. chs 20–23. Cf. Held, *Models of Democracy*, 177–98. Dunn, *Western Political Theory*, 17, 28.
14. Cf. Dunn, *Setting the People Free*, 164–72. Patterson, *The Vanishing Voter*. Dalton, *Democratic Challenges*. Cf. also an interesting critique of modern democracy in Micklethwait and Wooldridge, *The Fourth Revolution*.
15. *Gnōme*: Thuc. 2.65.8. Cf. Farrar, *Origins of Democratic Thinking*, esp. 158ff. It is worth noting that two of the world's greatest theorists, Plato and Aristotle, left no imprint on the politics of their day. Their only engagement with real-life politics was in tutoring two absolute rulers. Plato, towards the end of his life, was tutor to Dionysius II, tyrant of Syracuse (cf. *Epistle VII*), and Aristotle was tutor to Alexander the Great. Neither would have considered his efforts successful.
16. Arist. *Pol.* 1281a40–1281b15. Cf. above, p. 103.
17. Syme, *Roman Revolution*, 7. Michels, *Political Parties*, chs 5–9.
18. Arist. *Pol.* 1295a40, 1310a15–17, 1337a10–18. Aristotle believed that the constitution in a sense represented the way of life of the state. Cf. above, p. 106. Ober, *Democracy and Knowledge*, esp. ch. 4.
19. Cf. Lloyd, *What the Media Are Doing to our Politics*. Association of European Journalists, *Goodbye to Freedom? A Survey of Media Freedom across Europe*.
20. Arist. *Pol.* 1298a12–34. Aristotle emphasises that all the modes of popular rule that he cites are democratic (1298a34).
21. Dahl, *Democracy and its Critics*, ch. 23, esp. 338–41. Dunn, *Setting the People Free*, esp. 176–88. Farrar, *Origins of Democratic Thinking*, esp. 274–78; 'Power to the People'. Fishkin, *Democracy and Deliberation*. Elster (ed.), *Deliberative Democracy*. Papadopoulos, *Démocratie directe*. Macedo (ed.), *Deliberative Politics*. Fishkin and Laslett (eds), *Debating Deliberative Democracy*. Gutman and Thompson, *Why Deliberative Democracy?*

Bibliography

Amit, M., 'The Melian Dialogue and History', *Athenaeum*, n.s. 46 (1968), 216–35.
Andrewes, Antony, *The Greek Tyrants*. New York: Ebury Press, 1956.
——, 'The Mytilene Debate: Thucydides 3.36–49', *Phoenix* 16 (1962), 64–82.
——, 'The Opposition to Pericles', *JHS* 98 (1978), 1–8.
Annas, Julia, *An Introduction to Plato*. Oxford: Clarendon Press, 1981.
Badian, E., 'Harpalus', *JHS* 81 (1961), 16-43.
Bayliss, A.J., *After Demosthenes: The Politics of Hellenistic Athens*. London: Bloomsbury, 2011.
Berlin, Isaiah, *Four Essays on Liberty*. London and New York: Oxford University Press, 1969.
Boardman, John, *Greek Sculpture: The Archaic Period*. London: Thames and Hudson, 1978.
——, *The Greeks Overseas*. 3rd edn. London: Thames and Hudson, 1980.
——, *The Parthenon and its Sculptures*. London: Thames and Hudson, 1985.
——, *Greek Art*. 4th edn. London: Thames and Hudson, 1996.
Boedeker, Deborah, 'Presenting the Past in Fifth-Century Athens', in *Democracy, Empire, and the Arts in Fifth-Century Athens,* ed. Deborah Boedeker and K.A. Raaflaub. Cambridge, Mass.: Harvard University Press, 1998, 185–202.
——, and K.A. Raaflaub (eds), *Democracy, Empire, and the Arts in Fifth-Century Athens.* Cambridge, Mass.: Harvard University Press, 1998.
Boegehold, Alan, 'Resistance to Change in the Law at Athens', in *Demokratia: A Conversation on Democracies, Ancient and Modern*, ed. Josiah Ober and Charles Hedrick. Princeton: Princeton University Press, 1996, 203–14.
——, and Adele Scafuro (eds), *Athenian Identity and Civic Ideology*. Baltimore: Johns Hopkins University Press, 1994.
Boersma, J.S., *Athenian Policy from 561/0 to 405/4 B.C.* Groningen: Wolters-Noordhoff, 1970.
Bowra, C.M., *Greek Lyric Poetry*. 2nd edn. Oxford: Oxford University Press, 1961.
Bradeen, D.W., 'The Popularity of the Athenian Empire', *Historia* 2 (1960), 257–69.
Bruce, I.A.F., *An Historical Commentary on the Hellenica Oxyrhynchia*. Cambridge: Cambridge University Press, 1967.
Burnet, John, *Early Greek Philosophy*. 4th edn. London: A & C Black, 1948.
Calhoun, G.M., *Athenian Clubs in Politics and Litigation*. Austin, Texas: Bulletin of the University of Texas 262, 1913.
Carawan, Edwin, *The Athenian Amnesty and Reconstructing the Law*. Oxford: Oxford University Press, 2013.
Cargill, J.L., *The Second Athenian League: Empire or Free Alliance?* Berkeley: University of California Press, 1981.
Carter, L.B., *The Quiet Athenian*. Oxford: Clarendon Press, 1986.
Cartledge, P.A., *Sparta and Laconia: A Regional History, 1300–362 B.C.* London and Boston: Routledge & Kegan Paul, 1979.

——, *Agesilaos and the Crisis of Sparta*. London: Duckworth; Baltimore: Johns Hopkins University Press, 1987.

——, 'Comparatively Equal', in *Demokratia*, ed. Josiah Ober and Charles Hedrick. Princeton: Princeton University Press, 1996, 175–85.

——, 'Democracy, Origins of: Contribution to a Debate', in *Origins of Democracy in Ancient Greece*, ed. K.A. Raaflaub, Josiah Ober and R.W. Wallace. Berkeley: University of California Press, 2007, 155–69.

——, *Ancient Greek Political Thought in Practice*. Cambridge: Cambridge University Press, 2009.

Cawkwell, G.L., 'Notes on the Social War', *C&M* 23 (1962), 34–49.

——, 'Eubulus', *JHS* 83 (1963), 47–67.

——, 'Epaminondas and Thebes', *CQ*, n.s. 22 (1972), 254–78.

Cohen, David, *Law, Sexuality and Society: The Enforcement of Morals in Ancient Athens*. Cambridge: Cambridge University Press, 1991.

Connor, W.R., *The New Politicians of Fifth-Century Athens*. Princeton: Princeton University Press, 1971.

——, *Thucydides*. Princeton: Princeton University Press, 1984.

Constant, Benjamin, *Political Writings*. Cambridge: Cambridge University Press, 1988.

Crosby, Margaret, 'The Leases of the Laureion Mines', *Hesperia* 19 (1950), 189–312.

Dahl, R.A., *Democracy and its Critics*. New Haven and London: Yale University Press, 1989.

——, *How Democratic Is the American Constitution?* New Haven and London: Yale University Press, 2002.

Dalton, R.J., *Democratic Challenges, Democratic Choice: The Erosion of Political Support in Advanced Industrial Societies*. Oxford: Oxford University Press, 2004.

Davies, J.K., *Athenian Propertied Families*. Oxford: Oxford University Press, 1971.

——, *Wealth and the Power of Wealth in Classical Athens*. New York: Arno Press, 1981.

Dover, Kenneth, *Greek Homosexuality*. New York: Vintage Books, 1978.

Dow, Sterling, 'Aristotle, the Kleroteria and the Courts', *HSCP* 50 (1939), 1–34.

Dunn, John, *Western Political Theory in the Face of the Future*. 2nd edn. Cambridge: Cambridge University Press, 1993.

——, *Setting the People Free: The Story of Democracy*. London: Atlantic Books, 2005.

Eddy, S.K., 'The Cold War between Athens and Persia', *Classical Philology* 68 (1973), 241–58.

Eder, Walter, 'Aristocrats and the Coming of Athenian Democracy', in *Democracy 2500? Questions and Challenges*, ed. Ian Morris and K.A. Raaflaub. Dubuque, Iowa: Kendall Hunt, 1997.

——, ed., *Die athenische Demokratie im 4. Jahrhundert v. Chr., Vollendung oder Verfall einer Verfassungsform?* Stuttgart: Franz Steiner Verlag, 1995.

Ehrenberg, Victor, *From Solon to Socrates*. London: Methuen, 1968.

Elster, Jon (ed.), *Deliberative Democracy*. Cambridge: Cambridge University Press, 1997.

Farrar, Cynthia, *The Origins of Democratic Thinking: The Invention of Politics in Classical Athens*. Cambridge: Cambridge University Press, 1988.

——, 'Power to the People', in *Origins of Democracy in Ancient Greece*, ed. K.A. Raaflaub, Josiah Ober and R.W. Wallace. Berkeley: University of California Press, 2007, 170–95.

Finley, J.H., *Thucydides*. Ann Arbor: University of Michigan Press, 1963.

Finley, M.I., 'Athenian Demagogues', *Past and Present* 21 (1962), 3–24.

——, *The Ancestral Constitution*. Cambridge: Cambridge University Press, 1971.

——, Introduction to *Thucydides: History of the Peloponnesian War.*, tr. Rex Warner, rev. edn. London: Penguin Books, 1972.

——, *The Ancient Economy*. London: Chatto & Windus, 1973.

——, *Early Greece: The Bronze and Archaic Ages*. 2nd edn. London: Chatto & Windus, 1977.

——, 'The Fifth-Century Athenian Empire: A Balance Sheet', in *Imperialism in the Ancient World*, ed. P.D.A. Garnsey and C.R. Whittaker. Cambridge: Cambridge University Press, 1978, 103–26.

——, *The World of Odysseus*. 2nd edn. London: Chatto & Windus, 1980.

——, *Economy and Society in Ancient Greece*, ed. Brent Shaw and Richard Saller. London: Chatto & Windus, 1981.

——, *Democracy, Ancient and Modern*. 2nd edn. New Brunswick: Rutgers University Press, 1985.

Fisher, N.R.E., *Hybris: A Study in the Values of Honour and Shame in Ancient Greece*. Warminster, UK: Aris & Phillips, 1992.

Fishkin, J.S., *Democracy and Deliberation: New Directions for Democratic Reform*. New Haven: Yale University Press, 1991.

——, and Peter Laslett (eds), *Debating Deliberative Democracy*. Oxford: Blackwell, 2003.

Fornara, C.W., *Archaic Times to the End of the Peloponnesian War*. 2nd edn. Cambridge: Cambridge University Press, 1983.

Forrest, W.G., *The Emergence of Greek Democracy 800–400 B.C.* New York and Toronto: McGraw Hill, 1966.

——, *History of Sparta, 950–192 B.C.* London: Hutchinson, 1968.

——, 'An Athenian Generation Gap', *Yale Class. St.* 24 (1975), 37–52.

Forsdyke, Sara, *Exile, Ostracism and Democracy: The Politics of Expulsion in Ancient Greece*. Princeton: Princeton University Press, 2005.

Francis, E.D., *Image and Idea in Fifth-Century Greece: Art and Literature after the Persian Wars*. London: Routledge, 1990.

Frisch, Hartvig, *The Constitution of the Athenians*. New York: Arno Press, 1976.

Fuks, Alexander, *The Ancestral Constitution: Four Studies in Athenian Politics at the End of the Fifth Century B.C.* London: Routledge & Kegan Paul, 1953.

Fukuyama, Francis, *The End of History and the Last Man*. Harmondsworth: Penguin, 1992.

Fustel de Coulanges, Numa-Denis, *The Ancient City*, 4th edn. Tr. Willard Small. Boson: Lee and Shephard, 1882.

Gabrielson, Vincent, 'The Naukrarii and the Athenian Navy', *C&M* 38 (1985), 21–51.

——, *Financing the Athenian Fleet: Public Taxation and Social Relations*. Baltimore: Johns Hopkins University Press, 1994.

Gagarin, M., *Antiphon the Athenian: Oratory, Law and Justice in the Age of the Sophists*. Austin: University of Texas Press, 2002.

Garlan, Yvon, *Slavery in Ancient Greece*. Trans. Janet Lloyd. Ithaca, NY: Cornell University Press, 1988.

Garland, Robert, *The Piraeus from the Fifth to the First Century B.C.* Ithaca, NY: Cornell University Press, 1987.

Garnsey, P.D.A., and C.R. Whittaker (eds), *Imperialism in the Ancient World*. Cambridge: Cambridge University Press, 1978.

Giovannini, A. 'The Parthenon, the Treasury of Athena, and the Tribute of the Allies', in *The Athenian Empire*, ed. P. Low. Edinburgh: Edinburgh University Press, 2008, 164–84.

Goldhill, Simon, *Reading Greek Tragedy*. Cambridge: Cambridge University Press, 1986.

——, and Robin Osborne (eds), *Performance Culture and Athenian Democracy*. Cambridge: Cambridge University Press, 1999.

Gomme, A.W., 'The Working of the Athenian Democracy', *History,* 36 (1951), 12–28.

——, *More Essays in Greek History and Literature*. Oxford: Blackwell, 1962.

——, A. Andrewes and K.J. Dover, *A Historical Commentary on Thucydides*. 5 vols. Oxford: Clarendon Press, 1945–81.

Grote, George, *A History of Greece: From the Earliest Period to the Close of the Generation Contemporary with Alexander the Great*. 12 vols, 1859–65. Reprint London: Dent; New York: Dutton, 1907.

Grube, G.M.A., *Plato's Thought*. Boston: Beacon Press, 1958.

Guthrie, W.K.C., *Socrates*. Cambridge: Cambridge University Press, 1971.

——, *The Sophists*. Cambridge: Cambridge University Press, 1971.

Gutman, Amy, and Denis Thompson, *Why Deliberative Democracy?* Princeton: Princeton University Press, 2004.

Hahm, D.E., 'Kings and Constitutions: Hellenistic Theories', in *Cambridge History of Greek and Roman Political Thought*. Cambridge: Cambridge University Press, 2006, 457–76.

Hamilton, Alexander, John Jay and James Madison, *The Federalist*. New York: Modern Library, n.d.

Hamilton, C.D., *Sparta's Bitter Victories: Politics and Diplomacy in the Corinthian War*. Ithaca, NY: Cornell University Press, 1979.

——, *Agesilaus and the Failure of Spartan Hegemony*. Ithaca, NY: Cornell University Press, 1991.

Hammond, N.G.L., *A History of Greece to 322 B.C.* Oxford: Clarendon Press, 1959.

Hansen, M.H., *The Sovereignty of the People's Court in the Fourth Century B.C. and the Public Action against Unconstitutional Proposals*. Odense: Odense University Press, 1974.

——, *Eisangelia: The Sovereignty of the People's Court in Athens in the Fourth Century B.C. and the Impeachment of Generals and Politicians*. Odense: Odense University Press, 1975.

——, 'Did the Athenian *Ecclesia* Legislate after 403/2?', *GRBS* 20 (1979), 27–53.

——, 'How Often Did the Athenian *Diskateria* Meet?', *GRBS* 20 (1979), 243–46.

——, 'Seven Hundred *Archai* in Classical Athens', *GRBS* 21 (1980), 151–73.

——, 'The Athenian Heliaia from Solon to Aristotle', *C&M* 33 (1981–82), 9-47

——, 'Demographic Reflections on the Number of Athenian Citizens 451-309', *AJAH* 7(1982), 172-89.

——, 'The Number of Rhetores in the Athenian Ekklesia, 355–322', *GRBS* 25 (1984), 123–55.

——, 'Athenian *Nomothesia*', *GRBS* 26 (1985), 345–71.

——, *Demography and Democracy: The Number of Athenian Citizens in the Fourth Century B.C.* Herning, Denmark: Systime, 1986.

——, 'The Ancient Athenian and Modern Liberal View of Liberty as a Democratic Ideal', in *Demokratia: A Conversation on Democracies, Ancient and Modern*, ed. Josiah Ober and Charles Hedrick. Princeton: Princeton University Press, 1996, 91–104.

——, *The Athenian Assembly in the Age of Demosthenes: Structure, Principles, and Ideology*. Norman: University of Oklahoma Press, 1999.

——, *The Athenian Democracy in the Age of Demosthenes: Structure, Principles, and Ideology*. 2nd edn. Bristol: Bristol Classical Press, 1999.

——, *Polis: An Introduction to the Ancient City State*. Oxford: Oxford University Press, 2006.

——, and T.H. Nielsen (eds), *An Inventory of Archaic and Classical Poleis*. Oxford: Oxford University Press, 2004.

Hanson, V.D., 'Hoplites into Democrats: The Changing Ideology of Athenian Infantry', in *Demokratia*, ed. Josiah Ober and Charles Hedrick. Princeton: Princeton University Press, 1996, 289–312.

Harris, E.M., 'The Constitution of the Five Thousand', *HSCP* 93 (1990), 243–80.

——, 'Pericles' Praise of Athenian Democracy: Thucydides 2.37.1', *HSCP* 94 (1992), 152–67.

——, *Aeschines and Athenian Politics*. New York: Oxford University Press, 1995.

——, *Democracy and the Rule of Law in Classical Athens: Essays in Law, Society and Politics*. Cambridge: Cambridge University Press, 2006.

Harris, W.V., *Ancient Literacy*. Cambridge, Mass.: Harvard University Press, 1989.

Harrison, A.R.W., 'Law-Making at Athens at the End of the Fifth Century B.C.', *JHS* 75 (1955), 26–35.

——, *The Law of Athens*, Vol. 2: *Procedure*. Oxford: Clarendon Press, 1971.

Held, David, *Models of Democracy*. 2nd edn. Cambridge: Polity Press, 1996.

Henderson, Jeffrey, 'Attic Old Comedy, Frank Speech and Democracy', in *Democracy, Empire, and the Arts in Fifth-Century Athens*, ed. Deborah Boedeker and K.A. Raaflaub. Cambridge, Mass.: Harvard University Press, 1998.

Hölscher, Tonio, 'Images and Political Identity', in *Democracy, Empire, and the Arts in Fifth-Century Athens*, ed. Deborah Boedeker and K.A. Raaflaub. Cambridge, Mass.: Harvard University Press, 1998, 153–83.

Hornblower, Simon, *Thucydides*. London: Duckworth, 1987.

——, *A Commentary on Thucydides*. 3 vols. Oxford: Oxford University Press, 1991–2008.

Jacoby, F., *Die Fragmente der griechischen Historiker*. 3 vols. Berlin and Leiden: Brill, 1923–58.

Jaeger, Werner, *Paideia*, trans. G. Highet. 3 vols. Oxford: Oxford University Press, 1944.

Jameson, M.H, 'Agriculture and Slavery in Classical Athens', *CJ* 73 (1977–78), 122–45.

——, 'Religion in the Athenian Democracy', in *Democracy 2500? Questions and Challenges,* ed. Ian Morris and K.A. Raaflaub. Dubuque, Iowa: Kendall/Hunt, 1998.

Johnson, W.A., and H.N. Parker (eds), *Ancient Literacies.* Oxford and New York: Oxford University Press, 2009.

Joint Association of Classical Teachers (JACT), *The World of Athens: An Introduction to Classical Athenian Culture.* 2nd edn. Cambridge: Cambridge University Press, 2008.

Joint Association of European Journalists, *Goodbye to Freedom? A Survey of Media Freedom across Europe.* Published by the Association of European Journalists, 2007.

Jones, A.H.M., *Athenian Democracy.* Baltimore: Johns Hopkins University Press, 1977.

Jones, N.F., *Rural Athens under the Democracy.* Philadelphia: University of Pennsylvania Press, 2004.

Kagan, Donald, 'The Origin and Purposes of Ostracism', *Hesperia* 30 (1961), 393–401.

——, *The Outbreak of the Peloponnesian War.* Ithaca, NY: Cornell University Press, 1969.

——, *The Archidamian War.* Ithaca, NY: Cornell University Press, 1974.

——, *The Peace of Nicias and the Sicilian Expedition.* Ithaca, NY: Cornell University Press, 1981.

——, *The Fall of the Athenian Empire.* Ithaca, NY: Cornell University Press, 1987.

——, *Pericles of Athens and the Birth of Democracy.* New York: Free Press, 1991.

Kallet, Lisa, 'Accounting for Culture in Fifth-Century Athens', in *Democracy, Empire, and the Arts in Fifth-Century Athens,* ed. Deborah Boedeker and K.A. Raaflaub. Cambridge, Mass.: Harvard University Press, 1998, 43–58.

Kallet-Marx, Lisa, 'Did Tribute Fund the Parthenon?', *CA* 8 (1989), 252–66.

——, 'Money Talks: Rhetor, Demos, and the Resources of the Athenian Empire', in *The Athenian Empire,* ed. P. Low. Edinburgh: Edinburgh University Press, 2008, 185–210.

Kallet-Marx, R.M., 'Athens, Thebes, and the Foundation of the Second Athenian League', *CA* 4 (1985), 127–51.

Kamen, Deborah, *Status in Classical Athens.* Princeton: Princeton University Press, 2013.

Kerferd, G.B., *The Sophistic Movement.* Cambridge: Cambridge University Press, 1981.

—— (ed.), *The Sophists and their Legacy.* Wiesbaden: Hermes Einzelschrift 44, 1981.

Kirk, G.S., J.E. Raven and M. Schofield, *The Presocratic Philosophers.* 2nd edn. Cambridge: Cambridge University Press, 1983.

Kroll, J., 'What about Coinage?', in *Interpreting the Athenian Empire,* ed. J. Ma, N. Papazarkadas and R. Parker. London: Duckworth, 2009, 195–210.

Lambert, S.D., *The Phratries of Attica.* Ann Arbor: University of Michigan Press, 1998.

Lesky, Albin, *A History of Greek Literature,* trans. James Willis and Cornelis de Heer. New York: Crowell, 1966.

Lewis, D.M., 'Cleisthenes and Attica', in *Athenian Democracy,* ed. P.J. Rhodes. Edinburgh: Edinburgh University Press, 2004, 287–309.

——, 'The Athenian Coinage Decree', in *Coinage and Administration of the Athenian and Persian Empires,* ed. I. Carradice. Oxford: BAR Series, 1987, 343, 53–63.

Lewis, John, *Solon the Thinker: Political Thought in Archaic Athens.* London: Bristol Classical Press, 2006.

Liddel, Peter, *Civic Obligation and Individual Liberty in Ancient Athens.* Oxford: Oxford University Press, 2007.

Lloyd, John, *What the Media Are Doing to our Politics.* London: Constable, 2004.

Locke, John, *Two Treatises of Government,* ed. P. Laslett. 2nd edn. Cambridge: Cambridge University Press, 1970.

Loreaux, Nicole, *The Invention of Athens: The Funeral Oration in the Classical City,* trans. Alan Sheridan. Cambridge, Mass.: Harvard University Press, 1986.

Low, Polly, *Interstate Relations in Classical Greece.* Cambridge: Cambridge University Press, 2007.

—— (ed.), *The Athenian Empire.* Edinburgh: Edinburgh University Press, 2008.

Luce, J.V., *Introduction to Greek Philosophy.* London: Thames and Hudson, 1992.

Ma, J., N. Papazarkadas and R. Parker (eds), *Interpreting the Athenian Empire.* London: Duckworth, 2009, 67–88.

McClelland, J.S., *A History of Western Political Thought.* London and New York: Routledge, 1996.

MacDowell, D.M., 'Law-Making at Athens in the Fourth Century B.C.', *JHS* 95 (1975), 62–74.

Macedo, Stephen (ed.), *Deliberative Politics: Essays on Democracy and Disagreement*. Oxford: Oxford University Press, 1999.

Manville, P.H., 'Ancient Greek Democracy and the Modern Knowledge-Based Organization: Reflections on the Ideology of Two Revolutions', in *Demokratia: A Conversation on Democracies, Ancient and Modern*, ed. Josiah Ober and Charles Hedrick. Princeton: Princeton University Press, 1996.

Maurizio, Lisa, 'The Panathenaic Procession: Athens' Participatory Democracy on Display?' in *Democracy, Empire, and the Arts in Fifth-Century Athens*, Deborah Boedeker and K.A. Raaflaub (eds), Cambridge: Harvard University Press, 1987

Meiggs, Russell, *The Athenian Empire*. Oxford and New York: Oxford University Press, 1972.

——, and D.M. Lewis (eds), *A Selection of Greek Historical Inscriptions to the End of the Fifth Century B.C.* Oxford: Clarendon Press, 1988.

Merritt, B.D., H.T. Wade-Grey and M.F. McGregor, *The Athenian Tribute Lists*. 4 vols. Cambridge, Mass.: (1) Harvard University Press and (2–4) Princeton: American School of Classical Studies at Athens, 1939–53.

Michels, Robert, *Political Parties: A Sociological Study of the Oligarchical Tendencies of Modern Democracy*, trans. Edan and Cedar Paul. New York: Hearst's International Library Company, 1915.

Micklethwait, John, and Adrian Wooldridge, *The Fourth Revolution: The Global Race to Reinvent the State*. London: Penguin, 2014.

Missiou, Anna, *Literacy and Democracy in Fifth-Century Athens*. Cambridge: Cambridge University Press, 2011.

Mitchell, T.N., *Cicero the Senior Statesman*. New Haven and London: Yale University Press, 1991.

Moreno, A., *Feeding the Democracy: The Athenian Grain Supply in the Fifth and Fourth Century B.C.* Oxford: Oxford University Press, 2007.

Morris, Ian, 'The Strong Principle of Equality and the Archaic Origins of Greek Democracy', in *Demokratia: A Conversation on Democracies, Ancient and Modern*, ed. Josiah Ober and Charles Hedrick. Princeton: Princeton University Press, 1996, 19–48.

——, and K.A. Raaflaub (eds), *Democracy 2500? Questions and Challenges*. Dubuque, Iowa: Kendall/Hunt, 1998.

Mossé, Claude, 'How a Political Myth Takes Shape: Solon, "Founding Father" of Athenian Democracy' (trans. Rosh Ireland), in *Athenian Democracy*, ed. P.J. Rhodes. Edinburgh: Edinburgh University Press, 2004.

Murray, Oswyn, *Early Greece*. 2nd edn. Cambridge, Mass.: Harvard University Press, 1993.

North, Helen, *Sophrosyne: Self-Knowledge and Self-Restraint in Greek Literature*. Ithaca, NY: Cornell University Press, 1966.

Ober, Josiah, *Mass and Elite in Democratic Athens*. Princeton: Princeton University Press, 1989.

——, *The Athenian Revolution: Essays in Ancient Greek Democracy*. Princeton: Princeton University Press, 1996.

——, 'Revolution Matters: Democracy as Demotic Action', in *Democracy 2500? Questions and Challenges*, ed. Ian Morris and K.A. Raaflaub. Dubuque, Iowa: Kendall/Hunt, 1998, 67–85.

——, *Athenian Legacies: Essays on the Politics of Going On Together*. Princeton: Princeton University Press, 2005.

——, 'I Besieged That Man: Democracy's Revolutionary Start', in *Origins of Democracy in Ancient Greece*, ed. K.A. Raaflaub, Josiah Ober and R.W. Wallace. Berkeley: University of California Press, 2007.

——, *Democracy and Knowledge*. Princeton: Princeton University Press, 2009.

——, and C.W. Hedrick (eds), *Demokratia: A Conversation on Democracies, Ancient and Modern*. Princeton: Princeton University Press, 1996.

Osborne, M.J., *Naturalization*. Verhandelingen Kon. Acad. voor Wetenschappen van België, Klasse der Letteren, vol. 43, no. 98, 1981.

Osborne, Robin, *Demos: The Discovery of Classical Attika*. Cambridge: Cambridge University Press, 1985.

——, 'Archaeology and the Athenian Empire', in *The Athenian Empire*, ed. P. Low. Edinburgh: Edinburgh University Press, 2008, 211–24.

——, *Athens and Athenian Democracy*. Cambridge: Cambridge University Press, 2010.

Ostwald, Martin, *Autonomia: Its Genesis and History*. Chico, Calif.: Scholars' Press, 1982.

——, *From Popular Sovereignty to the Sovereignty of Law: Law, Society and Politics in Fifth-Century Athens*. Berkeley: University of California Press, 1986.

——, 'Stasis and Autonomia in Samos: A Comment on an Ideological Fallacy', *Scripta Classica Israelica* 12 (1993), 51–66.

——, 'Shares and Rights: Citizenship Greek Style and American Style', in *Demokratia: A Conversation on Democracies, Ancient and Modern*, ed. Josiah Ober and Charles Hedrick. Princeton: Princeton University Press, 1996, 49–61.

Paine, Thomas, *The Rights of Man* [1791]. Harmondsworth: Penguin, 1984.

Papadopoulos, Yanis, *Démocratie directe*. Paris: Economica, 1998.

Papazarkadas, N., 'Epigraphy and the Athenian Empire: Reshuffling the Chronological Cards', in *Interpreting the Athenian Empire*, ed. J. Ma, N. Papazarkadas and R. Parker. London: Duckworth, 2009.

Patterson, Thomas, *The Vanishing Voter*. New York: Vintage, 2003.

Pélékides, Chrysis, *Histoire de l'éphébie attique des origines à 31 avant Jésus Christ*. Paris: de Bocard, 1962.

Perlman, S., 'The Politicians in the Athenian Democracy of the Fourth Century B.C.', *Athenaeum* 41 (1963), 327–55.

——, 'Political Leadership in Athens in the Fourth Century B.C.', *PP* 22 (1967), 161–76.

——, (ed.), *Philip and Athens*. Cambridge: Heffer, 1973.

Pickard-Cambridge, A.W., *The Democratic Festivals of Athens*. 2nd edn, revised by John Gould and D.M. Lewis. Oxford: Oxford University Press, 1988.

Pleket, H.W., 'The Archaic *tyrannis*', *Talanta* I (1969), 19–61.

Podes, Stephan, 'The Introduction of Jury Pay by Pericles: Some Mainly Chronological Considerations', *Athenaeum* 82 (1994), 95–110.

Pomeroy, Sarah, *Goddesses, Whores, Wives and Slaves: Women in Antiquity*. New York: Schocken, 1975.

Pritchard, D.M., 'Costing Festivals and War: The Spending Priorities of the Athenian Democracy', *Historia* 61 (2012), 18–65.

—— (ed.)'The Symbiosis between Democracy and War' in *War, Democracy and Culture in Classical Athens*. Cambridge: Cambridge University Press, 2010, 1–62.

—— (ed.), *War, Democracy and Culture in Classical Athens*. Cambridge: Cambridge University Press, 2010.

Pritchett, W.K., *The Greek State at War*. 5 vols. Berkeley: University of California Press, 1971–91.

Raaflaub, K.A., 'Equalities and Inequalities in Athenian Democracy', in *Demokratia: A Conversation on Democracies, Ancient and Modern*, ed. Josiah Ober and Charles Hedrick. Princeton: Princeton University Press, 1996, 139–74.

——, 'The Thetes and Democracy (Response to Josiah Ober)', in *Democracy 2500? Questions and Challenges*, ed. Ian Morris and K.A. Raaflaub. Dubuque, Iowa: Kendall/Hunt, 1998, 87–103.

——, 'Power in the Hands of the People: Foundations of Athenian Democracy', in *Democracy 2500? Questions and Challenges*, ed. Ian Morris and K.A. Raaflaub. Dubuque, Iowa: Kendall/Hunt, 1998, 31–66.

——, 'The Transformation of Athens in the Fifth Century', in *Democracy, Empire, and the Arts in Fifth-Century Athens*, ed. Deborah Boedeker and K.A. Raaflaub. Cambridge, Mass.: Harvard University Press, 1998, 15–41.

——, 'Poets, Lawgivers, and the Beginnings of Political Reflection in Archaic Greece', in *The Cambridge History of Greek and Roman Political Thought*, ed. Christopher Rowe and Malcolm Schofield. Cambridge: Cambridge University Press, 2005, 23–59.

Raaflaub, K.A, Josiah Ober and R.W. Wallace (eds), *Origins of Democracy in Ancient Greece*. Berkeley: University of California Press, 2007.

Randall, R.H., 'The Erechtheum Workmen', *American Journal of Archaeology* 57 (1953), 199–210.

Rawson, Elizabeth, *The Spartan Tradition in European Thought*. Oxford: Oxford University Press, 1969.

Rhodes, P.J., 'Thucydides and Alcibiades', *Revue des études grecques* 65 (1952), 54–96.
——, 'The Five Thousand in the Athenian Revolutions of 411', *JHS* 92 (1972), 115–27.
——, '*Eisangelia* in Athens', *JHS* 99 (1979), 103–14.
——, 'Athenian Democracy after 403 B.C.', *CJ* 75 (1980), 305–23.
——, *A Commentary on the Aristotelian Athenaion Politeia*. Oxford: Clarendon Press, 1981.
——, '*Nomothesia* in Fourth-Century Athens', *CQ* 35 (1985), 55–60.
——, *The Athenian Boule*. Oxford: Clarendon Press, 1985.
——, 'Political Activity in Classical Athens', *JHS* 106 (1986), 132–44.
——, 'The Ostracism of Hyperbolus', in *Ritual, Finance, Politics: Athenian Democratic Accounts Presented to D.M. Lewis,* ed. R. Osborne and S. Hornblower. Oxford: Oxford University Press, 1994, 69–89.
——, *Ancient Democracy and Modern Ideology*. London: Duckworth, 2003.
——, 'After the Three-Bar Sigma Controversy: The History of Athenian Imperialism Reassessed', *CQ* 57 (2009), 500–6.
——, and R. Osborne, *Greek Historical Inscriptions, 404–323 B.C.* Oxford: Oxford University Press, 2003.
Roberts, J.T., *Accountability in Athenian Government*. Madison: Wisconsin University Press, 1982.
——, *Athens on Trial: The Antidemocratic Tradition in Western Thought*. Princeton: Princeton University Press, 1994.
——, 'Athenian Equality: A Constant Surrounded by Flux', in *Demokratia: A Conversation on Democracies, Ancient and Modern,* ed. Josiah Ober and Charles Hedrick. Princeton: Princeton University Press, 1996, 187–202.
Robertson, Martin, *A History of Greek Art*. 2 vols. Cambridge: Cambridge University Press, 1975.
Robespierre, Maximilien, *Discours et rapports à la convention*. París: Union Générale d'Éditions, 1965.
Robinson, E.W., *The First Democracies: Early Popular Government outside Athens*. Stuttgart: F. Steiner, 1997.
Romilly, Jacqueline de, *Thucydides and Athenian Imperialism,* trans. Philip Thody. Oxford: Blackwell, 1963.
——, 'Thucydides and the Cities of the Athenian Empire', *Bulletin of the Institute of Classical Studies* 13 (1966), 1–12. Reprinted in P. Low, *The Athenian Empire*. Edinburgh: Edinburgh University Press, 2008.
Ryder, T.T.B., *Koine Eirene: General Peace and Local Independence in Ancient Greece*. Oxford: Oxford University Press, 1965.
Saïd, Suzanne, 'Tragedy and Politics', in *Democracy, Empire, and the Arts in Fifth-Century Athens,* ed. Deborah Boedeker and K.A. Raaflaub. Cambridge, Mass.: Harvard University Press, 1998, 275–95.
Schumpeter, Joseph, *Capitalism, Socialism and Democracy*. 3rd edn. London: Allen & Unwin, 1950.
Scully, S.P., 'The *Polis* in Homer', *Ramus* 10 (1981), 1–34.
Sealey, Raphael, 'The Revolution of 411 B.C.', in *Essays in Greek Politics*. New York: Maryland, 1967.
——, *Demosthenes and his Time: A Study in Defeat*. New York: Oxford University Press, 1993.
Shapiro, H.A., 'Autochthony and the Visual Arts', in *Democracy, Empire, and the Arts in Fifth-Century Athens,* ed. Deborah Boedeker and K.A. Raaflaub. Cambridge, Mass.: Harvard University Press, 1998.
Sinclair, R.K., 'The King's Peace and the Employment of Military and Naval Forces 387–78', *Chiron* 8 (1978), 29–54.
——, *Democracy and Participation in Athens*. Cambridge: Cambridge University Press, 1988.
Snodgrass, Anthony, 'The Hoplite Reform and History', *JHS* 85, (1965), 110–22.
Solmson, Friedrich, *Hesiod and Aeschylus*. Ithaca, NY: Cornell University Press, 1949.
Ste Croix, G.E.M. de, 'Demosthenes' *timema* and the Athenian *eisphora* in the Fourth Century B.C.', *C&M* 14 (1953), 30–70.
——, 'The Constitution of the Five Thousand', *Historia* 5 (1956), 1–23.
——, 'Notes on Jurisdiction in the Athenian Empire', *CQ* 55 (1961), 94–112 and 268–80.
——, *The Origins of the Peloponnesian War*. Ithaca, NY: Cornell University Press, 1972.

——, 'The Character of the Athenian Empire', *Historia* 3 (1954–55), 1–41. Reprinted in P. Low, *The Athenian Empire*. Edinburgh: Edinburgh University Press, 2008.

——, *The Class Struggle in the Ancient World*. London: Duckworth, 1981.

——, *The Class Struggle in the Ancient Greek World: From the Archaic Age to the Arab Conquests*. Ithaca, NY: Cornell University Press, 1983.

——, *Athenian Democratic Origins*, ed. David Parker and Robert Parker. Oxford: Oxford University Press, 2004.

Stockton, David, *The Classical Athenian Democracy*. Oxford: Oxford University Press, 1990.

Stone, I.F., *The Trial of Socrates*. Boston: Little, Brown, 1988.

Strauss, B.S., *Athens after the Peloponnesian War: Class, Faction and Policy 403–386 B.C.* London: Croom Helm, 1986.

Syme, Ronald, *The Roman Revolution*. Oxford: Oxford University Press, 1960.

Thomas, R., *Literacy and Orality in Ancient Greece*. Cambridge: Cambridge University Press, 1992.

Thompson, H.A., 'The Pnyx in Models', *Hesperia*, Suppl. 19 (1982), 133–47.

Thomsen, Rudi, *Eisphora: A Study of Direct Taxation in Ancient Athens*. Copenhagen: Gyldendal, 1964.

Todd, S.C., *The Shape of Athenian Law*. Oxford: Clarendon Press, 1993.

Too, Yun Lee (ed.), *Education in Greek and Roman Antiquity*. Leiden: E.J. Brill, 2001.

Traill, J.S., *The Political Organisation of Attica: A Study of the Demes, Trittyes and Phylai and their Representation in the Athenian Council*. Princeton: American School of Classical Studies at Athens, 1975.

Trevett, Jeremy, *Apollodorus, the Son of Pasion*. Oxford: Clarendon Press, 1992.

Vlastos, Gregory, 'The Theory of Social Justice in the *Polis* in Plato's Republic', in *Interpretation of Plato*, ed. H. North. Leiden: E.J. Brill, 1977, 1–40.

Wallace, R.W., *The Areopagus Council to 307 B.C.* Baltimore: Johns Hopkins University Press, 1989.

——, 'Law, Freedom and the Concept of Citizens' Rights in Democratic Athens', in *Demokratia: A Conversation on Democracies, Ancient and Modern*, ed. Josiah Ober and Charles Hedrick. Princeton: Princeton University Press, 1996, 105–19.

——, 'Solonian Democracy', in *Democracy 2500? Questions and Challenges*, ed. Ian Morris and K.A. Raaflaub. Dubuque, Iowa: Kendall/Hunt, 1997, 11–29.

——, 'Revolutions and a New Order in Solonian Athens and Archaic Greece', in *Origins of Democracy in Ancient Greece*, ed. K.A. Raaflaub, Josiah Ober and R.W. Wallace. Berkeley: University of California Press, 2007, 49–82.

Webster, T.B.L., *Everyday Life in Classical Athens*. London: Batsford, 1969.

——, *Athenian Culture and Society*. London: Batsford, 1973.

West, M.L., *Iambi et Elegi Graeci*. 2nd edn. 2 vols. Oxford: Clarendon Press, 1991–92.

Whitehead, David, *The Ideology of the Athenian Metic*. Cambridge: Cambridge Philological Society, 1977.

—— 'Sparta and the Thirty Tyrants', *Ancient Society* 13/14 (1982–83), 106–30.

——, *The Demes of Attica, 508/7–ca. 250 B.C.: A Political and Social Study*. Princeton: Princeton University Press, 1986.

Will, Wolfgang, *Athen und Alexander: Untersuchungen zur Geschichte der Stadt von 338 bis 322 v. Chr.* Munich: Verlag C.H. Beck, 1983.

Williams, Bernard, *Plato: The Invention of Philosophy*. London: Phoenix, 1988.

Wood, E.M., *Peasant-Citizen and Slave: The Foundations of Athenian Democracy*. London: Verso, 1988.

——, 'Demos vs "We the People": Freedom and Democracy, Ancient and Modern', in *Demokratia: A Conversation on Democracies Ancient and Modern*, ed. Josiah Ober and Charles Hedrick. Princeton: Princeton University Press, 1996, 131–37.

Wood, Neal, *Cicero's Social and Political Thought*. Berkeley: University of California Press, 1988.

Yunis, Harvey, 'The Constraints of Democracy and the Rise of the Art of Rhetoric', in *Democracy, Empire, and the Arts in Fifth Century Athens*, ed. Deborah Boedeker and K.A. Raaflaub. Cambridge, Mass.: Harvard University Press, 1998.

Index